T0418474

Charismatic Leadership in Singapore

Dayan Hava · Chan Kwok-bun

Charismatic Leadership in Singapore

Three Extraordinary People

 Springer

Dayan Hava
Hebrew University of Jerusalem
Jerusalem, Israel
havadayan64@gmail.com

Chan Kwok-bun
Chan Institute of Social Studies
Hong Hong, China
ckb@ci-ss.org

ISBN 978-1-4614-1450-6   e-ISBN 978-1-4614-1451-3
DOI 10.1007/978-1-4614-1451-3
Springer New York Dordrecht Heidelberg London

Library of Congress Control Number: 2011940694

Printed on acid-free paper

Springer is part of Springer Science+Business Media (www.springer.com)

Preface

This book offers a narrative of the unusually transformative lives of three extraordinary Singaporeans: community work volunteer Sister Prema, dramatist Kuo Pao Kun, and architect Tay Kheng Soon. With a few exceptions, sociological studies have neglected the concept of charisma, and the idea has never been incorporated into other major theoretical sociological discussions. Although Weber's definition of charisma[1] forged what is for many writers the starting point for any appreciation of the concept, his conceptualization of charisma has not been very useful to sociology because it deals with charisma more as a psychological than a social phenomenon.[2] Even the growing interest in leadership and charisma within organizational behavior studies[3] is mainly oriented to messo level analysis and is still principally concerned with psychological concerns rather than sociological ones. With the exception of Edward Shils and Smuel Eisenstadt who employ charisma as a concept to analyze power in terms of the symbolic social order, the interest of mainstream sociology in charisma studies ended before the end of the 1960s.[4]

In contrast to the prevailing attitude of sociologists, the basic assumption of our book is that the study of charisma can make a significant contribution to several central sociological topics because, in the real world, charismatic leadership is closely related to important sociological concerns such as action, power, and influence and to social symbolic meaning, the social construction of reality, and transformation. But, by way of its nature, the concept takes in the individual, small groups, various social institutions and organizations, and the macro social system. That means aspects and agents from different social levels. Because of this, it has the

---

[1] Writing in 1924, reprinted in 1947.

[2] See Friedland (1964, p. 18), Moscovici (1993, p. 125 and 221–222).

[3] House (1977); Bass (1985); Conger and Kanungo (1988); Sashkin (1988); Avolio (1995); and others.

[4] Even the subsequent sociological studies are based either on Weber (Friedland 1964; Fabian 1969; Tucker 1970) or on Shils's approaches (Geertz 1977; Willner 1984) and do not offer major theoretical reformulation.

potential to enable meaningful discussions with regard to the intricate and complex intersections between these various agents and with regard to the interplay within the various levels of society.

It is our intention to pick up the sociological study of charisma right from the point where it was left off – with Shils's symbolic reformulation and Eisenstadt's inclusion of institutionalizational dimensions in the process of the agency of charisma.[5] This book will offer a framework that deals with the symbolic and institutionalized aspects of charisma (thus incorporating the approaches of both Shils and Eisenstadt),[6] yet that still retains Weber's distinct micro-level and "revolutionary" aspect of charisma. In the process, we will attempt to clarify the revolutionary aspect of charisma, both conceptually and empirically, by linking it to the realm of ideas, perceptions, and underlying basic social assumptions. From the conceptual point of view, this attempt can be seen as trying to synthesize[7] the core arguments of the writings we have mentioned – of Shils, Eisenstadt, and Weber – with the additional application of structural conceptualizations of basic social assumptions.[8] In addition, this book will attend to micro–macro relations – the relations that occur through and with charisma – and will thus explore an area that has been severely neglected: the intersections between context and charisma. Indeed, both the traditional sociological as well as the recent organizational behavior treatments of charisma require a more dialectical approach to unravel or explicitly demonstrate the dual interactions between charisma and structure.

While the traditional sociological approaches typically tend to place greater emphasis on the structural constraints (and less on the subjective, intentional nature of micro-level agents and the ways that they can shape structure),[9] recent approaches in organizational behavior seem to emphasize the "omnipotent," individual nature of such leadership and neglect possible macro contextual[10] impacts on such agency's nature, form, and process.[11] This book will make a case for treating charisma and social structure as both influencing and being influenced by each other.

---

[5] See Shils (1965) and Eisenstadt (1968).

[6] Their theories still require theoretical reformulation in order to apply to the analysis of change, and in that respect, they significantly depart from Weber's initial formulation of charisma as a revolutionary force.

[7] Admittedly, we think that Eisenstadt's (1968) approach also tried to offer a possible synthesis between Weber ([1924] 1947) and Shils (1965) (through an institutional perspective on the process of charisma and social change). However, this reconceptualization "lost," as it happened, the revolutionary notion of charisma and is less applicable for the analysis of social changes of a revolutionary kind.

[8] See the writings of Kluckhohn and Strodtbeck (1961).

[9] With the exception of Weber, who indeed emphasized the individual subjective aspect yet neglected the other side of the dialectics.

[10] Not in the messo, situational, or organizational confines, but particularly when referring to macro contextual factors such as history, culture, politics, society, and others.

[11] There is indeed an inconclusive, ongoing dispute and treatment of the relation between crises and the emergence of charisma (see Chap. 6), but other possible dimensions and interactions are severely neglected.

The conceptual synthesis between the micro and macro aspects of charisma will rely on sociological approaches that deal with the way social reality is constructed.[12] An underlying assumption for such an analysis of charisma is that, since reality is not predetermined[13] but (to use Weber's concept) a matter of "elective affinities," it posits the quest and the challenge for its social construction. Charismatic leadership can therefore be seen as a social mechanism that constructs social reality by negotiating the macro structure.

The approaches of both Berger and Giddens may benefit from their incorporation into the analysis of charisma as they are not clear with regard to revolutionary types of reality construction, a point that will be pursued in this book. There have been sociological treatments that have dealt with charisma's revolutionary agency, but whether it is implicit (as by Weber) or explicit (as by others),[14] they all seem to argue that such changes are intrinsically correlated with mass social movements. We will review such argumentation both conceptually and empirically because there may be particular cases of charismatic revolutionary changes that do not engage mass social movements nor large-scale transformations, yet still play a major role in the construction of social reality.

Strategically, this book will make a case for presenting charisma as a useful idea and concept in the study of a number of social processes, namely, the social construction of reality and meaning (and its interrelation with social transformation), and the ongoing dialectics between macro-level structure and micro-level agency. For such an understanding to develop, the conceptualization of charisma should move from the traditional orientation of the discipline (whether that be a macro- or a micro-type of analysis) and venture into the zone where macrosociology and social psychology intersect. This conceptual intersection, which engages both micro and macro approaches to the analysis of the phenomenon at hand, seems a fruitful ground for the proper treatment of the dialectical nature of charisma.

Dayan Hava   Chan Kwok-bun
Jerusalem, Israel   Hong Kong, China

---

[12] See Berger (1966, 1981) and Giddens (1984).

[13] As was pointed out by several sociologists (Berger 1967, 1981; Eisenstadt 1968; Giddens 1984), reality is not predetermined because macro-level factors, although posing substantial constraints, do not totally determine micro-level action.

[14] For an example of explicit treatment, see Friedland (1964), Fabian (1969), Tucker (1970).

Contents

Chapter 1
Charisma Revived

Until recently, the subject of charisma has suffered from a serious lack of attention. Stodgill's *Handbook of Leadership*, published in 1959, combed through 5,000 studies, but only a dozen of them referred to charismatic leadership.[1] And in spite of the great body of literature on leadership in organizations, the charismatic, as a particular type of leadership, was given scant attention until the second half of the 1980s. In the mid-1970s, a growing number of scholars began to explore leadership in relation to organizational issues,[2] and the research focus shifted from leadership in general to a special kind of leadership, one that is exceptional and extraordinary. And whether the emphasis was explicit or implicit, the new genre of theories focused on charisma as a central concept. The focus on such leadership was perhaps related to the transformation and revitalization of organizations, which became especially relevant after many executives in the United States finally acknowledged the need to make major changes in the way things were done in order to survive increasing competition from foreign companies.[3] Boaz Shamir describes it in this way:[4]

> In the mid 1970's, a major paradigm shift in leadership research took place. Attention was shifted from an emphasis on the relationship of leader behavior to follower cognitions to an emphasis on exceptional leaders who have extraordinary effects on their followers and eventually on social systems. Such leadership—alternatively called 'charismatic' or 'visionary' or 'transformational'—is claimed to affect followers in ways that are quantitatively greater and qualitatively different than the effects specified in past theories.

Within the new genre of leadership theories, three central versions of an extraordinary leadership have been identified, albeit with certain unifying ideas: "the charismatic,"

---

[1] In *Stodgill's Handbook of Leadership* (Bass, 1981).

[2] House (1977); Bass (1985); Conger (1989); Conger and Kanungo (1988); Peters and Waterman (1982).

[3] For a discussion of this, see Conger's *The Charismatic Leader: Behind the Mystique of Exceptional Leadership* (1989).

[4] In his 1992 article, "The Charismatic Relationship: Alternative Explanations and Predictions."

Dayan Hava and Chan Kwok-bun, *Charismatic Leadership in Singapore:*
Three Extraordinary People, DOI 10.1007/978-1-4614-1451-3_1,
© Springer Science+Business Media, LLC 2012

"the transformational," and "the visionary." [5] Although our particular concern is with charisma, we will briefly describe the other two versions because many of their major themes correlate with the notion of charisma.

Charismatic Leadership

One of the earliest attempts to include charisma in the organizational sphere can be found in the 1961 writings of Amitai Etzioni, although even there it was not a major concern. In it, he provides a very general definition of charisma, which facilitates its exploration in the context of "complex organizations." For Etzioni, charisma is defined as the ability of an actor to exercise diffused and intense influence over the normative orientations of other actors, and this suggests that charisma is a form of normative power that ultimately depends on the power of an individual.[6] Etzioni's treatment is important because he makes a significant distinction, and this transcends the specific definition that he provides by distinguishing between charisma of office on the one hand and personal charisma on the other. Somewhat extending this distinction, it implies that there may be three manifestations of charisma in an organizational setting: charisma of office, personal charisma that arises during the incumbency of an ordinary office, and personal charisma that arises during the incumbency of a charismatic office—for example, a high-ranking position in a prestigious or powerful organization.

An important elaboration of charisma in an organizational setting comes from William Oberg.[7] He is concerned to show how the concept of charisma could be divested of its religious overtones and applied to secular, profit-seeking organizations, and he mentions five factors that can lead to the attribution of charisma. First, there are a number of personal qualities including the ability to demonstrate significant past achievements and the ability to empathize with followers. Second, he includes factors related to the followers, such as employees' fears and troubled feelings, their ages, and the length of their service. Thirdly, he refers to contextual factors such as when charismatic leadership is most likely to emerge—for example, when decisions involve unclear means and goals—and where charismatic leadership is most likely to emerge (most likely at the apex of an organization). Fourth, he includes the employment of symbols denoting prestige, such as the use of rituals and "executive dramaturgy." And fifth, he refers to some kind of corporate creed, or ideology, such as a mission statement.

---

[5] "The charismatic" is described in Conger and Kanungo (1988); "the transformational" in Burns (1978); Bass (1985); Avolio and Bass (1988); and Avolio (1995); and "the visionary" in Sashkin (1988); Bennis and Nannus (1985); and in Nannus (1992).

[6] See "A Comparative Analysis of Complex Organizations: On Power, Involvement, and their Correlates," (1975, p. 305).

[7] Writing in 1972.

We count Oberg's analysis as important because it lists a mixture of different factors, which could be personal, situational, social, interpersonal, organizational, or institutional. But it is not quite clear how they interact together, nor what is the relative importance of each one. There is a sense in which we are left with a catalogue of factors which are relevant to charisma, but which still await systematic analysis.

Writing around the same time, David Berlew[8] provides a significant treatment of charisma, and he sees charismatic leadership as exhibiting three forms of leadership behavior. He argues that such leaders develop a commonly shared vision for the organization—and that this vision expresses a set of goals that are valued by the organization's members—that there is a creation of value-related opportunities and activities within the vision's frame of reference, and that the leader makes members of an organization feel stronger and less powerless.

But probably the major application of charisma in the study of formal organizations can be found in Robert House's *A 1976 Theory of Charismatic Leadership*. In his work, he develops a number of testable hypotheses concerning the situational characteristics, the traits and the behavior of charismatic leaders. According to House, the personal characteristics that contribute to charismatic leadership are a high level of self-confidence, a tendency to dominate, a need to influence others, and a strong conviction in one's own beliefs.

He also specifies a number of aspects of the personal behavior of charismatic leaders—for example, he mentions "role modeling" (through which the leader represents the values and beliefs to which he wants followers to subscribe), "image building" (that creates an impression of competence and success), the leader's high expectations and high confidence in his followers (by exhibiting confidence in their ability to accomplish the lofty goals that they have been set to achieve), and the leader's engagement in the arousal of motives that are relevant to the execution of the mission. Such motives may include a need for affiliation or achievement, a need to overcome an enemy or competitor, or a need for the achievement of excellence in one's work.

Of particular significance is the fact that in this, and in later work, House studies charismatic leaders from the point of view of the followers (and does not rely only on the descriptive account of their traits and behavior).[9] In fact, House bases his definition of charismatic leadership on its effects on followers. He associates charismatic leadership with a strong affection for the leader and a similarity of follower beliefs with those of the leader. These effects describe a sort of bonding or identification with the leader's personality and a parallel psychological investment in a goal or activity (a "cause") bigger than oneself. As a consequence, the followers' identities or self-concepts become defined in the terms of the leader. Being like the leader, or being approved of by the leader, becomes an important part of self-worth, and House therefore concludes[10] that the effects on the followers can help us identify charismatic leaders.

---

[8] Writing in 1974.

[9] See also the 1988 essay, "Charismatic and Non-charismatic Leaders: Differences in Behavior and Effectiveness" by House, J. R. and Woycke J. and Fodor, M.E.

[10] Ibid., pp. 105–106.

This is significant because followers of charismatic leaders will express effects that go well beyond what might be expected from typical contractual or exchange relationships between most supervisors and subordinates. They will express a high degree of loyalty, commitment, and devotion to the leader; they will identify with the leader's mission; they will emulate his values, goals, and behavior; they will see the leader as a source of inspiration; they will derive a sense of high self-esteem from their relationship with the leader and his mission; and they will have an exceptionally high degree of trust in the correctness of the leader's beliefs.

This process clearly links leadership to the construction of a self-concept. By emphasizing the notion of self-concept as a crucial element in the charismatic leadership, both House and Boaz Shamir assert[11] that charismatic leaders achieve transformational effects, not only by specifying the intrinsic valence of effort and goal attainment, but also by implicating the self-concept, self-worth, and self-efficacy of the followers. The leaders increase the intrinsic valence of efforts and goals by linking them to valued aspects of the followers' self-concept, their relations with the organization, the society, and the world.

Jay Conger and Rabindra Kanungo[12] also provide an important framework for the study of charismatic leadership: one that is specifically concerned with its emergence in business and other complex organizations. Their starting point is that charismatic leadership is primarily an attributional phenomenon (an attribution made by individuals who work in organizations, in respect of certain leaders), and they relate these attributions to the behavior of the leader.[13] Hence, for Conger and Kanungo, the key issue becomes that of revealing the types of behavior that are most likely to lead to the attribution of charismatic leadership. They argue that the starting point is a vision: an idealized goal that the leader wants the organization to achieve in the future, and which breaks with the status quo, and often uses unconventional methods to move toward achieving the vision.[14] The charismatic leader then portrays the

---

[11] See Shamir's (1992) essay, "The Charismatic Relationship: Alternative Explanations and Predictions," and the 1993 essay of House and Shamir, "Toward the Integration of Transformational, Charismatic and Visionary Leaders."

[12] In their 1988 essay, "Behavioral Dimensions of Charismatic Leadership."

[13] They imply in their model that charismatic leadership is not only a perceptual phenomenon but also it has real motivational and behavioral effects on followers. The attributions by the followers are considered the essential link between leader's behavior and the followers' tendency to have faith in the leader, obey him, and invest efforts on behalf of the leader's mission.

[14] The ground assumptions of this approach have very close affinities with Weber's theory of charisma. What Conger shares with many recent writers is a preoccupation with vision. He describes vision as "the cornerstone of charismatic leadership" (1989: 36) and is entirely consistent with Weber's formulation that vision should be regarded as the central aspect of charisma. But contrary to Weber who perceives the extraordinariness of the charismatic leader as central, Conger does acknowledge this aspect but only in the context of its being a device for creating a sense of trust in the leader's vision. For Weber, the belief in the extraordinary quality of the charismatic leader was much more central; it was not simply a device or artifice for getting one's mission across.

status quo as insufferable and his own vision as leading to a viable alternative.[15] Other behavioral expressions include confidence in his own capacity to lead and a concern for the needs of his followers. Rather than his own position, the charismatic leader uses personal power to influence others, and often engages in entrepreneurial or exemplary behavior to exert that power.

Conger and Kanungo's theory represents an attempt to apply ideas from the substantial literature on charisma to business and similar organizational settings, and this factor is of considerable significance. In emphasizing the behavioral precursors to the attribution of charisma, they appear to imply that charisma is not a mystical quality exhibited only by very special individuals. While leaders may differ in terms of their capacity to transmit their vision, Conger and Kanungo seem to argue that charisma is a fairly mundane pattern of behavior that enhances the likelihood of being deemed charismatic and which is, therefore, potentially learnable.

Transformational Leadership

Researchers are in agreement that there is a fair chance that charisma would have remained a fairly marginal category in leadership research, had it not been for the growing interest shown in the notion of "transforming leadership"—a term coined by the political scientist James Burns,[16] in the context of a contrast with another approach to leadership, which he dubs "transactional leadership." In "transactional leadership," there is an exchange between the leader and the follower, entailing a kind of implicit contract beyond which the followers are not prepared to venture. Through such an "implicit contract" leadership takes place, but it does not bind the "leader and follower together in a mutual and continuing pursuit of a higher purpose."[17]

The "transforming leader" seeks to engage the follower as a whole person, and not simply as an individual with a restricted range of basic needs and motives. This kind of leadership entails both leaders and followers raising and inspiring each other's motivation and sense of higher purpose—a higher purpose in which the aims and aspirations of leaders and followers merge into one. And in this way, "transforming leadership" addresses the higher-order needs of followers and looks to the full range of motives that move them. Burns argues that, in the pursuit of goals that express aspirations with which they can identify themselves, it is not only the followers but both the leaders and the followers who are changed.

Taking Burns as his starting point, Bernard Bass has written and conducted substantial research into "transforming leadership."[18] Like Burns, he also draws a

---

[15] But at the same time, according to Conger and Kanungo, since the charismatic leader is sensitive to the organization's environment and threats and the opportunities that it offers, he may seek to implement his vision when the time is ripe.

[16] In his 1978 book, *Leadership*.

[17] Ibid., p. 20.

[18] See his 1985 work, *Leadership and Performance Beyond Expectations*.

distinction between "transactional" and "transformational" leadership, but while Burns conceives of them as two types of leadership, Bass views them as separate dimensions within "transformational" leadership. Hence for Bass, a leader can be both "transactional" and "transformational," and "transactional leadership" is only one of the components in "transformational leadership."

Bass defines the transactional aspect as the expected performance and the establishment of the ground rules for rewards. The other dimensions of transformational leadership are "charisma"[19] (as a vision and a sense of mission, and inspiration), "individualized consideration" (giving personal attention to followers and their needs, trusting and respecting them, and helping them to learn by encouraging responsibility), and "intellectual stimulation" (providing a flow of new ideas which challenge followers and which are supposed to stimulate a rethinking of old ways of doing things). He also adds two other transactional aspects to the definition of the transactional dimensions, namely, "contingent reward" (where the leader rewards followers for attaining specified performance levels) and "management by exception" (which refers to an approach in which the leader takes action when there is evidence of something not going according to plan).

An important implication of Bass's writings on this subject is that charisma alone is not sufficient for generating change, and that includes both system-wide change and the alteration of the follower's moods and propensity to effort. However, most of Bass's research on "transformational leadership" concentrates on the effects on the followers, and in particular, he developed the Multifactor Leadership Questionnaire (MLQ), a diagnostic tool to define such leaders in terms of their personal attributes, behavior, and their effects on followers. But his research does not analyze the process of transformation of organizations or system-wide changes, and in this respect, the field still seems to be lacking.

Visionary Leadership

By and large, researchers are in agreement that charismatic leaders are often characterized by a sense of strategic vision,[20] that is, a futuristic idealized goal for the society or organization.[21] While leaders with a mission (in the sense of a particular goal) can be charismatic as well, leaders with a vision are prone to charismatic attributions because of the ideal component of their mission. Jay Conger[22] says that the

---

[19] Note that for Bass, charisma is only one of the components in "transformational leadership."

[20] In reality, it is sometimes very difficult to distinguish between mission and vision, but it is important to make an analytical distinction between the two in order to define what vision is.

[21] This can be found in the writings of Weber ([1924] 1947); Berlew (1974); Zaleznik and Kets de Vrie (1975); House (1977); Willner (1984); Bass (1985); Bennis and Nannus (1985); Sashkin (1988); Conger (1989).

[22] 1988: 85–86.

idealized vision, in turn, makes the leader an adorable person who deserves respect, and is "worthy of identification and imitation by the followers"—thus reinforcing his attribution as being distinctly charismatic.

Focusing on organizations, Conger has argued that what makes vision unique in relation to ordinary tactical goals is that it provides a broad perspective on the organization's purpose. Unlike tactical goals, which often aim at a greater return on assets, increased market share, or the introduction of certain products, vision encompasses goals that are abstract. He introduces a typology of visions which relates to different focuses of inspiration, and argues that the most strategic visions can be categorized into four types (or an amalgamation of these four types) in relation to their main focus: whether that be on a particular product, on the revitalization of an organization, on a contribution to the work force itself, or on a contribution to society.

Although Conger's writings are more related to the "charismatic approach," his dealing with vision as "the cornerstone of charismatic leadership"[23] is entirely consistent with Weber's formulation of vision (or, in his terms, "charismatic ideas") as a central aspect of charisma. In his view, a leader is charismatic when his vision represents an embodiment of a perspective shared by followers in an idealized form. He argues that "the greater the degree to which the vision is shared by employees and addresses their deepest aspirations, the greater the likelihood the leader will be seen as charismatic." [24]

The most prominent scholar in the "visionary leadership" approach is Marshall Sashkin, and he elaborates a complex model that includes the leader's traits, behavior, and the nature of their vision. In his essay "The Visionary Leaders," Sashkin argues that the visionary leaders' primary concern is the transformation of an organizational culture according to a vision that he foresees. He also says that visions vary in their specific content, so that it is possible to identify some underlying common themes that refer to the processes of organizational operation or functioning. That means that certain basic issues must be dealt with by any vision, if it is to have a substantial impact on the organization. The three basic underlying themes that he identifies in visions are "dealing with change" (visions that work in helping the organization deal with change), "ideal goals" (incorporating goals not in the sense of clearly defined ends but in terms of ideal conditions or processes), and "people working together" (a focus on people, both as organization's members and as customers).

Sashkin correlates these three basic themes to Talcott Parsons's "action framework" theory[25] and its classification of the four functions of every social system (i.e., adaptation, goal attainment, integration, and values). For Sashkin, the visionary element that deals with change refers to the adaptation function (in which all organizations must adapt to meet the demands of changing environments). The second thematic

---

[23] See "The Charismatic Leader: Behind the Mystique of Exceptional Leadership," 1989: p. 36.

[24] Ibid., p. 48.

[25] See his 1960 *Structure and Process in Modern Societies*.

element—the ideal goals—refers to the function of goal attainment; the third deals with "people" and refers to the integration function, and the fourth function in the action framework (values) does not refer to a specified thematic element in the vision but is treated as the most basic of all, and as such is threaded into all the other three elements.

According to Sashkin, visionary leaders are characterized by two basic personal attributes. The first is a personality orientation focused on obtaining power (as in social power that refers to people and not for himself or herself). This socialized power ensures that the vision is shared and enacted by others. The second attribute is the cognitive skill of visioning. By this he refers to abilities such as taking advantage of opportunities as they appear, thinking and planning over a long period of time, expressing the vision through behavior, explaining the vision to others, and the ability to expand the vision.[26]

Sashkin also suggests that visionary leaders generate specific behaviors, which stimulate and enhance the enactment of the vision. This will include behaviors like focusing attention on specific key issues: effective interpersonal communication of the vision (like active listening); demonstrating trustworthiness by showing consistency in their actions; displaying respect for others; and creating and taking calculated risks (and making clear and strong commitments to these risks once they are decided on).

Reflecting on the New Leadership Theories

Yet in spite of Bass's insistence that charisma is just one of the components of "transformational leadership," there is a discernible tendency among scholars of leadership to treat the two as synonymous. Even in Bass's research on transformational leadership, charisma is by far the major component of that leadership, so the treatment of the two is at the very least difficult to distinguish. This tendency for charismatic and transformational leadership to be confused or at least indistinguishable from one another manifests itself in a number of other ways. Some writers, for example, use the formulation "charismatic/transformational leadership"[27] and by this imply that the two concepts are barely distinguishable. As an indication of this tendency to treat the two as interchangeable, Alan Brynman[28] points to the subject index to the *Academy of Management Review*, Volume 14, 1989, and cites the following entry: "Leadership, Transformational. See leadership, charismatic."

---

[26] This means that the leader applies the vision not just in one limited way or not even in a variety of essentially similar ways but applies it in many different ways, in a wide range of circumstances and to a broader context.

[27] Avolio and Gibbons (1988) provide one example of this.

[28] In *Charisma and Leadership in Organization* (1992).

Against this tendency to treat charismatic and transformational leadership as synonymous, an attempt to draw a distinction between the two has come from Harrison Trice and Janice Beyer,[29] who suggest that while both forms are essentially innovative, charismatic leaders typically create new organizations, whereas transformational leaders are concerned with the change of existing organizations. But still the affinities between the two are greater than the distinctions, and there are overlapping focuses within the three versions of leadership. For example, Conger's view of vision as the most significant component in charismatic leadership overlaps Sashkin's treatment of visionary leadership. At the same time, Sashkin's treatment implies similar notions to those of the transformational leadership approach (as expressing values and ideals and working toward a meaningful purpose). There are also clear affinities between Sashkin's approach and many of the central ideas in the charismatic and transformational approaches to leadership, even though Sashkin argues that his emphasis on visionary leadership differs in the way he combines three central features: the distinctive personal characteristics of the leaders, their decisive impact on an organization's functioning (such as changing the organization's culture), and their distinctive behavioral patterns.

To add to this, both Brynman and Shamir argue that a number of terms are currently being used to describe what are essentially very similar phenomena, yet different labels are given to the kind of leadership that exhibits these revered qualities. Thus, the argument is that when writing about leadership that is charismatic or transformational, or visionary, many authors employ similar themes and motifs to those who write about charismatic leadership in organizations. To some extent, the themes overlap—for example, charisma is often depicted as a component of transformational or visionary leadership, or certain unifying ideas, like vision, are seen as common to charismatic and other leadership approaches. And the authors acknowledge that while there are differences between the various labels used, they are mainly a matter of emphasis. Yet even though these different labels do share various common motifs, and while the distinctions between them are not clear-cut, neither Brynman nor Shamir suggests that charismatic leadership is the same as transformational or visionary leadership.

Perhaps what we should do is not to try so much to find differences or distinguish between these recent approaches, but to distinguish them from the previous, traditional approaches to leadership and see how they promote the study of charisma. It is perhaps only then, when seeing them as a new reconstruction of the theoretical paradigm of leadership, that we can recognize the collective strength of all these recent approaches. Alan Brynman,[30] for example, argues that in comparison to earlier approaches, a much greater attention has been given to the issue of "exactly what leadership is" and a greater emphasis to "vision" as a central motif, and that a more complex view of leadership (as an amalgam of both personal and behavioral

---

[29] In their 1986 essay, "Charisma and its Routinization in Two Social Movements Organizations."

[30] This argument can be found in Brynman (1992: 144).

factors)[31] is offered. The fact that Brynman "lumps" all these approaches into one term—namely, "the new leadership" approach—indeed is based on the close affinities between the approaches. But more significantly, Brynman's term implies that there has been a paradigmatic shift in the theoretical treatment of leadership.

It is in this respect that attempts to synthesize the three versions by distinguishing them from more traditional theories of leadership[32] imply once again that the way leadership is defined, and the treatment of leadership as a concept, have both been transformed. Boaz Shamir, for example, argues[33] that while traditional theories take performance, satisfaction, and cognition of subordinates as their dependent variables, the new leadership theories generally focus on the self-esteem of followers, their trust and confidence in the leader, their motivation to perform beyond the call of duty, and their emotional responses to work. While traditional leadership theories describe leaders in terms of task-oriented structuring behavior, the new approaches describe leaders in terms of articulating a vision and a mission, empowering followers, setting challenging expectations for them, and creating positive and inspirational images in their minds.[34] But there is also a difference in the behavior specified by the new approaches. While earlier theories describe leadership as a "transactional,"[35] instrumental kind of exchange relationship between the leader and the followers, the new leadership approaches emphasize symbolic leader behavior.[36]

Overall, Brynman seems to argue that with these recent approaches, leaders that are charismatic/transformational/visionary seem to be able to transform the needs, values, preferences, and aspirations of followers from self-interest to collective interests. They empower others, inspire, challenge the status quo, and adopt a proactive stance. Such actions cause the followers to become highly committed to the leader's mission, to make significant personal sacrifices in the interest of the mission, and to perform above and beyond the call of duty. The emphasis in the recent leadership theories, or the exceptional notion of leadership (as having vision as a core aspect and as an interactive process based on social attributions and perceptions), is, as we shall see in the next chapter, aligned with Weber's initial formulation of the nature of charisma and its social processes of transformation.

---

[31] This would suspend the old question of whether leadership is a matter of born traits or behavior that can be learned.

[32] Examples of this can be found in Brynman (1992); Yukl (1989); and Shamir, House, and Arthur (1993).

[33] In his 1992 essay, "The Charismatic Relationship: Alternative Explanations and Predictions."

[34] For example, rather than treating leaders as transforming organizations who affect the cognition or the task environment of followers, by offering incentives or the threat of punishment – leaders are said to transform organizations by infusing into them ideological values and moral purpose (and by inducing a strong commitment to mission and transformation).

[35] Like the provision of direction and support, and the reinforcement behaviors.

[36] Like emphasizing vision, values, intellectual stimulation, high confidence in followers, and high expectations from followers. This shift parallels the sociological shift between Hollander's approach and his treatment of leadership as a social exchange process [In Hollander E.P (1964) *Leaders, Groups and Influence*. New York: Oxford University Press] – to Shils's (1965) symbolic treatment of charisma.

All this work carried out by scholars of organizational behavior has brought the study of charisma to the mainstream of leadership studies. The theoretical emphasis on cognition, values, ideals, and meaning is of utmost relevance to the focus of our own research and will continue to prevail throughout our analysis. It provides a core link to the understanding of charisma in its philosophical, existential notions, as well as charisma's links with the socio-psychological aspect of identity formation.

Yet what still seems to be missing in this new genre of approaches is a broader, macro perspective, both in terms of contextual implications on the nature and form of charisma, and also in terms of how the leaders engage with society in a wider sense. Most of the studies cited tend to be confined to the organizational, messo level and do not address the larger possible interactions of charisma with the structure. This lack could be attributed to the point of departure of most of these scholars, and with their being organizational behaviorists. Such a perspective seems to confine itself to the study of social messo level (that of organizations), and to be less developed in the fields of the macro dimensions of charisma.

Indeed little has been said and studied with regard to contextual factors related to charisma. The modest amount of attention given to date mainly discusses the existence of a social crisis as a possible contextual precondition influencing the emergence of charisma.[37] Much less attention, if at all, has been granted to the analysis of other possible contextual factors interacting with the nature of the charismatic leadership and its concrete manifestation. This analytical "vacuum" is not unique to the research on charisma, but to the research of leadership in general. Although Richard Osborn and James Hunt[38] try to work out a classification of relevant macro factors that may effect management,[39] they do not make any propositions or empirical validations, and their model stays as just a suggested list of possible contextual factors.

Some studies that do take into consideration contextual elements seem to focus more on situational factors on the messo level of the organization. For example, an analysis of processes of leadership and of the nature of the situations in which people are especially sensitized to the appeal of the leader has been conducted by scholars like House, and by Fred Fiedler.[40] These theories are based on the assumption that different behavior patterns (or trait patterns) will be effective in different situations and that the same behavior pattern is not optimal in all situations. They emphasize the importance of contextual factors, such as the leader's authority and discretion, the nature of the work performed by the leader's unit, the attributes of subordinates, and the nature of the external environment. These approaches describe

---

[37] We will elaborate on this precondition in Chap. 6.

[38] In "Toward a Macro-Oriented Model of Leadership: An Odyssey" (1982), "Environment and Organizational Effectiveness" (1974), and "An Adaptive-Reactive Theory of Leadership: The Role of Macro Variables in Leadership Research" (1975).

[39] Note that these dimensions may differ when dealing with leadership and with charismatic leadership in particular.

[40] See "A 1976 Theory of Charismatic Leadership" by House (1977), and Fred Fiedler's article "The Contingency Model and the Dynamics of Leadership" (1978).

how aspects of the situation may moderate the relationship between the leader's behavior (or traits) and the outcomes. Although the studies yielded inconsistent findings, they have contributed to the conceptual expansion of leadership such that it encompasses a larger scope of analysis.

However, because these studies emphasize organizational factors such as the nature of the organization, the task definition, and the particular nature of the followers, they do not usually extend the messo level of analysis,[41] and they do not deal with elements of macro societal factors, and their possible interplay with charisma. Even Edgar Schein's treatment of leadership and culture,[42] though important in introducing the cultural dimension to the study of leadership, is mainly confined to an organization's cultural messo level of analysis.

Contextual factors which are societal, political, cultural, historical, and economic may have an impact on various dimensions of leadership. To name just a few that come to mind, there may be an impact of social dimensions on the concrete content of the social category of leadership (for example, the traits attributed to this category, or what it takes to be a leader). There may be cultural and social impacts on the nature and form of the charismatic relationship with the followers, on the kind and degree of social manifestations toward the leader, on the kind of behavior that the leaders display, and on the mode of vision articulation and its themes. There may also be a political impact on the legitimacy of a certain type of leadership and on the type of questions that leaders can and cannot deal with, and there are many other such possible contextual impacts.

For one thing, macro contextual factors are difficult to define and analyze operationally because in reality, they not only overlap but also form and reform in an ongoing change process. Yet, it is nonetheless important to clarify the various possible factors and their actual influence, at least analytically, and it is here that a macro-level sociological perspective may contribute to their clarification. We will begin the next chapter by giving an overview of the macro sociological approaches to charisma.

---

[41] Also Brynman, Stephens, and Campo (1996) – recent research yielded inconclusive findings with regard to the impact of the context, but even their research was mainly confined to messo level factors, rather than macro-level factors such as culture, history, society, politics, and others.

[42] See his *Organization Culture and Leadership: A Dynamic View* (1985).

Chapter 2
Explaining Charisma: A Macro View

Weber on Charisma: The Introduction of the Concept to the Field of Social Power

It is through Weber's exposition of charisma in the sociology of religion and his historically based account of the nature of modernity that he forges what is for many writers the starting point for an appreciation of the concept.[1]

The term charisma is derived initially from the New Testament where it was used to refer to the "gift of grace." It is the evidence of having received the Holy Spirit, as manifested in the capacity to prophesy, to heal or to speak in tongues. However, Weber's use of the term moves it well beyond this somewhat specific range of religious phenomena. With charisma, according to Weber, allegiance is owed to persons who possess charisma by virtue of their unique attributes and abilities. And it is these individual and specific features that result in the special allegiance shown by the followers of charismatic leaders.

The initial stimulus for his exposition of charisma was Weber's interest in the mechanisms by which power comes to be seen as legitimate by those to whom it is applied. When power is viewed as legitimate (a situation which can be contrasted with power that has to be enforced), those who possess power can be said to have authority. Weber recognized three types of authority: rational, traditional, and charismatic, each type representing a different claim to the legitimate exercise of power.[2] Unlike traditional, rational, or legal leaders who are appointed or elected under existing traditions and rules, a charismatic leader is chosen by the followers out of the

---

[1] Although it has been stretched far beyond its original meaning and context in many later treatments for example Shils's demystification of charisma (1965).

[2] Each of these types should be viewed as a "pure" or "ideal" type, that is, an extreme delineation of the chief characteristics of the phenomena it stands for and which may never be found in such a form in reality.

Dayan Hava and Chan Kwok-bun, *Charismatic Leadership in Singapore: Three Extraordinary People*, DOI 10.1007/978-1-4614-1451-3_2, © Springer Science+Business Media, LLC 2012

belief that he is extraordinarily gifted, and authority, based on charismatic grounds, rests on devotion to the exceptional sanctity, heroism, or exemplary character of the individual. It also rests on the normative patterns or order that are revealed or ordained by him. The charismatic bases of power are therefore personal:

> The term 'charisma' will be applied to a certain quality of an individual personality by virtue of which he is considered extraordinary and treated as endowed with supernatural, superhuman, or at least specifically exceptional powers or qualities. These are such as not to be accessible to the ordinary person, but are regarded as of divine origin or as exemplary, and on the basis of them the individual concerned is treated as a 'leader.'[3]

In contrast to the tendency nowadays to treat charisma as a sole characteristic of the charismatic individual, Weber did in fact recognize the importance of the leader's validation by his followers. In this way, in order for a charismatic relationship to exist, the charismatic person must establish a relationship in which the governed submit because of their belief in his extraordinary qualities. But an important corollary of the charismatic leader's need for his claims to be validated is that, should his powers or abilities desert him, his followers will likewise abandon him and this implies that the relationships between the followers and their leader are not simple; they are complex, ambivalent,[4] and can be volatile.

Since the leader has to be constantly re-approved, he needs his followers, and this dependency is tricky, since he does not wait for them to recognize him but sees it as their duty to make this recognition. Since the leader is capable of evoking a sense of belief, he can thereby demand obedience. According to Weber, this acknowledgment is, in a way, an "imposed expectation" of the leader since he believes it is their duty to obey him: "However, he does not derive his claims from the will of his followers, in the manner of an election; rather, it is their duty to recognize his charisma."[5] In other words, potential charismatic leaders do not passively await recognition by their followers, but demand it. Weber says:

> Every true leader in this sense, preaches, creates, or demands new obligations (…) recognition is a duty (…) but where charisma is genuine, it is not this which is the basis of legitimacy. This basis lies rather in the conception that it is the duty of those who have been called to a charismatic mission to recognize its quality and to act accordingly (…) No prophet has ever regarded his quality as dependent on the attitudes of the masses toward him. No elective king or military leader has ever treated those who have resisted him or tried to ignore him otherwise than as delinquent in duty.[6]

Reinhard Bendix has argued[7] that the above passage suggests that both the recognition by followers and the leader's own claims and actions are fundamentally ambivalent because for the charisma of a leader to be present, it must be recognized

---

[3] Weber *The Theory of Social and Economic Organization* ([1924] 1947) p. 241.

[4] They are not of a total mastery by the leader (since he needs his followers' constant recognition) yet once accepted as such, he gains mastery over the followers' beliefs, emotions, and actions.

[5] Quoted in Runciman and Matthews (1978: 113).

[6] Ibid., pp. 242, 244.

[7] In his 1968 essay, "Reflections on Charismatic Leadership."

by his followers.[8] But even a personal devotion of followers is easily "contaminated" by the desire for a "sign" that will confirm the existence of charisma. In turn, the leader demands unconditional devotion from his followers, and he will construe any demand for a sign or proof of his gift of grace as a lack of faith on their part and a dereliction of duty.

In Weber's writings, the charismatic leader has a mission or a task which "inverts all value hierarchies and overthrown custom, law and tradition."[9] Weber argues that success and failure contribute to this transitory nature of charismatic authority. Failure is a serious challenge to the charismatic's authority since it reveals a less than superhuman character on the leader's part: "Above all (...) his divine mission must 'prove' itself in that those who surrender to him must fare well. If they do not fare well, he is obviously not the master sent by gods."[10] Conversely, success confirms the powers of the leader and is therefore critical to sustaining charismatic authority.

In Weber's eyes, charisma is usually a revolutionary force that involves a radical break with the preexisting order, regardless of whether that order is based on traditional or legal authority. While legal and traditional authorities are capable of a considerable degree of continuity (because of its institutionalization and its detachment from specific individuals), charisma can easily burn itself out. This is related to Weber's view of charisma as contrary to bureaucracy. To him, they represent divergent positions in relation to rules, saying: "Bureaucratic authority is specifically rational in the sense of being bound to intellectually analyzable rules, while charismatic authority is specifically irrational in the sense of being foreign to all rules."[11] Also, the absence of an administrative staff of technically trained officials (who could have helped to routinize the charismatic authority), contributes to its temporary and transitory notion.

Weber does argue that charisma can be routinized (e.g., in the preselection criteria for the successor, a choice of successor through revelation, designation, and so forth) but only at the cost of its depersonalization. No longer is it a characteristic that applies to a special individual but instead it becomes a quality that can be transferred or acquired, or is attached to a position in an organizational setting, adding to its bureaucratic attributes.

The question that arises here is whether Weber's notion of charisma is relevant to an understanding of leadership in the modern world. Many scholars argue that the type of charisma he describes is not viable in modern societies. They rely for this argument on the fact that the examples Weber used were mainly from ancient societies and on Weber's own predictions that charisma as a social historical force will wane with the onrush of modernity (and its omnipotent bureaucracy). However, Weber did not perceive charisma to be in the exclusive province of the past because,

---

[8] Again, it is intrinsically ambivalent because the recognition of the leader in the ideal typical case is a matter of duty.

[9] Weber ([1924] 1947), op. cit., p. 117.

[10] Quoted in (in Runciman & Matthews, 1978: 243).

[11] Op. cit., ([1924] 1947), op. cit., p. 244.

along with many premodern illustrations (such as the prophets in ancient Judaism), Weber used other modern cases of charisma, one example being that of President F.D.R. Roosevelt.

Shils on Charisma: Introducing a Macro Symbolic Notion

Weber's elaboration of charisma was developed by Edward Shils by proposing a "sociological symbolic approach" that connects charismatic leadership to the question of social meaning, social structure, and power,[12] and the latter's view of charisma is more dispersed and less intense than Weber's theory. While Weber's writings imply that charisma as an attribution toward a certain individual has a temporary or transitory notion, Shils makes a systematic attempt to stretch the concept of charisma beyond the very specific meanings and concepts upon which Weber had concentrated.

Compared to Weber, who emphasized charisma as a temporary and individualistic phenomenon, Shils enlarges the scope by arguing that charisma can also be found in modern societies and in nonpersonal social entities such as permanent social structures like positions, organizations, and institutions. He treats charisma as a metaphysical quality attached to what is regarded as the center of society, and as a universalistic, common social characteristic of every society, in its everyday life.

This enlargement resulted in the reduction of both the intensity and extreme rareness of charisma, as they had been emphasized by Weber. Whereas Weber tended to view charisma more as an essentially revolutionary force, Shils proposed that it is present in the ordinary, everyday operation of the society, and as such, it does not necessarily imply a tendency to disrupt the status quo.

With this approach, the concept of charisma was demystified into a more mundane and common phenomenon, spread throughout various spheres of social life. But this treatment of charisma did not ruin its mystic notion altogether because in this treatment charisma is intrinsically connected to a symbolic realm of meaning. According to Shils, within the whole notion of charismatic attribution is a component of evoking awe and reverence. These two elements—awe and reverence—are invoked by "social objects" (institutions, symbols, or people) that help us understand the condition of man in the universe and the exigencies of social life and, as such, strike at the very heart of the need for symbolic social order. In other words, those persons, roles, and institutions possessing charismatic attributes embody the core or central values of the societies to which they are attached. They are therefore instrumental in helping people understand the nature of their social condition.

Shils's approach to charisma is very much related to the human need for meaning and order, which forms a human predisposition to accept and legitimize charismatic leadership. And this conceptualization partially bridges the gap between charisma

---

[12] See his 1965 essay, "Charisma, Order and Status" and his 1968 essay, "Charisma."

as an extraordinary event or quality and as a constituent element of any orderly social life. The search for meaning, consistency, and order is not something extraordinary, like something that exists only in extreme disruptive situations or among pathological or rare personalities. The search exists in all stable social situations even if it is focused within some specific parts of the social structure (like in the hands of a few in power) and not only in times of crises. In other words, this approach addresses charisma as a fundamental part of every "normal" society and not as a phenomenon related to disturbed phases of crisis or revolution. In Shils's words:

> A great fundamental identity exists in all societies and one of the elements of this identity is the presence of the charismatic element. Even if religious belief had died, which it has not, the condition of man in the universe and the exigencies of social life still remain, and the problems to which religious belief has been the solution in most cultures still remain, demanding solution by those who confront them. The solution lies in the construction or discovery of order (…) the need for order and the fascination of disorder persist, and the charismatic propensity is a function of the need for order.
> Whether it be God's law or the society as a whole or even a particular corporate body or institution like an army, whatever embodies, expresses or symbolizes the essence of an ordered cosmos or any other significant sector thereof awakens the disposition of awe and reverence, the charismatic disposition.[13]

This idea has been explored by Smuel Eisenstadt, who seems to agree with Shils's underlying assumptions on the symbolic nature of charisma. He argues that the human need for meaning is linked to the egoistic wishes of human beings[14] and that a very important part of human needs seems to consist of their quest for and conception of the symbolic order, of the "good society," and of the quest for participation in such an order. This calls for a rather special response from those who are able to respond to this quest. Therefore, the charismatic quality of an individual, as perceived by others or by himself, lies in what is thought to be his connection with some very central feature of man's existence and the cosmos in which he lives. The centrality coupled with intensity makes it extraordinary, and thus charismatic.

Charisma's centrality is constituted in its formative power in initiating, creating, governing, transforming, maintaining, or destroying what is vital in man's life. Shils argues, "That central power has often, in the course of man's existence, been conceived of as God, the ruling power or creator of the universe, or some divine or other transcendent power controlling or markedly influencing human life and the cosmos within it exists."[15] In other words, the "center" is represented as a distinct aspect of any institutional framework and as the structural locus of the macro societal institutionalization of charisma.

According to Shils, the close relation between charisma and the power center is rooted in the fact that both are concerned with the maintenance of order and with a

---

[13] In Shils's (1965) essay, "Charisma, Order and Status," p. 203.

[14] See his 1968 work, *Max Weber: On Charisma and Institution Building*, and his 1995 book, *Power, Trust and Meaning*.

[15] Shils, op. cit. (1965: p. 201).

provision of some meaningful symbolic and institutional order. The contact with the center can be attained through various ways and not only through the incumbent of positions in the power center. The symbolic center of the society can be touched also through reflective wisdom, through disciplined scientific penetration, artistic expression, forceful and confident reality-transforming action, and other possible forms. Shils says:

> This contact through inspiration, embodiment or perception, with the vital force which underlies man's existence, his coming to be and passing away, is manifested in demeanor, words and actions. (…) The person who through sensitivity, cultivated or disciplined by practice and experience, by rationally controlled observation and analysis, by intuitive penetration, or by artistic disclosure, reaches or is believed to have attained contact with that "vital layer" of reality is, by virtue of that contact, a charismatic person.

The attributional aspect and the divine nature of the charismatic attribution are emphasized by both Shils and Weber. But Shils suggests that the roots of divinity are related to the symbolic and power center of society, and he argues that Weber was referring to a very special form of charisma that occurs relatively infrequently, while normal charisma is an active and effective phenomenon, essential to the maintenance of the routine order of the society.

Seeing the demise of pure personalized charisma in advanced societies, Shils suggests that the sheer size, complexity, and power of modern bureaucratic organizations engender, in the individual, a sense of mystical wonder and "awe" toward those who hold positions of power and responsibility in these omnipotent systems. According to Shils, then, charisma has not died out in modern societies but rather has adapted itself to the predominant social form of bureaucratic organization (as in charisma of the office).

This symbolic approach to charisma established a new framework for its analysis and consequently influenced a whole generation of sociologists. Clifford Geertz, for example, showed how kings used rituals and symbols of power to evoke a connection with the social center,[16] and in *The Spellbinders: Charismatic Political Leadership*, A.R. Willner used a symbolic approach to study charismatic leaders at the macro level of society and showed how the leaders' charisma is correlated to their ability to symbolically evoke and invoke core social values and myths.

But not everyone accepted Shils's approach, and it was subjected to a detailed critique by Joseph Bensman and Michael Givant who argued that he "stretches the idea of charisma to such a degree, and in such a way, that it encompasses a host of different manifestations and becomes almost indistinguishable from the notion of legitimacy, of which charisma was only one expression according to Weber."[17] They also argued that such a conceptualization loses its personalized dimension, which is one of the core arguments in Weber's treatment of charisma.

---

[16] See his *The Interpretation of Cultures* (1973).

[17] See their 1975 essay, "Charisma and Modernity: The Use and Abuse of a Concept."

Eisenstadt on Charisma: Introducing the Institutional Dimension

In most of the literature on charisma,[18] the stages of social changes and institutionalization are separated, referring to institutionalization as the aftermath of change or the succession of charisma. In fact, Weber argues that charisma's essence is its opposition to institutions and rules. He also refers to the problem of a routinization of charisma as the stage where charisma cannot operate any longer through the personification of the leader and must undergo transformation to develop into a different type of authority (such as traditional or legal), for it to continue to exist.[19]

Against this tendency to separate charisma and institutionalization and to see the latter as a successor to the former, Eisenstadt has argued that charismatic leadership is in fact impossible without the application of different modes of institutionalization and that although order and change may be analytically distinct, in reality, they interact closely.[20] His treatment introduces the relation of charisma to order and institutions and not only to change or to unstable forces, and he argues that creativity and freedom (of which charismatic leadership is one example) do not exist outside the institutional framework, saying:

> The antithesis between the regular flow of organized social relations and of institutional frameworks on the one hand, and of charismatic qualities and activities on the other, is not extreme or total (…) While analytically this distinction between 'organized' routine and charisma is sharp, this certainly does not imply total dichotomy between concrete situations.[21]

While it is common to find the terms "routinization" and "institutionalization" being employed interchangeably in the literature on charisma, Eisenstadt argues that institutionalization is not a "post-mortem" phenomenon, but a process through which charismatic leaders (or their successors) try to retain the original vitality of charisma. Thus, institutionalization does not refer to the aftermath of charisma but to its operating social mechanisms while emerging and "in vivo." Although charisma is regarded as juxtaposed to stability and institutions, charisma is treated as a phenomenon which actually acts and maintains itself via institutionalization. By institutionalization mechanisms, he refers not only to concrete formal institutions but also to different forms of formalization, including initial social patterns or what Peter Berger and Thomas Luckman have called "typificatory schemes."[22]

---

[18] With very few exceptions – see for example Bradley's (1987) research on the organization of communities with or without charismatic leaders.

[19] See Weber ([1924] 1947) op. cit.

[20] A point implied also by Kanter's (1984) analysis of leaders as "Change masters," and the techniques that they use to implement change. It is also implied by Schein in his treatment of leadership's construction of organizational culture (1985) and by Giddens (1984) in his notion of structuration as an ongoing process of intertwined change and patterning of structure.

[21] See *Max Weber: On Charisma and Institution Building*, p. xx.

[22] In *The Social Construction of Reality* (1969), p. 29.

This is a "revolutionary" treatment of charisma, particularly in the light of Weber's emphasis on the noninstitutionalized, anti-institution nature of charisma. It treats institutionalization as an essential mechanism for social phenomena to operate at all. The institutionalization of charisma, according to this view, is inherent in its nature, and the organizational and institutional mechanisms are regarded as essential also in the initial stages of the emergence of leadership as well as throughout the ongoing process of social change itself. Eisenstadt, for example, argues that the leader works through a group or a band that institutionalizes itself, as well as through the institutionalization of the charismatic mission and symbols that have to be institutionalized at least partially, in order for the leadership to be effective.[23] Eisenstadt says:

> The test of any great charismatic leader lies not only in his ability to create a single event or great movement, but also in his ability to leave a continuous impact on an institutional structure—to transform any given institutional setting by infusing into it some of his charismatic vision, by investing the regular, orderly offices, or aspects of social organization, with some of his charismatic qualities and aura. Thus here the dichotomy between the charismatic and the orderly regular routine of social organization seems to be obliterated.[24]

Hence, according to Eisenstadt, institutionalization is also inherently embedded in the need for the reconstruction of the new transformation because a crucial aspect of the charismatic personality or group is not only the possession of some extraordinary, exhilarating qualities but also the ability to reorder and reorganize both the symbolic and the institutional order. In other words, he refers to the leader's engagement with the construction of reality, not only with its deconstruction but also with the institutionalization of a new order. In his view, this engagement is a crucial aspect of charisma.[25]

Reflecting on the Major Sociological Explanations of Charisma

Indeed Weber's introduction of the concept to the social analysis of influence triggered a whole new appreciation of the leadership studies, and it forged what is for many writers the starting point for an appreciation of the concept. However, as William Friedland and Serge Moscovici both argue,[26] Weber's concept of charisma

---

[23] Bass mentions Chang's paper (1982) where Mao Tse-Tung is mentioned as an illustration to the argument that institutionalization does not bring routinization as Weber maintains. Rather, in fact, charismatic leadership such as Mao's was legitimized, reinforced, and maintained through institutional efforts.

[24] See *Max Weber: On Charisma and Institution Building* (1968), p. xxi.

[25] Also, Burns (1978) argues that true leadership is not merely symbolic or ceremonial: "The most lasting tangible act of leadership is the creation of an institution – that continues to exert moral leadership and foster needed social change long after the creative leaders are gone" (1978: 454).

[26] See Friedland's (1964) essay, "For a Sociological Concept of Charisma," p. 18 and Moscovici's *The Invention of Society* (1993) pp. 125, 221–222.

has not been very useful to sociology because Weber dealt with charisma more as a psychological than a social phenomenon. (According to Weber, allegiance is owed to persons who possess charisma by virtue of their unique attributes and abilities as perceived by their followers.) On the other hand, with the exception of Shils, Eisenstadt, and Geertz, who separately employed charisma as a concept to analyze power in terms of the symbolic social order,[27] sociological studies have been neglecting the concept of charisma, and it was never incorporated into other major theoretical sociological discussions.

Weber's emphasis on the subjective element in the attribution of charisma forged a "mythological" aspect in charisma whereby the ontological condition of the phenomena is referred to as being more of a social fantasy than of a real objective "social fact" (to use Durkheim's concept). This made it even harder for charisma to be incorporated in sociological analysis. This notion has even been treated by some researchers (e.g., James Meindl)[28] as an extreme subjective phenomenon: a mythical fantasy constructed totally in the followers' minds, having nothing to do whatsoever with external and objective reality. In this approach, the charismatic leader himself is not relevant at all: only the follower's attributions creating his image and acting accordingly. This conception of leadership (termed also as the "romance of leadership") is grounded on the human "fundamental attribution error,"[29] which results in a biased preference to understand important but ambiguous and causally indeterminate events in terms of salient individual factors which can be plausibly linked to these events. This leadership, according to this explanation, is a convenient explanatory category, and nothing more. In other words, the leader's behavior or personality may have very little to do with the charismatic effect—an effect that derives primarily from its "mythical" aspect.

However, even if charisma is a myth (which it is not), myth itself is not a matter for sociological indifference, least of all because myth and ideas represent social constructions of reality and because they enfold potential transformational social power. In Moscovici's words: "It is a proven truth that an idea, no matter what form it assumes, has the power of making us come together, of making us modify our feelings and modes of behavior and of exercising a constraint over us just as much as any external condition. It matters little if it appears irrational, dissenting, and even having undergone censorship." Thus, the mythical attribution to leadership cannot serve as a serious academic excuse for not including the analysis of the phenomena in social or sociological frameworks of analysis, since as Moscovici argued, "even if charisma is no more than a word, if we accept its existence whilst knowing

---

[27] Shils's essay, "Charisma, Order and Status" (1965), Eisenstadt's *Max Weber: On Charisma and Institution Building* (1968), and Geertz's "Centers, Kings and Charisma: Reflections on the Symbolics of Power" (1977).

[28] See his 1990 essay, "On Leadership: An Alternative to Conventional Wisdom" and his earlier 1985 essay, "The Romance of Leadership" coauthored with Ehrlich, S.D. and Dukerich, J.M.

[29] A term coined by Leo Ross in "The Intuitive Psychologist and his Shortcomings: Distortions in the Attribution Process" (1977).

little or nothing about its nature, has not the time come to acknowledge that we have been subscribing to a fascinating myth? It certainly contains myth. But myth itself is not a matter for indifference."[30]

Shils's approach was seminal in reframing charisma in a macro perspective.[31] His macro perspective introduces charisma's social agency and suggests that even if charisma is undoubtedly a personal relationship (resting upon individual characters), its nature still contains a sociological dimension, which, importantly, represents the central social core values, central principles, and social foundations that order the construction of reality. It places charisma studies in a macro perspective that enables the study of the relations between the leader and the society, as well as the interactions between the leaders and the macro structural context (both influencing and being influenced).

Furthermore, the symbolic dimension that he suggests, between charisma, core social principles, and the human quest for meaning,[32] is extremely significant in constructing a meaningful sociological framework for the analysis of charisma. Such a framework enables a study on charisma that can expound from the typical tendency to explain leadership by describing the mere traits and behaviors of the leader and his influence on the followers.

Following one line of argument, Shils's symbolic conceptualization of charisma would seem to offer a "second-degree" theoretical construct. This view comes from Billy J. Calder who says that all too often social science theory confuses first-degree constructs with those of the second degree.[33] The scientific confusion stems from the simplistic elevation of the explanations of everyday life (which actually represent the people's nonscientific efforts to understand and give meaning to their world) into a scientific status. According to Calder, the systematic and consistent use of everyday thought (with only minor redefinitions) consequently led to a simplistic analysis of leadership. For example, the study of leadership in terms of defining what the leader's traits, behavior, style, tasks, and the like are, is a kind of first-degree theoretical construct that does not achieve a real scientific development of the understanding of what leadership is about.

Eisenstadt's approach is significant to the reconceptualization of charisma as part of ordinary life. It reframes the seeming paradox or dichotomy between charisma and institutionalization so that instead of just being juxtaposed, charisma and institutionalization presuppose and complement each other. This conceptualization may suggest that charismatic leaders do not oppose institutions per se. They perhaps oppose the specific and concrete content and ideas of specific institutions but do not

---

[30] The quotes in this paragraph come from pages 115 and 125 of Moscovici's *The Invention of Society* (1993).

[31] As we have said in Chap. 1, this is still severely lacking in the new genre of leadership theories.

[32] For example, the suggestion that objects that exhibit charismatic attributes function to help us in understanding the condition of man in the universe and the exigencies of social life (Shils, 1965: 203).

[33] Calder bases his arguments on Cicourel's (1964) and Schutz's ([1932] 1967) criticism of social science. See his "An Attribution Theory of Leadership" (1977).

categorically oppose institutions as such. Their agency at least acknowledges the inevitable leaning on institutionalizational mechanisms as such. For one, we would guess that charismatic leaders do not oppose efforts that pattern and objectify their vision. This is a strong suggestion that charismatic leadership, eventually (or even, initially), engages in some kind of organization and institutionalization throughout. It is impossible otherwise to understand charisma without taking these processes into account.

One problem with regard to the approach of both Shils and Eisenstadt is that they seem more suitable for the study of leaders who preserve social order and are less useful for the study of social change, particularly those of a revolutionary type. In this respect, there seems to be a great departure from Weber's original formulation of charisma as revolutionary.[34] Although theoretically, both writers suggest that the symbolic framework caters to social transformational cases, even the sociological studies that followed their approach[35] place more emphasis on order (by pointing to the interactions between the leaders and the social symbolic center), and less on processes of social transformation. This is more so with regard to social changes of the revolutionary type, which seem to be a distinctive aspect of charisma.

Willner even makes special effort to reinterpret Weber's writings in light of the symbolic approach to show that it is possible that Weber himself was implying that charisma can be linked also to social order and its preservation and not only to revolutionary breaks. In her discussion on the definition of charismatic leadership, she attests that there is a very common error in the understanding of Weber's ideas regarding charisma, where his ideas are treated as a state of definition rather than a theoretical state. And she says that unless proved, Weber's suggested definition is a theoretical proposition that is still subjected to verification, "to lock these propositions immutably into the definition is to deprive us of the chance to test their validity."[36]

From this point of departure, Willner argues that some of Weber's discussions about the conditions and enactment of charisma were mistakenly regarded as part of the definition. The condition for its emergence, a requirement for its maintenance, a probable consequence, and some of the modes by which a charismatic leader exercises authority were unfortunately, and mistakenly, incorporated by some scholars into the definition of charismatic leadership itself. For example, the assimilation of the mission or the distress situation as part of the definition is a mistake, since they are possible explanations of its origins, and not part of its definition. The same holds for the revolutionary phenomenon: it is a possible consequence of charismatic leadership and not part of its definition.

---

[34] Also, Bensman and Givant (1975) argue that Shils's approach is in total contradiction to Weber's "pure-charisma," since pure charisma, in the Weberian sense, may have order to the extent that it has coherence, but pure charisma inevitably and by definition attacks the "order" of the society. And even Geertz's approach (1977), which is derived directly from Shils, agrees on this matter, suggesting that it is not just involvement with the center that may engender the attribution of charisma – but also oppositional involvement with the center.

[35] See for example, Geertz (1977) and Willner (1984).

[36] See her *The Spellbinders: Charismatic Political Leadership* (1984) p. 10.

Willner's position is that these aspects of charisma can be regarded as antecedents or contributory factors or consequences of the typical emergence of charismatic
phenomenon. In the same line, she argues that social revolutions are a possible consequence and not part of the definition. Her conclusion, therefore, is that there can
be atypical cases of charismatic leaders who seek to preserve[37] a prevailing social
order from falling apart (or who seek to revive one from the past, or in Shils's terms,
to symbolize the current order).

In trying to show that Weber viewed charisma as a phenomenon that could
engage in the presentation of order, Willner suggests that slight modifications in the
translation of Weber's writing contribute to some other errors in the translation.
While the translation emphasized more the notion of change,[38] she argues that a
more accurate translation could have stressed the possibility of the linkage between
charisma and order, with charisma as the symbolization, manifestation, or revelation
of order.[39] Her retranslation (and reinterpretation) of Weber's writings reinforce the
notion of charisma as being linked to the symbolic representation and preservation
of the social order.[40]

The approaches of both Shils and Eisentadt incorporate the study of charisma in
a sociological macro perspective (such as in the power center, existential dilemmas,
social structures and organizations, and others) much more than was the case in
Weber's approach. But all the three major sociological approaches to charisma still
require elaboration, clarification, and validation with regard to the nature of the relations between charisma and the context. As we argued in the introduction, the treatment of such an area is well within the discipline of sociology but has been still
substantially neglected.

In the next two chapters, we will conceptualize a framework that would enable
a sociological study of charisma that looks at both the macro and symbolic aspects
as well as human, individual intervention, and social transformations and change
generated by micro-level agency. The framework will rely on Shils's and
Eisenstadt's symbolic approaches to charisma and integrate Weber's revolutionary

---

[37] Her argument is in agreement with Oomen's (1968: 86) suggestion that it is possible to see
charisma as linked to order and not only to change.

[38] According to Willner, the first original German passage, in which Weber defines charisma, was
translated somewhat more than literally, using the word "normative", which has no equivalent in
German. But this does stress more the connotation of "created" or "shaped" which, while not
incorrect, does not clearly suggest an already created or established order. Willner argues that if the
German text had been translated somewhat more literally, it would have been very clear that Weber
specified two specific possibilities: the "revealed order" (that which the charismatic projects) and
the "created order" (that which the charismatic has established).

[39] She relates to the passages in Weber ([1924] 1947), pp. 202–208.

[40] Burns would have probably agreed with such an interpretation but for other reasons, to him,
charisma as the "revealed" order does not mean, by definition, stability because order can be very
dynamic in preserving or expressing the governing rules of structure (Burns, 1978: 415–416), a
view similar to that of Giddens (1984).

aspect. This emphasis is in line with current treatment of exceptional leadership by scholars of organizational behavior (whether that leadership is termed as "visionary," "transformational," or "charismatic") as consistently correlated with values, ideals, meaning, and organizational change.[41] In doing so, it will also incorporate the conceptualizations of Peter Berger and Anthony Giddens with regard to the nature of social reality as being intrinsically dual and dialectical.[42]

---

[41] See Sashkin (1988); Burns (1978); Bass (1985); Avolio Bruce (1995); Bruce and Gibbons (1988) Avolio Bruce and Bass Bernard (1988); Conger (1988, 1989); House (1977); Shamir, House, and Arthur (1993).

[42] See Berger's (1967) *Invitation to Sociology: A Humanistic Perspective* and his 1981 title *Sociology Reinterpreted* and Giddens' *The Constitution of Society: Outline of the Theory of Structuration* (1984).

Chapter 3
Explaining Charisma:
A Nondeterministic View

It is possible that mainstream sociology neglected charisma because it has never really fitted into the macro or micro sociological paradigms. The macro theories that ruled sociology until the last quarter of the twentieth century treated social phenomena as given facts that shape and determine human behavior and clearly had no room for the conceptual appreciation of a social phenomenon that puts at its forefront, prominent individuals. Similarly, micro theories developed in the last quarter of the century also could not deal with charismatic leadership, because its consequences on the social change of macro-level society were out of the scope of their emphasis on a micro-level analysis of the individual, reflective consciousness and the voluntaristic element of human reproductive action and their responses to situations.

The time, however, has come for the inclusion of charisma into sociological analysis for at least two reasons. First, it fits perfectly into the growing understanding, developed over the past 20 years, of the need to see the interactional processes between macro and micro theories (or levels of analysis) which constantly shape and reshape reality.[1] The concept of charisma enfolds, by way of its very nature, aspects and agents from different social levels—the individual, small groups, various social institutions and organizations, and the macro social system. Because of this, it has the potential of enabling meaningful discussions on the interactions and interplay between the various levels of society.

Second, charisma enfolds both micro, subjective dimensions as well as macro, objective ones. And even though charisma may have subjective aspects (arising from followers' attributions and perceptions)—it includes external and objective social aspects that are within the core of its nature and power. Once socially constructed, charisma is part of the external reality, imposing itself on individuals and the structure, and has generalizable and law-like relationships waiting to be discovered by social scientists.[2] It is in these aspects that a sociological treatment of

---

[1] See George Ritzer 1990: 348–350 for a discussion of this.

[2] That is, in spite of the individual's subjective and idiosyncratic consciousness aspect in reality construction.

Dayan Hava and Chan Kwok-bun, *Charismatic Leadership in Singapore:*
Three Extraordinary People, DOI 10.1007/978-1-4614-1451-3_3,
© Springer Science+Business Media, LLC 2012

charisma triggering micro, messo, and macro change, and all facing structural constraints in all these levels, can be relevant and analytically meaningful.

This chapter will comb through possible philosophical and conceptual perspectives that can serve as a ground and language for the treatment of charisma in a micro–macro dialectical perspective (that is capable of dealing with social change that is originated by individuals). In doing so, the chapter will attend to the endemic dialectics between micro and macro levels of society, or in other words, it will try to synthesize sociological approaches that are capable of attending to both the subjective and objective aspects of reality in general and of charismatic leadership in particular.

This will not be an easy task because most sociological macro perspectives (e.g., those of Durkheim) do not seem to see the individual as a significant social agent. Rather, to explain social change, they tend to rely on either structural or other external causes, and do not accord any such significant role to micro-level agents. However, a theoretical compromise can be achieved by synthesizing various approaches into a kind of humanistic, nondeterministic, nonmechanistic macro approach.

Placing Leadership Analysis in the Dilemma of Freedom vs. Determinism

As leadership is situated in a macro–micro dialectic, it embeds a philosophical (and ontological) discussion regarding human determinism vs. freedom. This is a dilemma that is sociologically reflected in the long battle between different interpretive action theories—the macro deterministic vs. the micro subjective.

It is quite reasonable to assume that research on charismatic leadership cannot be based on the idea of "fatalism," simply because fatalism would leave no role for human intervention (not even of a leadership kind). Fatalism implies that the future is always beyond our control, meaning that all events are irrevocably fixed and predetermined, and cannot be altered in any way by human beings.

Scientific determinism is spread through various disciplines, as well as among macro and micro approaches such as Newton's physics, Darwin's genetics and biology, Hegel's history, Skinner's behavioral psychology, Hospers' philosophy, the sociology of Durkheim, and others. But none of these approaches can serve as a point of departure. Although they relate to human action, they do not acknowledge the possibility of freedom or intentional choices, which are fundamental to leadership, and in these deterministic approaches, all events have external causation which means that there can be no such thing as freedom, free will, or human intention and intervention.

A common characteristic of all these approaches is that the researchers do not find the basic causes for any event or action within human control. These other external, nonpersonal causative factors are actually outside the control of the person's choice or action and determine both the way he is and the way he acts. These approaches treat humans as programmed to choose and act in certain ways, predetermined by other (micro or macro) forces.

Durkheim, for example,[3] concentrated mostly on social constraints in his various discussions of the nature of sociology, arguing that the structural properties of society form constraining influences over an individual's action. To him, this is because societal totalities, not only preexist and postdate the lives of the individuals who reproduce them in their activities, but also stretch across space and time away from a particular individual. In Durkheim's conceptualization, social facts have properties that confront each single individual as "objective" features that limit that person's scope of action. The "objectivity" of the institutional world confronts the individual as undeniable facts. Whether he likes it or not, the institutions are there, external to him, persistent in their reality. These external world's "thinking-like" properties define what he will or will not do, as well as each individual's incorporation of what is, or is not, proper to do.

Contrary to such fatalistic or deterministic approaches, a basic conceptual assumption for our research is that leadership enacts not only from macro constraints (such as environmental, social, or historical constraints), or micro constraints (such as the physiological or the psychological)—but also out of reflective awareness, and personal intentions, which cannot be reasonably explained, either by macro, structural and deterministic approaches or micro deterministic ones. Although acknowledging that leadership is not altogether a process free of external or internal constraints, a fruitful analysis of leadership would require sociological frameworks that introduce the role of individuals, their ability to act, to reflect, and to make individual choices.

A moderate deterministic approach will suit the framework somewhat better. Such an approach would maintain that although there is universal causation, some of this causation originates with human beings. This approach would therefore give meaning to the phrase: "human freedom." Of course, no one is completely free. If there is freedom, it is by nature limited, since freedom by definition refers to some structure; otherwise it is chaos. People are both free and constrained, yet this freedom to choose does not mean that people act in a totally free environment. Rather, people possess the human ability to make personal choices within defined situations, albeit constraining as they are, choices that, consequently, can make a difference in the world. According to the existentialists, if human beings can be said to cause some of their actions by means of their own minds and wills—then it can be said that they have some freedom.

Søren Kierkegaard[4] asserted that "the most tremendous thing which has been granted to man is: the choice, freedom." Existentialists agree with Kierkegaard that freedom and choice are pivotal concepts in the description and interpretation of human existence, and indeed, freedom for Sartre[5] is indistinguishable from human reality. Sartre linked this human "freedom" to consciousness as directional and creative, in the sense that consciousness "intends" things rather than merely passively

---

[3] Quoted in Giddens's *Emile Durkheim: Selected Writings* (1972).

[4] Quoted in O.C. Schrag's *Existence and Freedom* (1961).

[5] In *Existentialism and Humanism* (1952).

receives them. Hence, to him, the human mind is capable of directing itself in different ways and selecting its objects of reference. It can be said to create its own experience, and thus experience is not just waiting (in a deterministic sense) to impinge itself on human consciousness.

Existence and freedom are, therefore, inevitably interrelated, and there is no difference between man's being and his being free.[6] In Sartre's words, "Man is condemned to be free."[7] He is "condemned" because he did not create himself, yet in other respects, he is free because once thrown into the world—he is responsible for everything he does. To Sartre, human beings are condemned because they cannot cease being "free" in the sense of having the capacity and possibility to choose. In Sartre's words, "What is not possible is not to choose. I can always choose, but I must know that if I do not choose, that is still a choice."[8] It is quite clear that freedom in this sense cannot be understood as a quality or property which is somehow "attached" to man's being. Rather, freedom is seen as the very stuff of human reality. In other words, Man does not "have" freedom; he is freedom.

It is important to emphasize that this perception or notion of freedom is not possible without social action and without active participation in the world. The notion of choice stemming from existential freedom is related to human action, because it is through action that humans get to know about themselves and develop their individual consciousness. Following existentialist thinking, we know ourselves, in our existence, only through resolved and decisive action:

> Man is nothing else than his plan; he exists only to the extent that he fulfills himself; he is therefore nothing else than the ensemble of his acts, nothing else than his life (…) There is no reality except in action (…) (and) it defines man in terms of action (…) man's destiny is within himself (…) and the only hope is in acting and that action is the only thing that enables a man to live.[9]

This kind of subjectivism does not direct primary attention to the knowing mind in epistemological abstraction from existence, but gives priority to ontology, being, and being through action. This notion of existentialism is very different from Descartes's notion of "cogito ergo sum" because it does not refer to humanity as a special cognitive subject (thinking as being). It is not preoccupied with the thinking self, but with the existing subjective self. Sartre did not deny the validity of thought, but he objected to its reduction to a kind of rational, objectifying, theoretical activity. Instead, he argued that since we live our existence, and at the same time we think about it—knowing one's self is a mode of being.

According to existentialist philosophy, the existence of man is rooted in his interaction with the world he lives in,[10] and the fundamental phenomenon in such a view

---

[6] Schrag, op cit., pp. 177–178.

[7] See his 1992 essay, "Existentialism" (p. 273).

[8] Sartre and Mairet (1952), op cit., p. 48.

[9] Sartre, 1992, op cit., pp. 276–278.

[10] A point emphasized also in Berger and Kellner (1981) *Phenomenological Theory of Reality Construction.*

is the primordial consciousness of being-in-the-world.[11] Hence, the self and the world are regarded as correlative concepts,[12] or in Schrag's words, "Without the world there is no selfhood; without the person, there is no world."[13] This means that the world is already disclosed through man's existential immediacy. He has his world with him, so to speak, in his preoccupations and concerns. Intentionally speaking, the world is never there without man, and man is never there without the world. Therefore, as Schrag describes it, man's being is always a being-in-the-world.

Berger's phenomenological approach is very similar to these basic themes, saying that "the capacity for freedom is an inherent and universal human trait."[14] He also attests that at least certain human acts are their own cause, and therefore cannot be explained by antecedent causal chains. In Berger's "1981 version" of phenomenological existentialism, the notions of freedom and choice are linked to the human's ability to oppose or to say "no" to the given determined situation. He treats the human ability to say "no" as probably one of the most essential human statements of the prerogative to choose even in utmost constraining situations. Berger said:

> Homo sapien occupies a very peculiar position in the animal kingdom, and this is the root condition of his ability to say no to the world ... human beings are capable of doing and thinking genuinely new things. This is the capacity of saying no—be it to supernatural forces, to the forces of nature, to one's own body, and of course to all aspects of society. Man can only be free by saying no, by negating, the various systems of determination within which he finds himself or (using the language of existentialism) into which he has been thrown. Man's freedom only makes sense if it implies this transcendence of causalities.[15]

For Berger, it is possible for human beings to rebel against society because the network of social controls is not perfect, and it is possible for human beings to think genuinely new thoughts because socialization is never complete. In a way that is similar to Sartre, he undertakes a more minimal philosophical concept of freedom, proposing that human will can essentially (or in certain acts) transcend the systems of determination in which man finds himself, thus potentially making a difference in this world. Berger's phenomenology is ultimately derived from Hegel, and reflects a rich tradition of philosophical theorizing about the human condition (as evidenced in the works of Sartre, Alfred Schutz, and others).[16] Many of their works are concerned with questions of ontology and epistemology, that is, with issues oriented toward the very basis of being and knowing.

---

[11] As was also suggested by Mead (1934) and Berger and Luckman (1966).

[12] This is very relevant to the framework of this book because it implicitly emphasizes the significance of the interactional aspect of being and meaning, as well as between the self and the world (a relation that, as we shall see, is central to the understanding of charisma).

[13] Schrag, op cit., p. 26.

[14] Berger and Kellner (1981) p. 95.

[15] Ibid., pp. 95–96.

[16] The work of Schutz ([1932] 1967), for example, reemphasizes the call that had been put forth earlier by Weber ([1924] 1947), Mead (1934), and others, to give special consideration to the role of subjective meanings in social life. It stresses "intersubjectivity" or shared understandings on which social interaction is based. It also argues for descriptive research oriented toward a more empirically grounded understanding of the ordinary perceptions and intentions of social actors in daily life.

There is, in fact, a distinct theological flavor to much of this conceptualization, in that it is deeply concerned with questions of ultimate meaning, existence, and transcendent being. Berger linked this "theological flavor" of dealing with existential notions to the "human craving for meaning that appears to have the force of instinct."[17] To him, men are compelled to impose a meaningful order upon reality, and humans necessarily infuse their own meanings into that reality. The individual therefore attaches subjective meaning to all of his actions, and in concert with others, these meanings become objectified (in the artifacts of ideologies, belief systems, moral codes, institutions, and so on). Hence, the very heart of the world—that the human creates—is socially constructed.

The concept of individuals as intentional and powerful actors as a prerequisite for a proper sociological framework for leadership analysis is also emphasized in Giddens's structuration theory, but when Giddens refers to these abilities, he refers mainly to the nature of structural dualities. His structuration approach[18] may have a relevance for leadership studies because it does not present actors as behavioral reflections or as manifestations of social rules, but accords to individuals—both to leaders and followers—the ability to act upon structure. In this perspective, the behavior of individuals does not only reflect on the social constraints and rules but also acts upon them. Such a role is possible because for Giddens structures are not predetermined but subjected (in varying degrees) to the individual's reproduction.[19]

This implies that structure entails untapped opportunities, along with its constraints. Giddens does not deny the fact that structure can be constraining on action, but he feels that sociologists have exaggerated the importance of this constraint. They have failed to emphasize the fact that structure "is always both constraining and enabling."[20] Structures often allow agents to do things they would not otherwise be able to do. Thus, dual structures are potentially mutable by the action of actors. Although structures shape people's practices in varying degrees, it is also the people's practices that constitute (and reproduce) structures. In this paradigm, human agency and structure, far from being opposed, in fact presuppose each other. In Giddens's words, "The constitution of agents and structures are not two independently given sets of phenomena, a dualism, but represent a duality (…) the structural properties of social systems are both the medium and outcome of the practices they recursively organize."[21]

It is here that we can see another connection to leadership studies: while most people are generally aware of the more constraining sides of structure, leaders, by contrast, are masters in spotting the enabling sides of the structure. And within the current literature, charismatic leaders are said to be experts in seeing untapped

---

[17] In *Invitation to Sociology: A Humanistic Perspective* (1967), p. 22.

[18] See his *The Constitution of Society: Outline of the Theory of Structuration* (1984).

[19] An idea also captured by Homans (1950) as well as Parsons (1960).

[20] In *New Rules of Sociological Method: A Positive Critique of Interpretive Sociologies* (1976), p. 161.

[21] Giddens (1984) op cit., p. 25.

opportunities and being able to take advantage of opportunities they encounter. With regard to visionary leaders Sashkin says, for example:

> This type of leader looks for useful bits of 'rubbish' as he or she makes his or her daily rounds (…) Their luck consists of finding especially good or useful bit of 'garbage,' and their skill is in watching for opportunities and taking full advantage of those they find… While visionary leaders certainly take advantage of opportunities as they appear, such leaders are even more attuned to construction of opportunities; they create the future as much as they adapt to it.[22]

In Giddens's conceptualization, this notion does not refer only to leaders, because followers are no longer passive recipients of the leader.[23] And seeing the individual's role in the production of the structure not only helps us to better understand possible micro–macro links but also places the individual in a position in which he makes a difference: whether maintaining or transforming the structure, he plays an active and vital role in the construction of reality. It does not mean that individuals totally shape structure, but that to some extent, they definitely interact with it and influence it. In this respect, charismatic leaders are one such dramatic example, and the particular analysis of their action can promote further understanding of human agency within social, dual structures in general.

This kind of human agency is consistent with Giddens's emphasis on agents that are active, intentional, knowledgeable, and powerful. His agents have the ability to make a difference in the social world, and he says:

> Action logically involves power in the sense of transformative capacity … to be an agent is to be able to deploy a range of causal powers, including that of influencing those deployed by others. Action depends upon the capability of the individual to 'make a difference' to a pre-existing state of affairs or course of events.[24]

To him, agents make no sense without power, and that means that an actor ceases to be an agent once he loses the capacity to make a difference. Giddens certainly recognized that there are constraints on actors, but this does not mean that actors have no choices at all and that they make no difference. In fact, we think that Weber would also have agreed with this emphasis on power. Indeed, Weber's initial stimulus for the exposition of charisma was his interest in the mechanisms by which power comes to be seen as legitimate, and he saw charisma itself as a personal base of power, with which one individual is capable of triggering social change.

Weber and Giddens are not alone, and several other scholars have postulated that charismatic leaders possess high needs for power or influence.[25] Amitai Etzioni, for example, contended that charisma is the ability of an actor to exercise diffused and

---

[22] See his 1988 article, "The Visionary Leaders," p. 127.

[23] As was initially implied by Weber's treatment of the ambivalent leader–follower relations ([1924] 1947), and elaborated by scholars like Bendix (1968), and to a greater degree Meindl, Ehrlich, and Dukerich (1985); Meindl (1990).

[24] Giddens (1984) op cit., pp. 15–16.

[25] For example, House, 1977; Sashkin, 1988; Howell, 1988.

intensive influence over the normative orientations of other actors.[26] Robert House argues that charismatic leaders have extremely high levels of dominance and need for influence over others; J. M. Howell suggests that charismatic leadership has either a "social power" drive (which is "socialized," in the service of others) or a "personal power" drive (characterized by the exertion of personal dominance), and similarly, Sashkin argues that a prerequisite for effective visionary leadership is a strong need for power (along with the desire to use power in positive, prosocial ways).[27]

This notion of "power" brings us back to the points concerning action as the core mode for existential consciousness. It is in this respect that the literature on leadership relates to the leaders' power drive[28] and to high levels of activity. In David McClelland's view, the motivation or need for power is related to levels of activity. Therefore, individuals with a high need for power take an activist role with respect to their work environment. This argument echoes the treatment of leaders' active orientation. Leaders are regarded as "doers," and high levels of activity are generally attributed to them; "they do not only think, they also do: they implement what they think."[29]

For one thing, powerful active actors contribute to the generation and transformation of recurrent social practices, which, in turn, create the "visible pattern" that constitutes the social system. Giddens attributes the production of recurrent social practices to agents, who summon up a picture of the "routedness" of routine action (whether static or just maintaining a situation). He also refers to them the possibility of engaging in the metamorphosis—the generation of radically new practices when "agency rides on the coat-tails of structural facilitation to produce social change of real magnitude."[30] But Giddens does not postulate any propositions regarding the process of this change. This type of structural change, as we will elaborate in the next chapter, may be related to charismatic leadership's agency in particular.

The dialectical perspective in Berger's and Giddens's treatments of social structure and reality construction is very similar to the approach of Phillip Bosserman who asserts that "First, the dialectic concerns social reality. This means that such reality is conceived or studied in its totality, in its various dimensions, expressions and manifestations. As a real movement the dialectic is the way followed or taken by human groups."[31] He argues that a dialectic scientific approach has advantages

---

[26] See his *A Comparative Analysis of Complex Organizations* (1961), p. 203.

[27] See House's "A 1976 Theory of Charismatic Leadership" (1977); Howell's "Two Faces of Charisma: Socialized and Personalized Leadership in Organizations" (1988); and Sashkin's "The Visionary Leaders" (1988).

[28] Examples can be found in, for example, House, 1977; Sashkin, 1988; and Howell, 1988.

[29] For example, Maranell (1970) found that charismatic presidents were seen as more active and taking significantly stronger actions than noncharismatic presidents. Similarly, Peters and Waterman (1982) found that high activity levels coupled with strong self-confidence, determination, and a sense of mission lay behind the success of chief executive officers turning around their organizations.

[30] In M.S. Archer's *Structuration Versus Morphogenesis* (1985).

[31] See *Dialectical Sociology: An Analysis of the Sociology of Georges Gurvitch* (1968), p. 227.

for sociology by delineating the different facets of social reality that could be understood and analyzed, saying:

> Dialectical analysis permits the study of the unexpected and the unanticipated and in fact makes the quest for such occurrences a central concern. It permits the incorporation of complementarity and contradiction into the analyses of social reality. Contradiction is part of social life and this contradiction, when it is included in analysis, makes the study much more relevant and authentic.

A dialectical conceptualization permits the analysis of ambiguity and ambivalence as an essential aspect of social reality. It further makes it possible to understand antinomies, dichotomies, and opposites, "in short the processes of polarization as part of the same reality rather than seen as intrusions and invasions." Hence, in the analysis of social reality, whether using historical data or not, one must use perspectives that encompass contradictory and ambiguous situations. As Kenneth Burke has said, "Accordingly, what we want are not terms that avoid ambiguity, but terms that clearly reveal the strategic spots at which ambiguities necessarily arise."[32]

One must therefore examine the charismatic dialectical presentations of social attitudes, actions, and interactions of the charismatic leaders,[33] to be able to grasp the phenomenon in its full totality, which includes, we think, an account of its antinomies, ambiguities, and dialectics. The analysis of puzzling patterns of interaction would require a reflective perspective that is first and foremost willing to confront and deconstruct the conventional and traditional notion of reality as constituted of clear, unilineal patterns.

A consistent thread should therefore underlie the treatment of charisma: a distinct dialectical flavor that at times may even seem to run the risk of bearing incomprehensive paradoxes and ironies. Indeed, such a perspective should not be so foreign to charisma, as some scholars have already argued that the concept of charisma intrinsically interweaves paradoxes, ambivalence, and dichotomies. For some, this is all too much, and some researchers have gone as far as to reject charisma altogether as a hopelessly confused, and therefore, useless concept, except as a residual category for describing what we cannot fully understand or explain.[34]

---

[32] In *A Grammar of Motives and a Rhetoric of Motives* (1962), p. xx.

[33] For example, Perinbanayagan and Wilson (1971) argue that it is obvious that the Hindu masses saw Gandhi in a "state of grace." Gandhi's devotion to Hindu–Muslim unity and his repeated sacrifices on behalf of the Muslim minority and its rights also impressed some Muslims. However, along with this following, he created structures that were indifferent or hostile because they felt that Gandhism was only refurbished Hinduism or Brahminism or worse. In other words, the very processes that created his charismatic appeal also created antinomous audiences, which often saw him in terms of what could be termed counter-charisma. "Not only is it untrue that all classes and groups were integrated by Gandhi's charisma, but it was inevitable that the same processes that created the charisma of Gandhi should create antithetical structures (groups, classes, individuals, institutions, etc.). Charisma emerges in a field of conflict and contradictions and is so sustained" (1971: 395).

[34] See Bradley's *Charisma and Social Structure: A Study of Love and Power, Wholeness and Transformation* (1987), p. 29.

But instead of discarding the academic usefulness of charisma on the grounds of its unbearable dialectics or admitting to them as analytical faults, its treatment should explore various dimensions of such aspects, or at least acknowledge the fact that they are part and parcel of reality and the phenomenon alike. We are reminded here of Serge Moscovici's statement that "taking paradoxes as a starting point, as is true of every paradox, can be a fruitful way of looking at phenomena."[35]

One such dimension that will be treated in this book relates to the dialectical nature of the relations between charismatic leadership and social structure. These relations reflect the intrinsic dialectic between man and society or between micro and macro factors, both shaping each other. Another possible dimension for the dialectics of charisma can refer to the nature of the leader–followers interactions. Indeed a close look at the current literature would reveal that there are some indications to the possibility of charisma as being inherently ambivalent, rather than unanimous. Such a postulate is given scarce attention in the literature and need further treatment. Shamir (1995: 23), for example, included in his research a proposition in regard to the nature of close leader–followers relations as including ambivalence, arguing that "the perceptions of close, as compared to distant, charismatic leader may even contain social negative evaluations." Bendix (1968: 25) transforms Weber's implicit assumption into an explicit one by arguing that "all types of leadership are alike in that they involve an ambivalent interaction between leaders and led. A leader demands unconditional obedience, because he does not want his performance to be tested against criteria over which he has no control. Such tests jeopardize his authoritative right to command. On the other hand, the led withhold an ultimate surrender of their will (if only in the form of mental reservations), because they do not want to forego their last chance for a 'quid pro quo,' i.e., for a gain through effective leadership in exchange for the obedience shown. The ambivalence is a core aspect of such relations, to the extent that the followers' desire for a sign— born out of their enthusiasm, despair, or hope—may interfere with, modify, or even jeopardize their unconditional devotion to duty" (1968: 20). Perhaps followership is not a clearly defined, objectified, monolithic, infallible, and unanimous entity. A somewhat critical inspection of the treatment of followership in the current literature may reveal that it has been covered in a too simplistic unidimensional framework and has possibly even been "romanticized" to the point of reflecting the scholar's own fantasized version of followership. This is in fact a twist of Meindl's (1990, 1985) arguments on the myth of charisma. While Meindl focused on the leader as an illusive fantasy constructed by followers, the emerging findings suggest that it is also possible that the followership as a unified symbiotic entity is in itself a "romanticized fantasy" version of leader–followers relation that may have been constructed by leadership scholars themselves. This can be a presumptuous argumentation, or worse, a wrong accusation, but to the extent that scholars are human, it is possible that we all adhere to the human attributional biases resulting in the tendency to see things as more consonant than they really are.

---

[35] See his 1980 article, "Towards a theory of conversion behavior" p. 237.

From a micro–macro perspective, we acknowledge that certain micro-level agents have special capacities to interact with the macro level, in such a way that they are not merely constrained by it but act upon it to change it. Though this kind of micro–macro influence may be rare, charismatic leaders are one such dramatic example.

The micro perspective is rooted in the individualized and personalized way of this social interaction. It is a very personal experience which each of the followers and the leader goes through and, at the same time, is a general social process of which a whole group of members are a part. The macro perspective represents itself in the matter with which the leaders deal (the symbolic societal core) and the way that structure shapes charismatic agency. The macro and micro perspectives or levels of analysis are practically interrelated, since part of what each individual goes through is affected by group influences and macro structure, and vice versa.

It seems that it is only through an understanding of the inherent dialectical nature of man and society (as in Berger's notion of "reality construction" and as in Giddens's notion of "structuration")—both influencing each other and being influenced by—that one can understand any social phenomenon adequate to its empirical reality. Hence, concepts such as duality, paradoxes, ambivalence, liminality may be embedded within the nature of social reality (and charisma alike), and thus reflected in our treatment of charisma.

The theoretical significance of this dialectical view of social reality (as Berger himself posits) is the integration of fundamental insights of two seemingly opposed approaches to sociology, the Weberian and Durkheimian—that is, social life as subjectively meaningful activity and social life as thing (or in Durkheim's words, "social facts"). Berger maintains that reality is in a constant "dialectic," referring to an interaction, or interplay within itself. The two dialectical processes that are important to the human experience in the world are a dialectic between the self and the body (or organism and identity) and the dialectic between the self and the sociocultural world. The dialectical interplay between the individual and the sociocultural world is more conspicuous in Berger's writings for it is out of this dialectic that social reality in its totality is constructed and maintained.

The dialectical conceptualization of the social world posits two central questions in the analysis of leadership and human condition and of leadership in particular. The questions are: how is charismatic leadership formed by the constraining aspects of structure within which it acts? And at the same time, how does charismatic leadership form and transform the mere constraining structure within which it acts? These two questions seem to be the core conceptual issues for research investigation.

In this chapter, we have tried to find a sociological language and framework for a treatment of charismatic leadership that has a macro perspective on societal issues and structures and at the same time allows space for human intervention, and we have concluded that it is possible to somewhat synthesize to some extent the sociological perspectives of Berger and Giddens in the study of charisma. Berger's phenomenological treatment enables meaningful discussions of concepts such as human choice, intention, reflection, subjectivity, and notions of humanity (as well as the implied dialectic between man and society); and Giddens's structuration theory enables a meaningful macro discussion of the dual and dialectical relations within the structure (as well as concepts such as individual intention and action).

Yet something remains unanswered. Neither of these approaches seems to offer a clear conceptualization with regard to social changes that are of a "revolutionary type." Giddens's notion of structuration and Berger's notion of the construction of reality as an ongoing process do not offer an adequate conceptualization for the treatment of changes that break the status quo, or in other words, break the mere ongoing, reproductive processes of structuration, or for that matter, reality construction. The next chapter will attempt to attend to this issue and will start by laying a working definition of charismatic leadership that stems from the conceptualization we have just described.

Chapter 4
Explaining Charisma: A Constructivist View

In this chapter, we will offer a sociological working definition of charismatic leadership. Conceptually, this definition is situated within the dialectical dimensions of social reality that we discussed in the previous chapter, and it offers a framework for the treatment of a social phenomenon that intrinsically embeds micro, messo, and macro aspects.

Our point of departure will be Shils's symbolic approach to charisma, and we will further clarify how leaders engage with and construct symbolic order simultaneously. The clarification of their agency will incorporate anthropological concepts like "social basic assumptions," constructivist notions related to processes of reality and meaning construction, and Foucault's conceptualization of social discourse.

In addition, the definition will attempt to link these anthropological and sociological concepts with the "revolutionary" notion of charismatic leadership and its agency in social transformation and change. This link will also promote the conceptual clarification of the "revolutionary" aspect of charisma as one that is capable of encompassing cases of social transformations that involve neither mass movements nor large-scale structural change. The first part of this chapter will lay the ground between charisma and the construction of reality, and the second part will link charisma with social change.

Leadership and the Construction of Social Structure and Meaning

The perception of the phenomenon of leadership as related to structure formation was pointed out early in the literature. In the 1930s, the observations of La Pierre and Farnsworth on leadership situations[1] concluded that they may be distinguished

---

[1] In R.M. Stodgill's *Individual Behavior and Group Achievement* (1959).

Dayan Hava and Chan Kwok-bun, *Charismatic Leadership in Singapore: Three Extraordinary People*, DOI 10.1007/978-1-4614-1451-3_4, © Springer Science+Business Media, LLC 2012

by the extent to which they are organized by one member of the group, and they consequently defined leadership as the process of originating and maintaining the structure of a situation. A focus on structure appears in the work of John Hemphill. Writing in 1954, he defined leadership as the initiation of structure in interactions and said that "to lead is to engage in an act that initiates a structure in the interaction as part of the process of solving a mutual problem." This emphasis on structure is pointed out also by Ralph Stodgill, who defines leadership as the initiation and maintenance of structure in expectation and interaction saying that "Group structure and operations control are determined to a very high degree by leadership."[2] In the same way, Alvin Gouldner argues that leaders have a higher probability of structuring a group's behavior due to the group-endowed belief that he or she—the leader—is a legitimate source of structuring. Gouldner links the concept of structuring to patterning of behavior, saying that the actual content of the structuring is not relevant as long as it patterns behavior:

> A leader will be considered as any individual whose behavior stimulates patterning of behavior in some group. By emitting some stimuli, he facilitates group action toward a goal or goals, whether the stimuli are verbal, written or gestural. Whether they are rational, non-rational or irrational in content is also irrelevant in this context, whether these stimuli pertain to goals or to means, cluster about executive or perceptive operations, is secondary consideration, so long as they result in the structuring of group behavior.[3]

Collectively, these writers attempted to define leadership in terms of variables which give rise to the differentiation and maintenance of role structures in groups. And they treated leadership in relation to their influence on behavioral patterning and goal setting of group behavior. Their point can be reasonably generalized by saying that leaders are able to structure the formation, differentiation, and maintenance of social systems in general. But what would be defined as unique to charismatic leaders, as suggested by a number of scholars of organizational behavior,[4] is that such leaders construct structures that offer symbolic social meaning.

These two ingredients—social structure and meaning—are regarded as basic characteristics of human action and interrelate symbiotically. They appear both in structures and institutions, reflecting the duality of structural characteristics (as in "what" and "how" things are done) and their meaning orientation (their underlying content and the reasons for why they operate in that way). Yet if meaning and structure are interrelated, it does not mean that they are consistent, as discrepancies and inconsistencies may exist as well, and in fact, such discrepancies may well be the charismatic leader's arena for social action.

---

[2] Ibid., p. 212.

[3] See his *Studies in Leadership* (1965), pp. 17–18.

[4] See, for example, Shils (1965), Eisenstadt (1968), House, Woycke, and Fodor (1988), and Conger (1989).

The Existential Sources for the Construction of Meaning

According to both Peter Berger and Smuel Eisenstadt,[5] there is a human need for social meaning—a meaning whose roots are related to the concept of reality's "indeterminacies." Reality, they argue, consists of both determinant and indeterminate elements thus leaving space for voluntary human action in the construction of the indeterminacies of its reality.

For them, the root of that human need for structure and meaning is related to the basic derivative of the openness of the human biological program, which is the existence of very wide, indeterminate spaces.[6] For example, despite the obvious physiological limits to the range of possibilities of becoming man, there are different cultural manifestations and different sociocultural systems in the world (which are in turn indicative of the very existence of indeterminate spaces in the human biological and physiological program). Eisenstadt argues, for example, that "The existence—in all arenas of human action—of open spaces between the general propensities of human beings and the concrete specifications of these propensities means that the crux of concrete human activity is the 'filling in' of such spaces."[7]

The question of structure and meaning as descending from the indeterminacy of society has been addressed by Peter McHugh. He argues that there is "no one to one" correspondence between an objectively real world and people's perspectives of that world. Therefore, the consequence of the vague relation between a sign and its social meaning is that the character of an object is not self-evident (and thus does not unilaterally determine the meaning that comes to be assigned to it). He says, "An object is nothing of course, until it has *meaning* and thus can be differentiated in some way, treated in some way, can provoke a response, can serve to indicate something else and so forth."[8] And since society has a role in situational definitions, it is the social discourse that provides a baseline of the reality interpretation for its members.

A social discourse is formed on the ground of nature's indeterminacy because it does not enfold predetermined, given answers. In the words of Smuel Eisenstadt:

> There does not exist a simple one to one relation between cosmological visions and visions of social order and the range of preferences which prevail among members of a society, or the ground rules of social interaction on the other. Rather, there are strong elective affinities between them.[9]

---

[5] See Berger's *Sociology Reinterpreted* (Berger & Kellner, 1981) and Eisenstadt's *Power, Trust and Meaning* (1995).

[6] Of which one possible manifestation is the immense plasticity of the human organism's response to the environmental forces at work.

[7] Eisenstadt, op. cit., p. 331.

[8] See his *Defining the Situation: The Organization of Meaning in Social Interaction* (1968), pp. 9–11.

[9] See Eisenstadt's *Power, Trust and Meaning* (1995), p. 349.

In fact, elective affinities are grounded on a volatile and potentially conflictual basis. The indeterminacies suggest some sort of a state of chaos (potential or latent) and invite order and decisions to be taken (implying a state of potential conflicts). "If man in society is a world-constructor, this is made possible by his constitutionally given world-openness, which already implies the conflict between order and chaos."[10] This potential chaos is the reason for the "indeterminacies" constitution of conscious concern and awareness in all human societies. This potential chaos and the human awareness of it, "gives rise among human beings to the propensity, the quest, the construction of meaning, and the search for 'meta-thinking,' for 'meta-meaning,' i.e., thinking about thinking."[11] These structural arguments imply that leadership's social function is related to the "filling-in" of the open spaces. In other words, leaders can be seen as a social mechanism that attempts to cope with the general existential condition of society and human beings.

Following the argument of charismatic leadership as a social mechanism for reality construction (which in turn is grounded on "indeterminacies" of structure and the structural chaos and potential conflict), Foucault's treatment of social discourse may be relevant.[12] Foucault argues that in every society the production of discourse (which can be seen as a means for reality construction) is at once controlled, selected, organized, and redistributed by a certain number of procedures whose role is to ward off its powers and dangers and to gain mastery over its chance events. The discourse channels the social discussions and probably operates upon structural rules regarding procedures and content of the discussion: who can talk, where, when, about what, how, and how long. Foucault says:

> We know quite well that we do not have the right to say everything, that we cannot speak of just anything in any circumstances whatever, and that not everyone has the right of the speaking subject. In the taboo on the object of the speech, and the ritual of the circumstances of speech, and the privileged or exclusive right of the speaking subject, we have the play of three types of prohibition which intersect, reinforce or compensate for each other.[13]

Seen as such, charismatic leaders are actors who have social legitimacy, firstly, to discuss and interpret basic existential questions of the human condition in the world and, secondly, have the legitimacy and propensity to suggest and implement structures or constructions in the light of their interpretations. There is another interesting applicable perspective in the characteristics of Foucault's social discourse to leadership discussion. Foucault says that the discourse (possibly read as leadership) becomes an object for power exercise, desire, and admiration. He says:

> Discourse, far from being that transparent or neutral element in which sexuality is disarmed and politics pacified, is in fact one of the places where sexuality and politics exercise in a privileged way some of their most formidable powers. It does not matter that discourse

---

[10] See Berger and Luckman's *The Social Construction of Reality* (1966), p. 96.

[11] Eisenstadt (1995) op. cit., p. 349.

[12] See Foucault's *From the Order of Discourse* (1989).

[13] Ibid., p. 221.

appears to be of little account, because the prohibitions that surround it very soon reveal its link with desire and with power (…) There is nothing surprising about that, since, as psychoanalysis has shown, discourse is not simply that which manifests (or hides) desire—it is also the object of desire; and since, as history constantly teaches us, discourse is not simply that which translates struggles or systems of domination, but is the thing for which and by which there is struggle, discourse is the power which is to be seized.[14]

In accord with Berger's and Eisenstadt's view, this in itself would be an implication of the leaders' engagement with the existential need for meaning and order. This may mean that leadership as a mechanism for social discourse not only functions as an interpreter or constructor of reality—but also that leaders themselves become worthy of social adoration by way of being "polluted" by the "sacredness" of the content of their engagement. This point significantly resembles Shils's correlation of social awe and reverence with objects that exhibit a connection with the symbolic and the power center of the society. This perspective on charisma and social adoration is also in agreement with Clifford Geertz's treatment of charisma as combining concrete human activity with an orientation to what is perceived in human society as the "sources of being"—the sources of human existence.[15] Such charisma "interprets" the nature of the relations between human activity and structure (and the meaning of the existence). It is regarded as a "vital and serious" thing (and hence, charismatically attributed).

It is the constructivist dimension of the elements of the structure and meaning which make them prone to the role of charismatic leadership. The mere fact that they are not previously determined, combined with their vitality to human nature, invites the role for their formation and triggers the role, as well as the attribution, of charismatic leadership. All these arguments imply the following:

It is when leaders engage in the social process of ongoing and continuous discourse, interpretations, negotiations and constructions of the structure and meaning of their society—that the core of their charisma is constituted.

The Nature and Content of the Construction of Social Meaning

According to Peter Berger,[16] man constructs what was not provided for him in his biological constitution; he constructs a world in its sociocultural and psychological formations. The world that people construct in this process possesses a "thing-like" quality, the quality of objective facticity. But this process of construction and reconstruction is an ongoing one, because it remains real, not out of its intrinsic quality, but only if it is confirmed and reconfirmed by oneself in one's relation with social others.

---

[14] Ibid., p. 221.

[15] See Shils's *Charisma, Order and Status* (1965) and Geertz's *Centers, Kings and Charisma: Reflections on the Symbolics of Power* (1977).

[16] In *Sociology Reinterpreted* (1981).

However massive institutions may appear, because of their constructed nature, these realities can never be firm and independent. Despite the objectivity that marks the social world in human experience, it does not, thereby, acquire an ontological status apart from the human activity that produced it. This means that the "logic" of the institutions does not reside in them, but in the way that they are treated and reflected by people.[17] Since the given constructions are artificial, they are therefore in constant threat of being revealed as such by other human conditions or social agencies—leadership being one such example.

Leaders engage in the construction of reality by structuring and organizing patterns of interaction and order of and between objects, and between behaviors and concepts—pointing to their relative location, their priorities, and hierarchies. But they also point to their meaning, their specific content, and their relationship to values and to the notion of cosmological order.

The first management theorist to discuss charismatic leadership in some detail and to specifically link it to social "meaning" was David Berlew.[18] He argued that charismatic leaders are people-oriented (as opposed to task-oriented), with a pronounced emphasis on their ability to provide meaning and esteem for subordinates. According to Berlew, charismatic leaders develop a vision shared by organizational members and create activities that have a value or meaning for both organizational members and the organization. In this regard, the leader's vision, for example, can be regarded as containing the two main components of social constructions, that is, social structure and social meaning. The social construction of structure can be seen as articulated by the goal or the mission stated by the leader, or "what" has to be done. The social construction of meaning can be seen in the articulation of the ideals, values, and reasons, which relate to the explanation of the leader regarding "why" the mission is worth social implementation.

Generally speaking, the crux of charisma seems to surround existential dimensions that involve questions regarding the nature of the self, the society, the world, and the relations between them. Smuel Eisenstadt suggests that human action focuses on two axes that are inherent in the nature of human existence.[19] The first of these two poles or axes is the cosmological or ontological one. The main problems related to this axis are the definition of the nature of the cosmic order and the relations between this cosmic order and the human and mundane world. This relation could be, for example, between nature and culture, time and human and social time, and the subjective vs. the objective world. The second axis is the social order that focuses on the problems and tensions inherent in the structuring of social relations and human interaction. This axis could include the tensions that are inherent in the construction of social order, in the relations in social division of labor, in the regulation of power, and in the construction of trust and meaning.

---

[17] Ibid., pp. 57, 60.

[18] See his 1974 essay, "Leadership and Organizational Excitement."

[19] Eisenstadt (1995) op. cit.

Similar in concept but differing in terms, these basic existential parameters are referred to by Edgar Schein as "basic underlying assumptions." Chris Argyris identifies them as "theories in use" that act as a deep structure or basic general orientation or assumptions that actually guide the behaviors, perceptions, and feelings of the group; Florence Kluckhohn and Fred Strodtbeck treat them as "dominant value orientations" that reflect the preferred common solution or interpretation among several basic alternatives coexisting within a culture.[20]

Whether we speak of "dominant value orientations," "basic underlying assumptions," or "theories in use," they all seem to suggest a similar conceptualization of the social realm and the world. Altogether, they seem to suggest that human activity constructs deep underlying structures that contain particular interpretations of the various existential dimensions and that this deep structure, once constructed, acts very powerfully on human activity (as the deep underlying structure).

It is in following this line of thinking that we suggest the following:

> The charismatic leaders' construction of meaning is related to a social discourse regarding the nature of the mundane and the cosmological world, in particular trying to relate the self concept, the individual identity and the social dimension of life—to a larger scheme of things.

Argyris argues that because the "theories in use" (or underlying social basic assumptions) tend to be nonconfrontable and nondebatable, to relearn in the area of "theories in use," to resurrect, reexamine, and possibly change basic assumptions is intrinsically difficult.[21] It is in this respect that if Argyris' argument is correct and it is indeed extremely difficult to debate, contest, and reinterpret the basic underlying assumptions, it only adds a substantial "dramatic fragrance" to those who do engage in such a process. In fact, we suggest that:

> One of the distinguishing characteristics of charismatic leadership is precisely their ability to question, dialogue and negotiate with the basic underlying assumptions of their society, as difficult as this process can be. Furthermore, charismatic leaders not only reflect or question the basic assumptions but also implement their existential and structural engagement by actively seeking its transformation.

Charisma and Social Change

In his treatment of charisma, Weber stresses its innovative and even revolutionary character. Charisma is alien to the world of everyday routine, and calls for new ways of life and thought. Whatever the particular social setting, be it religion, politics, business, art, and so on, charismatic leadership rejects old rules and issues a demand for change. Weber claimed that charismatic authority, within the sphere of its claims,

---

[20] See Schein's *Organization Culture and Leadership: A Dynamic View* (1985); Argyris' *Increasing Leadership Effectiveness* (1976); and Kluckhohn and Strodtbeck's *Variations in Value Orientations* (1961).

[21] Argyris, ibid.

"repudiates the past, and is in this sense a specifically revolutionary force." It preaches or creates new obligations, and addresses itself to followers or potential followers by implying a break with the official status quo: "it is written (…), but I say unto you."[22]

It has been argued that charisma is crucial to Weber's system of analysis as the basis for the explanation of social change.[23] While his other types of authority are stable systems and can account only for micro-level changes, charisma can account for a large-scale social change. Indeed, Weber seems to point to a specific type of change, particularly the change "of" the rules of the system. By overthrowing traditional rules (and thus implying a change of the mere structure), the charismatic leader "inverts all value hierarchies and overthrows custom, law and tradition."[24] Also, many recent scholars agree that the notion of charismatic leadership is very much embedded in the notion of change.[25]

The potentially revolutionary type of change that was implied by Weber (who occasionally even used the phrase "charismatic movement") brought Robert C. Tucker to equate charisma with revolutionary social movements, arguing that they are symbiotic in nature. In his view, "Charismatic leadership inherently tends to become the center of a charismatic movement—that is, a charismatic movement for change. To speak of charismatic leaders, is to speak of charismatic movements; the two phenomena are inseparable."[26] Other recent scholars have also mentioned this "revolutionary" aspect. Bernard Bass, for example, attests that charisma carries with it a challenge to the old order, a break with continuity, a sense of risky adventure, continual movement, ferment, and change.[27] And Roberts and Bradley take the point further to associate this potential for social change to a possible wild power, to a "genie" taken out of a bottle: "As a transforming force, charisma is charged with explosive, unpredictable potential that, like the genie when released from the bottle, is beyond our control."[28]

Serge Moscovici goes even further than that and associates the nature of charisma with a "primitive atom," a primordial matter that possesses a fabulous energy, which can generate social innovation and changes. That primordial energy is akin to the "big bang"—the explosion that was the origin of our world billion of years ago; an explosion of energy that is the origin and the starting point for all subsequent phenomena.[29] In his discussion on charisma as a mass psychology phenomenon, he points out that "Charisma usually signifies a change in the direction of opinion or in

---

[22] See Weber's *The Theory of Social and Economic Organization* ([1924] 1947), p. 362.

[23] By William Friedland in *For a Sociological Concept of Charisma* (1964).

[24] Weber, op. cit., p. 1113.

[25] For example, see Sashkin, 1988; Friedland, 1964; Tucker, 1969; Bensman & Givant, 1975; Kanter, 1984; Roberts & Bradley, 1988.

[26] *The Theory of Charismatic Leadership* (1970), pp. 75–76.

[27] In *Leadership and Performance Beyond Expectations* (1988), p. 55.

[28] See *Limits of Charisma* by Roberts, N.C. and Bradley, R.T. (1988), p. 273.

[29] See Mosocovici's *The Invention of Society* (1993), pp. 124–125.

facts, an entirely different orientation given to all positions taken up regarding every particular form of life and the world."[30]

Abraham Zaleznik is another who seems to agree with the argument connecting charisma to radical changes.[31] Following this assumption, he makes a distinction between charismatic leaders who seek radical reforms for the achievement of their idealized goals and noncharismatic leaders who may advocate change but change that will usually be of an incremental type and within the bounds of the status quo. In fact, they may even be seen as "nudging" their followers towards established and more traditional goals. In a similar way, Jay Conger and Rabindra Kanungo attest that "charismatic leaders must engage in unconventional, *counter-cultural*, and therefore innovative behavior while leading their followers toward the realization of their visions (…) Charismatic leaders are not consensual leaders but active innovators and entrepreneurs, their plans (…) have to be novel and unconventional." They see charismatic leaders as embracing revolutionary rather than evolutionary change and even question whether an evolutionary leader (one who leads slow changes *in* the system) can truly be considered as transformational or charismatic.[32]

It seems that collectively, both Weber and most of the recent organizational behavior scholars of charismatic leadership[33] point at an implicit distinction between two types of change. The first type refers to changes within the given structure (that is, making changes that do not alter the rules of the system), and the second type of change refers to changes of the system itself, in the sense that it changes the rules it operates on.[34]

The anthropologist Alfred Radcliffe-Brown notes that changes within structure do not affect the structural form of society, and he makes a sharp distinction between "system maintenance" (the kind of readjustment that is essentially an adjustment of the equilibrium of a social structure) and "system change" or "change of type" which is "a change that when there is enough of it, the society passes from one type of social structure to another."[35] Another useful distinction comes from the political sociologist Lewis Coser—a distinction between changes "of" systems which occur, "when all major structural relations, its basic institutions, and its prevailing value system have been drastically altered" and changes "in" the system, which take place more slowly and affect smaller sectors of the system.[36] He admits, however, that given

---

[30] Ibid., p. 127.

[31] See Zaleznik's "Managers and Leaders: Are they Different?" (1977).

[32] See *Behavioral Dimensions of Charismatic Leadership* (1988), pp. 88–89, 327.

[33] Other scholars, such as Harrison Trice and Janice Beyer (1986), as well as David Nadler and Michael Tushman (1990: 82–83), see charismatic leadership as having an important role in organizational change which involves innovation and "re-orientation."

[34] These two types of change (change within the given structure and change of the structure) were analytically discussed by several scholars, for example, Coser (1967), Radcliffe-Brown (1957), Watzlawick, Weakland, and Fish (1974), and Morgan (1986).

[35] See his *Natural Science of Society* (1957), p. 87.

[36] In *Continuities in the Study of Social Conflict* (1967), p. 28.

enough time, changes in the system, through mutual stimulation and adjustment, can produce extensive change, if not a fundamental transformation of system.

This classification of change is conceptually similar to James L. Morgan's (1986) classification of learning.[37] He argues that the "single-loop" learning allows a person to detect and correct an error in relation to a set of operating norms, while on the other hand, the "doubled-loop" learning system, not only does everything that the single-loop system does but also takes a "double-look" at the existing situation by questioning the operating norms themselves. Similarly, Watzlawick et al. (1974) terms changes "in" systems as "first-degree" changes (which are made within existing rules), whereas a change "of" system is a "second-degree" kind of change that alters the operating rules themselves.

Following this conceptual classification of social changes, we can reframe the charismatic formulation to suggest the following:

> One of the major distinguishing attributes of charismatic leaders is, actually, their ability to question, revise, and transform the rules or basic assumptions that they themselves are operating upon. In other words, charismatic leaders will tend to engage in changes 'of' the social system.

The formulation may be simple, but it is not at all a simple task. Such actions require, as Edgar Schein puts it, "the ability to step outside one's own culture even as one continues to live within it." It requires emotional and cognitive abilities since in order to work at the level of the group's deepest assumptions about the nature of reality, its own identity, and its relationship with its environment, "a leader must have a great depth of vision and extraordinary insight into thoughts and feelings that are normally taken for granted and therefore not articulated."[38]

In addition to the cognitive abilities to analyze given structures and rules, the leader must also possess emotional abilities to overcome his own inhibitions. In Herbert Mead's terms,[39] the leader should overcome the "Me" part in his own self—the part that is a reflection of the "generalized other"—or in other words, the societal level as reflected in his own self-concept. Following this line of thought, the "I" part (which, in Mead's conceptualization, represents the more individualistic, idiosyncratic, surprising, and even astonishing or shocking part) is probably the part in the self that has to "overcome" the social inhibitions and the taken-for-granted formulations of the "Me" part. By the same token, the "I" part in the self of the leaders is the one which enables them to overcome the constraints of social structure of which they are a part and which gives them the ability to change it. This is an intriguing

---

[37] See his *From Simple Input to Complex Grammar* (1986).

[38] In *Organization Culture and Leadership: A Dynamic View* (1985), p. 325.

[39] In *Mind, Self and Society from the Standpoint of a Social Behaviorist* (1934) Herbert Mead suggested that the process of social interrelations between the self and society as the "generalized others," can be seen as the internalization and reflection of the interrelations between micro and macro levels. In fact, he went further to claim that these interrelations are reflected in the inner structure of the self. The self actually consists of two parts: the "I" part and the "Me" part. Both parts interact continuously to shape and form the actual self.

process since it means that in order to "step out" of the social structure of which they are a part, charismatic leaders have to shock and overcome themselves—that inner part, the "me" which reflects the "generalized others" and the given social rules. In other words, they must divorce themselves from the current social structure of which they are a part and which previously shapes and still continue to shape the "Me" component of their self. Another perspective on this comes from Bernard Bass. Using Freud's concepts, he refers to the leader's ability to "step out" of the structure and draws a similar inner process requiring the leader to overcome social inhibitions reflected in the self and says:

> The ability of charismatic leaders to see around the corners stem from their relative free-dom, from internal conflict that ordinary mortals are likely to experience between their emotions, impressions, feelings, and associations (Freud's id), and their strong, controlling conscience (superego). Freedom from the id-superego conflict makes for strong ego ideals and assurance of what the leader values as good, right and important.[40]

Hidden in this kind of change is a potential social conflict because changes of structure include the changing of current institutions and underlying taken-for-granted basic assumptions. This is a difficult task not only because institutions act as constraints on a leader and because he has to overcome taken-for-granted formu-lations but also because institutions are encapsulated within social structures that are themselves responses to earlier needs or to the needs of other groups in the social system. This implies that charismatic transformations are potentially conflictual and destructive to the current structure and systemic assumptions.[41]

A further distinction can be made to differentiate change processes by their veloc-ity and their spectrum. Large, wide-spectrum changes, by virtue of their sheer size, have the propensity for charisma attribution, even though they are not changes "of" the system. This is because, to a certain point, large quantities become distinctly qualitative. Moreover, different velocities of change processes may result in different types of change. These may be accumulative change processes (slow changes on a longitudinal perspective), or they may perhaps be more acute, abrupt, and sudden.

We can assume that charismatic leaders are probably related to all types of social changes "of" the system, whether abrupt or accumulative, small or large-scale. (These changes would probably be abrupt and wide-spectrum social changes "in" systems because of their sheer notable break of stasis.) But what is of significance to the research we are describing is that this type of classification enables us to study charismatic transformations that do not involve mass social movements or large-scale changes (that may, for instance, be difficult to achieve in systems that effectively repress social action of such type). In other words, this means that:

> Small-scale social transformation may also be revolutionary and charismatic as long as the change engages the 'rules' of the structure or its underlying basic assumptions.

---

[40] In Bass, Bernard M. (1988). "Evolving Perspectives on Charismatic Leadership." In Conger and Kanungo (Eds.), p. 48.

[41] Although on the other side of the dialectic, charismatic leaders soothe the human needs for mean-ing and symbolic order; and by constructing meaning, they are also a "creative" social force.

Clarifying the Charismatic Revolutionary Aspect

From the above clarification, it seems that the crux of the leaders' charisma is rooted in their revolutionary constructivist engagement with basic social assumptions. In other words, this is a strong indication for the possibility of locating the charismatic revolutionary aspect within the realm of the ideas articulated by the leaders, and this aspect gives charisma a strong cognitive, perceptual flavor. This is entirely consistent with the new genre of leadership theories that we have described in Chap. 1, and which emphasize vision as core component in extraordinary leadership. This is not to say that all visionary leaders are charismatic by definition. Only leaders whose visions are revolutionary (i.e., those who engage with the underlying basic assumptions) are charismatic. This perspective contradicts other sociological treatments that interpret the revolutionary aspect of charisma as the activation of mass social movements and large-scale social changes.

To further clarify the distinctive revolutionary aspect of charisma, we will offer a possible reinterpretation of Weber's writings and show that it is possible to analyze charisma in a symbolic approach without neglecting its revolutionary notion. This reinterpretation of the revolutionary aspect is not entirely new, as we think that it is grounded or at least implied in Weber's writings. But Weber did not clarify the aspect, and it has remained vague even in recent works.

Weber indeed starts his discussions on charisma by mentioning the extraordinary, supernatural, or at least specifically exceptional qualities of the individual who possesses charisma—a description that somewhat resembles Carlyle's "Great Man" theory,[42] and one that mainly bases leadership on the specific traits of an individual. However, it is of significance that in the passages describing the exceptional aspects of charisma, Weber refrains from the term charisma and instead uses the generic term "leader," saying:

> These (exceptional qualities) are such as are not accessible to the ordinary person, but are regarded as of divine origin or as exemplary, and on the basis of them the individual concerned is treated as a leader.[43]

The omission of the term suggests that Weber may have felt that however extraordinary these qualities may be, they are insufficient for an analytical classification of charisma. Though they may be part of charisma (or a prerequisite of it), they are insufficient for a distinct classification between leaders in general, virtuosi individuals or charismatic leaders. It is probably because of this reason that instead of continuing to discuss charisma in terms of its exceptional qualities—Weber turns his discussion into a distinct additional notion, namely, its "revolutionary" aspect. The relatively extended emphasis on this revolutionary aspect vis-à-vis the other

---

[42] See Ralph Stodgill's *Individual Behavior and Group Achievement* (1959).

[43] This is in Talcott Parsons's *Max Weber: The Theory of Social and Economic Organization* (1964), pp. 358–359.

exceptional qualities that he had previously mentioned implies not only that he regards it as a crucial part of charisma, but also that the revolutionary aspect of charisma was and perhaps is still vague.

This obscure nature of the revolutionary aspect, coupled with the fact that Weber mentions some revolutionary movements, may have led to subsequent sociological treatments of charisma as cases of revolutionary social movements.[44] However, the revolutionary aspect of charisma should not be equated with revolutionary mass movements. Though such treatments of charisma retain Weber's notion of charisma as a revolutionary "creative historical force," they seem to ignore the distinction between the charismatic revolutionary *attitude* and revolutionary social *action* (of which mass revolutionary movements are only one such possibility).[45] A revolutionary social movement may be a possible and plausible outcome of charisma, but it is not essentially so and is certainly not a defining aspect of charisma itself.

Such an analytical distinction is imperative because although Weber relates to charismatic movements in his discussions of charisma, he does not go so far as to equate charisma with revolution, nor, we should add, with social change per se. And he does not argue that social change is solely facilitated by charisma, although he certainly sees charisma as a creative force and a historical force for change. Throughout his writing, he shows that social change could be the outcome of rational, bureaucratic, and traditional forces as well. For example, in regard to bureaucracy he says that "bureaucratic rationalization can also be, and often has been, a revolutionary force of the first order in its relation to tradition."[46]

Also, the translations of Weber's writings that use terms such as "attitude" and "will" in relation to charisma's revolutionary aspect suggest that Weber may have thought about the revolutionary aspect as a frame of mind or a general attitude and not only as the actual realization and activation of social revolutionary movements. Such indication is implied by the usage of terms such as saying that the charismatic "attitude is revolutionary"[47] or in the general reference to charisma's "revolutionary will."[48] Another indication for the interpretation of the revolutionary aspect as grounded in ideas is implied in Weber's comment on charisma as being "a revolutionary revaluation of everything."[49] Indeed, the usage of the term "revaluation" suggests that the revolutionary aspect is situated in the realm of perceptions and ideas.

---

[44] Examples of this treatment can be found in William Friedland's "For a Sociological Concept of Charisma" (1964), Johannes Fabian's "Charisma and Cultural Change" (1969), and Robert Tucker's "The Theory of Charismatic Leadership" (1969).

[45] In this regard, we think that Willner (1984) was correct in arguing that people tend to mix up various aspects of the phenomenon, such as possible antecedents (as social crisis) and possible outcomes (social change and mass revolution) with the mere definition of charisma.

[46] In Runciman, Walter Garrison. (Ed). *Weber: Selections in Translation* (1978), Cambridge University Press, p. 23.

[47] Weber ([1924] 1947) op. cit., p. 249.

[48] Runciman and Matthews (1978) op. cit., p. 231.

[49] Ibid., p. 230.

The probability of seeing the revolutionary aspect in the realm of ideas is reinforced also by the fact that such an interpretation is in keeping with Weber's emphasis on the role of perceptions and ideas in social action in general (and not only with regard to charisma). Weber says, for example, that "The power of charisma (…) depends on beliefs in revelation and heroism, on emotional convictions about the importance and value of a religious, ethical, artistic, scientific, political or other manifestation, on heroism, whether ascetic or military, or judicial wisdom or magical or other favors." Though it may seem at first glance that this passage does not squarely deal with the notion of ideas, in the following passage it is clearly indicated that Weber refers to all these "manifestations" as ideas. In other words, whether "rational" (as scientific) or "nonrational" (as religious, artistic, ethical, political, and other), all these social forces are manifestations of "ideas."[50]

As we have already implied, it should be no surprise that Weber links the revolutionary aspect to the charismatic ideas because this is consonant with his entire general emphasis on the place of ideas in society and their particular historical efficacy in the form of social change. Indeed for Weber, ideas have an autonomous state in the course of history and are capable of facilitating social change of a major scale. It is in this respect that Reinhard Bendix, for example, argues that the charismatic figure and his ideas represent the cornerstone of Weber's attempt "to make intellectual allowance for the role of ideas and innovation in human affairs."[51]

It is of significance that Weber attempts to define the particular characteristics of the nature of the charismatic ideas as having a revolutionary aspect or, in Weber's terms, as being "unheard of." The term "unheard of" may be a factual objectivist conceptualization or assessment of an idea as something "new," nonexistent before, or at least rare and uncommon. But at the same time, such a concept may equally refer to a *normative* aspect of the idea, as one that is *being juxtaposed to all taken-for-granted assumptions and paradigms*. The normative interpretation of the term "unheard of" would be the kind of interpretation that might apply in Weber's own examples of the ancient Israelite prophets as charismatic. The ancient prophets did not articulate entirely "newly created ideas" but referred to ideas that were counter-normative and not acceptable from the point of view of the official, institutionalized version of the religion that the priests tried to represent.[52] Their ideas were both "unheard of" as in "rare" (and thus enfolded a certain "newness" in relation to their context) and also "unheard of" in the normative, social, cultural sense (what would be, in Conger's and Kanungo's term, "counter-cultural").[53]

---

[50] Weber says: "For all the vast differences in the areas in which they operate, the psychological origins of ideas are the same, whether they are religious, artistic, ethical, scientific or of any other kind: this is especially true of the organizing ideas of social and political life" (references in this paragraph are from Runciman 1978 op. cit., pp. 231–232).

[51] See *Max Weber: An Intellectual Portrait* (1962), p. 183.

[52] Berger speaks of this in *Charisma and Religious Innovation: The Social Location of the Israelite prophecy* (1963).

[53] See *Behavioral Dimensions of Charismatic Leadership* (1988), p. 88.

These indications suggest that not all unique ideas and perceptions are by definition charismatic. Weber tried to define the nature of these ideas by pointing at the
close affinity between the charismatic, the ideas, and revolution. He says:

> Everyone knows that anyone with sufficient power can always replace these rules with oth-
> ers, equally deliberately created, and so that they are not in any sense 'sacred.' By contrast,
> charisma, in its highest forms, bursts the bonds of rules and tradition in general and over-
> turns all ideas of sacred.[54]

In other words, Weber draws a distinction between the "profane," nonrevolution-
ary, noncharismatic nature of ideas that target realms that are intrinsically interchangeable, and the "sacred" nature of the ideas that the charismatic revolutionary
attitude tries to deconstruct. This does not mean that charismatic revolution targets
sacred ideas as in the spiritual or religious sense. Such ideas may, or may not, have a
religious flavor, but even a "secular" idea can be socially sacred in the sense of being
considered as "unchangeable." We can therefore talk about the charismatic revolutionary notion as overturning "sacred ideas" which have the qualities of *underlying
paradigms or underlying social basic assumptions*. In other words, charismatic ideas
question the socially "taken for granted" or *question the "unquestionable."*

Indeed, as we shall see, interviewees in this research of ours use terms that
collectively describe the notion of "basic social assumptions" when they describe
this particular characteristic of the leaders' action. For example, they refer to the
leaders as people that "push social *taboos*,"[55] "push the *boundaries* of what is
considered right or wrong here," "argue against the *sacred cows*," and "rock the
status quo, the norm, or what is considered norm," and *rock the boat*.

However, as we shall later see in our case studies, the leaders' engagement with
the deconstruction of basic social assumptions is not the only component in their
charisma. Equally so are their synthetic, unique, alternative ideas. This deconstruction of basic assumptions together with the construction of alternative unique ideas
turns them from being mere leaders (with "followership" and with exceptional attributions) into charismatic leaders. This suggests that there is a simultaneous, almost
symbiotic, intertwined relation between the deconstruction and the reconstruction
of reality and that this aspect may be related to the constructivist and transformative
social processes that these leaders lead.[56]

---

[54] Runciman and Matthews (1978) op. cit., p. 232.

[55] For the purposes of anonymity, we used a code to refer to the numbering sequence of the interviews. The first letter (A/B/C/D/E) stands for the particular volume of interview transcriptions.
The middle number represents the number of the interview in the particular volume, and the third
number stands for the page number in the transcript of an interview. (Using this system, "B/10/8"
would mean that the citation refers to volume "B," interview number 10, page 8.) References in
this paragraph come respectively from transcript B/10/8, B/10/9, The Business Times 22 November
1997, transcript D/16/8, and transcript D/16/15.

[56] As we shall see later on, it is also a crucial component of the nature of their charisma. For the
purpose of analytical clarity, we will try to make an ongoing distinction between reality deconstruction and reconstruction. However, we shall see in Chaps. 7–9 that the empirical data suggest
that they are essentially inseparable.

To sum up, the definition of charismatic leadership obtained in this chapter is a combination based on theories from various fields: charisma, social structure, leadership, and social change. It is based on theories on charisma from Weber, Shils, and Eisenstadt; on Sartre's existentialism; on the structuration theory of Giddens; on Berger's constructivist phenomenology; on the new genre of organizational behavior theories on leadership (most notably their emphasis on vision); on Klukhohn's and Strodbeck's anthropological conceptualizations of social basic assumptions; on conceptualizations of social change from Coser and Burns; and on a reinterpretation of Weber's writings on the revolutionary aspect of charisma.[57]

Our analysis of charisma is grounded within a perspective on the social construction of reality and meaning and that this perspective focuses on the study of such construction as intrinsically embedded within a revolutionary notion. Also, the particular notion of revolution is different in that it does not rely on mass movements or large-scale changes but emphasizes perceptions and ideas as the main framework for analysis.

---

[57] The Weber reference is from ([1924] 1947), op. cit.; Shils (1965), op. cit., and Eisenstadt (1968), op. cit. For Sartre's existentialism, see *Existentialism and Humanism* (1952); the Giddens's reference comes from *The Constitution of Society: Outline of the Theory of Structuration* (1984); Berger's constructivist phenomenology is in his works (Berger, 1967; Berger & Luckman, 1966; Berger & Kellner, 1981); for Klukhohn and Strodbeck, see their *Variations in Value Orientations* (1961); for Coser see his *The Functions of Social Conflict* (1956); and for Burns see his *Leadership* (1978).

Chapter 5
Methodological Operations

The discussion so far, on the subjective, perceptual, and dialectical nature of reality, seems to indicate that a framework for the analysis of charisma requires a qualitative approach and that, more particularly, a case study approach may suit the analysis of charismatic leadership.

In this chapter, we will present the case study approach and, in addition, offer an operationalization of the definition of charismatic leadership to explain the selection of cases for the empirical analysis. We will also describe the procedures for the selection of the particular cases and the methodological procedures that were applied in the course of the data collection.

The Usage of a Qualitative Approach to the Study of Charisma

Writing in the early nineteenth century, Auguste Comte asserted that the new field of sociology was an extension of natural science[1] and that sociological study should generate the same kinds of law-like propositions and explanatory methods as in natural science because all things are capable of being known (not only natural phenomena, but human phenomena as well), through the techniques of observation and measurement.

---

[1]Concerning Western social science, there are at least two major epistemological traditions: the humanistic and the positivistic. The humanistic tradition on the one hand (especially influenced by Kant) posits a distinction between different types of reality: the phenomenal and the noumenal. The phenomenal includes the many dimensions of the natural and human environment, and animal bio-chemistry; it is governed by "laws of nature" and is capable of being known and understood through the systematic use of the senses. The noumenal includes the social world, is governed by "laws of freedom," and is capable of being understood principally if not exclusively through "sympathetic reason." The positivistic tradition, on the other hand, sees no qualitative distinctions in reality.

Dayan Hava and Chan Kwok-bun, *Charismatic Leadership in Singapore:*
Three Extraordinary People, DOI 10.1007/978-1-4614-1451-3_5,
© Springer Science+Business Media, LLC 2012

However, although social reality is limitless in its detail, positivistic or derivative quantitative approaches base their explanations on a limited set of theoretical ideas, principles, and variables. It is in this respect that different writers have argued[2] that in contrast to the rich and complex reality, what "analytical research" results suggest are, in fact, a simple chain of correlations between a few variables (instead of a comprehensive analysis of the complex reality). Andrew Abbott says that "behind the extremely analytic statements couched in terms of variables, are pseudo-narrative statements that are actually simple descriptions of the correlations."[3] He adds that in such approaches, the cases themselves are largely undifferentiated and uniform, since in most models, they all have to follow the same narrative, and the explanation is couched as a narrative of acting variables, not of acting individuals. In quantitative approaches, "cases" are characterless since "they have no qualities other than those hypothesized to determine the dependent variable."[4] Since even those qualities act in isolation from one another, they thus have little to offer in terms of meta-conceptualizations of leadership.

In contrast to simple chains of causation and explanation, the study of leadership requires a more complex set of tools. It is a study in which the subjective sphere plays a crucial role in social sequences and consequences and where many aspects and dimensions interact, and it should move beyond the search for "recurrent sequences" or clear quantifiable correlations between a set of a few variables. Moreover, as we suggested in Chaps. 3 and 4, the emphasis on the subjective meanings that leader and followers impute to their activity and to the construction of reality implies that they are "rational," therefore "free" and not mechanistically determined. Such "rationality" and "freedom" is, however, inaccessible to the tools of positivistic science.

This, however, does not mean that we should abandon science, but that we should try to transcend scientific reasoning and methodology which reduce human life to simple causal sequences. Instead we should use approaches[5] whereby the description itself is problematic, and in which theory assumes a more tentative, inducive character. It follows then that the analysis of charisma should concern itself with an understanding of the subjective meaning[6] or intentionality of those engaged in

---

[2] See Abbott (1992) and Brynman, Stephens, and Campo (1996).

[3] See Abbott's (1992) essay, "What Do Cases Do? Some Notes on Activity in Sociological Analysis." p. 55.

[4] Ibid., pp. 61–62.

[5] Weber argues that a meaningful understanding of a phenomenon that entails more than a concrete relation between variables requires "the empathetic understanding of which is naturally a problem of a specifically different type from those which the schemes of the exact natural sciences in general can [solve] or seek to solve" (In Shils & Finch, 1949: 74).

[6] Human activity (in the broader, Weberian sense of the term) must therefore be "understood" ("Verstehen") as being meaningful to the actors in society, or in Weber's terms, it must be "interpreted." Weber developed the idea of "Verstehen" – the importance of understanding the full dimensions of social life in social and historical research.

everyday life and employ an approach that is capable of attending to complex,[7] multifaceted, and multidimensional phenomena.

Hence, it seems that the usage of a case study approach suits the analysis of charisma with its dynamic, phenomenological, and processual aspects. Indeed, the case study approach seems suitable to the analysis of complex action, multifactor social processes, and transformational processes and is thus suitable also for the analysis of charismatic leadership.

Abbott, for example,[8] argues that cases allow for contingency over several steps or between variables or events (as opposed to a social analysis of specified variables, that reduces activity to a "one-step rational-action" model and which does not involve actors with substantial complexity and variability). Since the case study approach does not consider transformational processes as a linear transformation but as a complex and loose one, it allows for an analysis of a process where the "case" may be transformed in fundamental and various ways (e.g., micro transformations, structural, macro transformation, and so forth).[9] Within the case study approach, transformation in attributes can be so extreme that it even suits the analysis of cases which begin as belonging in one category, and may then subsequently completely transform into another category: a state can become a nation, an individual may become a leader, and as we shall see, an individual's idea may become social reality.

Cases are not only specific individual events but can be both situationally grounded and theoretically general. Howard Becker argues that ideas and evidence are mutually dependent. He says that "we transform evidence into results with the aid of ideas, and we make sense of theoretical ideas and elaborate them by linking them to empirical evidence. Cases figure prominently in both of these relationships."[10] Cases can thus help us discover knowledge about how phenomena are specific and particular, but can also be representative of the larger phenomenon of charismatic leadership, and of such leadership's agency and nature in tight constraining structures.

In this respect, we will use cases as an opportunity to empirically validate conceptualizations with regard to charismatic leadership (as have been put forward in this research) and to discover meta-themes, meta-structures, and meta-processes in the charismatic leadership's agency in the construction of reality, and in its interactions with the contextual factors within which it operates. The originality

---

[7] Weber understands that "as soon as we attempt to reflect about the way in which life confronts us in immediate concrete situations, it presents an infinite multiplicity of successively and coexistently emerging and disappearing events, both within and outside ourselves" (In Shils & Finch, 1949: 72).

[8] Abbott, op. cit., p. 61.

[9] Ibid., pp. 63–64.

[10] See his essay, "Cases, Causes, Conjunctures, Stories, and Imagery" in *What is a Case? Exploring the Foundations of Social Inquiry*, 1992. pp. 217–218.

and idiosyncrasy of the cases should not keep us from discovering patterns and models and, in fact, may serve as vivid clues and hints for such general patterns waiting to be discovered.

Having said that, we think that to be able to generalize observations it is important to ensure that the case will be as close as possible to an "ideal type." This means that the choice of the cases should follow a defined set of criteria as strictly as possible.

Operationalizing a Definition of Charismatic Leaders

The definition of charismatic leadership that we offered in the last chapter can be divided into six analytically distinct dimensions. Our research does not aim to focus on the verification of each of these dimensions or the types of interactions between them, but uses them to establish criteria for the selection of cases.

The first criterion refers to the requirement of idiosyncratic personal charisma. The second dimension, the "leader-image," refers to the beliefs that followers have about the person that they identify as a charismatic leader. The third dimension (the "followers-engagement") refers to the different modes by which the followers engage with the leader and with the social action that he leads. The fourth dimension refers to socially objectified constructs and artifacts (such as texts, ideas, institutions, and organizations) that were created by the leaders. The fifth dimension refers to the leaders' articulation of a unique set of ideas. The sixth dimension refers to the leader's social action in terms of attempting to transform the underlying structure of which they are a part.

The dimensions offered include both aspects of the charismatic leaders as social entities (who they are, their characteristics, what they think), as well as aspects that relate to charismatic leadership as a social agency (what they do, how they influence reality and society, what their role in the process is, etc.). Though each of these dimensions appears analytically independent from the others, in reality, overlaps exist, often appearing in the form of a constellation rather than in isolation in a given leadership.

For example, the "leader-image" dimension emphasizes the leader, but also implies phenomenological aspects (that is, followers' perceptions) because even the extraordinary attributions ascribed to the leader's ability have to be accredited by the followers, and their conceptions and perceptions[11] are a critical component in the social process of reality construction. Similarly, the dimensions that deal with

---

[11] This phenomenological aspect further reinforces the argument that charismatic leaders cannot be efficiently measured by positivistic methods, because it is basically a social phenomenon in which the reality is inevitably filtered through a process of social perception, and therefore what establishes a charismatic relationship is not only the "factual" characteristics of the leader, but also their reconstruction and perception in the followers' minds.

the leaders' agency (social action, ideas, and socially objectified artifacts) were presented above as analytically distinct, but in actual processes of social transformation, they overlap and intersect.

Idiosyncratic Charisma

One important point of departure to the particular choice of the cases is our belief that a follower's devotion to the leader is due to the charismatic leader, qua individual,[12] and not due to his status or position.

The operationalization of the criteria, therefore, should include a requirement for "idiosyncratic charisma." That means that the leaders should exercise "pure" personal charisma that has not been "contaminated" by the bearing of office roles, or "office charisma." "Office charisma" is used here in Amitai Etzioni's terms to refer to charisma that stems from the fulfilling of certain established central roles and positions. (This is different from Weber's concept of "charisma of office," which typically relates to the aftermath of pure charisma: the routinized form of charisma once transformed into traditional, legal, or hereditary charisma).

The elimination of office bearers is sought to enable a clearer theoretical analysis and argumentation and ensures that the selected cases would be the closest possible to an "ideal type" of charisma[13] (at least "ideal" in the sense of following the conceptualization we are using in this research).

This, however, does not mean that the leaders in the cases did not hold organizational positions. They did, in fact, but the roles that the leaders held were a result of their own founding of new social institutions. For example, one of the cases, Kuo Pao Kun, founded and managed "The Substation—A Home for the Arts"; Sister Prema, a second case, founded and managed both the "Home for the Aged Sick" and, later on, the "Heart to Heart" social welfare service; and Tay Kheng Soon (the third case) managed the "Akitek Tenggara" architectural company. But these institutions were part of their own vision implementation and were constructed by their own idiosyncratic charisma.

This requirement restricted severely the number of possible cases because (as we will elaborate in the next chapter) most of the outstanding people in Singapore have been invited at one time or other to join the establishment (and in the context of Singapore, that is an offer that is hard to refuse). Although it does not follow that such cases should be an "alternative authority" to the power center, the elimination of office bearers resulted (in this research) in dealing with people outside the

---

[12] Therefore, to understand the essence of leadership, we should focus on the individual perspective, while we may need to look into the psychological aspects at times.

[13] Weber's definition is an ideal classification that does not necessarily exist as such, but to make a critical theoretical analysis of the concept and the phenomenon it is of good sense to focus mainly on cases that are as close as can be to the ideal type.

establishment. This has probably a lot to do with the particular context of the Singapore system as one highly centralized and controlled by a one-party regime (as we will elaborate in Chap. 6). In such a situation, the cases may, almost by definition, have been perceived as an "alternative,"[14] contesting authority.[15]

The Leader Image

The "leader-image" dimension consists of beliefs that identify the leader with extraordinary realms (traits, abilities, behaviors, and deeds), and there are a number of personal factors that may come into play in relation to the question of who becomes a charismatic leader. So we may ask whether a charismatic leader possess a distinctive collection of physical and psychological characteristics that determine who becomes such a leader. Although the attempts to define a clear profile or a cluster are still inconclusive,[16] recent scholars on leadership have put forward evidence for a number of personal characteristics associated with the propensity to become a charismatic leader.

As we have seen in the first chapter, the individual characteristics cited by the various organizational behavior scholars are a personal vision or the appeal to ideological goals; behavior that instills confidence, empowers, inspires, and creates inspirational activities; high activity levels; qualities of dominance; self-confidence;

---

[14] The definition of "alternative" is formed in relation to the definition of the mainstream and hence inherently relativistic. Although charisma can be considered as yet another type of alternative authority (as was Weber's initial stimuli for the classification of charisma), there is a particular aspect that defines the cases from other alternative authorities: they differ in being an agency that engages in the deconstruction and reconstruction of the basic underlying assumptions of the society of which they themselves are a part. Not all alternative authorities seek to change the underlying basic assumptions. The theme of charisma as engaging with the underlying assumptions was dealt with in Chap. 4 and will be empirically treated in Chaps. 7 and 8. This dimension seems to be the most distinguishable aspect of charisma and is clearly not an integral part of alternative authority as such.

[15] The notion of "alternative" is different from the normative aspect that the concept of "variety" bears; while "variety" refers to something that has common similarities and can basically coexist or collaborate within the mainstream, an "alternative" implies a contention of the mainstream. In a centralized social system, such a situation underlies a question in relation to the notion of opposition: how far can this "pure" charisma function and insist on being outside the centrally controlled establishment without being considered as yet another version of subversive sociopolitical opposition? The boundaries are notoriously unclear, and the notion of "subversiveness" may constantly hover above such leaders' heads.

[16] Some writers even deny that there is a charismatic personality type. Willner (1984), for example, argues that there is a common misconception about charisma that links it directly to the personality of the individual who is credited with it. She argues that apart from similarities, the variations in the individual personalities seem so great that the probability of teasing out a composite "charismatic personality type" seems small. Moreover, the fact that charisma consists of social interactions (as well as based much on impression formation and social attributions) means to her, that it is not what the leader is, but how people see the leader.

a need to influence; self-determination; and a strong conviction in the moral righteousness of their beliefs.

Though Weber explicitly states that charismatic traits should be "supernatural," or at least extraordinary, we do not think that this "extraordinariness" should be equated with unnatural sources.[17] "Supernatural" traits can be reasonably operationalized by substituting them with human normal traits that, although being "normal" and "normative," are considered "extremely positive"[18] and create an aura of myth. B. J. Calder, for example, says that leaders, like deviants,[19] cannot conform in their behaviors, otherwise there would be no basis for judging them different; "Yet leaders are not deviates. Their behavior is perceived to belong to a special class of functionally positive behaviors."[20]

Though a specification of concrete abilities is difficult because of cultural variation,[21] some general abilities can be pointed out, not least because they have to be in some way instrumentally related to the leadership nature or process. A publication like the Guinness Book of Records may list all individuals acquiring unusual and outstanding achievements, and yet they are not by definition charismatic leaders.[22] In other words, extraordinary traits and deeds must be perceived as relevant to the leadership process. Their relevance can be related either to the content of the leader's vision, to the process of leadership (as reinforcing the validity of the nomination of someone as leader), to the means of effecting the social change, or to any other leadership dimension.

Using the conceptualization of charismatic leadership in this research, the "leader-image" dimension includes the ability to engage with the underlying structure of which they are a part (that is, reflecting on it, analyzing it, redefining it, and attempting to transform it). More particularly, we can expect to see individual traits that enable the leader to "step out" of structure (such as emotional courage, cognitive

---

[17] In this respect, it is much closer to the view of the recent new genre of leadership theories. See Chap. 1.

[18] Extreme nonnormative human traits might lead to negative social labeling, such as deviance.

[19] In his essay, "An attribution theory of leadership," Calder said: "Hollander (1958) has advanced the well-known premise that leaders obtain "idiosyncrasy credits," that is, implicit permission to differ in their behavior in order to benefit the group. Granting of these credits is related to the supposed earlier conformity of leader (…) perhaps one of the most frequent distinguishing characteristics of evidential behavior is simply the extremity of that behavior. People who do more of something are likely to be perceived as leaders (or else deviants)" (1977: 188–189).

[20] Ibid., p. 188.

[21] As argued by Schein (1985), Willner (1984), Bensman and Givant (1975). Attributes considered truly exceptional in one culture may be seen as no more than relatively rare in another. Similarly, different cultures may have different measures for how much of any quality so far surpasses the normal human range as to be considered as transcending human potential.

[22] Hence, qualities such as a great sense of humor, great musical talent, a gift talent for painting or dancing or running (although being positive traits and skills, and even if being outstandingly virtuosi) are indifferent in terms of leadership. They might deliver a great artist or comedian but not by definition a charismatic leader.

ability to analyze and question the "taken for granted," the ability to see the enabling sides of structure or to reveal structural hidden opportunities). This also includes the individual ability to construct objectified artifacts (the ability to translate abstract notions into forms that have a "thing-like" quality, e.g., texts, organizations, products, and such) and an individual ability to relate to symbolic social meaning (like philosophical and metaphysical reflection).

In addition to the defining qualities, charismatic leaders may possess other qualities such as rhetorical skills, a high need for power, self-confidence, or a high IQ, but these are not considered as essential to the charismatic definition, though they may reinforce extraordinary attributions.

The "Leader-Followers" Dimension

The following categories would construct evidence of a charismatic relation: emotional attraction (referring to deep feelings of admiration, adoration, or awe, and reverence for the leader: a personal desire to be part of the leadership phenomenon and process), cognitive internalization (referring to a deep internalization of the leader's ideas and beliefs, or when the leader's ideas become a core foundation of the followers' self-concept and self-perception), and a behavioral manifestation of the bond through active participation in the implementation of the leader's ideas.

The "Socially Objectified Artifacts" Dimension

Since this dimension is less self-explanatory and is important to the understanding of the charismatic leadership's agency in the transformational processes, we will discuss it in a more detailed manner. This dimension refers to the leader's ability to implement and transform ideas into factual, "thing-like" form and refers to the creation of concrete objectified artifacts that are institutionalized (at least to a degree that they can "act back" upon society and, theoretically, even upon the leaders themselves). Some examples for such artifacts can be ideas, texts, designs, institutions, organizations, products, and others.

These man-made, "thing-like" constructs are, in Berger and Luckman's terms, "externalized," "objectified reifications." Berger argues that externalization is the essence of human being,[23] and Berger and Luckman say:

> The objectivity of the social world means that it confronts man as something outside himself. The decisive question is whether he still retains the awareness that however objectivated, the social world was made by men and, therefore, can be remade by them. Reification can be described as an extreme step in the process of objectivation, whereby the objectivated

---

[23] See his *Invitation to Sociology: A Humanistic Perspective* (1967), p. 4.

world loses its comprehensibility as a human enterprise and becomes fixated as a non-human, non-humanizable, inert facticity.[24]

In the terms used by Berger and Luckman,[25] these messo level constructs are then "internalized" by people and become part of their (constructed) social reality. They argue that to speak of an externalized product is, however, to imply that beside the product being an externalized projection, it has acquired a measure of distinctiveness from the one who produced it and said: "as man externalizes himself, he constructs the world into which he externalizes himself. In the process of externalization, he projects his own meanings into reality."[26]

In the terms of Karl Popper and Mark Notturno, these "thing-like" man-made constructs are "world 3" objects,[27] and they acquire a semiautonomous nature by being able to "act back" upon both "world 1" (the material, external reality) and "world 2" (the human subjective world).[28] Popper argues that although such ("world 3") objects are abstracts (even more abstract than physical forces examined in physics), they are nonetheless real, at the least because they are powerful tools for changing the world (the material, external world, "world 1"). He says:

> Once produced, they have a certain degree of autonomy; they may have objective consequences of which nobody so far has thought of, and which may be discovered: One may say that world 3 is man-made only in its origin, and that once they exist, they begin to have a life of their own; they produce previously invisible consequences, they produce new problems.[29]

The "Unique Ideas" Dimension

This research's emphasis on "ideas" is in keeping with the emphasis made in the new genre of leadership theories on vision as a core component of charisma, but we would like to stress the "alternative," revolutionary nature of these ideas. The charismatic leaders in this research promote and articulate a set of "unique ideas" that not only deal with their professional field but also offer an alternative look into society and the self. We prefer to refer to the ideas that the charismatic leaders articulate as "unique" rather than "new," because "new" is an absolutist determination, while uniqueness is endemically relative and contextual and, as such, allows room for a contextual and subjective perspective.

---

[24] See Berger and Luckman's *The Social Construction of Reality* (1966), pp. 82–83.

[25] Ibid., p. 94.

[26] Berger and Luckman (1966) op. cit., p. 96. Berger has summarized this dialectical process saying: "it is through externalization that society is a human product. It is through objectivation that society becomes a reality 'sui generis.' It is through internalization that man is a product of society" (1967: 4).

[27] In *Knowledge and the Body-Mind Problem*, 1994, p. 7.

[28] Popper, K.R. and Eules, J.C., *The Self and Its Brain* (1977), pp. 39–40.

[29] Ibid.

The uniqueness of the leaders' ideas is not rooted in their absolute "newness" but in the fact that the ideas do not deduct their logic from given traditional, professional, or legal structures. This dimension includes ideas that are "new" in the context (as in rare), are "unheard of" (in the sense of questioning certain dominant, normative basic assumptions), and have "an internal logic of their own" (in the sense that they offer coherence and meaning).

The Social Action Dimension

This dimension refers to the leaders' engagement with the social transformation of society[30] and structure, and as such follows most of the theories that link leadership with change. Yet from the point of view of this research, what is important is that these transformative attempts should bear a revolutionary aspect: not by the mere sheer size of the achieved transformation, but by the fact that these attempts correspond to an attempt to change the paradigms, social assumptions, or structure that they are part of.

The leaders' social action should bear an active[31] attempt to transform the mere structure that underlies social reality. Note that we prefer to use the term "attempt" because this distinction enables a discussion of charismatic leadership that acts within constraining structures. This means that the transformation may be reflected in the change of people's attitudes and behavior but also indicated (at least) in the attempts to negotiate the macro structure and its underlying paradigms.

Procedures for the Selection of Cases

In order to accumulate a list of cases that are still alive and active (so that they can be interviewed and possibly observed while in action), a preliminary survey preceded the final selection of the cases. For that purpose, interviews were conducted with 13

---

[30] Burns (1978), for example, suggests that such transformations should be defined by the existence of changes in specific aspects of life: in the psychological arena (a change in the individual's attitudes and behaviors) and in the social arena (the reflection of the change at the institutional level, either by new institutions or by the change of institutions). He says: "By social change I mean here real change – that is, a transformation to a marked degree in the attitudes, norms, institutions, and behaviors that structure our daily lives. Such changes embrace not only new cultural patterns and institutional arrangement and new psychological dispositions, but changes in material conditions, in the explicit, felt existence, the flesh and fabric of people's lives (…) real change means a continuing interaction of attitudes, behavior, and institutions, monitored by alterations in individual and collective hierarchies of values (1978: 414)."

[31] In the action-inclined perspective, individuals are not defined as charismatic leaders merely by their ability to articulate a vision, disapprove of the current circumstance, or preach for a change, but by their active attempts (at least) to implement new structures.

people[32] who were considered as knowledgeable in the area of public life in Singapore. The interviewer, first author of this book, introduced herself, the research and its definition of charismatic leaders and asked the following questions:

1. Whom would you name as people who are perceived by the public or a certain group as outstanding and exceptional?
2. Are these people held in awe or emulated by (a more or less) defined group of people?
3. What is the approximate size of this group? How does this group manifest its high regard and awe toward the leader?
4. Did these people articulate any unique set of ideas? What were these ideas? What constitutes their uniqueness?
5. Did the people create any particular institutions or organizations that can be attributed to their sole action? What were these institutions? How were they significant?
6. Would you say that these people actively engaged in attempts to change? How? What type of change did they manage to trigger, and achieve, if at all?

A list with the names that were most frequently mentioned as charismatic added to a sum of 15 people. Thereafter, we studied more particularly each of these people, gathering and verifying information on the five dimensions of the set criteria. We relied for the final selection on newspaper articles and other written data[33] and then categorized the people according to their proximity to the set criteria.

Of the 15 people, two were lacking in individual extraordinary attributions (the leader-image dimension), two did not have a clear unique set of articulated ideas (the "unique ideas" dimension), and of the rest, eight people bore "office charisma" in that they occupied positions in either the government or its related agencies (and hence did not establish cases of clear-cut, idiosyncratic, ideal-type charisma). The only three cases that met all the six dimensions of the set criteria were Sister Prema, Kuo Pao Kun, and Tay Kheng Soon.

Each of these three worked in a different field of action: Sister Prema is in the social service field; Kuo Pao Kun worked in the arts and theater scene; and Tay Kheng Soon works in the field of architecture. These three cases shared the following set of criteria: (1) They did not belong to the establishment or its related agencies and thus did not bear "office charisma." (2) They were perceived as outstanding and exceptional in their own field. (3) They were regarded with awe and emulated by a more or less defined group of people. (4) They created messo level constructs that were attributed to their sole action (organization, body of ideas, texts, and so forth). (5) They articulated and promoted a synthetic set of ideas that was seen as "new" in

---

[32] Eight were academics, two journalists, and three social activists.

[33] With regard to three of the 15 nominees, we did not have enough written data to substantiate the extent of their proximity to the set criteria. We therefore interviewed three additional people who were considered knowledgeable about these particular people (most of whom were considered to be in close relations to these people).

the context, offered an "internal logic" of their own and questioned the given paradigms in their fields. (6) They all engaged in social action that (at least) attempted to transform their own field of action.

This is not to say that all three cases represent the "ideal type" of charismatic leadership, as even Weber acknowledges that the ideal type is only an analytical construction. It would be more appropriate to say that the leaders met the criteria with close degrees of approximation,[34] and to a sufficient extent as to be defined as charismatic leaders and to enable an analytical clarity as almost "clear-cut," "ideal-type" cases of charisma.

The likelihood of attributing charismatic leadership to a person depends on the number of the components manifested (or attributed) in each dimension. Overall, the three selected cases manifested more components in each of the dimensions in the set criteria, but even within the three cases, gradation and variation exists. For example, in the "leader-image" dimension, the number of different extraordinary traits attributed differs among the cases. The realms, for instance, for extraordinary attributions in Prema's case consist of five different realms (expertise knowledge, spiritual aura, physical abilities, unique ideas, and life-style), while in Kuo's and Tay's cases, the realms of extraordinary attribution relate mainly to three (professional expertise, "moral courage," and unique ideas). Likewise, the "leader-follower" dimension differs in the scope of the group of people who perceive themselves as followers. In Kuo's case, for example, the group of followers is larger than in the case of both Tay and Prema. Similarly in the dimension of "social constructs," the number of components related to the objectified artifacts constructed differs. Kuo and Prema constructed two public organizations while Tay constructed one private company, but both Kuo and Tay constructed more objectified artifacts than did Prema (Kuo's playwriting, productions, artistic projects, and comments; and Tay's designs, articles, and texts).

The level of each case's proximity to the "ideal type" depended also on the level of intensity of each component. Overall, the intensity of the three cases chosen, in all the dimensions, seemed higher than in the rest of the nominees. But even within the three chosen cases, there are variations and gradations of intensity. For example, in Prema's case, the followers express higher degrees of emotional bond and higher levels of personal transformation. Also, the extraordinary attributions seem more intense in Prema's case (as the usage of words such as "Goddess," "Angel," and other such terms may suggest).

With regard to the level of personal manifestation of the bond, it seems that in Kuo's and Prema's cases, the level of active personal engagement in the process is higher than in Tay's case. On the other hand, the revolutionary aspect (of ideas

---

[34] For example, Tay Kheng Soon was a leading figure in a number of organizations (such as the Singapore Planning and Urban Research group and the Singapore Institute of Architects) but he was not the founder. He did set up his own firm (which can be seen ultimately as a kind of a social institution) but its degree of proximity to the dimensions of "social constructs" is less solid than in the case of Kuo Pao Kun and Sister Prema.

and attempts for transformation) is more intensely attributed to Tay than to Kuo and Prema. Also with regard to the scope of social action and transformation, there are differences in kind. In Kuo's case, for example, the transformation seems to address the macro level because it introduces a cultural dimension to society. In Tay's case, the transformations are more confined to the messo (professional) level, and in Prema's case, the transformations seem to be more confined to the micro (individual) level.

Each case therefore seems to exhibit a different cluster of intensity and of components in each of the dimensions of the set criteria, and thus each case has its own particular points of strength and weakness. But overall, the proximity of the three selected cases to the "ideal type" was the highest among the list of all the potential nominees.

Research Questions

The research questions do not take the form of precise propositions with simple and clear correlations of variables, but are considered as general guidelines toward the analysis and understanding of the dynamics, as well as the symbolic and the subjective meaning that are woven within the phenomenon.

Our research attempts to analyze two main questions: the first question is based on the assumption that leadership is one dramatic example of reality construction. In this plot, we need to clarify how defined actors (such as leaders and followers) play essential roles and what substantial consequences are related to this type of social activity (namely, the social construction and transformation of meaning and reality).

The second main question is based on the assumption that charismatic leaders are not totally "born" nor totally "made" by the context, but are influenced by both. Still, a question pertains to the very nature of the interactions between charisma and contextual factors—an interaction that is itself a matter for theoretical and empirical inquiry.

With regard to charisma's constructivist agency, some of the questions are: How do the leaders construct social meaning? To what extent is reality transformed in that process? What are the patterns of such reality and meaning construction? In which areas does transformation take place? What is the role of the objectified artifacts (that the leaders constructed) in the process? Are there additional mechanisms that play a role in this process?

With regard to the interactions between charisma and the context, some of the questions are: How do charisma and its context interact? (e.g., do these relations have the nature of a "zero-sum game?" Are they complementary or ambivalent, or do they constantly "deter" or push each other?) Which dimensions of charisma are affected by the context? How? To what extent? Which structural dimensions are affected by charismatic leadership? How? To what extent?

Framing the Research Within Time

A related problem with the usage of cases which have to take into account dynamic, multifactor processes is that they require artificial subsections of the social process (a unilineal matrix with clear-cut beginnings, middles, and ends). Yet reality is more complex and its proper conceptualization should treat it as being and bearing "endless and intersecting middles." This issue is a major problem, especially when the case is not a biological individual but a social entity,[35] and is particularly complicated in cases of the social analysis of change and transformation.

Indeed the analysis of change as interactively intertwined with order is conceptually difficult. Static phases, as well as change phases, occur only in analytical spheres, while in reality, we will always find them interrelated.[36] It is notoriously hard to measure change accurately, for example, how do we know when it started and ended? Furthermore, since changes themselves are not only technical procedures, but also subjective and symbolic, they are even harder to operationalize. In *The Change Masters*, Rosabeth Moss Kanter says, for example:

> Innovation and change, I am suggesting, are bound up with the meanings attached to events and the action possibilities that flow from those meanings. But that very recognition—of the symbolic, conceptual, cultural side of change—makes it more difficult to see change as a mechanical process and extract the 'formula' for producing it.[37]

For purposes of analytical clarity, the research was framed in certain "time brackets," which, though artificial, are not totally arbitrary. Here, we will mainly focus on the years between 1980 and 1997, which are considered as the "hey days" of all three cases, and also because Kuo was released from detention[38] only that year and Tay had returned from his "self-imposed exile"[39] around the same time. We will confine the cases to 1997, the year that Tay announced his official retirement, and also because it was shortly after Kuo had stepped down, in 1995, from the running of "The Substation"—an artistic public organization that he founded.

---

[35] Abbott (1992) cites the following example: World War II has come to its end, but have its consequences?

[36] See Berger and Luckman (1966) and Giddens (1984). This assumption excludes from reality, the mere possibility of a static equilibrium phase, because even this "static" equilibrium needs actions to be taken for it to remain stable (either in the form of reproduction or in the form of preventing the oppositional processes of different possible variants within the social reality). It means that the equilibrium homeostasis is practically an ongoing reproduction process, in spite of its pseudo static-phase image.

[37] In *The Change Masters* (1984) p. 281.

[38] Kuo was a political detainee between the years 1976 and 1980.

[39] Tay says that sensing a "feeling of danger" he left Singapore in 1975 and returned around 1980. (During that period, he was in and out of the country but he only fully resumed work in Singapore a few years later).

Data Collection Procedures

Our first case study was Sister Prema, and the period between February and July 1998 wase spent with her. This included studying and transcribing relevant parts of the nine hours of in-depth interview that the Oral History Department (from the National Archives) had had with her during April and May 1994, as well as transcribing a recorded tape of one of her public talks in the Buddhist library, back in September 1991. At the same time, we gathered written material that included newspaper articles on her between the years 1982 and 1998 and a chapter devoted to her in Khng Eu Meng's book, *Singapore's Extraordinary People*.[40]

When we met Sister Prema, we asked for her permission to study her, and though she was quite hesitant (she would rather we study the social service, and was not so comfortable with the emphasis on her as the main focus of the research), she agreed and offered a few names and contact numbers to start with. She also suggested that we get the help of her long-term, close volunteer, Mr. Thanaraja. We should acknowledge that he assisted us tremendously by making introductions to people and asking them to allocate an hour of their time for the purpose of an interview. Our time with Sister Prema included visiting her social service three times (during the monthly meetings with the volunteers) and joining her twice in her private weekly visits to the poor people. During this period, we had the chance of "seeing her in real action" as well as the chance to have a few short talks with her.

Twenty-five semistructured interviews were conducted in English with 25 of her volunteers in the period 2–18 February 1998. Except for one interview that was tape-recorded (although with many requests to "close the tape" or "pause the recording"), all the other interviews with her were not recorded. While interviewing, the interviewer took notes and, immediately after each interview, wrote from fresh memory as much as she could recall (attempting to "reconstruct" the interview). The interviews lasted, on average, about an hour, with three longer ones of three hours each, and two shorter ones of 40 min each.

The interviews were terminated at Prema's request, when she felt that "enough people" had already been interviewed for the purpose of understanding what she is or what the social service is about. We tried to negotiate and requested more interviews, but since she was very firm, our decision was to respect her wish. Those interviews in progress were stopped,[41] and another eight that were already scheduled were then canceled. Three months were then devoted to the typing of the interviews and their analysis, and this gave time for reflection on the procedures for data

---

[40] Khng Eu Meng, *Singapore's Extraordinary People* (1995).

[41] We could have perhaps insisted more, but were afraid that she might withdraw her approval for this study. The interviewer therefore stopped right then and there, feeling that Sister Prema had perhaps hit a nerve when she the interviewer had spoken with an ex-volunteer who was critical of Sister Prema, or perhaps it was that Sister Prema was really uncomfortable with the fact that the interviewer was talking "about her" with "so many people."

collection in the next two cases. Our decision was that in the next two cases, we should try as much as possible to use a tape recorder, and that we would explain to the leaders that it is important to continue to interview people, at least until a theoretical saturation is achieved. We also decided to clarify with the leaders the possibility of encountering interviewees who opposed them and suggested that these differences in views are to be expected and, in fact, balance the nature of the data.

With both Kuo and Tay, there were abundant written and published materials: hundreds of newspaper articles (mostly in *The Straits Times*), published papers, public comments, and articles written by Kuo and by Tay. There were also Tay's own texts on architecture and Kuo's plays. (In addition, in Kuo's case, there was a large amount of published material concerning the "Substation"—the artistic organization that he founded).

We received their permission to study them and their approval for long, in-depth interviews with them as well. The interviews with Kuo and Tay were done in parallel between October 1998 and March 1999. But, in both cases (and unlike in Prema's case), we had no "close assistant" who could "arrange" interviews and introductions.

Forty people were interviewed in Kuo's case and 24 people in Tay's case. In Kuo's case, more people were interviewed because his influence seemed to cut across many diverse art groups (including Malay theater practitioners, installations artists, intellectuals, Tamil theater practitioners, music performers, English theater practitioners, Chinese theater practitioners, and others), and that fact enlarged the scope of the people who had to be interviewed. Also in Kuo's case we started the interviews with a preliminary list of a few names which had been suggested by Kuo's administrative assistant (after double-checking that list with Kuo himself). From then onward, at the end of each interview, we requested that each interviewee suggests other people whom he or she knew, that they could recommend as a potential interviewee, and whom they thought would add significant input to the research.

In general, the interviews covered various groups that came in contact with Kuo and not only with the so-called "followers." For example, over and above the theater practitioners already mentioned, the interviews encompassed art administrators, arts experts, members of the board of directors in his organizations, other playwrights, and people who worked in "The Substation—Home for the Arts." Each such group of interviewees was enlarged until the content of the interviews reached thematic saturation.

Most of the interviews on Kuo (a total of 37) were recorded, and all (40) were transcribed. At the request of the interviewees, the other three interviews were not recorded, and only general notes were taken down. All the interviews were done in English. In two cases, the interviewees were concerned that their English may not be sufficient so they brought along a "translator" to assist. Three interviewees requested, and were given, a copy of the taped interview. The average length of the interviews was 60 min. There were two longer interviews: 1 of 8 hours (in four meetings) and 1 of 3 hours (in one meeting) and two shorter interviews (of 25 min each). Four people refused to be interviewed, and though three others initially agreed, they somehow could "never find a time slot to schedule an interview."

Twenty-four people were interviewed with regard to Tay. We started with a preliminary list of people that Tay had given us—a list that consisted of people whom he considered as having had influence on him, or having been influenced by him, and from then onward, every interviewee suggested an additional person to interview. Representative groups of interviewees included lecturers who had taught him or worked with him, colleagues, young architects, architects from the public sector, critics, architects who were members of the Singapore Planning and Urban Research group, and journalists. With the exception of one interviewee who requested not to be tape-recorded, all other interviews (23) were recorded, and all were transcribed. (The interview that was not tape-recorded was written up in notes taken during the interview and immediately after it.) All the interviews were conducted in English, at times and places that were convenient to the interviewees. The average length of interviews was about 50 min (The longest was 90 min and the shortest was 30 min). No one refused to be interviewed. One interviewee requested, and was given, a copy of the tape-recorded interview.

Altogether, for the three cases, 89 people were interviewed, and repeated long in-depth interviews were conducted with two of the leaders—Kuo and Tay. Tay's interview came up to 10 hours (divided into five meetings). Kuo's interview was 8 hours (divided into three recorded meetings and two meetings that were unrecorded, at his request). The recorded interviews were transcribed, but both Kuo and Tay requested that the tapes be discarded once we had finished using them. We asked their permission to keep the tapes until the research was finished and received their approval provided the tapes were discarded afterward.

In the case of both Tay and Kuo, many of the interviewees were in high-ranking positions and had very busy schedules, so we had to be patient with their own time allocation. All the interviews were requested in writing and followed by a letter thanking them for the time and effort that they had invested in the interviews.

As we have said, at the end of each interview, the interviewees were requested to suggest additional names of potential interviewees. One further request made to each one was for their permission to use their name as a reference when approaching these potential interviewees whom they had proposed. It seems to us that this personal, incremental ("snowball") method of interviewing was in accord with the culture[42] and also cleared the initial suspicion[43] that people might have had about the

---

[42] Whereby its social interactions are based on the inclination to incorporate personal relationships in decision making, a "guanxi" interpersonal mode that is defined as a base on which two or more persons have a commonality of shared identification, which facilitates social exchange interaction. See Tong and Yong (1998: pp. 2–3).

[43] Also, at the time of these interviews, the interviewer was in an advanced stage of pregnancy. It could be that the "softer," "round," "feminine," "motherly," "containing" connotation of pregnancy did some good in this respect and "disarmed" them (or the interviewer herself). However, this is not to say that in order to facilitate cooperation, interviewers should be pregnant, as equally so it may have also "impaired" the interviewer's "professional appearance" in the interviewees' eyes. Alternatively, of course, it may have made her "less penetrating" and thus "less threatening."

interviewer's "intentions" (Was she an "undercover" government "agent provocateur?" Were their comments going to land in the "wrong hands?")

The interviewees were promised that any formal citation that might be made would be done in a way that would prevent their disclosure and preserve their anonymity. For this reason, all the possible clues about particular speakers were erased, and all the interviews were arranged in a numbering sequence, amounting to five volumes: three volumes for interviews on Kuo (volumes A, B, and C), one volume for interviews on Tay (volume D), and one volume for interviews on Sister Prema (volume E). Throughout this book, each citation is numbered in a way that identifies the interview. For example, a citation "B/17/6" would indicate that it is taken from volume B, interview number 17, and is on page 6 in that interview.

The interviews also usually included an "off the record" phase, where interviewees asked that the tape be turned off, and when they talked more freely (usually about sociopolitical issues concerning the leaders and leadership in Singapore). However, we could not make explicit use of these comments since we were asked to keep them confidential.

The following questions were guidelines that were used at the interviews, although the focus changed according to the particular interviewee and the particular issues discussed in that interview.

The "Leader Image"

How would you describe the leader? His/her Traits? His/her Behavior? His/her Beliefs?

How would other people (that are in contact with the leader) describe him/her? How would his/her critics describe him/her? How would the public describe him/her? Why do you think that he/she is perceived as such by these different people? What is so unique about him? What would you say to his "quest"/"vision?" What drives him/her?

Socially Objectified Artifacts

How would you describe the institutions/organizations that he/she founded? What is their uniqueness? Why do you think that he/she wanted to found these organizations/institutions? How did he/she found them? What was his/her role in their foundation? With whom did he/she work to found and run them? How did he/she run them? How would you describe the people that joined (or helped in other ways) and their attitudes toward the institutions'/organizations' foundation and running? What was the scope and degree of their engagement with these institutions? How did these people engage? How long did they engage?

Social Influence

How would you describe your relationship with him/her? How does this relationship translate into your daily behavior? Would you say that you were influenced by him/her? Would you say that your life has changed as a result of your engagement with him/her? How would you describe this change? Is this change significant? What are the behavioral manifestations of this change? Are there other people who were influenced by him/her? Who are these people? How were they influenced? How did people manifest their involvement with him/her? Did these various people interact among themselves? How? Did he/she influence the particular professional field or other fields? How? Did he/she change the Singapore society? (If yes: How? if no: Why?).

Chapter 6
Contextualizing Charisma: Theoretical and Empirical Indications

As we pointed out in the first chapter, research on the contextual factors of leadership is scant and inconclusive. This is all the more so in regard to the study of charisma. We maintain the correlation between the context and the characteristics of charisma could and should be further investigated, to which this chapter hopes to contribute in terms of some theoretical and empirical insights. However, to start with, some preliminary contextual indications will be pointed out in particular relation to Singapore.

Admittedly, it is too early for the following conceptual indications to form a theoretical model, but they may help to promote the analysis and the understanding of the particular case studies, and may also suggest some possible dimensions for the conceptualization of the relations between context and charisma. In formulating conceptual indications that are applicable to the analysis of the case studies and compatible with the Weberian notion of pure charisma, some analytical dimensions such as the degree of control, degree of bureaucracy, and ideological orientation will be extrapolated from Weber's implicit indications and references,[1] and additional ones, such as cultural social tendencies, and perceptions, will be proposed.

More specifically, the structural indications aim to help us understand a few aspects of the case studies: the lesser frequency and intensity of "pure," idiosyncratic "non-office" charisma; the increased tension between such leaders and the power center; and the high degree of structural constraints for social action at the macro societal level.

The following structural indications do not stem from a theoretical model nor aim to become one. They constitute a conceptualization that derives from various sources

---

[1] Weber feels that it would be difficult to make generalizations on the issue of charisma vs. political parties and their structure, saying: "It is impossible to generalize about this topic. Each individual case is affected by too close an association between the intrinsic laws of the particular party machine and the economic and social conditions prevailing in the concrete situation" (in Runciman, 1978, p. 246). However, he still manages to indicate some generalizations with regard to the nature of charisma in such structures.

Dayan Hava and Chan Kwok-bun, *Charismatic Leadership in Singapore:*
Three Extraordinary People, DOI 10.1007/978-1-4614-1451-3_6,
© Springer Science+Business Media, LLC 2012

(from the very few writings on contextual factors, from observations that stem from empirical data, and from related writings on Singapore). The following conceptualization is restricted mainly to the years between the early 1970s and the mid-1990s,[2] more or less to cover the 17 years that are within the scope of our research.

Generally speaking, the following indications point at structural constraints for the rise and function of alternative authority in general (alternative in the sense of not being part of the power center) and of alternative charismatic authority in particular (that in its "pure" Weberian type is antiestablishment and revolutionary). A few facilitating aspects will be mentioned, but even these do not relieve the constraints nor the tension that such leadership faces vis-à-vis the power center.

Placing the Discussion in Theoretical Dilemmas Regarding Charisma

Before we proceed, we will briefly relate the theoretical question of the relationship between context and charisma and offer a possible conceptualization.

A conceptual dilemma still exists in regard to the origins and operation of charisma: Is it related to the leader's personality or to contextual factors? Thomas E. Dow, for example, argues that people must recognize, accept, and follow the leader before he can be spoken of as truly charismatic. Yet he says, "The question is why do they do so? Do they do so because the times are particularly propitious for revolutionary change, or do they do so because of their belief that the charismatic figure, because of his extraordinary gifts, can achieve the transcendent image contained in his message?"[3] To this day, these questions have not been fully resolved.

In his treatment of charisma, Weber implies that the origins of the charismatic phenomenon are probably a corollary of both aspects: the leader and the context. On the one hand, Weber initially suggests that charisma is manifested under *certain circumstances* more than others,[4] for example, more frequently in ancient societies, in the religious field, and in times of distress. He notes that "Charismatic domination in the 'pure' sense (...) is always the offspring of unusual circumstances— either external, especially political or economic, or internal and spiritual, especially religious, or both together."[5]

---

[2] We think that since the early 1990s, some changes have begun to appear in the degree and scope of the Singapore government's control, for example, an increased latitude for civic groups, the "speaker's corner" – opened in August 2000 (where people can articulate their views on a variety of matters), and others.

[3] See his essay, "The Theory of Charisma" in *Sociological Quarterly*. Vol. 10 (1969), p. 315.

[4] See *The Theory of Social and Economic Organization*. [1924] 1947, p. 370.

[5] See *Weber: Selections in Translation*, ed. by Walter Runciman, 1978, pp. 235–236.

He links this contextual influence to the relevance of the leader's vision and to the leader's power in his followers' eyes, arguing that these two aspects are by definition contextual. He said:[6]

> Charisma can be, and of course is, qualitatively particularized (...) In meaning and in content the mission may be addressed to a group of men who are delimited locally, ethnically, socially, politically, occupationally, or in some other way. If the mission is thus addressed to a limited group of men, as is the rule, it finds limits within their circle.[6]

At the same time, Weber also explicitly states that charisma is something that "knows only inner determination and inner restraint," it has a "purely personal basis," and that "pure charisma does not know any 'legitimacy' other than that flowing from personal strength."[7] Following this line of thought, some attempts have been made to locate the charismatic context,[8] but the findings are inconclusive and are unable to explain why charismatic leadership arises in one situation and not another, even though both situations apparently contain the same necessary preconditions.

For example, it has been argued that social crises are antecedents to charisma, but to this date, findings are inconclusive, though there has been a consistent, long-standing discussion[9] on social crises as a particular contextual factor influencing the emergence, the vision, and the particular form of relations between the leader and the followers in such cases. Weber was the first to suggest that charismatic impulses in general are most likely to occur in times of distress. His correlation of charisma to acute phases of social life theoretically implies that charisma may wane as life returns to normal and that the periods of charismatic outburst may be relatively few and short. He mentions a list of causative factors that operate both at the macro level and the micro level, for example, "psychic, physical, economic, ethical, religious, or political."[10]

Indeed, Weber recognizes that eruptions of charisma are frequently associated with periods of social crisis, and a central focus of attention in the mission of

---

[6] This is quoted in *From Max Weber: Essays in Sociology* by Gerth and Mills (1947, p. 247).

[7] The first and third quotes here are from Gerth and Mills (Ibid., pp. 246, 248) and the second quote from Runciman (op. cit., p. 237).

[8] See Friedland (1964); Berger (1963); and Boal and Bryson (1988). Friedland (1964: 18) even suggests focusing primarily on the context: "the concept (of charisma) can be useful (...) in the analysis of social change if (attention is focused) on the social context within which charisma develops rather than on charisma or charismatics."

[9] Another reason for the inconclusiveness about crisis as a precondition may stem from the disagreement regarding the definition of the crisis. The concept of crisis can take a number of different forms, but the most prevalent is that of profound social dislocation and the discontent that accompanies it. Distress occurs in such a wide variety of forms that it seems hardly feasible for a theorist of charismatic leadership to catalog them. They range from physical and material distress caused by persecution, catastrophes, and extreme economic hardship to such diverse forms of psychic or emotional distress as the feelings of oppression in peoples ruled by foreigners, or the radical alienation from existing order experienced by revolutionaries.

[10] See *The Theory of Social and Economic Organization.* [1924] 1947, p. 1112.

charismatic leaders is their program for relieving the current and the prospective followers of the circumstances associated with crisis. The interpretation of the connection between charisma and crisis (or discontent) is that charismatic leaders gain a following by fitting their message or mission to the situation at hand (or to the followers' needs), and the followers are said to be more willing to accept the authority of someone who claims to have a solution or answer to their needs.

Robert Tucker, for example, uses the term "situational-charisma" to refer to instances where a leader evokes a charismatic response simply because he offers hope in a time of acute distress.[11] Here, leadership is perceived as a source and a means of salvation from distress. Referring to social movements (with masses of followers), Tucker argues that it is at times of crisis or of extremely serious widespread distress that charismatic leadership movements for change develop in profusion and attract masses. It seems especially likely that charismatic movements attain their greatest force at the confluence of multiple forms of distress in society.

Alternatively, leaders may draw attention to critical situations of which their followers were only dimly aware of at the outset by referring maybe to a "latent crisis" and bringing it out into the public consciousness. Indeed, much of the charismatic literature explicitly or implicitly argues that there must be a crisis situation for charismatic leadership to be established.[12] Bernard Bass cites literature supporting crises or at least distressful situations in transition stages as opportunities for transformationally oriented leaders (for whom, as we saw, an important dimension of their characteristics is charisma). He also says that charismatic leaders are more likely to appear in failing organizations or in newly emerging ones that are struggling to survive. More recently, also Stewart McCann finds a correlation between social crises and the election of charismatic leaders in the United States, suggesting that crises are indeed correlated with charisma.

Nancy Roberts and Raymond Bradley argue that their case study supports this view, seeing crisis as a contextual "imperative." They show a case study that examines a leader's charismatic leadership: first, when she was a direct superintendent of education and then, when she was promoted to head of the education system of an entire state. The researchers presented evidence suggesting that, at the district superintendent level, the leader was very charismatic. However, after her promotion to the state level, she was not seen as charismatic at all, even though she was able to get much accomplished. The authors argue that there was a crisis at the district level but not at the state level and that the leader's charisma therefore could not be transferred.[13] In fact, they take a very strong position, arguing that charisma cannot be manufactured by a leader or an organization and needs a crisis to set it on.

---

[11] See his essay "The Theory of Charismatic Leadership." 1970, pp. 82–83.

[12] Conger and Kanungo (1988) even argue that if there is no crisis, the leader may need to create one or something very close to one if he is to be able to exert charismatic leadership.

[13] Nevertheless, there is a possibility that the result of the charisma loss of the superintendent was not because of the absence of crisis but actually due to her inability to have effective mass audience communication on a macro level. Perhaps her expressive behavior was suited more to micro-level, interpersonal relations. If this is indeed the case, the findings correlating her charisma to the social crises are still inconclusive.

On the other hand, it is possible that both deficiencies and opportunities in the context can account for some aspect of the charismatic leadership phenomena. In this respect, Ann Ruth Willner, for example, argues that social crisis and psychic distress may logically link together proximate causes for the generation of political charisma.[14] Her empirical investigation shows that only two out of the six cases that she examined (namely, those of Hitler and President Franklin D. Roosevelt) seem to conform sufficiently to the conditions of crisis and psychic distress. This finding implies that the other charismatic leaders may have emerged from noncrisis grounds and that if this is so, crisis may be a possible antecedent to the rise of charisma but not an imperative prerequisite.

Indeed, other scholars in organizational behavior recognize the possibility of charismatic leadership emerging from a noncrisis context. In such cases, the "unexplored opportunities" within the larger context may facilitate the emergence of a charismatic leader. The relation of noncrisis charisma and untapped contextual opportunities is mentioned by Jay Conger,[15] who finds charismatic leaders both in contexts of crisis and contexts without crisis. In the latter, the charismatic leaders are associated with high opportunity or entrepreneurial environments.

K.B. Boal and J.M. Bryson contribute an interesting argument to this discussion. They suggest that crisis and noncrisis contexts may stand for different processes leading to the emergence of charismatic leadership. They opine that besides visionary leaders (those evolving from a clear ideal vision), there is another "crisis-produced" form of leadership in which it is the extraordinary circumstances that create charismatic effects. "Crisis leaders" evolve from a situational problem that requires a solution. They handle a crisis situation through detailing the actions to be taken and the expected consequences of those actions.

In contrast, visionary-charismatic leaders first link the individual's needs to important values, purposes, or meanings by the articulation of a vision and goals and only then point out how individual's behavior can contribute to the fulfillment of those values, purposes, or meanings. In other words, while "crisis leaders" start with action and then move to interpretations and values, visionary leaders start with "theory" —with ideas and the ideals—and only then move to action.

The inconclusive findings and arguments with regard to crisis and charisma suggest that it is possible for charisma to occur in relatively ordered situations and, at the same time, it may evolve in situations that involve military, political, economic or other forms of disorder.[16] In either case, such situations have not uniformly produced charismatic departures and have as often resulted in noncharismatic as in charismatic phenomena.[17]

---

[14] In her *The Spellbinders*. 1984, p. 46.

[15] In the essay, "Behavioral Dimensions of Charismatic leadership."

[16] See the 1988 essay by Boal and Bryson, "Charismatic Leadership: A Phenomenological and Historical Approach."

[17] This is discussed by Jay Conger in "Behavioral Dimensions of Charismatic Leadership" (1988).

We are in agreement with Thomas E. Dow who argued that any analysis which solely concentrates exclusively on the social context in which charisma is supposed to develop "risks misunderstanding the fundamental nature of the charismatic movement, i.e., the relative independence of both the exceptional individual and his ideas."[18] Similarly, Peter Berger and Walter Runciman referred to charisma's autonomous nature, saying that charisma is neither old nor new, but an omnipresent possibility in all ages, places, and social conditions (therefore, not entirely contextual). Also, Reinhard Bendix implied this independent and autonomous notion by relating to the fact that charismatic phenomenon cuts across time and place. He said that "charisma has been a recurrent phenomenon because persons endowed with this gift of grace (for better or for worse) —have asserted their leadership under all historical conditions (…) in all phases of history."[19]

Charisma's autonomous notion can be related to Weber's emphasis on the autonomy of ideas and the ideas as being a core element in charisma. He says: "There is hardly ever a close connection between the interests or the social origin of the speaker (…) with the content of the idea during inception (…) there is no pre-established correspondence between the content of an idea and the interests of those who follow from the first hour."[20]

Weber's other comments on the autonomy of ideas seem to reinforce the notion of charisma's semiautonomous nature from the particular social context. That is, if we accept Weber's conceptualization of charisma as having a strong element of ideas. For example, in his discussion on religious ethic, he emphasizes the essence of ideas as stemming from their content and not from the context. He says:

> It is not our thesis that the specific nature of a religion is a simple 'function' of the social situation of the stratum which appears as its characteristic bearer, or that it represents the stratum's 'ideology,' or that it is a 'reflection' of a stratum's material or ideal interest situation (…) However incisive the social influences, economically and politically determined, may have been upon a religious ethic in a particular case, it receives its stamp from religious sources, and first of all, from the content of its annunciation and promise.[21]

Indeed, throughout his work in the sociology of religion, Weber is concerned to demonstrate that religious ideas have a historical efficacy of their own and cannot simply be understood as a "reflection" or even a "function" of some underlying social processes.

He therefore refuses "to conceive of [the ideas] as being 'mere' reflections of psychic or social interest."[22] For both Peter Berger and Smuel Eisenstadt, this is the reason why Weber seeks to show the religious factors in the genesis of what he

---

[18] In "The Theory of Charisma." *Sociological Quarterly*. (1969) Vol. 10, pp. 306–318, 316.

[19] This reference is from Bendix's 1962 work, *Max Weber: An Intellectual Portrait*, pp. 326–327. Berger's reference to this comes in "Charisma and Religious Innovation: The Social Location of the Israelite Prophecy," while Walter Runciman's reference is from his 1963 essay, "Charismatic Legitimacy and One Party Rule in Ghana."

[20] Weber (1947). op. cit., pp. 62–63.

[21] Ibid., pp. 269–270.

[22] See Weber's *The Theory of Social and Economic Organization* (1947), p. 62.

considers to be the two great innovating forces in history—charisma (e.g., in the case of the ancient Israelite prophets) and rationalization (e.g., in connection with the role of Protestantism).[23]

To add to this, Thomas E. Dow argues that the very essence of charisma is not rooted in the leader's "appearance in the right time" but in an individual who can inspire belief in his message not because of particularly facilitating conditions but in spite of tremendous odds. Dow suggests that such a man is followed not because a revolutionary departure is imminent, likely, or normally to be anticipated but because he can demand support for such change in spite of its improbable character. He said:

> Thus Christ makes God believable; Mohamed, Allah; Churchill and De Gaulle make victory seem possible; while Kenyatta and Gandhi do the same for freedom and independence. It is not the inchoate feeling for freedom which makes such men believable, but the men who inspire belief that freedom can be obtained in spite of all odds—and the odds are always long![24]

We can therefore agree that since charismatic phenomenon is not bound necessarily to any particular historical period or social condition, charismatic leadership can be understood as a social phenomenon where the leader, the followers, and the content of ideas cannot be explained as following directly from a specific context or constellation of interests. Both Berger and Runciman, for example, suggest that charismatic leadership existed and still exists within complex institutional structures. Runciman states that "under a (modern) bureaucratic or rational-legal system, the situations where charismatic leadership still finds expression are those where a leader can by his personal and exemplary qualities create further legitimacy for actions going beyond his stipulated office."[25]

In this regard, the relative independence from the setting makes charisma an important potential for social change because it is able to trigger a departure that is independent of the given constraints and context. Charisma may then represent the sudden eruption into history of quite new forces, often linked to new ideas. Far from being "reflections" or functions of already existing social processes, the charismatic forces may powerfully act upon the preexisting processes and initiate new processes of their own. It is precisely the fact that charisma is not a necessary development from any set of present circumstances that makes it a truly potentially revolutionary departure.

However, having said all that, it does not mean that charisma is completely asocial or ahistorical. Although the occurrence of a specific charismatic episode can be indeterminate as to time and place, some characteristics of charisma may vary along contextual factors. As we shall see later in our case studies, severe restrictions do put a lot of impediments on charisma and are probably expressed in the particular

---

[23] For their comments on this, see Beger's 1963 essay, "Charisma and Religious Innovation: The Social Location of the Israelite Prophecy" and Eisenstadt's book, *Max Weber: On Charisma and Institution Building* (1968).

[24] Dow, op. cit., p. 317.

[25] Runciman, op. cit. (1963), p. 149.

form that charisma takes. This is probably implied in Weber's understanding of the relation between ideas and history (as can be seen in his notion of "elective affinity" that refers to the way in which certain ideas and certain social processes "seek each other out"). In other words, it means that even if autonomous social forces such as charisma or religion do not stem from the context, they still correlate with it in ways that require further exploration.

We know from studies on leadership that indeed there is some kind of correlation between the context and the specific style and operation of leadership.[26] Since charismatic leadership is also a type of leadership (although a distinct one), we can infer that even if charisma is able to cut across time and place, its particular context may interfere with aspects such as the vision's content, the form and intensity of the relations and interactions, the mode of operation and other possible influences.

For example, in arguing that charisma can appear in a variety of intensities (of which Weber mentions only the very extreme type), Edward Shils proposes a correlation between the context and a certain aspect of charisma—its intensity and frequency—and attests that a less intense and a more frequent case of charisma can develop and function in a rational or even a bureaucratic context. Likewise, a correlation may be detected between historical context and charismatic visions; for example, the visions of Lee Kuan Yew, Sukarno, and Gandhi would probably contain a similar meta-theme of independence. These charismatic visions contain a strong plea for an independent formation and expression of identity, and we can assume its correlation with the macro historical colonial context that these charismatic leaders faced.

The following discussion will show that the most salient observation in regard to the charismatic cases relate to the structural constraints on the rise, maintenance, and operation of alternative charisma, that is, charisma that is outside the establishment or, in other words, idiosyncratic charisma. However, it would be too simplistic to argue that Singapore's structure only restricts and represses "pure" charisma. Although this may be a general pattern, it is only partially true. A closer observation and inspection of the structure and its social processes may reveal that concomitant to the structural constraints on charisma, there are less obvious, latent structural aspects that enable and even facilitate the attribution of charisma to alternative leaders.

The structural enabling sides do not make charisma's rise and operation any easier, but they offer an unintended reinforcement of charisma if and when indeed such leaders do succeed to rise. Parts of the latent enabling aspects are given in the structure, and parts are a kind of "boomerang effect" from the intended repression of any alternative authority as such. Such effects are, paradoxically, repercussions from the efforts to control and repress alternative authority that, in a structural ironic twist, facilitate the rise and attribution of alternative charisma.

The facilitating aspects coexist in parallel to the structural constraints and create a dialectical structure that both constrains and facilitates charisma (in a way that

---

[26] This has been explored in the writings of Jyuji Misumi and Mark Peterson (1985) and Edgar Schein (1985).

resembles Giddens's notion of "structure's dualism"). Hence, instead of a structure that represses alternative charisma, we can see a combined structural pattern that both overtly constrains and partially and latently facilitates such charisma.

Having said that, this does not mean that the dialectical forces have the same weight. Generally speaking, alternative charisma faces many structural constraints that result in difficulties for the rise and operation of charisma, particularly at the macro level of society. It is thus less frequent in Singapore and takes particular forms that will be described later on. In Chap. 9, we will offer some clues with regard to how such leadership finds indigenous ways to work within a constraining structure. This unique form of "working with the structure" stems from the leaders' ability to act even in tight constraining conditions and is itself a sign of their charisma (i.e., if we refer to charismatic leaders as being able to step out and rise even in constraining structures).

Structural Constraints on the Rise and Operation of Charismatic Leadership

The general pattern of constraints on charisma stems from the few aspects that influence in the same direction. Political, social, and cultural aspects seem to create a strong resisting structure for the frequency, rise, and operation of the Weberian "pure" type of charisma. The following section will describe some of these sociopolitical and cultural dimensions. These will include aspects such as a highly centralized control, a high degree of bureaucracy, social compliance tendencies, and Singapore's perception of survival.

A Highly Centralized Controlled Social System

The centralized character of the social system is an indication for the restriction of charismatic leadership and of a greater friction with the power center. This proposition can be supported by extrapolating from Weber's line of argumentation in relation to charisma and party structure.[27] In that discussion, Weber indicates that the relations between the charismatic leaders and the power center would be of greater tension in cases of highly centralized social systems.

This dimension is applicable to Singapore as a highly centralized sociopolitical system whereby "all regions of social life are open to state administrative intervention"[28] and where almost all spheres of life are touched upon by the government's policies.

---

[27] For Weber's line of argumentation, see his (1947, pp. 247–248).

[28] This reference is from, Chua Beng Huat's 1995 essay, "Communitarian Ideology and Democracy in Singapore," p. 68.

This tendency may be linked to a more general observation on centralized social systems. David Rosen, for example, argues that social systems with centralized power control would normally tend to utilize the state apparatus in which they function to eliminate (insofar as it is possible) autonomous, independent sources of power, which do not emanate from the state system itself. He says, "In all systems where authoritarian leadership existed, such leaders attempted to consolidate state power by breaking up alternative sources of power and authority."[29]

However, it does not follow that the measures for the elimination of alternative sources of authority will be harsh. They can also be based on a softer mode of "elimination," as the Singapore's "unofficial co-optation policy" may suggest. The lesser frequency and intensity of "pure" charismatic leaders should not be taken as a sign that Singaporeans are less potentially outstanding. Rather, it can be related to what Douglas Sikorski terms the "unofficial policy of the power center to co-opt any potential, promising young leader."[30]

Once co-opted, these cadres are groomed and developed within the establishment, eventually posing no real threat for any other alternative source of social influence. Sikorski argues that "Singapore has a political culture where the best talent tends to join rather than oppose the establishment. Individuals who excel professionally are invited to be members of the PAP (the People's Action Party) —the dominant political party in Singapore —and it is an invitation that is difficult to refuse." He quoted a high-rank official saying: "It is not the function of the PAP to nurture or promote (political opposition). In fact, our task will be to identify and co-opt all such people into PAP."[31] This unofficial policy of co-optation is also echoed by our interviewees, one of whom says:

> Other (people) play with the rules by *bending themselves and obliging quite readily* because they argue with themselves and convince themselves; 'okay, let me get inside and then change from within,' and I have seen too many of them and most of them have *become seduced by the system, they just become co-opted*.[32]

In such a system, there seems to be little space for non-co-opted leadership and, once co-opted, outstanding personalities are no longer a potential "threat" in terms of alternative authority to the power center. Even people who do not join the PAP are still in various ways co-opted into the establishment and seen as representing it in some way. In such cases, even if they continue to be perceived by the public as charismatic, they are no longer clear cases of idiosyncratic charisma because they bear what Amitai Etzioni has termed "office charisma" —charisma that is, in this case, intrinsically intertwined with their degree of closeness to the establishment.

---

[29] See Rosen's *Leadership Systems in World Cultures* (1984), p. 57.

[30] See his 1991 essay, "Resolving the Liberal-Socialist Dichotomy: The Political Economy if Prosperity in Singapore," pp. 418–419.

[31] The references here come from Sikorski's essay, "Resolving the Liberal-Socialist Dichotomy: The Political Economy of Prosperity in Singapore," pp. 418–419.

[32] Transcript A/6/12.

For example, in this respect, interviewees in the survey preliminary to the research were inconclusive with regard to the idiosyncratic charisma of people who were appointed as ambassadors as they felt that they may have lost, "tainted," or "polluted" their "pure" charisma upon joining the establishment. After being "co-opted," outstanding people are eventually considered by the public as representatives of the establishment, and their ideas cease to be a pure sign of their own personal qualities or vision. Their partial co-optation is a serious impediment for the development of idiosyncratic charisma attributions since they no longer possess the internal, individual aspect that is so crucial to the attribution of charisma.

A Highly Bureaucratic System

It is important to refer to this structural aspect separately because bureaucratization is not by definition synonymous with centralized control. And although centralized systems require organizational structures, these are not by definition bureaucratized, though they may be institutionalized in varying degrees. The Singapore system can be truly referred to as a highly bureaucratic system where much of its functions are efficiently run by a large apparatus of standardized and regularized methods.

Indeed, Weber's treatment of charisma is in juxtaposition to bureaucratic authority, which he depicts as diametrically opposed to charisma in all respects: in its general orientation, its origins, its mode of operation, and its function, and this is something we have elaborated further in Chap. 2. Weber says, "(charisma) naturally runs up to the resistance of the normally dominant apparatus of the professional politicians (…) it is easy for the party organization to achieve this castration of charisma."[33] In his view, charismatic leadership is necessary and essential to modern society because it has the capacity to resist the omnipotence of bureaucracies.[34]

Weber regards the trend toward bureaucratization as dangerous to societal creativity, particularly its omnipotence, which even charisma does not have the strength to defeat: "charisma is fated to decline as permanent institutional structures increasingly develop."[35] The radical contrast that Weber sees between charisma and bureaucracy implies that this inherent tension may further intensify in systems with high bureaucratic structures.

Taking into consideration Singapore's highly institutionalized, semipolitical, bureaucratic center, it is also reasonable to expect a higher degree of tension and friction between alternative charismatic leaders and the bureaucratic power center. Such systems allow less role and social space for charismatic leaders and possibly even restrict their rise and operation altogether. While a bureaucratic notion rests on rationalized rules and regulations, charismatic leaders call for ideological and ideal

---

[33] This reference is from Runciman (1978). op. cit., pp. 247–248.

[34] For a discussion of this, see Stanley Tambiah's *The Buddhist Saints of the Forest and the Cult of Amulets* 1984, p. 321.

[35] See Runciman (1978). op. cit., p. 248.

visions that do not lend themselves easily to rationalized structures and orientations. Chan Heng Chee argues that in bureaucratic systems, there is no need for charismatic leadership but a need for a technocrat, saying, "We do not need a demagogue or charismatic leader. We need a systems man."[36] In such a systemic constellation, the friction between the two different types of leadership, charismatic leaders and the "system's man," is bound to collide.

Having said all this, it is important to emphasize that the difficulties that a pure charismatic leader might face in such systems not only derive from the bureaucrats themselves but from the public as well. This is because the "bureaucratic notion" (i.e., a rational, regularized, standardized method of social action) has probably been internalized by the public as the "taken-for-granted" way for the implementation of policies and for social interaction with the power center. This social orientation toward bureaucracy has become a kind of basic assumption with regard to the way that social matters should be addressed and treated. As such, the friction of the leaders is not only with the bureaucratic representatives but, by and large, also with the public.

Tendencies Toward Social Compliance

Singapore's society seems to enfold collectivist social tendency for compliance and cultural tendencies for harmony and conflict avoidance that result in a general attitude of abidance and conflict avoidance.[37] In his book, *The Spirit of the Chinese Capitalism*, Gordon Redding says, for example, that the notion of unquestioning obedience, reserved in the Western case for unusual circumstances (such as the parade ground or the protocols of a court law), is still common in much of Chinese life, including Chinese immigrants in Hong Kong and Singapore.[38]

We can infer the notion of "Chineseness" to Singapore for three reasons. First, the fact that the majority of its population is of Chinese descent is at least indicative of cultural inclinations and tendencies. Second, according to Redding, Singapore is an "overseas Chinese society, as a kind of offshore version of traditional Chinese society that preserves its verticality and its distinct form of order, and preserves also the legacy of weak horizontal cooperativeness."[39] Third, the "Chineseness" aspect of the society may have been reinforced, at least officially, by the fact that the

---

[36] The references in this paragraph are from Chan Heng Chee's essay, "Politics in an Administrative State: Where Has the Politics Gone?" (1975), p. 68.

[37] For discussion of the first point (collectivist social tendency for compliance), see Hofstede (1980); Smith and Peterson (1988); Hofstede and Bond (1989); Bond (1991); and Smith and Bond (1993). For discussion of the second (cultural tendencies for harmony and conflict avoidance), see the work of Redding (1990); Bond (1991, pp. 65–66); Emmerson (1995); and Erez and Early (1993).

[38] See Gordon Redding's *The Spirit of the Chinese Capitalism*. (1990), p. 185.

[39] Ibid., p. 187.

Confucian notions and values were officially embraced and "reintroduced" by the PAP government in the mid-1980s[40] as values that both express and reinforce the substantial essence of Singapore's cultural and social roots.

The Confucian emphasis on obedience means that the person comes second to the order itself. Redding argues that from this flow the ensuing advantages that decision-making rights are not normally disputed, and authority in general is looked for and more or less followed. Similarly, Chan Heng Chee notes that in Asian cultures, "there is a greater acceptance of and respect for authority and hierarchy whether it is in India, China, or Japan and the countries of Southeast Asia. Adversarial opposition against the state and people in positions of power are not absent but certainly not a normal reflex."[41]

This compliance pattern is commonly correlated with the paternalistic style of the government, which both Sikorski and Chan treat as a style that is intolerant of dissension and the questioning of authority and its decisions.[42] For Redding, the paternalistic political style of Chinese government "rests on a long Confucian tradition sponsoring familism and authoritarianism, which creates norms of dependence and acceptance of hierarchy." He argues that the most immediately understandable aspect of social structure for the Chinese are the rules governing vertical relationships, and they are conveyed in the notion of *hsiao* (or filial piety) and seen commonly as the foundation stone of Chinese society. The book of filial piety—which was a key text in Chinese schools for 2,000 years—is all about a person's duty to a role, and the way in which a total system can be sustained only if all those in it remain faithful to the demands that their role places on them.[43]

In the case of China, throughout the history of the Confucian state, the emphasis has remained on the duties as a core aspect of a social role. This emphasis has depersonalized the structure and introduced a great deal of ritualistic role-copying, in which the individual's personal interests were sublimated, and where obedience, in which the person comes second to the order itself, was emphasized. To Redding, the insistence on appropriate role behavior all through the system reduced the need for harsh dictatorial methods. He says, "if society were successful in socializing people, then the son's behavior to the father was automatically deferential. (Therefore) the need for discipline was relatively rare, given all the surrounding influences which encouraged conformity to the order."[44]

---

[40] According to Sikorski, it was to "avoid the internal contentiousness" of the West, as Lee Kuan Yew stressed in August 1984. According to Sikorski (1991, p. 418, 423), Lee Kuan Yew himself attributed Singapore's success, at least indirectly, to the Confucian cultural tradition. This was in his speech on 12 December 1986.

[41] It does not mean that adversarial opposition is absent, as the cases of Korea and Japan (having changed long-term parties) may imply. But even that speaks of this phenomenon being relatively rare. It is certainly not a common social feature of these societies. See p. 22 of Chan Heng Chee's 1993 essay, "Democracy: Evolution and Implementation, an Asian perspective."

[42] See Sikorski (1991, pp. 418–420) and Chan (1993, p. 22).

[43] The two references here are from Redding, op. cit., pp. 117, 128.

[44] Ibid., p. 129.

That this should be such a dominant theme in Chinese societies derives from the nature of what Weber saw as the "patrimonial" state. To Weber, the distinguishing feature of such a state was that the ultimate power that rested with the head of state was personal and was dispensed and dispersed by representatives who also interpreted it personally. To remain stable, such a system required a form of authority seen as legitimate by those subjected to it. The Chinese solution to the problem of authority and stability therefore lies in the legitimacy of strict role compliance by both parties. Weber says in this regard that "to be without filial piety is the only 'sin' in a society otherwise devoid of such a transcendental concept."[45]

In such a system, the open challenge to formal authority is rare. This is not to say that compliance is mute and unthinking (as there are endless possibilities for subtle resistance and for disguising the unwillingness to conform), but the general tone is that there is not an issue of principle at stake about rights and duties and that the concentration on conformity per se is intense. It follows that alternative authority as such (pure charisma included) squarely confronts the characteristic of social and political compliance.

Singapore's Perception of Survival

Here we shall see how Singapore's perception of survival influences the latitude and reaction toward alternative voices in general and of alternative leadership in particular.[46] Weber argues that a crisis condition propels people toward charisma. His argument is initially a general comment in regard to the possibility of crisis being a contextual antecedent to charisma, but he does not elaborate on how such condition may affect the relations between charismatic contentions and a centralized and legitimate power center.

In this regard, George Simmel's and Lewis Coser's theories on social conflict may shed some light on the social reaction toward alternative views in times of perceived distress.[47] But for this, we would have first to establish that Singapore's government, as well as its public, perceived itself to be in a constant state of external threat. Moreover, we will try to distinguish between two sets of survival threats,[48] an

---

[45]This reference comes from Hans Gerth's 1951 study, *Max Weber: The Religion of China: Confucianism and Taoism*, p. 228.

[46]Note that we refer to the case studies as a type of pure charisma because our three cases had not been bearing "office charisma" and have not been co-opted in the established, centralized power center. See Chap. 5.

[47]For Simmel's theories on social conflict, see his *Conflict* (1995), and for the theories of Lewis Coser, see his *The Functions of Social Conflict* (1956) and *Continuities in the Study of Social Conflict* (1967).

[48]The distinction between internal and external perceptions of threat is for the purpose of analytical clarity. In reality, the various threats may intertwine.

external and an internal, and show how these two perceptions may correlate with reactions toward the leaders (both the reactions from the power center as well as from the public).

The "External Threat"

In her book, *Singapore: The Politics of Survival*, Chan Heng Chee argues that the term "survival" has been suggested as the dominant theme in Singapore politics because, in the context of Singapore's "forced independence" in 1965, it seems to be the most apt description. She notes that the obsession with the survival of Singapore can only be understood if one bears in mind certain basic facts about the island. Such facts would usually include its relatively small size, its strategic position on the Straits of Malacca (linking the Indian Ocean with the South China Sea), its position (at the tip of the Malayan peninsula and north of the Indonesian archipelago), the fact that its population is 78% Chinese (surrounded by non-Chinese races particularly in countries immediately around the island), and that it possesses no natural resources.

Implicit in this description is an underlying question with regard to Singapore's ability to survive as a city-state and as a nation.[49] Chua Beng Huat concludes that the historically determined condition at the time of Singapore's political independence in 1965 was distilled and conceptualized by the PAP into an issue of the "survival of the nation" —one that could only be resolved by successful capitalist industrial development. The fact that it had served "as the basic concept for the rationalization of state policies, even those that extend beyond economics to other spheres of social life" only speaks for the salient role of this perception in the eyes of the power holders.[50]

Moreover, Chua argues that the survival perception is not only a private perception of the power center. In fact, it is deeply shared as a basic social assumption among the population as well. Indeed, interviewees in our research echoed such a collective perception, and even the more critical interviewees seem to share (in varying degrees) this "survival perception." This "sharing of perception" between the public and the power center is in itself evidence of the fact that this perception has already been deeply constructed as the "correct" representation of reality.

This means that even if the perception were factually fallacious it would still be crucial in terms of the social outcomes, because what really matters is the mere

---

[49] Chan (1971) adds that the intensive PAP indoctrination campaign has had disturbing effects on the Malaysian leaders, saying: "The alliance government is highly irked by the 'mania of survival' in the Singapore leaders who have the annoying habit of bringing up the question at every opportunity. Implicit in the survival ideology is the call to strengthen a Singapore front against an unnamed external enemy, and the Malaysian leaders have many reasons for believing the survival exercise is directed at them" (1971, p. 54).

[50] Chua Beng Huat, op. cit., p. 4.

perception of and the belief in a threat (rather than a real such situation). This is in accordance with Simmel and Coser who argue that outside conflict need not even be objectively present. Coser says, "All that is necessary is for members to perceive or be made to perceive that there is an outside threat. Threats may or may not exist in objective reality, but the group must feel that they do."[51] Indeed, although Singapore is not in a state of war, it certainly perceives its existence as being vulnerable, fragile, and under constant threat of survival.[52]

This perception is relevant to our discussion because it seems to interfere with the particular context for charismatic leadership's rise and function. To Simmel, such groups[53] cannot afford to be "tolerant," and they become radical and intolerant toward any slight deviation. The reaction toward such people is expected to be harsh because "groups in any sort of war situations are not tolerant. They cannot afford individual deviations from the unity of the coordinating principle beyond a definitely limited degree." Simmel argues that this radicalism is not ideologically rooted but sociologically related to the perception of survival.[54]

Our interview data indicates such reactions, for example, in the way that an interviewee recalls the government's reactions toward SPUR as an independent think-tank in the late 1960s. (The group consisted mainly of architects and urban designers who offered alternative plans for public housing and public transportation in the late 1960s.)[55] The interviewee says:

> The (Spur members) were more into 'ideals,' whereas the government I believe, was more of a 'survival.' So you already see that the people who were pro-active to what was going on, were not ready to tolerate any contradictions or questions (…) I don't think they were ready for any opposing or contradictions at that time (…) I don't think that anybody would allow any inkling of contentious issues to form (…) that time was so sensitive, Oh! It was a crisis situation! (…) I think that at that time the government was so serious, it was very serious really. Let's face it, its life and death of a country (…) (so) you become very guarded,

---

[51] Coser (1956), p. 104.

[52] Both Chan Heng Chee and Chua Beng Huat have commented on this, Chan in *Singapore: The Politics of Survival* (1971) and Chua in *Communitarian Ideology and Democracy in Singapore* (1995).

[53] We can infer from this argumentation on groups as messo level social entities to Singapore's case as a macro-level social entity because although Simmel (1955) talks about groups, Coser (1956) enlarges this conceptualization to larger social entities including states as well.

[54] Simmel (1955) says that the "Radicalism here is sociological in its very nature. It is necessitated by the unreserved devotion of the individual to the rationale of the group against other nearby groups (a sharpness of demarcation required by the need for the self-preservation of the group), and by the impossibility of taking care of widely varying tendencies and ideas within a narrow social framework. Of all this, the radicalism of *content is* largely independent." The references in this paragraph are from pages 93–98 of Simmel's book, *Conflict*.

[55] SPUR stands for Singapore Planning and Urban Research Group. The group was officially started by William Lim, but soon after Tay Kheng Soon joined, and they were both the most outspoken people of that group. The group consisted mainly of architects and urban designers and also of people from other disciplines like sociology, law, political science, and others. They sought to contribute to the planning and construction of Singapore and insisted on being an independent group that does not represent nor is willing to be co-opted by the government. This group was eventually disbanded in 1974.

you are on your toes, and the slightest things get on the nerves—you would say. That is no more question of rationale. And I think Singapore to an extent at that point was sort of on to edge to an extent. It was too edgy.[56]

As we can see in the interviewee's citation as well as in Simmel's theoretical comment, the group's radicalism in times of survival perception will be expressed in the degree of the violence or degree of intolerant reactions toward inner dissensions (or, in our case, toward alternative charismatic leaders expressing different views).

Such survival perception may increase the already-given friction and tension with the power center because along such perception, the charismatic leaders appear to endanger the concerted efforts for the survival struggle. Hence, they are endemically considered as a nuisance, an impediment, a sort of obstacle to the group's continued struggle for existence.

The notion of being perceived as a "nuisance" was also echoed by interviewees as well as by Tay's own comments on SPUR. He says, for example: "It was not accepted! We were a nuisance. We were regarded as a nuisance, and an ungrateful lot"[57] (…) "We were an *irritation!* Froth! We irritated. We kind of *polluted* the tranquility of the space! So, we were a *nuisance!* We were *impediments.*"[58] Other interviewees echoed this perception saying that, in hindsight, they could see how they were seen as "wasting the time" and energies of the government in their efforts to fight for survival. Note how the following interviewee uses a metaphor of shooting, to express the extent to which he thinks that they were seen as "disturbing." He says:

> It is like today you would go to Vietnam, and talk about all these (things); they would say; what?! How *idiotic you are, really*?! I mean you go and talk to them, and they will think: 'We got all these people that *don't even have basic essentials*, and you talk to me about this?' Don't you think you *will be thrown out? Or maybe even shot! 'You are wasting my time* and not only that, you are trying to tell me that I'm wrong! No way!' (…) I'm not a political person but its just that it was something whereby the *urgency of certain things was so great* (I'm talking about the politicians) that they just literally *flick* you aside and say; *'Don't waste my time!* Don't waste my time! *You are a bunch of idiots!'* I'm sure that that was how we were seen![59]

The "Internal Threat"

In addition to the perception of an "external" survival threat, there seems to be another aspect of threat: that of an internal origin. By an internal threat, we refer to an additional aspect of Singapore's survival perception that Chan had noted back in 1971, in *Singapore: The Politics of Survival*, though she did not elaborate it. She argues that when the PAP leaders speak of survival, they are interested in the survival

---

[56] From interview transcript D/10/1,13.

[57] See Tay Kheng Soon's in-depth interview, Section 3, p. 3.

[58] See Section 5, p. 11 of the same interview.

[59] Transcript D/10/6,14.

of an independent sovereign, an economically viable Singapore. In the introduction to the same book, she adds further that, though it is not explicitly suggested, "The PAP leaders seem to equate the survival of Singapore with the survival of PAP values for Singapore."

This aspect is totally different from the previous external threat as an aspect of the survival perception and introduces an additional element of threat to the survival perception. While the perception of external threats relates to the mere existence of the nation, the perception of possible internal threats relates to the nation's type and nature of existence (its social and political characteristics). This additional aspect complicates the survival perception not only because it intensifies the threat but also because there may be multiple "possible enemies" —different in kind, both from within and from outside.

The internal type of survival threat (i.e., Singapore in the terms of its PAP values) may well relate to Lewis Coser's sociopolitical comments on "dissenters" where he argues that the heretic calls forth violent hostility from his former associates not only because of the strength of previous affective identifications but also "because he symbolically, if not always in reality, threatens the very existence of his former group, just like an external threat does."[60] In other words, the threat on the group is not in terms of physical extermination but in terms of the group's definition, identity, and nature, *qua* group.

This kind of survival threat offers a conceptual resemblance between pure charismatic leaders and group dissenters as an internal threat to the group's underlying basic assumptions; while still contemplating to belong and claiming to be part of that mere group, they insist on questioning its basic assumptions.[61] Indeed, Coser argued that such dissenters create even more confusion than heretics who have left the group, because they claim belongingness. He said:

> In a small group, the dissenter who still claims belongingness threatens to break up the group from within, for he does not represent to it the clear-cut danger of the heretic or apostate, against whom the group may find it easier to act concertedly (…) The dissenter is unpredictable and creates confusion: Will he go over to the enemy? Or does he intend to set up a rival group? Or does he intend to change the group's course of action? His fellow-members can be sure only that he is 'up to something.'[62]

---

[60] See Coser's *The Functions of Social Conflict*, p. 101.

[61] Two such examples are Tay Kheng Soon and Kuo Pao Kun, who could have left Singapore for other countries but insisted on staying there as part of what they are, as an expression of belonging. Tay returned after a few years of "self-exile" and Kuo, for example, said that while being detained in prison, he could have been set free if he would have only agreed to leave the country and live in whichever country that would be willing to accept him. But he says that he rejected that offer, saying: "I had the choice of leaving Singapore from prison directly, to go to any country that is prepared to accept me. I didn't take that option. I said, 'I'll take that option when you release me. I'll think about it afterwards. I won't think about it now.' (You can go very soon if you, you know, just go away, because, it rids the government of its baggage.) I said no. And I am sure there are many reasons for me to respond that way. I am probably not very clear myself. One aspect, which I know, is that this place is important, apart from the fact that you don't want to go away because they want you to go away. I have as much right to be here as you guys, so why?" (Transcript K/2/16).

[62] Coser, op. cit.

The group's reactions toward such "internal threats" may be even harsher. Interviewees say, in regard to the fact that SPUR was eventually disbanded, that it may have been because it was seen as a "threat" to government (not in terms of political threat but in terms of an alternative authority and power).[63] In the words of Tay Kheng Soon, who was one of SPUR's prominent leaders:

> Oh, obviously it was threatening. If not, otherwise, why would they take all those actions against us? (Because) it was (threatening)! But from our naïve point of view, we were not threatening. We didn't set out to threaten anybody. We just wanted to express our research findings and our opinions, that's all. That is (politically) naïve, I suppose (…) We were not political in the sense (of seeking power), definitely not. We were not seeking power, but they (the government) never believed that. The government saw us as seeking political power, wanting to become the government.[64]

In Coser's view, the origin of any threat is not significant, because the pattern of a social entity's intolerance will come about whenever there is a perceived threat, regardless of its origins (not only when there is a perceived external type of threat but also with regard to an internally perceived one). However, Coser does not distinguish between these two kinds of threat, although in our opinion they may elicit different reactions in terms of the degree and scope of friction.

On the issue of the internal threat, the leaders are seen as the origin of the survival threat (or in other words, the mere threat). In the external perception of threat, the leaders are not considered to be the threat itself. They are merely considered as a nuisance and as an obstacle that exhausts the required energies for the outside struggle and are at no time the mere survival threat itself. Therefore, with regard to the external threat, the negative reaction may be of a lesser degree because after all, they are not the mere threat to be wary of. On the other hand, since this perception is shared by the whole group or population (as we have already established earlier in this chapter), the scope of friction is wider because it includes not only the power center but the general public as well.

A different scope and intensity may be related to charismatic leaders as an internal threat to Singapore's survival "à la PAP mode." The scope of friction may be smaller because this perception is not, by definition, shared by the whole population. The reason for this is that, in general, the public may have bigger latitudes toward variations in its identity and be more receptive toward various forms of existence. However, though the friction is confined mostly to the power center, its degree or intensity may be higher because, in this distinction, the leaders are seen as the threat itself.

Incidental evidence for the perceptions of internal dissent as being a threat to the group's form in terms of its PAP values may be seen in the fact that Kuo Pao Kun was detained without trial for allegations of Communism (that may have been seen by the government at that time as a threat to the values of the PAP's perception of

---

[63] Although when SPUR started, it had good working relations with the government, to the point of being given access to information and even being offered a public place to utilize as their office. Some interviewees say that it was the "independent," autonomous stance that the group proclaimed that began the roller-coaster of its final "un-synchronized tunes" with the government and for its being eventually disbanded.

[64] Transcript T/3/24.

what Singapore should be like, as well as to Singapore's survival). The fact that interviewees use the word "rehabilitation" to describe Kuo after his period of imprisonment is in itself an implication of the fact that he was previously "dangerous" and "threatening" and perhaps continued to be seen as such at the time of the interviews. For example, an interviewee says:

> He was seen for a long time as the guy on the wrong side of the establishment because he was put in jail and his wife also was put in jail. But it is highly significant that they gave him a cultural medallion. And the year before they gave him a cultural medallion, they did a documentary on him on television channel under state control. He was 'officially rehabilitated' and set up as a local paragon, a pillar of statehood.[65]

The term "rehabilitation" is associated with the notion of being a "criminal" or, at least, as being dangerous to society and, as such, a person has to be "treated" to be allowed to resume his place in the group's social life.[66]

Structural Properties That Enable and Reinforce Alternative Charisma

In this section, we will point at various social, cultural, and political aspects that, although different in kind, have a similar characteristic: they may facilitate the attributions and rise of charismatic leaders. Some of the aspects are given structurally, but others are an ironic "boomerang effect" of the general tendency to suppress alternative authority or alternative views as such.

It is important to emphasize that these aspects are not able to facilitate the rise and operation of charismatic leadership in a major way but only to a very limited extent. They enhance and facilitate charisma once it rises but they cannot solely trigger and enable its function. The structural aspects that may enable and even facilitate charisma relate to the following dimensions: the tight though not total control of the government, its pragmatic orientation, the dual implication of the "filial piety" notion, and sociopsychological processes of attributions and impression formation.

Tight But Not Total Control

No system is ever so total as to eliminate voluntary, social action, and there will always be enough opportunities for human intervention and change. In fact, the case studies are themselves sound evidence for the possibility of human action to strive

---

[65] Transcript B/6/6.

[66] Kuo recalls that when he worked at the Chinese Chamber of Commerce in the early 1970s, his father was very proud. But, he says, "then I was detained, and he felt so shameful. He felt so *shameful* that I was in prison (…) At first he couldn't understand, he felt so shameful that his son was arrested and put into prison. Of course he didn't understand 'detention without trial,' as a political detainee, and the convicted criminal. He didn't understand that" (Transcript K/1/19).

even in tight and constraining conditions. Furthermore, even in tightly controlled systems there will always be a variation in the degree and scope of control in any particular field, and it will always be possible to find niches of less control and, consequently, more space for social action.

This is all possible because the systemic properties in Singapore, although tight, are not totally controlling. The authoritarian aspects of the structure are different from the systematic and total control that totalitarian regimes aim for. Whereas totalitarian societies suppress all forms of autonomous organization and all independent sources of information, authoritarian regimes are confined mostly to a tendency to suppress organized opposition and public criticism. Although it tries to limit and confine activities within institutional orders, it does not attempt to control them completely. Moreover, even if the political power holders might recognize no constitutional limitations of state power, in practice, they do recognize some limitations to their power.[67]

We can therefore assume that within the authoritarian regime there are various social arenas that are less tightly controlled and that enable greater opportunities for alternative social action, charismatic leadership included. However, these opportunities are neither readily observable nor accessible. They are, in Giddens's terms, "hidden" within the structure and waiting to be untapped and utilized. It is here that the leaders' agency is reflected as their leadership comes about in terms of their ability to spot and manipulate such structural opportunities. Such a structure enables a wider latitude to initiate social action and change in less structurally constrained fields and thus facilitate its rise in those particular fields (e.g., micro and messo levels are less constrained in general). This is not to say that in more controlled fields, charisma is eliminated but that it is probably less frequent.

The Pragmatic Orientation of the Power Center

One of the aspects that may reinforce charismatic attributions relates to the "pragmatist" orientation of the power center, vis-à-vis the in-principle ideological, and somewhat utopian, orientation of the charismatic leaders. That this aspect may facilitate charisma can be extrapolated from Weber's discussions on charisma vis-à-vis social structures.[68] Weber argues that a pragmatist or ad hoc ideology structure results in the modification of the inherent tension between charisma and the power center.

---

[67] For example, Coser (1967) argues that such regimes might try to make the Church into a pliant instrument of their rule, yet they will not attempt to deny the religious order a measure of autonomy in regard to other worldly concerns. They may limit the exercise of proprietary rights and channel the allocation of scarce resources, yet they will not attack the legitimization of property as such. In authoritarian societies, the military order is typically somewhat independent of the political order; it may even tend to dominate it. Where totalitarian societies have "politicized armies," authoritarian societies often have a "militarized polity" (1967, pp. 192–193).

[68] This can be found in Runciman, op. cit., (1978).

Accordingly, charisma has greater chances to operate in cases where the ideology structure is loose (as in "unprincipled" and "ad hoc"). In his short discussion on the chances of pure charisma in bureaucratic systems such as political parties, Weber notes that:

> We can accept that the chances of charisma in its struggle with bureaucracy in a party depend to some extent on the general character of the party. The chances of charisma are very different in a simple 'unprincipled' party—that is, a party of place-hunters which formulates its program ad hoc in the light of the opportunities offered by the particular electoral contest—from what they are in a party which is primarily an association of notables based purely on status, or a class party, or a party which to a greater extent still preserves its idealistic program or ideology. In certain respects, its chances are greatest in a party which is primarily of the first type.[69]

In other words, pure charisma has greater chances of operating in structures that are "ad hoc" and "unprincipled," having loose and less rigidly systematic assumptions, than in structures with rigid routinized machinery of ideology.

In *Communitarian Ideology and Democracy in Singapore*, Chua Beng Huat attests that Singapore's PAP politics has promoted pragmatism as its main criteria for decision making. He defines pragmatism as referring to loose ideological orientation, saying that "briefly stated, pragmatism is governed by ad hoc contextual rationality that seeks to achieve specific gains at particular points in time and pays scant attention to systematicity and coherence as necessary rational criteria for action; whereas utopian rationality emphasizes the whole and at times sacrifices the contextual gains to preserve it, if necessary." Chua argues that the PAP style of operation is ad hoc because:

> The justification for intervention is always contextual and never based on principles of political philosophy (…) (and) each intervention in a specific region of social life aims to be effective in that region exclusively (…) as contextual and instrumental instead of 'in principle' interventions, they are discrete and discontinuous acts,[70] in the sense that a particular intervention in a particular region of social life may radically alter the trajectory that an early intervention may have put in place.[71]

It does not mean that there is no underlying ideological logic in the policies but that even if there were,[72] it is not readily accessible to the laymen. However, it can be said that the pragmatist policies have a popular legitimacy and are "constitutive of the ideological consensus between the PAP and the population." Its acceptance by the population is probably supported not only by the general level of compliance

---

[69] Ibid., p. 248.

[70] Chua (1995, p. 69) quotes Ow (1984) who noted that this ad hoc nature even led opposition members to perceive it as a pathological syndrome: "Contextual and discontinuous interventions are characteristics of what a PAP backbencher calls the 'crisis mentality' of his own government."

[71] The quotes here and in the previous paragraph are from Chua Beng Huat (1995), pp. 58, 69.

[72] In the same text Chua makes a systematic phenomenological attempt to decode the underlying ideology of the power center policies. His ability to decode the underlying ideology is probably related to his sociological acumen. But in the eyes of laymen, the underlying ideology, if indeed it exists, is encoded in such a way that is neither readily observable nor overtly comprehensible.

and conformity but also by what Redding refers to as the "Chinese cultural inclination to pragmatism." Gordon Redding argues that the Chinese value pragmatism, and this can be inferred (among other things) from cultural tendencies such as the Chinese perception as being especially "immediate" and sense-based and the Chinese morality as being contingent rather than being based on absolutes. Redding argues that this pragmatic orientation will be expressed in their mode of decision making, saying that "The taking of decisions on what appears as practical grounds is to be expected."[73]

Although Weber indicates that in loose ideological contexts charisma should have less tension with the center, he did not elaborate the reasons for his general indication. To understand how such context affects the rise of charisma, we need to refer again to the transcendental, meaningful nature of charisma. Following the symbolic approach to charisma,[74] we suggested in Chap. 4 that the essence of charisma relates to its ability to offer a meta-meaning by engaging with the underlying, basic social assumptions. The attraction toward charisma is rooted in the human quest and need for meaning and in its relation to values and ideals that are transcendental to the daily trivial pragmatic preoccupations.

Charisma therefore colors the daily life with an overarching coherent meaning. By the way that charisma relates to existential dilemmas and issues pertaining to the nature of the world, human beings, and the society, it not only drives people to action but also gives to their actions a valuable meaning that is coherent with a larger scheme of reference. It is in this respect that a system that offers social action cannot answer the human quest for an overarching meaning when its actions seem eclectic, ad hoc, or pragmatic. This in itself may result in people being "charisma hungry" or at least in a receptive predisposition to such charismatic leaders, and it may enhance the chances of such charisma to rise in spite of the very many structural constraints it faces.

The Dual Implications of the "Filial Piety" Notion

The preceding section of this chapter pointed at the general pattern of cultural compliancy as a power base of the rulers. It was also noted that this tendency toward conformity inhibits the rise of alternative authority or dissension and that this pattern probably stems from the Chinese notion of "filial piety." Although at first glance, this sense of verticality deriving from filial piety might appear stifling and constraining for the public, while deliberating for the rulers, filial piety is actually equally demanding on those in positions of power as well. The people in positions of power are bound by the same concept and are vulnerable and sensitive to public

---

[73] See Gordon Redding (1990), p. 71.

[74] As explored in Shils (1965); Eisenstadt (1968); Geertz (1977); and Willner (1984).

perceptions on their performance. They are therefore accountable and are expected to fulfill their role as benevolent rulers.

These mutual expectations actually gibe a picture of a more balanced account of the relative power between the rulers and the public. Although the public is expected to comply, the government is equally and reciprocally expected to perform in exchange for the legitimacy and compliance that they are accorded. This notion is supported by the Confucian aim of a peaceful, harmonious, ordered society that facilitates a form of paternalism that combines discipline with benevolence.

The core of that responsibility is the paternalist concern for the subordinates' general well-being—something for which much conformity is offered in return. It follows that any abuse of these responsibilities undermines the authority and destroys the allegiances of those below. Consequently, the rulers do not monopolize power in a totalitarian way without being subjected to any checks and balances, because these balances are given within the same paternalistic framework based on filial piety that both the rulers and the public comply with.

Hence, in this regard, it is not surprising to hear the following perception from an interviewee: "When you look at the government with such enormous power, (almost absolute power we would say in many areas), the fact that they have not yet used the iron block so often actually speaks quite well of them."[75] Withholding the use of power is possible because in the concept of filial piety, if roles are strictly followed, power is not abused, and Confucian doctrine aims to produce just such acceptable leaders, or powers that be, respected for their wisdom, humanity, and propriety.

By the same token, there is another less obvious implication for such a ruling style: such a concept seems to implicitly impel the rulers to be attentive and benevolent even to its, so to speak, "enfant terrible." Consequently, even in cases of rebels or "dissenters," the rulers would be driven to feel the obligation to "listen" and care for whatever such people may have in their hearts and minds. This role obligation stems from the very same paternalistic notion that perceives the rulers as fathers. Such a perception forms a symbolic equation whereby, if the ruler is a "father," equally the public are his "children." Therefore, even as deviant and as rebellious as a people may be, they are still the ruler's/father's children and as such ought to be taken care of by the father.

This mutually binding notion has, for example, been expressed in the media. An article in *Asiaweek* in June 1997 used the words "former bad boy" and "one time 'enfant terrible'" when referring to Kuo Pao Kun's past detention, and Singapore's *The Straits Times* used the words: "Time to honor this radical son" when referring to Tay Kheng Soon.[76] The phrases refer to Kuo and Tay as radicals, but more so, as sons, who nevertheless have to be at least embraced or accepted.[77] Such a call is

---

[75] Transcript B/11/10.

[76] The *Asiaweek* article was published 13 Jun 1997; *The Straits Times* article on 22 Jun in the same year.

[77] The fact that this publication coincides with Tay's retirement announcement may be in itself an indication of the difficulty to allow social space for such people.

only possible because it has been conceptually grounded in a prior basic assumption binding or defining each of the governed, as a son.

The reaction and the measures that such sons may be treated by is altogether a different question, but no matter how punitive these methods may be, they underlie the basic sense of a meaningful bond between the parties. Symbolically speaking, this tie is a kinship tie—one that can never be broken, however rebellious a son might be. The analogy of father-children means that the underlying relations between the rulers and the public are, in a very fundamental way, close.

Consequently, this familial kinship somewhat alters the power balance between the rulers and alternative leaders because the rulers are, to a certain extent, accountable to their children and because this accountability means that even the quests and views of rebellious kids have an initial legitimacy and an in-principle (though not total and unconditional) acceptance. In short, this underlying relation triggers a sublimation of the negative perceptions of the leaders and reactions toward them—at least from the point of view of the powers that be. This underlying notion may transform the perception of charismatic leaders from being perceived as dangerous, threatening political rivals, to a more forgiving, less dangerous kind of perception—that of rebellious, "naughty sons," "bad boys," or "terrible children."

Attributional Biases that Reinforce Charisma Attribution

Although the attribution of charisma may be well grounded in the individual characteristics and abilities of the leaders, the structural aspects further reinforce and facilitate the development of charismatic attributions. This happens because some structural aspects create a situation whereby the leaders seem relatively more extraordinary than they may really be. This point is crucial for charismatic perceptions because the attribution of being extraordinary—particularly one that is internally attributed—is a major aspect of charismatic attribution. In other words, if people cannot easily explain the leaders' behavior in terms of external factors, an internal attribution would take place and charismatic attribution may be reinforced accordingly. Here we will demonstrate how sociopolitical aspects affect social attributions of charisma toward such leaders in two possible attributional processes.

The general cultural and social tendency of compliance, coupled with the unofficial policy of eliminating the development of alternative authority (either via repression or co-optation of potential leaders) results eventually in the scarcity of any alternative authority including that of charismatic leaders.[78] Yet, paradoxically, the serious limitations on the frequency and intensity of alternative charisma reinforce

---

[78] Once again, pure charismatic leaders, according to Weber's definition, are inherently opposed to any establishment and power center.

the attribution of admiration and charisma to those who do actually take such a stand. An interviewee, for example, says:

> The societal conditions here make it easy for people to stand out, because there are very few people involved in certain kind of activity. So the minute you're involved in it—you stand out. I think that in Britain, there are so many critics of government, people criticize the government openly, in newspapers everywhere, so when you say something—you don't stick out. But in Singapore when you do that—you get stacked out, pretty much, you get slapped down too. So there are very few people who even dare to (…) Anything, which anybody does—sticks out.[79]

In other words, they are a priori respected because to take such a stand in such a constellation "takes *courage and strong principles*." Such people are actually considered by the interviewees as "sort of *great face* to stand up and speak up."[80] In this context, whoever stands up stands out and is predispositionally admired almost irrespective of the content of their vision. An example for that can be seen in the results of the preliminary survey in our research. When asked to nominate charismatic leaders in Singapore, people nominated, among others, the opposition Member of the Parliament, J.B. Jeyaratnam. Interviewees supported his nomination as being charismatic by the mere fact of his ability "to stand against the government and endure."[81] This specification does not refer to any of his ideas as a definitive sign of personal charisma, nor to a unique alternative vision, but only to his perseverance in standing as an opposition.

The relative scarcity of alternative leaders may contribute to the aggrandizement of the leader's impression formation due to an attribution bias known as the "contrast effect,"[82] where someone who is really only average may receive an outstanding appraisal, when evaluated in relation to others whose performance is poor. Implicitly or in an unintended way, this structural constraint actually reinforces the charisma attributed to leaders even though they may be only relatively, rather than absolutely, outstanding. Various interviewees expressed the reinforcement of the leader's charisma in relation to the context in which, relatively speaking, the leaders seem exceptionally extraordinary.

Tay, for example, in commenting on his own social perception as a leader says: "(If I am regarded as a leader it is because) in the kingdom of the utter silence the sound of a pin drop sounds like a thunderclap." Tay made this remark at the first meeting with our interviewer in November 1999, and in this metaphoric expression, he seems to imply that his own presence is "not an objective fact"; it is in fact just

---

[79] Transcript B/17/9.

[80] These two references are from transcript D/8/5.

[81] This is discussed in our description of the preliminary survey for the purpose of selecting charismatic leaders in Singapore (see Chap. 5).

[82] This bias refers to an attribution error that stems from the cognitive relativity of perception formation and can occur as a result of the contrast created in the mind of the person doing the appraisal comparing the very poor performer and the average performer. See Daniel Feldman and Hugh (1983).

as "quiet" as the sound of a pin dropping. However, it is the lack of any other "noise" or, in other words, "the sound of silence" that amplifies his presence. The relative sound of a pin dropping against a "deafening silence" transforms his "tiny tune" into an almighty thunder.

Interviewees echo this relative impression formation, saying, for example:

> I would say that because it is so difficult to find people in Singapore who are willing to stand up and articulate a dissenting view, that even someone who speaks on a very safe issue, let's say 'the preservation of rainforests in Bukit Timah' —(which is not political, it is miles away from defamation suits against an opposition politician)—such a person, if he attained some prominence, would be considered as an outspoken, daring or what have you, because there are so few people who are willing to stand up and challenge conventional thinking.[83]

Ironically then, the "loner position" not only increases the extraordinary perceptions but also increases the chances of them being heard or having social influence. Tay says in this regard:

> There is no politics in Singapore! I mean, there is no tradition of making a public stand on what one believes in. It doesn't happen! Very seldom! It is not the common thing. No one expects it (to happen) (…) there is so little of these public expressions of alternative views that whenever it takes place, even in, say, a closed forum, it is taken very seriously by the powers that be, precisely because expressions of alternative views are so rare.[84]

In spite of the fact that people may be aware of the relativity dimension in perceptions, they still perceive the leaders as extraordinary. This is because they implicitly relate to the context as a structural constraint that requires a great degree of social courage to speak up. Ironically then, the scarcity of alternative views symbolically evokes archetypal myths of victories, of triumphs, of the concepts of overcoming great odds that, in turn, elicit awe and admiration. One interviewee says, for example, of Kuo:

> Pao Kun takes on a greater influence and significance because of his own *personal background*. That, I think, is the *key* to Pao Kun's influence, what has happened *to him* and how he *has not given up his ideals*, since. The fact that he was locked up by the government, accused of being subversive, was never on trial in court for it (as far as I know), and then released eventually. *And then he goes back to the very same thing that he was more or less doing*. This is an *emotional appeal* to the *intellectuals 'to stick to your ideals,'* and he has *not been crushed*. The *kind of standing* that Pao Kun has, has partly to do with his background, the fact that he paid a *price for his beliefs*, but he continues to *hold on* to those beliefs. Now, this is not to say that everybody that challenges the government is now a new Nelson Mandela as such. It is nothing like that. I think it is just *the sense of respect that people give to a man, who has stuck to his beliefs*. Now, you may or may not like his beliefs, but the fact that this person stuck to his beliefs and was not crushed, always elicits a kind of respect from people.[85]

Paradoxically, the tendency for extraordinary attributions may further increase when there are certain systemic regulations and restrictions on group gatherings and

---

[83] Transcript D/21/4.

[84] Transcript T 5/6.

[85] Transcript B/11/1–2.

when the general political climate is not conducive to group action (e.g., the fact that certain social gatherings require official approval and through the nonenforced yet existing law that restricts the nature of certain social gatherings above five people). Although these regulations may originally or generally refer to the prevention of secret societies or subversive political action, they nonetheless seem to posit a climate that restrains group action as such. An interviewee expresses this sentiment:

> There is a political culture in Singapore where *group* activity is always viewed as something *very suspicious*, which is why we have very few Non Governmental Organizations and *we have very few civic groups*. You know that you even have these assembly laws where if you gather in too big a group you can be considered as illegal, etc. So for that reason, that's the kind of political *culture* that we have.[86]

These structural restrictions mean that social action may tend to be restricted to an individual, micro level. But micro-level type of social agency is itself a structural aspect that reinforces extraordinary attributions because it enhances internal causes as the explanation for the leader's behavior. Since their action cannot be accounted for as an expression of a group (at least not a defined group), it can thus only be seen as stemming from a certain individual; or in other words, it can only be internally attributed. This means that the leader will be perceived as its own "event maker," which in turn further reinforces his "standing out." An interviewee says, for example:

> It's a very special (context). It is different from other places. Under these conditions, anybody who writes a letter, (let's say one day there's somebody at the National University of Singapore who says okay; 'I'm going to write a letter')—*he is going to (be very lonely)*. There will be *no (social) support for him*. There is no background (and) nobody is going to defend him. So I suppose that that is what is also special about Kuo Pao Kun; he didn't mind (being a loner). He wasn't the *head* of a '*movement*.' It was Pao Kun.[87]

This kind of impression formation is linked to Ross's argument on a type of the "fundamental attribution error," which is a general biased tendency of observers to refer behavioral causality to the performers (i.e., an internal attribution), while the tendency of the performers themselves is generally to attribute their own behavior to external causes.

Though it may be argued, as Michael Bond has done,[88] that such fundamental attribution error may not be that dominant in Asian culture (because of intervening social and cognitive tendencies toward perceptions that are less internally inclined),[89] we still think that the tendency for internal attribution is more than compensated for in conformist, highly compliant societies. This is because, in conformist societies, social explanations of nonconformist behavior (either deviant or extraordinary) are

---

[86] Transcript D/22/14.

[87] Transcript B/17/10.

[88] See his *Beyond the Chinese Face: Insights from Psychology* (1991, pp. 42–43).

[89] Smith and Bond (1993, pp. 110–116) argue that the tendency in Asian cultures is to combine both internal and external causes in the explanation of behavior, a tendency that may alter the fundamental error that Ross has found in the West.

less compatible for the explanation of deviant nonconformist behavior by external attributions (since there is hardly any external factor that would encourage such behavior). Paradoxically then, the conformist aspect may reinforce the idiosyncratic social aspect of charisma by triggering internal attributions as the explanations for nonconformist, extraordinary behavior.

Some Structural Indications for the Case Studies

We will now briefly relate to the different structural constraints that each of the three leaders in our study faced in their particular context and relate also to their relation with the power center and to their social position.

By and large, as we have seen, extraordinary traits are attributed to all three leaders. (Attributions and impression formation processes that may have been reinforced by the above-mentioned structural aspects). There is also a variation in the degree of control in each of the social arenas that the leaders acted upon, and a different degree of latitude toward social action in each respective field.

The Latitude for Alternative Social Action in Each Particular Field

The most tightly controlled field, relatively speaking, was the field of architecture and urban planning in which architect Tay Kheng Soon acted. At least until recently, the constraints to promote alternative visions were most notable within this field, as there was very little latitude for alternative views on public housing and urban planning, these all being determined by central planning bodies such as the Housing and Development Board (HDB) and the Jurong Town Corporation (JTC). Tay's alternative architectural vision was often rejected. His social action seems to be confined mainly to the domain of the construction of "ideas," and many interviewees seem to lament the fact that most of Tay's ideas were not physically experimented nor executed.

Compared to Sister Prema and Kuo, Tay had never really succeeded in fully implementing his own ideas nor in constructing a public organization (like Prema's Heart to Heart service or Kuo's Substation), except his own private architecture firm. Though the firm tried as much as it could to focus on designs that enfold Tay's ideas, his ideas were never institutionalized in a public organization. Perhaps the metaphors relating to Tay as a "Don Quixote"[90] or as one who keeps "bashing (his) head against the wall" [91] are analogies of the nature of the odds that he faced—giant

---

[90] The metaphor of Don Quixote also implies a kind of a naivete, the naivete of a man who fights giant wind mills, a perspective which Tay himself seems to have internalized, saying: "I have the right to be politically naïve" (T/5/14).

[91] Transcript D/21/15.

windmills and solid walls. Eventually, his charisma stayed as a kind of "prophetic charisma"; a prophet who talks and talks but to whom very few listen, or he is, as an interviewee describes him, "a voice in the wilderness."[92] To what extent the inability to implement his alternative vision is a corollary of his own personality[93] is not clear, but it probably also has something to do with the very limited, restricted latitude for alternative social action in the field of architecture and urban design.

In comparison, Kuo, whose field of action is theater, faced a slightly less controlled space for action. Although there existed (and perhaps still exists) a basic political suspicion toward arts in general and theater in particular (as being inherently prone to social and political action and thus being potentially subversive), there was never a systematic effort to totally suppress art or dictate its content. Indeed, more centralized control was felt from the early 1980s onward when the government decided to step into the arts field and promote it in relation to the identity formation of Singapore. However, this centralized control has provided many more opportunities for the art and theater scene (as is evident in the infrastructure providing space and technical support for yearly Art Festivals from the early 1980s onward, various premises for art groups to perform and practice, and other initiatives).

In Kuo's case, the latitude for social action was restricted yet still containing considerable possibilities. The physical institutional implementation of his alternative vision was not impossible, as may be implied by the mere establishment and operation of the "Substation—Home for the Arts" and by the production of most of the plays that he wrote (other than those that were banned in the early 1970s). Yet, the many structural constraints still required a very talented, sophisticated manner of exploiting and manipulating structural opportunities and of overcoming or avoiding the many odds. The social perceptions of Kuo as a "shrewd, astute, sophisticated operator"[94] and as one that "has got to play the game and plays it very well"[95] may emphasize this point.

To turn to Sister Prema, at least until recently, social welfare in Singapore was more or less left to private individuals, and it was the responsibility of families themselves to support the needy and elderly people.[96] Sister Prema was (and still is) a leader in the social welfare field and was never perceived as being potentially subversive. In fact, her actions were more or less welcomed by the power center; although they did not actively support her, they did not restrict her either. She was not perceived as an alternative to the government because at that time there was no controlled mainstream in the field in which she operated.

The field was, structurally speaking, open or at least uncontested. Consequently, the latitude for her social action was larger. This latitude was additionally increased

---

[92] Transcript D/15/17.

[93] Many interviewees describe Tay's behavior as brusque, using, for example, words such as "arrogant," "stepping on people's toes," "does not beat around the bush," and other similar terms.

[94] Transcript A/6/12.

[95] Transcript B/10/19.

[96] Realizing that the percentage of the elderly population keeps growing, the government has lately stepped into this area as well and has begun to provide infrastructure as well as policies for their support. At the same time, the government still emphasizes the role and responsibility of the family members in attending to the elderly needs.

by the fact that she restricted her action to the micro-messo level and never "went big." The government's general attitude of religious flexibility to encourage the coexistence of various religions in a multiracial, multilingual, and multireligious society also gave Prema more room for social action. She has, therefore, never directly confronted the power center and enjoyed a wider (than the other two leaders) latitude of freedom and social space in which to operate (a latitude that, in constraining structures, is typically reserved for a private individual's social life).

Patterns of Ambivalence in the Relations Between the Charismatic Leaders and the Power Center

Though there exists, in principle, an initial close relation between charismatic leaders and the power center (which is rooted in the fact that both are concerned with the provision of a meaningful symbolic order and in that both strive to construct social reality), this close relation does not imply consensual relations. As we have already argued, such involvement with the symbolic center is not acquired only by its mere representation or invocation but also by way of a reflective mode that is inherently provocative: eternally calling for a reevaluation of dominant basic social assumptions.

Indeed, Weber's sociological starting point of the treatment of charisma is the recognition of the inherent tension that the charismatic engenders in any social system, stressing its disruptive effects, and its contribution to the destruction of existing institutions and to social change. As R.S. Bell argues, such leadership is at the very least, potentially subversive. He says:

> Pure charisma (…) must by its very nature be revolutionary or, at the very least, potentially subversive. This is due to the fact that pure charisma cannot recognize any competing claim, including that of the state, as legitimate.
> (…) It is easy to see why this extraordinary personalistic foundation to charismatic authority must, practically by definition, constitute a threat to the state or any existing legal structure, no matter how sublime, gentle, or pacific the doctrine taught by the master may be.[97]

Weber did not thoroughly pursue an extensive and comprehensive analysis of leader-center relations. This omission could not have been on the ground of dismissing charisma as historically esoteric, because Weber himself was interested in such temporary transitory categories.[98] Nor could such exclusion be on the account of charisma being perceived as bearing a minor role in society because Weber acknowledged charisma's substantive role as a transformative power in the chain of the social system's history of change and reform. In any case, we are still left without a comprehensive theoretical treatment of the relations between charismatic leaders

---

[97] See his essay, "Charisma and Illegitimate Authority" (1986), p. 59.

[98] Eisenstadt (1968) acknowledges one of Weber's major analytical contributions to sociohistorical studies in his treatments of the temporary and transitory as an important scientific explanatory category. In Eisenstadt's words: "He was able to insert the temporal dimension as a category inherent in the very structure of social systems and of social life. Not as something irrelevant to the major forms of social organization, or as an external force directing the destiny of societies, but as an inherent element of social systems and their tendency to change over time" (1968, p. xlix).

and power centers (other than the symbolic treatment of such relations made by Edward Shils).

Our interview data indicates that the relations between the leaders and the power center (at least with regard to Kuo and Tay) are of a dual ambivalent character.[99] On one side, there is a certain degree of "fear" and resentment toward the leaders and indications of being perceived by the power center as "potentially subversive." Such perceptions and attitudes are themselves indirect indications for the fact that the leaders are perceived as capable of social agency, as powerful, and maybe even as charismatic.[100] Otherwise, why bother repressing and deterring them? We can probably assume that the degree of fear from potential leaders is correlated with the belief in their omnipotent powers. In other words, we can argue that the measure of repression expressed toward leaders could serve itself as an evidence of their perceived charisma and powers.

However, it does not mean that the relations contain only tension, as the relations between the leaders and the power center also contain partial acceptance and collaboration. This dual, or ambivalent, relation means, broadly, that the power center does not regard the leaders as totally oppositional, destructive, social agents who must be eliminated. Rather, it sees them as potentially contributive agents, who nonetheless have to be constantly deterred, disarmed, contained and controlled—, and also emulated and even at times, evoked. In other words, both the leaders and the power center do not seek (or cannot) overthrow and exclude one another.

Indications for such ambivalence can be seen, for example, in reactions toward Kuo. As an instance of this, the play, *The Coffin is Too Big for The Hole* was published in full in *The Straits Times* newspaper[101] in spite of its interpretation as a criticism of Singapore's bureaucratic system (as "an inspired little story that takes a naughty dig at our sometimes overly regimented way of life.") The publication in *The*

---

[99] Wolfenstein (1967) argues that revolutionary leaders attract attitudes that combine both awe and fear. He uses Freud's concept of "the taboo of rulers" to refer to this pattern, arguing that the ruler, or leader, is a man who "must be both guarded and guarded against." He is a potential force of great beneficence, but it is also dangerous to trust him deeply. He possesses a "manna," a special gift of power from the gods, but this can be used for good or ill. He concludes: "relations between ruler and ruled are thus fraught with danger" (1967, p. 6).

The ambivalent patterns of admiration-rejection can be also related to a social process whereby the alternative leaders may be "acting out" some of the latent inert desires of the larger group members. Since these inert latent desires are expressed by the alternative leaders, other group members are "released" from the need to express their own covert desires, and thus, at the same time, can engage in a simultaneous overt condemnation of the member's overt behavior that they themselves may be covertly wishing for (since this behavior is usually "deviant" and nonconformist) (Moscovici, 1980).

[100] Perinbanayagan's (1971) insight on such a dialectical notion is relevant. He argues that it seems that Gandhi's opponents themselves were coming to believe in his powers, so much so that they thought that if they would eliminate him, their path would no longer be blocked. That to him, was an implication of the fact that even those that oppose Gandhi came to perceive him in ways similar to those of the followers: they define him as being powerful enough to ruin their own cause and mission. This indirectly shows that those who try to repress the leaders (to the extent of their total extermination) eventually "succumb to the notion that the leader is all-seeing, all-powerful, and awe inspiring. Gandhi's assassin, then, was a Hindu who paid obeisance to the leader and then shot him at point blank range" (1971, p. 397).

[101] In *The Straits Times*, 7 Dec 1995. The reference to it as "an inspired little story" comes from the previous day's newspaper.

Straits Times is not trivial. It can be taken as a valid indication of its acceptance by the power center since "the government voice dominates the press"[102] and since the "newspaper is widely recognized as an organ which put the government's position on issues."[103] An additional sign of acceptance and even evocation can be seen in the fact that the play has been approved as an "O" level (high school) text by the Ministry of Education and that it was included (together with *No Parking on Odd Days*) as the core artistic plan for theater productions in the Singapore Arts Festival 2000.

In other cases (from the 1980s onward) Kuo was repeatedly commissioned or received special grants or positions to lead projects. He had also been given a cultural medallion for his cultural work at the same time as his citizenship was still denied (this was reinstated only in 1992). One interviewee says about this relationship:

> I suppose, from the early '80s he had a school but he was already doing his combined plays for the Singapore Arts Festival. He would be given the responsibility of directing plays using the resources of a number of Chinese theater groups collectively and he would use sometimes his own play all the time directing it. So I suppose, the government has a rather curious relationship with him. On the one hand, he had been given that responsibility but was also being watched all the time. At the same time his passport had been taken away from him, he could travel outside, but had difficulties in getting legal documents.[104]

There are also indications of a constant, latent, "suspicious" attitude toward him, as can be seen from an official Arts administrator, who has this to say about Kuo:

> Sometimes we are quite worried... sometimes we are quite concerned about the kind of works that he puts up, you see, whether there are a lot of these political underlying messages. And that is what sometimes worries us, especially if his works are supported by the state. We do not want his works to have subtle messages or something that is critical of the government or it takes a dig at the government in a very subtle way and hope to get away with it. And he is able to cleverly camouflage his works. That is something we are quite concerned (...) he is somebody that I think the state respects. He is somebody that the state would like to honor, disregarding his personal beliefs, his political beliefs, and so on. And we feel that he is somebody whom we would like to cultivate the support for and who help the state to raise the profile of the artistic community in Singapore. He has a role to play in the cultural development of Singapore.[105]

The Leaders' Liminal Social Position

The discussion on the relations between the leaders and the power center seems to trigger an additional underlying question that compels us, in a way, to return to the theoretical question in regard to the social position of charisma.[106] Is charisma indeed, as Weber suggests, ipso facto, marginal?

---

[102] See Chan Heng Chee (1993, p. 16).

[103] Sikorski (1991). op. cit., p. 419.

[104] Transcript B/12/8.

[105] Transcript B/6/9.

[106] It should be of no surprise that the question of the social position of the charismatic leaders is triggered once again, given the methodological criteria for charismatic leaders as strictly bearing no office charisma (see elaboration in Chap. 5).

Weber insists on the marginality of charisma as stemming from its total rebuke and repudiation of the institutional center per se. Hence, "pure" charisma is essentially alternative to the power center of the society and inclined to be marginal. He grounded this argumentation by relying on the cases of the ancient "Israelite prophets" and explicitly rejected the notion that the prophets are to be understood as spokesmen of a social protest movement of the underprivileged strata. He understood the prophets as isolated individuals opposed to the established religion of the priesthood and emphasized their noninstitutional or even anti-institutional character.

However, later scholars doubted that conclusion. Peter Berger, for example, has reviewed the cases of the ancient prophets and, in his reinterpretation, rejected the stereotype connected with the image of the prophets as opponents of the priests and as brave individualists defying the religious authorities of their time. He argued that, in fact, the Israelite prophets were not socially located on some solitary margin but within the religious institutions of ancient Israel and acted from such a traditional office. He concluded, therefore, that they were not as marginal as Weber argues but somewhat closer to the center,[107] even if not "from" the center.

The social position of the leaders in our case studies,[108] particularly those of Tay and Kuo, is not by definition marginal; their social position is neither marginal nor central and yet is both.[109] In other words, it is liminal.[110] Victor Turner argues that

---

[107] In a similar but a more radical line, Shils (1965), Eisenstadt (1968), and Geertz (1977) argue that charisma is capable of rising and functioning in the center as well, and therefore, charisma is not by definition alternative nor marginal.

[108] Sister Prema is more marginal in the sense of having no obvious contact with the power center.

[109] We think that this notion was initially implied, though not explicitly, by Weber's relation to charisma as being intrinsically both supernatural and worldly at the same time, saying that "charisma lives in, though not off, this world" (1947, p. 247). This implied that the notion is carried throughout Weber's various translations as we can see in Matthews's translation (1978, p. 228) using other words but the same liminal meaning: "charisma lives in the world, but is certainly not of it." In a more explicit conceptualization of the social position of pure charismatic leaders, we can see that Weber had in mind the "liminal" concept though he did not use the specific terminology. He says: "In order to do justice to their mission, the holders of charisma, the master as well as his disciples and followers must stand outside the ties of this world, outside of routine occupations, as well as outside the routine obligations of family life. The statutes of the Jesuit order preclude the acceptance of church offices; the members of orders are forbidden to own property or, according to the original rule of St. Francis, the order have to live in celibacy, and numerous holders of a prophetic or artistic charisma are actually single. All this is indicative of the unavoidable separation from this world of those who partake of charisma" (1947, p. 248). Weber relates to the implied "liminal" social position of the charismatic leaders while trying to crystallize its unique form in comparison to other forms of authority and ground his arguments on the noneconomic, irrational, and noninstitutional structure of charisma.

[110] The usage of the concept of "liminality" in regard to the social position of the charismatic leaders is not solely an academic exercise in the old theoretical dispute in regard to the social position of charisma. It promotes Shils's (1965) and Eisenstadt's (1968) symbolic approaches for the analysis of charisma because it is capable of explaining how such leaders engage with the meaning center and yet retain Weber's notion of charisma as essentially revolutionary and non- or anti-institutional. Furthermore, it offers a more proper definition to charismatic cases that are not clearly located in the social power center.

what characterizes the peculiar unity of liminality refers to the "coincidence of opposite processes and notions in a single representation (...) that which is neither this nor that, and yet is both."[111] Liminality therefore contains contradictions (like being both things,and at the same time being neither of the things). He says:

> They are neither one thing nor another; or may be both; or neither here nor there; or may even be nowhere (in terms of a recognized topography), and are at the very least 'betwixt and between' all the recognized fixed points in space—time of structural classification.[112]

However, while Turner treated liminality as an interstructural phase (in between the social change of status and role), the leaders' liminality in our case studies is not temporary; it is essentially and fundamentally an endemic aspect of their social position.

The liminal social positions of Tay and Kuo are formulated on the grounds of their being neither central nor marginal. They are close to the power center[113] in terms of personal relations and potential influence on decision makers, yet they are not part of the establishment, both rejecting and being rejected by it.

Along with the interviewee's perceptions that the leaders are (to use our interviewee's words) "trouble makers," "a nuisance," and "potentially subversive," they also point out many times that Kuo and Tay have ongoing personal contacts with high-positioned figures in the power center. One interviewee says this about Tay[114]:

---

[111] This and the following quotation are from Victor Turner's 1967 essay, "Betwixt and Between: The Liminal Period in Rites De Passage." We owe an intellectual debt to Turner's highlight and elaboration of the liminal concept as a phase in "rites de passage" in which he developed the concept of liminality from an amorphous situation to an interstructural phase. His treatment introduced liminality not as a residual category to be dismissed but of a cultural and structural significance. Although Turner referred to situations or states, it is possible to transfer the concept into the discussion of charismatic individuals, as he himself related also to the "liminal persona" as a representation of the isomorphic aspect of liminality (1967, p. 95), and therefore, it is also possible to refer to liminality as a structural social position rather than a state limited in time and place.

[112] There is an aspect to the liminal characteristics of the leaders that may be related to the "negative" reaction that Turner found in regard to liminal beings (and that is echoed in the case studies in the form of dual reactions toward the leaders). The ambivalent reactions that social liminality triggers were initially suggested by Douglas (1966) in her book, *Purity and Danger*. She suggests that the concept of pollution "is a reaction to protect cherished principles and categories from contradiction." She argues that what is unclear and contradictory from the perspective of social definition tends to be regarded as "unclean." From this standpoint, one would expect to find that liminal aspects are particularly perceived as polluting since they are neither one thing nor another. As we have seen, the reactions to the leaders include positive but also negative perceptions, and these contradictory perceptions form an ambivalent pattern of relations that may well be a corollary of the leaders' liminal social position.

[113] A structural affinity that is different from the symbolic affinity suggested by Shils (1965).

[114] Apart from the fact that his late brother used to be a minister in the government, a fact that probably contributed to his contacts. However, the contacts he has had are more within his own profession, and through all the time that his brother was a minister, as well as the time when he was married to Chan Heng Chee, the Ambassador, he continued to be critical of the government. Still, these background factors did probably prevent a stronger repressive reaction from the government toward him.

If I'm in his company, he will answer the telephone half a dozen times, and this would be talks with people that are generally in positions which are quite important in terms of (it might be the Chairman of the EDB or it might be a government minister or it might be a politician who is in charge of a community center, or something like that)…(his) voice has been very much respected and he is very respected, and this is another aspect of him.[115]

Interviewees say that Tay has gained idiosyncratic respect to the point of being taken seriously whenever he offers his commentary or ideas to the government's officials. One interviewee says, for example:

There are very few in our profession who have that credibility and that edge and who would make people sit up and listen (…) *He can! He can* because of his views and his stand that he represents, he can go into a meeting with a *Minister* and the Minister would *listen to him.* At the end of the day, the Minister may not agree with him and may not adopt any of his ideas but you can never deny the fact that the Minister *will listen* to him and *treat him seriously* as a person who *is serious* about his views.[116]

Similarly, an interviewee says this about Kuo:

He is fortunate. Unlike many other artistes who are marginalized (…) he is as intellectual as most of these people are, and is very defiant. He is truly independent. Pao Kun has had the good fortune to be not marginalised. He is at the center. I mean, imagine the Ministry of the Information and the Arts having special lunches and discussions with him, one on one. He is *not* in any way marginalized, no, no. He cannot claim the martyr.[117]

The leaders' personal accessibility to the power center is not obvious and never "played up" officially but kept in a rather low profile. The dialectic relations are reflected in covert collaborations and the usage of nonofficial, nonpublic channels of operation such as closed-door sessions and personal contacts.

The leaders, for their own part, are not discouraged by this ambivalent and ambiguous relationship and are able to work under such conditions. They are able to tolerate the system's dualities not only with a compliant attitude but in a collaborative manner (that at times may even seem rather ironic). It is an attitude that is also reflected in the way that Kuo relates to the founding of the Substation. An interviewee says the following about Kuo:

He told me that in those days when he staged plays you know, the Internal Security Officers will be there to watch his rehearsals. He knows them, they had coffee after that. They want to let him know that they are watching him and so on, that's all. So, that's why this place is wonderful: (He would accept that these Internal Security Department people are sitting there and watching him), and then they can go and have coffee after that. If Pao Kun were to tell this to a Western journalist, for instance with no background, then the Western journalist won't trust Pao Kun, (and would probably say): 'you are also part of the government!' But he is *not* part of the government! He is part of this *place, this place*! And he's got to play the game! And he plays it very well, the way he manages the journalists, the way he manages his Internal Security Department trailers, I think he's done it very well.[118]

---

[115] Transcript D/13/5–6.

[116] Transcript D/15/15.

[117] Transcript A/6/13.

[118] Transcript B/11/18–19.

Similarly and in a rather macabre way, Tay Kheng Soon expresses his ability and willingness to "collaborate" with the structure and to express himself in spite of the constraints on public articulation of dissenting views. He says:

> I am not worried. When I talk on radio or TV, I know that they will always remove (certain words or sentences and in fact) they will be very helpful to me (…) They don't want me to get into *trouble*. They know that, I know that. So that gives me some interesting kind of *freedom*, so I don't feel emotionally so self-inhibited. I just say whatever I like, and *they will cut* it.[119]

Emerging Patterns

Along the contextual constraining structural factors, the leaders' action would tend to be more restricted at the macro level of the society, though they enjoy more latitude at the micro and the messo social levels. Indeed, as we will see in the next two chapters, the relations with the followers and the social transformations are more attainable at the micro and messo levels of society, and as we shall see in Chap. 9, it is more constrained at the macro social level.

That, however, does not mean that the leaders stay clear altogether from the macro level (especially Tay and Kuo). All these dual, ambivalent, and liminal indications mean, at the very least, that from the leaders' point of view, the structure is not seen only as restricting. Instead, it is seen by the leaders as partially and potentially workable. This perception or attitude toward the structure is crucial for engaging in social action and reflects how their engagement is uniquely correlated with the constraints and with the enabling structural sides. We will illustrate these relations in Chap. 9.

The next chapter presents a narrative of our three case studies. In so doing, some analytical dimensions and concepts that underlie the descriptive presentation will be teased out and serve as the foundation for the conceptual analysis in chapters to follow.

---

[119] Transcript T/5/18–19.

Chapter 7
The Charismatic Enigma:
Three Extraordinary Singaporeans

This chapter will describe our three cases and focus on their presentation as social entities (i.e., what their characteristics are rather than what their agency is). This chapter, then, is an empirical preparation for the constructivist and transformative conceptual analysis in the chapters that follow this.

The three cases in this research are regarded as leaders in their own fields of action. They each excel in their chosen profession or area of work and are perceived as being exceptional and outstanding. They all have a more or less defined group of "followers" in the sense of people who admire them and admit to being influenced by them. Those followers are not the leaders' formal employees and are in no way "obliged" to follow, and many of them even work in other organizations and in totally different social fields altogether. Yet they admit to being significantly influenced by the leaders, and actively participate, to various degrees and in different ways, in the promotion and implementation of the leader's vision.

However, in these two criteria of exceptional attributions and the existence of an active followership, there is nothing so new as to constitute a contribution to the study of leadership. Neither are these criteria sufficient to establish the classification of the cases as charismatic leaders. Consistent with the emphasis of this research on the perceptual substance of charisma (the charismatic "unique ideas" as we described in Chap. 4), the main focus of this chapter will be to unveil their ideas and their uniqueness. Their uniqueness is constituted not only on the meaning that they offer with regard to existential dilemmas but also grounded in the way that these ideas juxtapose and contrast the dominant assumptions.

Along with the empirical description of the cases in this chapter, a few notions will be implied in the data and further elaborated in the chapter that follows this. First, the various dimensions work in a sort of constellation, interaction, and intersection and not as separately as they are presented for purposes of analytical clarity. Second, there is a close relation between charismatic leadership and the social construction of meaning. Third, the content of the social construction of meaning is related to existential questions. Fourth, these existential dilemmas prompt a debate with the dominant systemic assumptions and deconstruct their content and validity. And fifth, this deconstruction itself is essentially intertwined with a simultaneous

Dayan Hava and Chan Kwok-bun, *Charismatic Leadership in Singapore:*   113
Three Extraordinary People, DOI 10.1007/978-1-4614-1451-3_7,
© Springer Science+Business Media, LLC 2012

articulation of an alternative yet coherent and meaningful corpus of ideas—ideas which, again for the purpose of analytical clarity, we will attempt to separate as much as possible.

Sister Prema

I have never met a person like her, so very selfless. Totally selfless. Like 'Mother Teresa.' I haven't met such a person in all my life. I would rank Prema in terms of her work, morality and service—very high. Certainly not lower than 'Mother Teresa.'[1]

Fact File

Teresa Hsu, or Sister Prema[2] (as she prefers to be called), dies in 2011 at the age of 113. She has never married and has spent most of her life doing charity work. Despite being illiterate until her teens and having had only three years of schooling, Prema managed to learn numerous languages—including four Chinese dialects, Bahasa Melayu (the Malay language), German, and Spanish. At the time of this study, she was learning Sanskrit.

Born in Guangdong, China at the end of the nineteenth century, she lived there until her 30s. She later moved to Hong Kong, and from 1933 to 1939, she worked there and studied in the evenings. While she was working, she used to keep only a small portion of the salary for her basic amenities (such as rental, transportation, and basic food), and the rest of the money was used to pay medical bills or school fees of poor families that she came across. In 1939, she left Hong Kong and went to mainland China, where she continued to work with a news agency.

However, having to live through the Second World War and seeing its casualties, she decided to leave her job in 1940 to help a group of English Quakers attend to the wounded, until the war ended. Quakers are pacifists and avoid "all external wars," and at the end of the war, at the age of 45, she chose to be trained as a professional nurse in England. To account for applying for such a position at such an age, she wrote to the Principal of the Nursing School, saying, "I know that I am grossly over-aged, but for me it is not for livelihood but as a dedication."[3] Upon graduation in the early 1950s,

---

[1] Transcript E/4/1.

[2] According to her, the name "Sister Prema" was given to her by a Hindu guru, who acknowledged her service to needy people and gave her the name Prema, which means "love" in Sanskrit. She also prefers to be addressed as "Sister," because it is coherent with her belief that all human beings are brothers and sisters.

[3] This quotation is taken from Prema's interview by the Oral History Department in 1995, which is kept by the National Archives in the form of reels. We will mention in each such quotation the exact location among the 11 reels of interview. In this case it is "4/464." This stands for reel number 4, and 464 stands for the location on the reel.

she joined the "International Voluntary Service for Peace," and during 1953–1960, she worked as far afield as Paraguay with a medical unit tending to the poor and sick. Most of the time, she has forgone a regular income, relying instead on food and lodging in exchange for her nursing services—in an equation that sounded like: "I will work for my heart and you will give me one meal a day, and a place to sleep."[4]

In 1960, she returned to Malaysia at her mother's request. Prema recalls: "For 29 years I was away from home. But my mother was so surprised that after 29 years away, I came home with a rucksack on my back, and my clothes were the poorest clothes. (My mother) was surprised, and said: 'Waw! What happened to you? After all these years is that all you have?' And I said: 'Yes. I went to look after poor people, so I am as poor as all of them'."[5]

Prema moved with her mother to Singapore in the early 1960s and volunteered, in 1963, to work in Kong Wai Shu Hospital. At the age of 65, together with her elder sister, she founded "The Home for the Aged and Sick" at Jalan Payoh Lai in Singapore, the first home to take sick, bedridden, poor old people. This Home was unique because it took care of people who were both old and sick. Before, there were either "Homes" or "Hospitals" but there was no place to take chronic, poor, old patients who did not need acute medical treatment (and were therefore unsuitable for hospital admission), nor did they have a home to stay.

For the next 20 years, Prema devoted herself to nurse, free of charge, over 100 poor and sick elderly patients who were in the Home. This was not a trivial task since the care of so many sick, old, bedridden patients required a constant and substantial amount of work as well as financial and other resources. Prema had much support and help from people around her, who volunteered to help her in many ways, for many years. To run an operation of such magnitude and for so long, in a voluntary mode certainly requires a large mobilization of human and nonhuman resources.

When the "Home for the Aged and Sick" had more than 200 patients, the Rotary Club of Singapore agreed to support it financially in exchange for a formal "take over." For that purpose, the Club founded an association called "The Society for the Aged Sick," and Sister Prema was appointed as the Matron of the Home. However, in 1984, she was forced by the association to retire because she was considered to be too old at the age of 85 to continue to run the Home, where many of its patients were much younger than she was.

Prema retired from the Home with some reluctance. However, that same year, she established the "Heart to Heart" service. This service, which she runs, is informal and unregistered and offers direct help. With the assistance of volunteers, she collects food, clothing, and funds to distribute among poor people, whom she regularly visits. Every last Sunday of the month, with the help of volunteers who drive her around, she brings rice, sugar, biscuits, beverages, and monthly cash allowances, taking regular care of 14 families and 28 elderly people.

According to Prema, the "Heart to Heart" service looks after people in their own homes: those who need help but do not qualify for organizational aid for various

[4] National Archives interview (1995). 4/470.

[5] National Archives interview (1995). 9/431.

reasons. She says, "technically, these people can fend for themselves, but really, they cannot."[6] These include, for example, noncitizens, or people who technically "have relatives to support them" but whose relatives are too poor themselves to give help or who do not want to help.[7] She may even take care of people who receive welfare aid but who find the monthly allowance far from sufficient for their needs.

For this service, she was awarded the "Guinness Stout Effort Award" in 1988 and the "Life Insurance Association Award" in 1994—an award given to "those who selflessly contribute to others."[8] In 1995, she was featured in a television program dedicated to "Singapore's Extraordinary People" and a publication of the same title followed this program.[9] In 1995, she was invited by the Oral History Department of the Singapore government for a long, in-depth interview on her life, ideas, and activities. In 1998, the news channel CNN featured her for its promotion of news and general information programs on Asia,[10] and in April 2000, she was voted as "the woman of the year" by *Her World* magazine.[11]

Followership

There is a more or less defined group of "followers" consisting of more than 20 volunteers who regularly participate in the "Heart to Heart" service. Their contributions take the form of donations, or services such as the distribution of food and resources. To this group, we can add an additional, larger group of volunteers who participate on a less regular basis. These volunteers come from all walks of life and from various religions, but they all share the passion and belief in Sister Prema's vision and mission. They respect her and revere her. The degree of her influence is reflected not only in the willingness to contribute in physical efforts and resources but also in the fact that many of them admit having changed their lives in the light of her ideas.[12]

They all manifest a high degree of personal trust in Sister Prema. One of the volunteers told us, for example, that the company in which she works, once gave a

---

[6] *The Straits Times*, 20 May 1993.

[7] "These may include cases like 'samsui' women (who never married and worked as domestic helpers) who, after their retirement, have to fend for themselves, or families that do not qualify for formal assistance, like young widows with children, or families where the father is 'an irresponsible odd jobber'" (ST 20/5/93).

[8] Reported in *The Straits Times*, 20 May 1993.

[9] See Khng Eu Meng (1995).

[10] In this promotion, she demonstrated complicated Yoga postures that she practices and also summarized her perspective on life.

[11] (Together with two other woman nominees.) The opening notes on her were "Carer of the aged and sick, nature lover, yogic mystic—and 100 years young. Rachelle Lau is humbled by the selfless, silver-haired ascetic the press calls Mother Teresa." (April/2000:178).

[12] We will elaborate on the leaders' agency in social transformations in Chap. 8.

donation of S$40,000 to Prema's "Heart to Heart" service, but since it is an unregistered organization, the check was forwarded to Sister Prema's personal bank account. The donor even recalls that Sister Prema asked to make sure that her name would be spelt correctly on the check because "otherwise she will not be able to deposit it into her own personal account."[13] The donations do not go to an official, formal account, and their distribution (as well as the distribution of other material resources) to needy people is done at Prema's sole discretion.

The volunteer's participation in such an unofficial organization without formal "checks and balances" is indeed an expression of the high degree of trust that followers have in her, and also speaks of the degree of the moral integrity that they attribute to her. Interviewees say, for example, "it is her show, she has the last word, she decides. I don't know what the guidelines are and I don't bother. I trust Sister Prema to judge and decide who is illegible to receive the benefit from her."[14] Another interviewee says:

> I leave [the decisions] entirely to her. She decides what to do with the donations. She has done it for so long, she knows the best. She gained a lot of experience and knowledge on how to do it. She is doing it for so many years that she really knows how to do it continuously and not just one time, and from all her experience, she really knows how to decide who are the people that are entitled to her help.[15]

Extraordinary Attributions

What is it that is so extraordinary about her? If we analyze the attributions about her, we can see three main clusters or areas of exceptionality: her way of life, her physical appearance, and her spiritual aura.

Khng Eu Meng has described the place where Sister Prema lives in the following words: "her abode is spartan. There are tables and chairs, a small television, a medium-sized fridge, a stove and cooking utensils. The flat is devoid of ornamentation." When we visited her during the years 1997 and 1998, we learned that this description was correct, except that the television was gone (and according to Prema, it was for a good reason) because "some other poor family needed it more than I do."[16] Her spartan and frugal way of life is remarkable, as she will not indulge in any material pleasure, and even rations her own food and restricts her intake to the minimum amount necessary for the physical maintenance of the body: basically only one meal a day, consisting of rice and raw vegetables. She says:

> *Never* would I touch that that is not *strictly* necessary for maintenance of life! I will maintain my body in a good working order, as a duty—but not to eat for pleasure. Not for socializing and eating (…) I wear what passes on from people, at least I don't spend good money,

---

[13] Transcript E/5/7.

[14] Transcript E/12/6.

[15] Transcript E/18/3,4.

[16] Transcript E/4/2.

and food wise—I will go for the cheapest, so I don't squander money (…) I have no resources that I can call my own, the only things that I can call *my own* are the things that my *body really needs to maintain itself*. Anymore than that—is not *mine*, so all *must go*! (…) So my needs at the moment are really rock bottom.[17]

All the money that she had earned during her years of work (in Hong Kong and China), the money and provisions that she managed to collect from personal donations, and the money and land that she inherited went directly to needy people. Meticulously, persistently, and with utmost perseverance, day after day, and year after year, she keeps devoting her physical, material, and moral resources to the poor. A long-term volunteer says that "she is very, very thrifty. She saves a lot on herself, but she is very generous to others."[18] Others say that she could have very easily been a millionaire with all the land that she inherited, but instead, she donated it for the purposes of helping the needy. Another volunteer says, "She devoted her life to others without a thought for herself. She is the kindest person I know. For me she is a fantastic role model, one of my biggest heroes."[19] And a long-term volunteer says this about her: "People talk about Lee Kuan Yew,[20] but she is as great as Mr Lee. Mr Lee is great in his own way but she is great in her own way."[21]

Sister Prema's physical appearance is also a source for exceptional attributions. She has an extraordinary young and healthy appearance for a woman of her age. In newspaper articles, she is described as someone of exceptional physical appearance and stamina. Some examples include a November 1997 article in *Be* magazine, describing her as, "looking decades younger than she is—and with incredible agility and sharpness of mind." And *The Straits Times* describes her, in 1993, as "a woman who does not look a day beyond 50, whose complexion puts to shame women half her age, and whose only concession to age was that she stopped driving 10 years ago."[22]

We were personally able to verify these attributes from our own (rather embarrassing) experience with her. Our interviewer once joined her on one of her weekly visits to the elderly poor people whom she takes regular care of. In what was a typical hot and humid day in Singapore, she had to climb quite a lot of stairs up and down to each person's place (sometimes even four floors to reach each one of them). For the record, we should admit that, at that time, the interviewer was hardly one-third of her age, but could barely keep up with her pace, literally "running" after her (not to mention having to catch her breath once in a while).

An additional source of Sister Prema's exceptional attributes resembles Weber's notion of the superhuman or supernatural aspect of charisma. The perceptions of her

---

[17] Oral Archives (1995), 5/250.

[18] Transcript E/4/1.

[19] Transcript E/10/6.

[20] Lee Kuan Yew was the first Prime Minister of Singapore as an independent country. He is considered the "founding father" of Singapore, and still widely regarded with great awe and a sense of reverence.

[21] Transcript E/6/4.

[22] *The Straits Times*, 20 May 1993.

include divine attributions such as "Saint," "Goddess," "Guru," "Angel," "Spirit," and other such transcendental terms. One volunteer, for example, says: "She is an extraordinary person, she sacrifices herself, she is a Bodhisattva;[23] like a Goddess, she is a human being but her attitude is like God." Or "She is unlike all worldly people. She is practically spiritual. She has good connections with God because of her pure and high energies. She is human but her spiritual part is bigger than her worldly part."[24] Or "I consider her very close to *God*. A *living Saint*."[25]

People revere her. Our second visit to her was in February 1998, and as it was around Chinese New Year, it was customary, as we have often seen, for Chinese to bless each other by offering a pair of oranges symbolizing prosperity. However, we were quite surprised to see a volunteer kneeling on her knees and bowing her head while offering the oranges to Prema. It was an act to which Prema reacted in embarrassment, urging the volunteer to get back on her feet, but never before have we seen such a gesture, other than when this was done in a temple and the oranges were offered to the gods. To us, this volunteer's gesture was an authentic expression of respect for, and awe toward, Prema. The spiritual aspect of Sister Prema does not naturally flow from her field of action, which is a social welfare service. It flows from her frugal way of life, her constant meditations, from the ideology behind this frugality, and most of all, from her extensive knowledge of various religions, including Christianity, Hinduism, Buddhism, which trigger reactions of awe and reverence.

Unique Ideas

Sister Prema is profoundly preoccupied with the quest to work for needy people. Speaking of her inner urge to help, she says, "This urge is so strong that I cannot rest until I have met people's needs within my strength, within my power."[26] Whenever she talks, she emphasizes the notion of poor, needy people, and the duty to help them. So much so, that she even considers the keeping of something—while someone else needs it—as stealing. This is a rather unique reinterpretation of the notion of sharing: one that is couched in moral codes of right and wrong that are not directly deduced from the normative moral codes, yet have an internal moral and philosophical logic of their own. She says:

> We know that there is always somebody in need. In many ways: financially, materially, physically, emotionally, spiritually. So there is plenty of work for us to do. We are never off duty because as long as somebody is in need in those ways we are never off-duty (…) there are always more people who need money than those who have money to give, and there is always someone in need…

---

[23] A Buddy Satua is a Hindu term for the reincarnation of a good spirit. This comment comes from transcript E/13/2.

[24] Transcript E/2/2.

[25] Transcript E/10/6.

[26] Oral Archives (1995). 18/50.

If I have more things in the house, that I don't need, if I have more food in the house, and I know that a friend is poor, and I keep that thing—that deed is stealing, because it does not belong to me. I am not hungry. There are other people who are hungry. Therefore I may not keep it. So whatever I don't need, I don't put my fingers on. I don't touch it. I put it away. That is for me, not right to keep it. If somebody else needs it (not want but needs it. There is a difference between them; 'want' and 'need' are not the same: You may want many things, but you don't really need all those things), so if somebody else needs it and I have it—I must give. I have no right to keep.[27]

Another example for constructing an alternative morality that has an internal logic (or that derives its logic from the philosophical notion of "sharing") can be seen in the examples that she uses in order to emphasize how important it is to help poor people. For example, lying in order to help a poor needy person is something she has considered a "good lie." It is not that Prema preaches that one should lie, but that in certain situations (especially when that lie would protect or help a needy or desperate, destitute person)—it is not a morally wrong "lie" to be condemned, but, in fact, a "Holy Lie" to be emulated (or at least for its cause to be emulated).

She gave one such example when she shared with an audience the tale of how she had once helped a poor woman who relied on illegal fishing in order to feed her family. At one time, when the police was searching for that woman, Sister Prema agreed to let her hide in her place, pretending to know nothing about her or that matter.[28] She said about this example: "What could that poor woman do? She had to feed her family (…) so that was a *GOOD* lie. *A HOLY LIE*."[29]

Prema's notion and articulation of "sharing" has a strong universal, humanitarian perspective. Her basic philosophy is that she has not traveled to this world alone, but with other "fellow travelers." Of these "fellows," she has said that, if in need, "I must help them as much as possible. I don't call it charity or service. I call it duty."[30] It should be noted that, for Prema, needy people are not downgraded but are equal. Thus, helping her fellow men is intrinsically intertwined with transcendental and metaphysical ideas about the nature of the world and humanity.

Though most of us would not think about social welfare work as an expression of philosophical, transcendental, spiritual ideas, Sister Prema manages to articulate the idea of social welfare service as an ultimate spiritual experience. Through the links that she establishes between this action and other metaphysical ideas from various religions, social welfare action becomes an expression of transcendental philosophical notions about the world, the society, and the self.

For example, since she sees the notion of sharing as intertwined with needy people, according to Prema if she is blessed with good health, she should not hold it

---

[27] Buddhist Library, 22 Sep 1991.

[28] She even shared with the audience the tale of how she reached an arrangement with the police that the fish that they would confiscate for illegal fishing would be donated to the "Home for the Aged and Sick," as a noncommercial organization that feeds poor, sick elderly patients. She said that with such an arrangement she could return the confiscated fish back to the woman, "legally" (Buddhist Library, 12 Sep 1991).

[29] Buddhist Library, 22 Sep 1991.

[30] "*Be*" magazine 11/97.

to herself. She asks, "Why shouldn't I share with those who don't have it?"[31] Her justification for that rhetorical question is expressed in her feeling that "what I have is a blessing entrusted to me not for my own use, but to share with those who don't have it. Therefore, if I see somebody poor, I should share with him (whatever I have)."[32]

She refers to these notions as a "theory of ownership," and we should note how she perpetually emphasizes terms that transmit the notion of sharing by using words and phrases such as "equally," "us all," "each one of us," and "for all." She says:

> There is this theory of ownership: we are here in this world equally blessed, should be. And great good nature, the fatherly loving good nature—looks on each one of us—as a child. Great good loving father is looking after us all. So sunshine is meant for all, rainfall is meant for all, nature with its greens and beautiful flowers is meant for all of us. So equally will be my ability that is entrusted to me, to share with all. Just like the flowers, giving out their fragrance, giving out the beautiful flowers, just like the rain giving out the water, so I share everything with them. Only when I do that—that I am part of the great good nature. So it is my duty to share my all with everybody, especially those who need…So that is, roughly, my basic philosophy; that the gift that you have is not for you to use for yourself— is to share with all, especially those who need. So if you faithfully keep to this theory of a great good loving father caring for all of us lovingly—we must in return also care for everybody else. Lovingly as we are loved and cared for.[33]

According to Prema, the literal interpretation of the Christian notion of God as "Our father in heaven" actually embeds and implies a universal perspective on human beings—a notion that cuts across nations, religions, and other boundaries. To her, this is because if "there is only one God, and if we call this God 'father,' then all of us are his children. So we are all brothers and sisters because we have the same God, the same father."[34] It follows then that the notion of brotherhood is not the exclusive property of any religion but encompasses them all.

According to her, a direct implication of this notion of God—that she prefers to call "father"—means that we need to share and assist everyone, including other religions and nations. Hers is a universal notion because it cuts across all religions, and, indeed, volunteers told us that Prema assists poor people in India, as well as Vietnam, and also helps foreign workers in Singapore. She says:

> All creation (whether you call yourself a Christian or not)—if you are a human being, you are part of the creation. And God does not create only the Christian, he creates all beings— (moving or not moving, trees and stones are created by him), so he is the father of all of us, whether in our heart we acknowledge him and call ourselves Christian, or even if a man calls himself a Buddhist, he is still created by the same God and therefore he has the same father. And the one that I call 'father'—is also the one that he calls 'father'—so all men are brothers and sisters. So my thought became universal: everybody who needs—and I can help—it is my duty to go and help![35]

---

[31] Oral Archives (1995). 14/320.

[32] Ibid., 14/335.

[33] Ibid., 14/344.

[34] Ibid., 5/180.

[35] Ibid., 5/203.

Another unique feature of her ideas is the combination of the Hindu notions of "Karma" and reincarnation, with the Christian notion of brotherhood and sharing. A "self-purification" process is achieved by the practical daily mundane engagement with helping poor and needy people. She says:

> I know from my own experience that only when I believe in reincarnation—that I can explain why am I here, and why this unquenchable thirst to go and help: That is my duty. So that is the answer, and I found answers to my questions: who am I? Why am I on this earth? I know that I am here because it's my duty to serve! So now I know why I am in this world, and what I have to do. And all I have to do is to put my head down, go forward and do it, and do it, and do, and do—until the duty is removed from me. So now I know my job. And I am doing it, and it gives me great joy.[36]

Sister Prema believes that the notion of helping the needy is related to a transcendental cosmic order that encompasses both life and death. She therefore applies the notion of "Karma" to social welfare service, saying:

> There is a purpose to life. The Hindus teach that if there is any stain on your soul, if there are any misdeeds that you have done in your past life—you have to come back into this world to expiate all of it. That is cause and effect; that is why there is reincarnation. You have to come back and pay back all the debts. Debts in misdeeds—(means that) if you hurt somebody—you have to come and be hurt, and pay interest in it. Therefore, if you hurt somebody—you have to suffer this hurt plus interest. If you cause great hurt—you have to spend more time. So, what is my duty to this world? A duty to this world is that if I have lived other lives and I have done wrong things—I am here, at this present lifetime to purify myself and get rid of all the stains of the past misdeeds, and to help each other to purify.[37]

The mixture of various ideas such as the Christian notion of "brotherhood," the Hindu theory of "karma and reincarnation," and the Buddhist notion of "service to humanity" is revolutionary—not only because it is unique but because in Weber's terms, it literally "turns all ideas of sacred."[38] Such an articulation deconstructs the sacred notion of religion as "untouchable" and non-re-interpretable. Her critical reflective inspection of teleological corpuses, together with the liberty that she takes to apply a selective attitude toward religious doctrines (and their reinterpretation in social welfare terms), is revolutionary.

By this, she deconstructs the idea of the religion as an untouchable "taboo" and implies that it can be critically analyzed, reinterpreted, and selectively applied. Prema takes the liberty to recompose various ideas from different teleological corpuses and yet, at the same time, seems to offer a coherent philosophical construction that in Weber's terms has "an internal logic of its own."[39] This "collage" or hybrid kind of attitude is revolutionary and deconstructive, but is also equally coherent and meaningful for the followers, and this is something we will elaborate on in the next chapter.

---

[36] (1995:18/90–100)

[37] Ibid., 18/30–40.

[38] See Walter Runciman (1978, p. 232).

[39] See Hans Gerth and Wright Mills (1947, p. 250).

Analytically speaking, Prema deconstructs religious corpuses and reconstructs a belief system that is a "religiousless religion." It is "religiousless," not in the sense that it is atheistic or secular, but in the sense of not being constrained to any specific religion. At the same time, it is religious because it bears recognizable transcendental themes and because it is equally "religious" in preaching and demanding social welfare service. Prema indeed perceives her ideas as a "religion" saying, "selfless service is my religion."[40]

Although none of Prema's ideas is new, their recomposition as part of one belief system would be, in Weber's terms, "unheard of." From the point of view of the respective "official" religion holders such as priests, monks, and others, the mere "borrowing" of certain ideas and their reinterpretation may be seen as a "sin" because her selective, hybridized attitude deconstructs the idea that each teleological corpus is exclusive and undisputed.

She says: "I do not belong to a specific religion, but will accept anything that teaches me to be good."[41] She also says, "I don't call myself a Buddhist. I study Hinduism—I don't call myself Hindu. I study Buddhism—I don't call myself a Buddhist. I study the Christian religion—I don't call myself Christian. I don't call myself anything."[42] She can therefore accept the Christian notion of an overall guarding entity by "believing in a Supreme Being"[43] but at the same time refuse to call him God.

In the same manner, she argues that there are various interpretations of the notion of reincarnation, and that none is absolutely right. What really matters to her is not the official doctrine but the content of the idea. If the content is meaningful—it is good enough. In a talk that she delivered in 1991, she said:

> It doesn't matter who reincarnates whom, if the teaching is good: take it. Analyze it. Absorb it. When Buddhist people come to talk to me, I listen happy with my mouth open. I listen so happily because they speak to me words that I have not known before. You have to be open because no one religion is exclusively right and everybody else is wrong. That is not right. I don't have any picture in my home, so nobody is offended. If a Christian comes—I don't have a Christ picture. If a Buddhist comes—I don't have a Buddhist picture. If a Hindu comes—I don't' have a Guru's picture. Nobody can say, what do you worship? I am free, and nobody has to condemn me or be sorry that I will go to hell because I don't worship their God.[44]

Sister Prema's ideas are unique in their way of combining different sets of ideas together. One such combination is the convergence between social welfare service and spiritual ascetic notions. In this sense, the mere uniqueness of her "Heart to Heart" service is its distinct theological flavor and its underlying

---

[40] Khng (1995) op. cit., p. 52.

[41] Reported in Singapore's *The New Paper*, 30 Mar 1994.

[42] Oral Archives (1995). 17/430–460.

[43] *The Straits Times*, 20 Nov 1997.

[44] Buddhist Library, 22 Nov 1991.

"ideology." The spiritual religious notion is, as it were, expressed by the social engagement and participation in the chain of universal mutual help and sharing. This is a humanitarian-oriented belief system that socializes transcendental and metaphysical aspects of religion into the idea of selfless service. The humanitarian-oriented version "loses" some of its religious sacredness and turns into a more spiritual, humanitarian philosophy. In this respect, the metaphysical hierarchic notion of "God" is socially reinterpreted into a more egalitarian notion of "brotherhood," which means that "if he is our father—we are all brothers and sisters."

Another surprising combination relates to the content of the spiritual ascetic notion. It is an eclectic and selective mixture of various other religious ideas from different sets of religions. This, however, does not mean that it loses its sacred aspect altogether. Rather, it loses the absolutist, institutionalized, official "sacred version" of each religion, while it retains the spiritual and metaphysical notions of various religions. Her ideas are somewhat secularized by being "taken out" from their institutionalized "sacred realms" and reinterpreted in a social, humanitarian perspective (rather than in metaphysical terms).

Her version thus demystifies the institutionalized regimented religious doctrines, secularizes them, and suggests the possibility of an interreligion conversion. Such reinterpretations of religious themes have won her admiration, awe, and attributions of a spiritual and religious guru and have also been a key factor in her influence on people. One long-term volunteer said, for example, that along the talks he had had with her, she convinced him that it "really does not matter how do we call it; whether we call it Jesus, Buddha or something else."[45] This person was brought up with the thought that "whoever does not believe in Jesus goes directly to hell," but then he realized that "if a person like Prema will go to hell just because she does not believe in Jesus—then certainly, *no one can go to heaven*!" This volunteer says that this insight triggered a whole series of thoughts and reevaluation of his own religious convictions. He says, "in the religion issue she has really affected and changed my life, and the meeting with her had given me a new perspective on religion. I realized that I can worship God in my own way, and after talking with her, I became more broad-minded and I do not condemn other religions."[46]

To sum it up, the idea of social welfare service is neither new nor unique. So it is for other metaphysical and transcendental ideas that Prema talks about, such as the notion of "God" (in inverted commas), brotherhood, reincarnation, and other concepts. But the combination of social welfare service as bearing a spiritual, religious, philosophical flavor is unique. Also the recomposition of different religious ideas into one synthesized, philosophical view is refreshingly "new" (and "new" in inverted commas as well). Although each of the components is not new, the whole combination or hybridization creates something that is altogether different, unique, and "unheard of."

---

[45] Transcript E/4/3.

[46] The last two references in this paragraph come from transcript E/4/4.

Kuo Pao Kun

In a sense he was a kind of cultural icon, cultural hero. In the West, and in other countries, cultural heroes are very important and they are also present all the time. Look at Pavel in Czechoslovakia, or T.S. Eliot during the First World War. They represented something, they represented a standard, they represented a way of looking at the world. They had a certain *moral weight*, they had a certain light which shone for the rest of the people. I think that Pao Kun is the closest person we have in Singapore to such a *cultural hero*.[47]

Fact File

Kuo Pao Kun was born in 1939 in Hebei province[48] in China, in what he describes as "a very, very poor, poverty-stricken village."[49] In 1947, he left this place and went to Beijing, en route to join his father who was already working in Singapore and doing well there. He arrived in Singapore in 1949 and was educated in Mandarin and English. In 1953, he was awarded the Green Chord award for being very active in the Scout movement. However, during 1954–1956, he participated in the student unrest,[50] and in 1957, his father decided to send him to Hong Kong to keep him away from student politics. But Kuo returned after a few months and, upon graduation, started to work at the radio station in Singapore.

From 1963 to 1965, he attended the National Institute for Dramatic Art (NIDA) in Sydney, and in 1965, he returned once again to Singapore and set up the Practice Performing Arts School (PPAS) together with his wife—the dancer-choreographer, Goh Lay Kuan. The school is uncommon in that it is both a producing and a training educational center for theater and dance. A theater practitioner says about the school that "the path remained as rugged as ever" and that even in the days when the country was experiencing an economic boom, "the school had barely managed to make ends meet with its dedicated small skeletal staff, and in times of recession it has struggled to keep its head above water."[51]

Yet, in spite of the financial difficulties that the school faced, quite a few of the present young theater directors, actors, and lighting designers in Singapore have gone through Kuo's training workshops before moving to claim their own independent place in theater.

---

[47] Transcript A/4/10.

[48] His birthplace was Xianguo Village, in Wuyi County.

[49] Transcript K/1/2.

[50] The first half of the 1950s was characterized by a general unrest linked both to the anticolonialist reactions (particularly demonstrated by high school students) and communist ideologies (particularly active among union workers).

[51] This undated commentary on the school comes from Han Lao Da—a Chinese-speaking theater practitioner who was awarded Singapore's Cultural Medallion (Drama).

In 1968, he was appointed TV producer at Radio Television Singapura (RTS). He created the RTS TV Debate for senior high schools, which was later on expanded to include debates for tertiary institutions. An interviewee says about the production of these debates that "it was a very daring thing to do" at that time.[52]

During 1970 and 1972, three of the plays that he wrote were banned from being performed. Subsequently, during Singapore's massive anti-leftist purge, he was detained in 1976 without trial, under the Internal Security Act for "subversive activities against the government,"[53] and in 1977, he was deprived of his citizenship. He was released from detention in 1980, albeit with conditions imposed restricting his residence and travel. Those restrictions were subsequently withdrawn in 1983, and his citizenship was reinstated five years later, in 1992.

Upon his release, he continued to write and direct plays in Mandarin and began to write also in English. In the mid-1980s, he wrote and directed four plays that dealt with indigenous Singaporean issues. These plays won him much reputation and fame. The two plays, *The Coffin is Too Big for the Hole* (1985) and *No Parking on Odd Days* (1986)—together with Stella Kon's play *Emily of Emerald Hill*—were unique in the sense that they were the first plays to celebrate the "local" Singaporean psyche. This uniqueness in Kuo's plays came from their presentation of indigenous issues in terms of dilemmas in the life of a Singaporean and through their usage of "Singlish"—a specifically Singaporean mixing of words and structures from English and different Singapore mother tongues, and a language style that had never before been used in such a medium, and was considered taboo in formal mediums.

The play *The Little Silly Girl and the Old Tree* was ground-breaking in the usage of what is called the Grotowsky method—a physical rather than a verbal language—and the play *Mama Is Looking for Her Cat* (1988) was the first play to introduce Singapore's multilingual nature on stage. (Tamil, Mandarin, English, and other local dialects were used in the play.) In addition to actively writing and directing plays, Kuo conducted countless drama, directing, and stage-lighting workshops and introduced local theater practitioners to the new theaters of China, Taiwan, and Hong Kong by inviting guest directors, actors, and organizing seminars and workshops. In 1989, the Singapore Broadcasting Corporation—the successor to RTS—produced a special TV feature on Kuo and his theater work.

---

[52] The interview (transcript B/2/1–2) says: "It was a very daring thing to do. If you talk about Singapore history, you know that period, even up to later on for the next two or three decades, you know that you've got to be very *careful* of what you *talk*, what *you say*. And when you do a debate *in Singapore, on television*, can you imagine? Even though it was not a live show, but still, it is television, and it's *viewpoints*, isn't it? When you want to debate it means that you are presenting different kinds of viewpoints, and when you talk about *viewpoints* during those periods (maybe even now) You've got to be *very careful*, isn't it? But it was *daring*, it was very daring to have produced or presented that kind of a program (...) And the topics were very sensitive, *very sensitive*. I mean, you must remember it's Singapore, and it is not easy for anybody to *talk freely*, and when you debate you've got to attack, and when you attack you got to use all kinds of arguments. How are you going to control? It's difficult to control."

[53] *The Straits Times*, 11 May 1994.

In that year, Kuo also set up and headed the "Substation—Home for the Arts," the first place in Singapore to have, under one roof, various art forms such as theater, music, dance, literature, painting, installation art, and others. It had all started in 1985 when Kuo (who was then the artistic director of PPAS) came by a former power substation (an electricity facility), which had been built in 1928 and abandoned in the late 1970s. "The vision of a community arts center immediately excited Pao Kun (...) he developed the idea and his conceptual proposal was accepted by the Ministry of Community Development."[54] Kuo managed to convince the government to partici-pate in the turning of the "Substation" into a "Home for the Arts" and to invest $1.34 million to renovate the Substation building. He also managed to engage foundations, corporations, and individuals in the community in raising another $1 million to equip the Substation to function as a "Home for the Arts." This included, for example, a 200-seat multipurpose hall, air-conditioning, computers, sound and acoustic systems, wooden flooring, and full-length mirrors for use in dance. Kuo also agreed that PPAS should manage the Substation to serve all artists and art groups.

The uniqueness of the Substation was by virtue of the fact that it brought under one roof a number of different strands in society, such as different languages, races, and cultures. It has as its aim to constitute a permanent space, and the name "Home" with its primordial connotations suggests that it is not only a physical place but also a social, intimate, secure, space. "The Substation will become a home not only for the arts from the various disciplines to interact but also a place where artists can mingle and exchange ideas—among themselves and with their audience. Or just 'live' there."[55]

The place devoted itself to the promotion of artists and arts in general and par-ticularly emphasized the development of new, experimental work. It presented itself in the following manner:

> The Substation will become a base where our diverse cultures and heritages can cross-pol-linate, and where the fine arts, folk arts and contemporary indigenous forms can co-exist. The substation will become a station where original new works can be launched, where young talents and innovative experiments are given special focus and nurturing.[56]

While as its artistic director, Kuo founded various new projects that allowed new groups to perform or new works to be staged. These were projects that invited artists to come and use the place to develop and perform their art. For example, the Dance Space project, catering to dance groups; the Raw Theatre project, catering to theater groups; the Music Space project, catering to various music groups, including rock bands; the New criteria project for visual artists and installation artists; and the September Arts Conference for those who wanted to spend some time in intellectual reflection on art issues and dilemmas. All these projects, or "spaces," aimed toward the construction of an infrastructure that would allow the development of the arts, without having to present productions that were commercially viable. These various

---

[54] This reference is from the Substation's fund-raising brochure, 1989: 1.

[55] Ibid.

[56] Ibid.

projects emphasized experimentation, development, and process-oriented art work, without any imposed expectations as to "end results"—particularly the commercial type of results:

> Open 365 days a year, the Substation welcomes a wide cross-section of Singapore's society to enjoy and participate in its many-faceted activities. It is hoped that each person could take back something entertaining, inspiring or challenging to counterpoint the pervasive consumeristic influence so visible in our modern day metropolis.[57]

Many artists interviewed refer to the Substation as the starting point of their professional artistic career, as well as a place that nurtured them at the initial and "beginners" stages of those careers. It seems that the Substation, as an institution, created a "social space" that enabled artists (as well as audience) to develop an authentic, indigenous artistic expression of what they are and feel. Indeed, the interviewee's frequent usage of the term "space" (when they refer to what the Substation meant to them back in the early 1990s) suggests that, as an institutionalized vision, it carved out a singular space for the art community, the audience, and society at large. This vision was of Kuo's emphasis on the need to develop an "intangible" cultural dimension in the social life of Singaporeans and will be elaborated later in this chapter.

In 1990, Kuo was awarded the Cultural Medallion (Drama) by the Singapore government for "outstanding contributions to and achievements in Singapore Theatre," and also in that year, Times Editions published a collection of five of his plays in English. In March 1992, he received an award from the Japan Chamber of Commerce and Industry for sustained contribution to Singapore theater and for pioneering the Substation, and, in 1993, he was awarded the Performing Arts ASEAN Cultural Award. In 1995, he resigned as the artistic director of the Substation and published a Chinese edition of *Images at The Margin*—a collection of 10 plays written between 1983 and 1992. In 1997, he was made a member of the Order of the Chevalier des Arts et des Lettres by the French government.

Followership

It is commonly agreed among theater practitioners that the current generation of young theater practitioners in Singapore are Kuo's "followers," being initially triggered into professional theater by him, or having been developed by his professional ideas and methods, or formally trained by him. By now, many of these theater practitioners have developed their own individual styles, yet they still regard him as a "founding father" and still look up to him and his views.

Other than this group, there are many other people who are not within the field of theater, nor even in the arts, yet who have been influenced by Kuo and have been actively participating in and helping to promote and implement Kuo's ideas. They are not "followers" in the conventional sense; instead, these people have been influenced

---

[57] Ibid.

by him to the point of regularly and significantly contributing efforts and resources toward the implementation of his ideas. They are, in a sense, "backstage" people who help Kuo to implement projects, and it is said that without these people (many of whom being in high-ranking positions and having high social status), Kuo could not have been able to realize the concept of the Substation, which required vast contributions of various resources in its initial stages in order to remain self-sufficient.

Extraordinary Attributions

Kuo is commonly referred as the "The doyen of the Singapore drama scene."[58] Other terms applied to him imply a leadership position, for example, "guru," "doyen," "pillar," "leader," "father," "founding father," "icon," "guide," "shepherd," and others. Krishen Jit, the Malaysian theater expert, says, "after almost three decades of strenuous labor in the field, Kuo has carved a singular presence in the modern theater of Singapore. He has broken so much new ground that an analysis of it would very nearly amount to a history of the 'new' in the theater of contemporary Singapore."[59]

An interviewee says, "both as a critic of the theater and a critic of culture in Singapore, as well as a playwright himself, Kuo has over the years, in that sense, singularly achieved quite a body of work. He has had 25 years of solid work in theater. Also, his one single act which would really have established him as a kind of leader (if all these other things had not established him) would be his creation of the Substation and that space, which is a living proof of the Kuo Pao Kun legacy."[60] According to Krishen Jit, Kuo has been a constant pioneer and has always explored new frontiers in art. He says that Kuo was the first to bring the works of Brecht to the Singapore stage, and possibly even the first director to have staged Brecht in Southeast Asia. He was the first to successfully use both English and Chinese in playwriting and directing; the first to creatively integrate Chinese, English, Malay, Tamil, Hokkien, and other Singapore languages or dialects in one production; and the first to systematically introduce the Grotowsky actor training method and theater concepts, bringing great impact to the Singapore theater scene.[61]

But Kuo is not only exceptional in the field of theater and with a presence that extends over the artistic community. He rises above his own professional field and has become, in the eyes of many, a social activist. One interviewee uses the term "national asset" to express Kuo's engagement with social issues that have a moral aspect, values, or principles, saying:

> I consider him a national asset (…) I don't consider him a national asset just because he produces very good plays or directs very good plays. I think it is, to me, it is even more important that he has this 'social activism.' His integrity is impeccable. Both his professional

---

[58] *The Straits Times*, 14 Nov 1989.

[59] Kuo (1990, p. 7).

[60] Transcript A/7/6.

[61] In Kuo (1990).

and personal integrity is an extraordinary asset (…) I think the amazing thing about Pao Kun is that he is not only seen as a leader by artistes themselves (like the people who have been his students in the directors' workshop or the arts community as a whole). He impresses a number of people who actually don't have anything to do with the arts, in the manner in which he conducts himself, from the language, from the body language, from the ideas he articulates, as a *total package*. He has this quality that makes people listen to him, and that is an extraordinary quality. I have such high regard for Pao Kun. He stands by (his principles) and in fact I know that there are very few people like Pao Kun in Singapore, which is a great tragedy. We need more people who stand by such principles. We need to mature as a society, and he is a guide, he is a shepherd for us.[62]

Kuo had grown with the years into a symbol representing the significance of intangible spheres of human existence and their relation with the collective social identity. Inadvertently, these notions engage with dilemmas about the self, society, and culture. In this respect, Jit says that for Kuo, "theater is nothing if not purposefully persuasive about social philosophy."[63] An interviewee who regards him as a cultural icon says that Kuo has a kind of "morality" that is not confined only to the realm of theater. A notion of "moral weight" and of "standing by principles" is accorded to Kuo's social activism in commenting on issues of culture, social identity, and values and ideals that underlie the way we live. An interviewee says:

My feeling of Pao Kun is that he has always come across as a person of *great integrity who seeks his own version of truth. And then he is going to state it and nothing is going to stop him from stating his vision of the truth.* I guess he just looks like a man who is not very bothered about what the world says or what the world does to him, as long as he goes for the truth. (…) I've always felt *highly over-awed by Pao Kun.* When I am in his presence, I tend to feel that *'here is a man of great idealism'* and this leaves me to question; 'hey what am I doing?' it makes me feel that I am not so *active,* not so *idealistic* as he is (…) His strength in any group seems to be that he will be the one who *is keeping his eye on the important values.* While other people would be running off talking about the materialistic angle, Pao Kun would keep very quiet, and at the end of the discussion, he would sort of very quietly say something *that would bring the discussion back to the main values underlying everything.*[64]

Unique Ideas

Kuo's ideas are rooted in the field of art and, specifically, theater, but they enfold larger issues of social concern. His social commentary and his plays deal with human complexities and dilemmas. For example, they deal with the question of tradition in times of social change, the notion of individuality vs. homogeneity, intergeneration and interethnic communication, and so on. What would constitute the core of his ideas is his preoccupation with the cultural dimension of society or, in his words, the "intangible sphere of life." In this sphere, Kuo includes theater and

---

[62] Transcript A/6/6, 10, 13.

[63] In Kuo (1990, Introduction).

[64] Transcript B/15/10, 12.

the arts, but he also refers to intangible dimensions like philosophy, literature, tradition, history, and mythology. In other words, Kuo's ideas are seen as related to an attempt to carve out a space for the articulation and promotion of a cultural/intangible dimension in the life and living of Singaporeans.

According to Kuo, although geographically and historically Singaporeans are supposed to be inheritors of four major civilizations of the world, they have only fragments that lack the fulsome philosophy, history, literature, and art of these civilizations. He says that since this missing link has never been restored, "As a people, we lack depth. We are too much economic animals. Somehow we are not full-fledged as people. There are possibilities or realms or areas of possibility in the person's growth that we have silenced or constrained, restrained, limited or suppressed too much. It is to *nobody's good*, including those who are leading efforts to do that. It is to nobody's good."[65]

In a way, he thinks that though Singaporeans call themselves "multicultural" (in an area where several great civilizations meet: Indian, Chinese, Malay, and Western)—actually none of the cultures inherited are whole. He also says: "Similarly we call ourselves 'multilingual'; but actually we only have some vocabulary that we can do business with. When you talk deeper, you have no language. I think probably this 'source' problem, not having been addressed, still bothers us on a very fundamental level."[66]

Kuo thinks that although such long-term cultural disorientation may have made the people more productive materially, it has also made them "drift rootlessly."[67] To him, the shrewd and fast political economic reshaping has indeed won material rewards, "but some *essential human elements have been lost on the way*, and that dislocation is eating into our very confidence as a people."[68] Kuo feels that Singaporeans have a malformed and partial mode of existence, and that the lack of such intangible dimensions in life results in people who are shallow and weak. He argues that if we accept culture as a systematic way by which man lives, by which man perceives himself in relation to the world, and with which man changes the world (and himself), "then it is clear that he who possesses a fragmented culture, or one with merely a subculture, could only have a very partial, narrow, short and low level of understanding of existence. And is therefore incapable of longer-range, high-vantage point perceptions of any kind, nor to conceive any change with vision."[69]

It is in this respect that he coined the term "cultural orphans" in regard to the particular nature of the human condition of Singaporeans. Kuo tried to articulate a whole dimension that he thought was missing from the social life in Singapore, and although he traces the roots of orphanage to the departure of the forefathers of Singapore from their motherlands (as Singapore's first cultural dislocation), he

---

[65] Transcript K/2/15.

[66] See Kuo (1993, p. 26).

[67] See Kuo (1994, p. 1).

[68] Ibid., p. 2.

[69] *The Business Times*, 27–28 Feb 1993, and in Kuo (1997a, p. 2).

argues that the push for modernization may have turned out to be Singapore's second cultural dislocation. He says, "so if our forefathers had become physical orphans, we have become cultural orphans"[70] and he laments that Singaporeans have treated their heritage as baggage, saying:

> And to lighten ourselves, we gave up our mother tongues as first language, staked our future in imported cultures, and then turned what remained of our physical heritage into theme park-like exotics. (Here I am referring to the rebuilding of places like Chinatown, Malay Village, Clark Quay, and Little India.) What has happened to us on our way to affluence and prosperity?[71]

The usage of the word "orphans" suggests a lack of something, but it is not a trivial thing that is missing. Orphanage is a state in which a person is missing one of the most important, if not the most important, links of his life. Links such as this are not confined to the merely physical but touch on emotions and essence, by referring to questions of identity definition like "who we are." Furthermore, such a term implies an utmost vulnerability and fragility because we do not usually use such a term to refer to adults, but to children who have lost the most meaningful and reassuring thing in their lives, at a time where they do not yet solidly "stand with both their feet on the ground." The usage of the word "orphan" therefore implies, by way of reference, the crucial meaning and weight that Kuo addresses to culture. A lack of it can turn a person into someone who has lost, in a very fundamental way, his biological, psychological, and existential roots.

Such a perception of culture's vital link with the human existence is also expressed by his various comments on Singaporeans as being malformed, saying, for example, "we have become handicapped people."[72] This is an expression of something that is seriously missing, although this sense of missing something may be hard to assess and may be physically invisible. According to Kuo, this missing of a cultural/intangible dimension in the life of Singaporeans, not only hinders other, deeper dimensions of existence, but also inhibits the social formation of a collective, wholesome, authentic identity. He says:

> Singapore talks about the corrosive effects of foreign cultures and the government is best at doing this for its own defense. But it never goes on to properly contribute to creating our own culture, and if you don't have your own culture, how can you defend yourself? We need to study ourselves and our complex, multicultural pasts. And without creating our own arts, we don't create our own culture (…) In fact, we cannot actually do the art and call it our own without delving into our own tradition, our own history, our own experience. It is all really one. Different dimensions, different ways of seeing. How can you assert yourself without knowing who you are? What are you asserting?[73]

Kuo would have liked to have seen the construction of a cultural layer or sphere in the consciousness of the people and the place, "by instituting a permanent space

---

[70] Kuo (1994) op. cit., p. 1.

[71] Ibid., p. 1.

[72] He says: "In our long struggle for material survival we had become handicapped people, sensitive only to material things." This quote comes from *The Straits Times*, 18 Sep 1993.

[73] Kuo (1997b, p. 141).

for things philosophical, historical, literary and artistic which perpetually exercise the mind, the senses and the body, and help make valid a cultural space; a space that has its own rights and laws of operation. A dimension that is not subservient to politics."[74]

By such a social space or dimension, he does not refer to a concrete physical space, but to a social space that is an integral part of the national life and the society's psyche. In other words, he would have liked to have seen such a space as coherent with, rather than in opposition to, the basic assumptions and infrastructure of society. He says: "We are so open and yet we are so sterilized. We as a people have been conditioned to feel that everything has to be planned. But should we not also have a personal space so free, like art, that you do not have to worry about results or what other people think? You need to have a space where you can allow your imagination and your ideas to explore, to try out things."[75]

Kuo's arguments seem to boil down to the need to cultivate and regenerate a layer of existence which cannot be materially measured, but which is nevertheless meaningfully crucial. He speaks about the existence of a whole different dimension of human existence, which values and allows space for processes of introspection and reflection into the complexities and deeper levels of human existence. To him, such reflective processes are often conducted in the form of prolonged and lonely reading, reflecting, criticizing, debating, fantasizing, and creating—and essentially, no tangible things are transmitted or produced. But in spite of the tangential form of this cultural layer, it is nevertheless important because it "provides further access into the complexities (or simplicities) of our existence—our inner world and our outer world."[76]

For such a social space to develop, Kuo argues that various aspects and dimensions should be included, for example, artistic and creative freedom, respect for the individual as a creative and reflective entity, a process orientation (rather than a "product obsession"), and the release of centralized control in the arts field. The underlying implication of such dimensions is that they bear an attempt to deconstruct or at least ease the centralized form of social control in Singapore. In other words, the main thrust of Kuo's plea for the development of cultural or intangible dimensions of life seems to deconstruct some dominant social assumptions. It relies on a need for a social infrastructure with less control and more freedom—particularly artistic and individual freedom—and on a reduction of the government's tendency to control the arts. As to the social aspect, Kuo calls for the deconstruction of the "merchant mentality," by which he claims the society to be possessed.

Kuo argues that since the very essence of art is to try and perceive differences, perceive new things, and challenge established concepts and behaviors,[77] the function of art in that context requires the allocation of an artistic "freedom." Therefore,

---

[74] Ibid., p. 132.

[75] *The Business Times*, 27–28 Feb 1993.

[76] Kuo (1997a) op. cit., p. 1.

[77] *The Business Times*, 27–28 Feb 1993.

"it must firstly be recognized that art activities are the locus of free expression, invention and creative imagination. In maintaining and advancing this spirit of exploration, artistic creativity must resist or avoid inflexibilities arising from exclusivist aesthetic doctrines or judgments or historical necessities."[78] To him, paradigms, conventions, and judgments can hinder the ability to reach realms that are not easily grasped or understood. Yet since this complexity is exactly what the arts address, art should be given free access to such realms and be given the possibility to question and reflect on human dilemmas and human complexities without, or with fewer, restrictions. Such freedom would allow reflection and the questioning of conventional wisdom and paradigms. To Kuo, such actions can be best achieved in a space that does not inhibit reflective tendencies by making art subservient to any other social dimension.

Implicitly, Kuo states that the government, as well as the people, tends to avoid (rather than treat) matters that relate to the complex nature of human beings. He argues that the current "avoidance attitude" tends to prefer "silence" (as in avoidance) over "noise" (as in the treatment of an issue), and therefore relies on banning, censorship, restrictions, and punishments. Contrary to this attitude, Kuo believes that "the most dangerous thing for human beings is silence, not noise,"[79] and says:

> Chewing gum, for example, creates problems. (So) what do we do? Ban it! it's a very dangerous signal. Anything that you feel is intolerable—ban. Literature, in particular, deals with the complexity of the human being; the deviations of human beings are part of reality. To suppress it only bottles the damn thing up and creates more problems. It's like pressing down the spring (…) we are so open and yet I think we are so sterilized (…) when you let out the human complexity, dark forces, deviations and radical ideas—may come out. But what's wrong with that? (…) Let me give you a comparison. We have so many stupid shows on TV and in the films. Sometimes people single out an R(A) film as 'very dangerous.' But have we reflected upon the long-term dangers of exposing our people to such stupidity in films? They are deemed as harmless, but actually pull down our intellectual capability.[80]

According to Kuo, this "avoidance" attitude "has so eaten into the people's initiative that the real issue in our censorship has become self-censorship."[81] On a different occasion, he has also said: "I think there is so much self-censorship that we have been just bottling up our potential. Somehow, a lot of people give me the impression that they are very careful not to touch the limits of censorship. What is the real purpose of writing if you do not explore an issue? What is the purpose?"[82]

Indeed when Kuo founded the Substation, he had a chance to implement his belief in the need to have a free social space for cultural exploration. One interviewee, for example, said that he was very impressed by what he considered as "very powerful public statements"[83] that Kuo had made on this regard, when he was the

---

[78] *The Straits Times*, 18 Sep 1993.

[79] Kuo (1993) op. cit., p. 20.

[80] *The Business Times*. 27–28 Feb 1993.

[81] Kuo (1997a) op. cit., p. 8.

[82] *The Straits Times*, 22 Nov 1990.

[83] Transcript A/7/10.

artistic director of the Substation. While some people complained about the kind of freedom that artists were getting in the Substation, Kuo defended the freedom of the space to create, saying: "There must be a space for that. Nobody is forcing you to come into the Substation. You can walk through Hill Street and not come in.[84] But if you want to come in, then you must allow people to do their thing."[85]

Along with this concern over artistic freedom, Kuo seems to try and reflect on the government's tendency to keep a tight centralized control on social life,[86] and its implications on the construction of a cultural layer. He says:

> The government wants to control everything. Now they want to produce arts programs and this is what I heard from the Singapore Arts Center people. You control all the theaters, all the time and space, all the grants, all the festivals, and now you are producing programs. Where is the arts community in all this? What say do we have? We are coming back to this lack of an autonomous cultural sphere.[87]

Kuo believes that such official policies can hamper creativity and will be certain to further encourage passivity. So much so that he thinks that right now "there exists a non-creative or an anti-creative policy."[88] He believes that undue interference inhibits cultural growth,[89] and that this is especially so with the arts component which exists in many forms, modes, aspects, and levels. In place of a system such as this, Kuo suggests that officials and government policies should concentrate on making available opportunities for other people to do things.[90] He says: "You should never judge your achievement by how much you have done—but by how much you made possible for other people to do." Following this line, the government's role must be a supportive one, "conceding the active role to the people. The government can be justly proud by saying; 'I gave such basic facilities and then all these have happened on their own'."[91] Kuo believes that even if such an approach produces an arts scenario that is "not as orderly as technocrats generally would prefer, the

---

[84] He is referring to the Substation's location in Hill Street.

[85] Transcript A/7/10.

[86] Kuo argues that this inclination is combined with their orientation to treat all matters, even intangible ones, with an economic, rationalized method. He says that "It has been repeatedly declared that culture and the arts will not be planned and engineered. But the instincts of national planning have become a habit, as declarations such as the Vision of 1999 show, a date when Singapore is 'scheduled' to become a cultured and refined society" (1997a, p. 4).

[87] Kuo (1997b) op. cit., p. 139.

[88] Kuo (1997a) op. cit., p. 5.

[89] He says: "Creative energies have been held back for too long because it's the big government that controls the entire national life. Officials seem to believe that unless you spend big money, you cannot develop—this isn't true" (1997b, p. 138). Kuo believes that if officials would simply learn "how to relax"—people will participate actively and expand spaces for themselves with less need to spend big amounts of money for this purpose.

[90] Kuo has said that "While Government and media reports of arts scene often trace successes to government programs, schemes, events, sponsorships and other facilitation like the festivals. It is imperative to understand that the source energy of the arts has always come from the people. And always will" (1997a, p. 7).

[91] The two preceding quotes are from Kuo (1997b) op. cit., p. 139.

long-term creative results of releasing indigenous ground energy will more than compensate for the 'extra bother'."[92]

Another type of 'freedom' that Kuo conceptualizes relates to his perception of the need for a social space for individualism. He sees the 'Singapore individual' as the most basic human building block of the future and a space for individuality being therefore necessary for the development of a cultural dimension. He believes that social constraints, and inhibitions on individuality, hamper artistic and cultural development because art is, by definition, a process experienced and articulated by individuals. He says, "by artistic creation, a person searches within his inner world, wielding all resources at his command, to express a personal impulse uniquely his own. Hence, art is always one only, original and personal, expressing an individuality which has no double."[93]

However, the construction of such a social space requires a prior deconstruction of the sociopolitical and cultural environment that according to Kuo has a "suspicious attitude towards individualism as such."[94] The social space for an independent, creative individual in a structure that emphasizes collectivity (as in the national anthem, "society/community above the self") seems to him as invariably limited and restricted. Kuo says that "the term individual has been tarnished by misuse, often been identified with selfishness, as if someone with a strong individuality is necessarily selfish."

Instead, Kuo argues that it is possible to conceive of a notion of individualism that is socially rooted and consciously intertwined with his own society. To him, it is possible to see individuality as endemically social, saying that "the very term 'individual' is premised by the recognition of a collective. One who could justly be called an 'individual' is he who is most conscious of his position as a responsible member of a group with a conscious understanding of his integrity as an autonomous being (and it is in this sense that) a mechanism has to be inset within the system to serve the creative character development of that Person."

In addition to the need to construct a social space with more freedom (or fewer restrictions), with respect to individuality (or less suspicion toward him), Kuo's ideas and arguments seem to deconstruct what he refers to as the current "merchant mentality." In giving examples for this kind of merchant mentality, Kuo says:

> I can't think of another affluent modern nation which could conceive of a national tertiary education without a presence in the fine arts, or build a university campus in the 1980s without an arts center or theater or auditorium; a nation with an official Tamil language for its population but whose national university would respond to a request to revive its Tamil Studies Department by saying, 'We'll see if there is a market demand.'[95]
> Even now we are studying language almost devoid of literature. We study civics almost devoid of history. Or rather we have made history part of civic studies. We don't study history as history. We study history pragmatically, as expedience.[96]

---

[92] Kuo (1997a) op. cit., p. 4.

[93] Ibid.

[94] The quotations in this and the next paragraph are from Kuo (1997a) op. cit., p. 5.

[95] Kuo (1997a) op. cit., p. 3.

[96] Kuo (1997b) op. cit., p. 131.

To him, such mentality constrains any possibility of constructing an intangible cultural dimension of social life. Kuo argues that it is this mentality (or what we can call the "underlying basic assumptions") that confines both the government as well as the people to relate to, and appreciate, only matters that can be measured in quantifiable terms, particularly in a material sense. He argues that while man exists on many levels, layers, and in many spheres and modes, the mentality of Singaporeans is conditioned to understand and negotiate only, or mostly, in political, economic, and technological terms. Kuo thinks that most Singaporeans have a mentality conditioned in themselves that politics and economics are everything, and referring to the levels that man exists on, he has said that "This complexity is exactly what the arts address. The complexity of the human being is much wider and richer than what we have taken ourselves to be, so much so that we have put ourselves into a straitjacket."[97]

In such a mentality, economics and politics get daily attention, "and they are the only reasons for national celebration, while culture is left to its own device, as if the temporary advantage of the limbo state will bring perpetual benefits."[98] To him, such a mentality creates a simplistic understanding of the human existence, which involves ignoring the arts in the wider sense of the word. Furthermore, he argues that "such partial and narrow mentality accounts for most of our acts of intolerance in personal, familial, community and national affairs such as censorship, intellectual and artistic freedom, and ethnic and cultural interaction."[99]

Kuo refers to the general Singapore mentality that wants to plan everything, and wants to achieve goals, and to Singaporean society as "programmed to think and value things in a tangible, quantifiable, material manner."[100] He says that "in Singapore, it's always the product that's important. I think we are too product- or result-oriented (and) that planners have been approaching the arts in much the same way as they approach business: create products, plan labor-supply and try to quantify everything."[101]

As an example of such a mentality, Kuo argues that indeed it is good that high-ranking people talk about making Singapore "more than Singapore Inc." because this means that they express an understanding of the need to become more than an economic, materialistic society. However, he adds, "It is good, it should be a nation, it should be a big family. But then we can't just say 'tomorrow we'll call it a family.' Today it's Singapore Inc.—and tomorrow it will be 'Singapore family'."[102] Kuo believes that the process is as important as the product and says: "when I say an artist should take writing very seriously I mean that he should pursue a thought, pursue an issue, think it through rather than just produce something."[103]

---

[97] Quoted in *The Business Times*, 27–28 Feb 1993.

[98] Kuo (1994) op. cit., p. 2.

[99] Kuo (1997a) op. cit., p. 3.

[100] Kuo (1997b) op. cit., p. 132.

[101] *The Business Times*, 27–28 Feb 1993.

[102] Kuo (1997b) op. cit., p. 132.

[103] *The Straits Times*, 22 Nov 1990.

Other theater practitioners also seem to share this view and argue that it is indeed frustrating to work in "an instant noodle' kind of culture"[104] that does not allocate nor respect the need for the artistic creation to evolve in its own natural mode and pace. The term "instant noodle" is an expression for a product orientation that "lacks" the natural evolution process. It is instantly ready for consumption: in one moment, it is not there; in the next moment, it is there, "as if" it had been there all along.

In addition to the "quick-product" approach, the "instant noodle" term implies a process of transplantation (rather than an indigenous process of evolution). The noodles in the "instant noodle packet" are not different from regular noodles. They too require a certain procedure preparation and a certain cooking time. However, a large part of the "instant noodles" preparation is done somewhere else, by someone else. The consumer who buys the instant noodles "prepares" them, but that kind of preparation lacks the fulsome experience and process of "getting the noodles done." While there is a quick sensation in their purchase and consumption, the reflection and insight that could have been gained from the fulsome process are retained by the "other," who has invested time, effort, and reflection in the "process" of their preparation.

Kuo points at the Singaporeans' "merchant mentality" as the source for the tendency and preference to purchase or "transplant" art instead of creating and developing an indigenous one. He says: "we have always been preoccupied with making money, making a better living (…) so much so that even today that we are so economically advanced, I think we still possess, or are possessed by, this merchant mentality that we work, make money, have a better living, and everything can be bought and sold, including culture. I think in these last ten years, especially these last few years, there has been a rapid process of buying art (…) I don't think, with all the money in the world, one can buy culture, or buy an identity."[105]

Contrary to this "merchant mentality," Kuo argues that art cannot be bought because by buying art, one does not go through the necessary process of creation, recreation, and intense involvement. He says:

> The process of making art is the act of 'getting.' Our general perception of art as acquiring an object—buying a painting, owning a piano, affording a Theater ticket, etc., really has nothing to do with art. They do not give you that intense, prolonged exercise where your senses, mind and body are subjected to a grueling experience of holistic gymnastics. The process of art sensitizes one's whole being. Buying an art object produces but a consuming sensation.[106]

Kuo argues that people are wrong if they think that they can be "cultural" by buying art products, without going through the whole development of the cultural process themselves. The process of creating one's own cultural space and dimension

---

[104] Transcript A/1/5.

[105] Kuo (1993) op. cit., pp. 27–28.

[106] Kuo (1997a) op. cit., p. 5.

of reflection and inquiry is not "instant" nor pleasurable (as the act of buying art may be), but a prolonged and a demanding one, of which Kuo says:

> You can't really assert an identity or a feeling of yourself (which are an aspect of the cultural layer) unless you go through a process of searching.[107] And I mean really applying the heart and the soul, and the body. This is a process which usually needs to be traumatic, maybe not in the most physical sense of the word, but traumatic nonetheless. Otherwise it doesn't leave a trace (...) I think we need to pay that price, you can't buy it.[108]

To deconstruct the "merchant mentality" as well as to construct a cultural/intangible social dimension, Kuo emphasizes the crucial role of the creative process. Instead of a market-oriented quantifiable product, it should be a reflective process that only results in intangible reflections. The process should be seen as an end that justifies itself, without being possessed by a need to show quick, tangible results. As such, the creative process is not a means to achieve a "product," but the very goal itself. To further deconstruct this "merchant mentality" toward art, Kuo advocates a respect for, and an appreciation of, failures. Coining the revolutionary phrase, "A worthy failure is more valuable than a mediocre success,"[109] he tried to articulate the notion that an artistic development, even if it did not produce profitable productions, is a "worthy failure" and far more important than a production that was commercially viable but did not promote any artistic contribution (and was thus a mediocre success). He says: "there should be recognition, even respect, in Singapore for people who produce worthy failures than mediocre success."[110]

When Kuo was the artistic director of the Substation, he defended the right of the artists to focus on the process of their work even at the cost of noncommercial results and productions. The various projects in the Substation aimed toward the provision of a platform that enabled a physical as well as a social space for an emphasis on process and development, catering to young art practitioners whose work was characterized by a "creative rawness"—ongoing projects like "Raw Theatre," "Dance Space," "Music Space," and "New Criteria" (for installation art) are examples of such institutionalized "spaces" that put, at their forefront, exploration, experimentation, questioning, creativity, reflection, and dialogue.

For example, the aim of one of the Substation's conferences—a conference on heritage in 1994—was presented with the rationale that "in doing so we hope to provide an opportunity for deep and honest discussion from different perspectives, and to achieve both an intellectual and a visual reflection on the richness and

---

[107] He says that art is an ongoing process of reflection and internalization. "Even as far as heritage is concerned, tradition can only be regenerated, it cannot be passed on per se. Traditions can always stay in the museum but the museum is no guarantee of genuine cultural absorption. We can only internalize tradition in a recreative, regenerating process. So how can we talk about tradition without promoting the creative arts?" (Substation, 16 Sep 1994).

[108] Kuo (1993) op. cit., pp. 26–27.

[109] We were told that even among the Substation's Board of Directors (who were all very supportive of Kuo's ideas), it was difficult to get full support for this idea.

[110] *The Straits Times*, 11 May 1994.

complexity of heritage in Singapore."[111] Likewise, "Dance Space" was introduced in 1993, "to explore dance concepts and to create dialogue between the artist and the audience. (…) The event is dedicated to establishing a platform for an informed and involved dialogue between the dancers and the audience, a 'space' where experimentation and discussion can take place."[112]

Similarly, the "Raw Theatre" project was conceptualized as "a platform to show innovative works by young practitioners. It aims to nurture Singapore's new theater generation by cultivating a serious attitude to research on contemporary theater making."[113] And music programs were presented, for example, in the following way: "with the objective of nurturing indigenous new talents and promoting local original compositions."[114] Also "New Criteria," established in 1992, was devoted to the exhibition of experimental and multimedia work by younger local artists:

> This visual arts program questions and challenges existing notions in art practice in a serious and consistent manner. It is an inquiry into the faiths, practices, structures and meanings of alternative art in Singapore, an exploration of work by artists on the margin who are exploring, reconstructing and reinterpreting contemporary history and art through their own experiences, and have, intentionally or not, become engaged in a dialogue among themselves and with the international art world.[115]

In other words, these physical spaces enabled a "social space"—for experimentation, innovation, development, and process-oriented works that were not judged by commercial, tangible aspects but by their quality in terms of being true to the artistic process and development. While this hallmark of new Singaporean artistic works was snubbed by some as "immaturity," Kuo persistently advocates that "the Substation chooses to see these works as 'sparks of originality'—which is something peculiar to all 'untried, new creations.' He explicitly points out that these projects are premised on the belief that failure in the arts (particularly in the context of a maturing, rapidly developing arts scene like Singapore's) is not necessarily a bad thing. He says: "Instead of shunning failure, the Substation endeavors to thrive on it. As a 'Home for the Arts' funded chiefly by the community, this non-profit arts base wishes to practice the belief that a worthy failure is more valuable than a mediocre success."[116]

In brief, Kuo is seen in the eyes of many as a professional theater practitioner who has promoted the field of theater. But more so, in so doing, he also articulated the need for intangible dimensions in the cultural and social life of Singaporeans and thus brought the realms of culture, social identity, and everyday life into his frame of reference. It was also in the course of the expression and articulation of his perspectives that he has juxtaposed his ideas with some basic political and social assumptions, and hence deconstructed many aspects of their validity, significance, and dominance.

---

[111] From the Substation's conference program, 17–18 Sep 1994.

[112] From the Substation's event program, Feb 1997.

[113] Raw Theatre 4, Substation. Nov 1995.

[114] Substation program, Jan 91.

[115] Taken from "New criteria III," Substation 1995, p. 4.

[116] The references in this paragraph are from *The Straits Times*, 11 May 1994.

Tay Kheng Soon

Arrogant. Brilliant. Radical. These are the words that are used again and again to describe architect Tay Kheng Soon, more often than not, all in the same breath. Arrogant for his brusqueness; brilliant and radical for his controversial ideas on what public housing should look like and what the design language of the tropics should be.[117]

Fact File

Tay Kheng Soon was born in 1940 in Singapore and graduated with a Diploma in Architecture in 1964. He was one of a group of five students to graduate that year from the School of Architecture: the first graduates of the Singapore Polytechnic, which had accepted its first students in 1959. After graduation, he joined Malayan Architects Co-partnership and became an associate a year later. In 1967, he joined Koh Seow Chuan and the prominent architect, William Lim, to set up Design Partnership—the forerunner of the modern-day DP Architects Pte. Ltd. During the period from 1966 to 1975, he was a leading and outspoken member of Singapore Planning and Urban Research (SPUR) group, and its chairman during the years 1970–1971. SPUR was an independent think tank formed by professionals, comprising particularly architects and urban designers who offered numerous ideas on urban matters, including such suggestions as the positioning of Singapore's airport at Changi rather than at Paya Lebar.

Tay has long been a vocal critic of a wide range of numerous social and urban issues, such as the transportation system, education, public housing, environment, and issues of heritage. Robert Powell, who wrote a book on Tay, refers to his "vocal stands," saying: "for Tay, modern architecture was simply inseparable from its social underpinnings and this carried over into other fields."[118]

In the early 1970s, and quite early in his career, two of his most well-known controversial critiques were his alternative ideas on public housing and mass transportation. He suggested an alternative form of urban design, a "low-rise high-density" as opposed to the "high-rise high-density" plans for public housing buildings. He argued that this form of public housing would have been cheaper. It would enhance social and cultural interactions, and still be possible within the same constraint of scant resource land.[119] This type of housing contradicted the government's formula for public housing, which had been rapidly developing throughout the HDB

---

[117] *The Sunday Times*, 22 Jun 1997.

[118] See Powell (1997, p. 18).

[119] The famous talk was given at one of the meetings of the Rotary Club and immediately attracted vast publicity and controversy.

estates[120] during this period. Tay also expressed reservations about the nature of the public bus transportation as a system that has high costs in terms of people's loss of quality time when traveling to and from work.[121] Tay attracted very strong opposition from government officials on both issues, as their assumptions and plans were being questioned by Tay's critical perspectives.

Shortly after these two vocal critiques—but not necessarily in direct relation to them—the partners in Design Partnership decided to dissolve the practice. However, it was set up again as DP Architects without Tay Kheng Soon. Tay then left Singapore for a while, according to him, in an "imposed self exile." He returned in the early 1980s and founded Akitek Tenggara with Chung Meng Ker. Together they designed, for example, the Ming Arcade, which was completed in 1982 and awarded the Singapore Institute of Architects Design Merit Award. Consequently, they designed other projects, many of which implemented new design concepts to deal with modernism and tropicality.

The Cecil Court development and the Serangoon Gardens Country Club, for example, were completed in 1986, and they both presented an attempt to deal with modern architecture in the tropics. Cecil Court's entire first storey was given over to the public as a sheltered plaza and was conceived as a prototype of large, covered, and linked verandah spaces in the city. Powell says, "It is a shaded interactive outdoor space, an oasis, which poses the question, why do so few modern office towers contribute to the public realm in this manner?"[122] Likewise, the Serangoon Gardens Country Club is a low-rise building with a large covered outdoor space. While many architects criticize this building for the heat that the overhanging glass roof traps, they cannot but acknowledge that this overhanging roof introduced a new language and morphology of how modern tropical architecture should look.

Tay was a visiting scholar at the Aga Khan Program at MIT in 1986 and 1989, as well as a research associate at the Institute of Southeast Asian Studies, which then published his book, *Mega Cities in the Tropics*, in 1989. The book deals with Tay's ideas, projects, and theories on how mega modern cities should look in the tropics and discusses the issues that he considers as being intertwined with architecture—for example, history, geography, climate, community, transportation, culture, environment, an international agenda, and others. In 1990, Tay was invited by the then Minister of National Development to prepare a Development Guide Plan for a 76-ha site known as Kampong Bugis on the fringe of the central area of Singapore. In this project, he had the opportunity to continue to explore the notion of tropical architecture and to implement these ideas within a modern mega-high-density city district.

Tay was the vice president of Singapore Institute of Architects during 1990–1991, and its president from 1991 to 1993, and the term of his presidency was regarded by many architects as the most exciting, energetic, and dramatic.

[120] The Housing Development Board is the authority responsible for the planning, development, construction, and supervision of public housing in Singapore.

[121] Tay Kheng Soon (1975).

[122] Powell (1997) op. cit., 23.

He has successfully achieved a "revolutionary change" in the redistribution of the design work between the private sector and the public sector, which traditionally had (and still has) control over 85% of the housing in Singapore. Though it was just the handing over of 10% of the work to private sector architects, it was considered a radical change to the underlying rules. Interviewees say that it was only Tay who could have led such a transformation. One interviewee, for example, says:

> It was he who wrote to the government to let the government release public housing to be built and designed by the private sector. That had *never been done* before and it was only *he* who could have done that! Only he could have that sort of stature and that sort of *dogged-ness* to approach the government and say "Look, you know, concerning this, you're getting more, you're getting variety—we are getting 'this.' And 'this and this'—is going to solve lots of problems." Nobody else would have *dared* or *nobody else would have been capable of articulating those concerns.*[123]

Tay has been constantly engaged in a range of professional committees. By way of example, in 1987, he was the chairman of the Taskforce to the Singapore National Museum; in 1988, he was the chairman of the Heritage Committee; a member of the Singapore Advisory Council on Culture and Arts from 1991 to 1995; member of the resource panel in the Government Parliament Committee (Ministry of National Development); member of the Advisory Committee of the Institute of Policy Studies (1990), and a member of the Museum Development Committee from 1990 to 1992.

In 1993, Tay was invited to be a judge of the prestigious Quarternario Awards, and in 1997, he was appointed Adjunct Professor of the Royal Melbourne Institute of Technology (RMIT). That same year Robert Powell published a book called *Lines, Edges and Shade*, presenting Tay's ideas and works and his theories on modern tropical architecture. This book was one of the few books about architects in Southeast Asia and the first about an architect in Singapore. In 1997, Tay announced his retirement.[124]

Followership

Interviewees say things like, "when you look around Tay's contemporaries, all of them are actually very successful, but he is the only one who is *really vocal* and who comes out in public. He is the one who *tries out new types of architecture*. The rest are more or less conventional. The rest don't attempt to influence and attempt to create a following or any of the kinds of activities that makes him a leader."[125]

---

[123] Transcript D/2/9.

[124] He did not explicitly explain his retirement but people assumed that he had been "finally broken down." Tay indirectly implies this by saying: "ninety per cent of our projects are never built. They are all attempts to get commissions to feed the office. Therefore we spend a lot of time doing speculative work and that's where the energy goes. It's something which at this stage of life, I don't want anymore. I don't enjoy anymore—in Singapore anyway." (*Business Times*, 22 Jan 1997).

[125] Transcript D/11/10.

It is clear that Tay has a following. An interviewee says, "I think that his standing and his status among the architects, (especially) the young architects is quite high. They guard him quite as a sort of *icon*, one of the *towering architectural figures*."[126]

Tay's followers seem to consist mostly of the younger generation of architecture students, who admire him, engage with his theories and ideas, and seek to develop themselves close to his presence. An interviewee says: "He has a following, there are people and students outside his own practice who go and work for him because of *him*, because *he* is there, so he has got that kind of stature."[127] To this group, he seems to offer an environment conducive to exploration, reflection, and the inquiry into architectural issues. Patrick Chia—for example, a partner in Tay's firm—said that when he came to Akitek Tenggara in 1981, "he was impressed by the atmosphere of discourse on ideas and the manner in which design was considered at so many levels, not the least at the intellectual level."[128]

At the same time, however, Tay seems to have gained many opponents through his many years of provocative discourse, on matters both social and architectural. The older generation of architects—in particular, those in the public sector—would rarely express public admiration for Tay, although interviewees say that they would probably, "secretly and privately admit that he is the most (outstanding architect)."[129]

Extraordinary Attributions

People say that Tay is not only an architect but a man of ideas—a true intellectual. "Few will argue—and this includes his critics—that he is one of the most significant architect-thinkers to come out of Singapore."[130] One interviewee says that he is one of the most recognized professional architects and is seen as an intellectual because he goes the concrete field of architecture with his ideas. "If you talk to architects you can see the difference. Architects are all bound up just with places and spaces they design but he is someone who actually goes into politics, economics, social issues related to space, cities, and the transformation of society because of the built form. So I don't think that he has ever been limited by the fact that he is an architect."[131]

To many who know him, Tay has been seen as someone ahead of his time. An architect says: "His ideas on urban planning and housing have always been way ahead of his time. He has done what all architects should strive to do, and that is to focus on the macro concerns of the environment, to push beyond boundaries of unconventional wisdom."[132] His ideas seem to be a crucial part of his outstanding status.

---

[126] Transcript D/8/12.

[127] Transcript D/11/9.

[128] Powell (1997) op. cit., p. 24.

[129] Transcript D/2/10.

[130] *The Business Times*, 22 Jan 1997.

[131] Transcript D/8/7.

[132] Quoting Edward D'Silva, former president of the Singapore Institute of Architects, in *The Sunday Times* (Singapore), 22 June 1997.

In a comment that highlights the way that Tay stands out, an interviewee says, "*very few* other architects have the same determination, the same articulateness in talking about his ideas and the same wealth of writings and ideas that you can read from his own book."[133] Another architect adds, "In the areas of architectural thinking, design, and professional issues of architectural education, Tay has no equal to match him. While some may have excelled in the quality of their work, none has attempted to reach as wide an audience through writing, teaching and discourse."[134]

Architects see him as a pioneer who tried to redefine architecture in a macro perspective, encompassing aspects such as society, environment, and culture. In this respect, one has said of him that "Kheng Soon is a pioneer. It is not easy being a pioneer because people think you're crazy, they think you're a dreamer. But we all have to dream. Kheng Soon was not scared to dream and, in the process, has given people the impetus to make changes in the architectural environment."[135] His ideas and theories are also the reason why some call him a "Renaissance man," saying that "he is the most passionate and the most important of all Singaporean architects, not just because of his architecture, but also because of his theories and the way he has influenced a whole generation of younger architects."

Most of Tay's colleagues would agree that he is more of a thinker than a doer,[136] and yet he has an influential status because, in the words of the architect William Lim, "he did so much writing and thinking over the last 20 years, and very often, the most interesting architects, like Le Corbusier, don't build much. Their theories are more important."

In his book on Tay Kheng Soon, Robert Powell says that he had been urging Tay for years to let him write a book about him because he thought that Tay's ideas were very important, but they had not been disseminated widely enough. For example, he thinks that Tay's ideas on alternative housing—that is, alternatives to the sort of public housing that is built in Singapore—and his ideas on the tropical city develop a consistent idea about living in the tropics in the contemporary modernist life.[137]

At the same time, Tay's engagement across a wide spectrum of social issues is invariably looked at warily by the government, who considers such issues as political. This is the more so because, more often than not, Tay's comments question the validity of governmental policies or, as a journalist says, "One can count on Tay for that unflinching opinion with a bit of bite."[138] This so-called "anarchist" approach has accorded "moral attributions" to Tay. This morality is not related to the content of his ideas or comments, but more to his persistent pursuit of social commentary, even at the expense of being unpopular or controversial in the eyes of both the

---

[133] Transcript D/15/7.

[134] This was a nominator's reason for nominating Tay Kheng Soon for the SIA gold medal lifetime contribution to architecture, 27 Feb 1998.

[135] The quotations in this and the following paragraph come from *The Sunday Times*. 22 Jun 1997.

[136] People mention this as the reason why he was less able to translate some of his ideas into concrete built forms.

[137] Transcript D/13/6.

[138] *The Business Times*, 22 Jan 1997.

government and the general public. One interviewee addressed this persistence when he said: "*He has no fear* of taking on the establishment if he thinks it is an issue that is worthwhile, for which I think he has the respect of many of the younger professionals. He has actually been sort of a great face to stand up and speak up (...) *It takes courage and strong principles*."[139] Addressing the same point, Robert Powell says that the passion with which Tay promotes the cause of an architectural language for tropical Asia "inevitably creates controversy; for it spills over into the spheres of culture and politics."[140] For Tay, however, his behavior is both a literal and a trivial implementation of what an architect should be and do, which is, to participate in the shaping of society, particularly in the built form, but not only there.

Unique Ideas

Tay Kheng Soon has been an active member of various social committees and has engaged in ongoing public discourse on social issues. He has used the platform of the newspaper extensively, and especially the section of public letters to the press in the "Forum" page of Singapore's *The Straits Times*, to promote and articulate his ideas and comments. To attempt to cover the spectrum of the issues that he had dealt with would be a project on its own. His texts deal with issues such as architecture, aesthetics, culture, creativity, education, arts, transportation, environment, conservation, economy, politics, philosophy, modernity, and others. He seems to have a unique view or comment on everything, which is probably the reason for his media appeal and also for his public profile as a social commentator. For Tay, his irresistible need to comment stems from his quest to participate in the shaping of his society, the way he wishes it to be. He says, "I have this belief that there is a possibility of a more enlightened society. And I want to live in such a society. And because I do not have such a society, I must try my best to do something to create such a society."[141] His comments, however, are often seen as radical because they contradict the government's stand and policies.

For example, when Tay argued in 1991 that Confucian values result in the architects' inability to innovate, he seemed to cut right through the nub of deep underlying Chinese cultural assumptions. Likewise, when he argued against the kind of "show-off," "bimbo" (or, in its local term, "obiang") architecture of the new middle class of Singaporeans, he tried to deconstruct some basic social assumptions of the "nouveau-riche" class and the way they use certain material elements to symbolize their social status.[142] Also when he commented on the regulations governing the escalators on the Mass-Rapid Transit System (MRT), he tried to unveil what is to

---

[139] Transcript D/8/5–7.

[140] Powell, op. cit., p. 18.

[141] Transcript T/4/6.

[142] *The Straits Times*, 16 Dec 1993.

him "the government's underlying technocratic attitude" and the effects it has on the human and social development of Singaporeans.[143]

Apart from this general kind of social commentary on a wide spectrum of issues, Tay's unique contribution is probably best concentrated in his effort to focus on the agenda of constructing an alternative modern tropical architecture. It is agreed among his colleagues that the most unique, coherent, and persistent set of Tay's ideas relate to his quest to construct a unique architecture that deals with a modern, tropical mega-city in Southeast Asia. In Chua's words, "Architect Tay Kheng Soon has only one abiding concern: the development of an architectural language for the tropics, under conditions of rapid urbanization, which expresses the national and regional identities of Southeast Asia."[144]

Tay argues that since Singapore has few precedents of advanced, modern, tropical Asian cities to go by, "it will have to invent its own style of architecture, city form and poetic statements which parallel the drama of its economic development and its geographical imperatives."[145] The new designs must produce a distinct style, promote self-expression, and project a sense of wholeness, well-being, and place value. According to Tay, such architecture can project modernity and tropicality.

The Tropical City concept that he tries to develop is an attempt to reconceptualize the relationship between architecture and city planning at the metropolitan scale in a sustainable, ecologically appropriate manner[146] and to forge the critical link between ecology, city planning, and architecture.[147] He argues that, as ecologically balanced small towns and settlements in the tropics become megacities through modernization, town-planning principles have not developed to enable them to support the growth of dense populations. Instead, city planning concepts were borrowed from developed cities in the West without any attempt to modify them to suit the tropical climate.

According to Tay, because of the heat and humidity, the main criterion for a tropical city should be to achieve compactness by reducing the need to move about. The resulting compact town center should then be a medium for intense cultural, social, and economic exchange. He argues that such conceptualization should begin with an understanding of established settlement patterns, particularly the "interlocking geometries of cluster human settlements in the form of court houses, urban

---

[143] See, for example, his letter to *The Straits Times*, "Let's be civic without the need for technocratic rules," 25 Jul 1998.

[144] *The Straits Times*, 18 Jan 1998.

[145] *The Sunday Times*, 29 Apr 1989.

[146] A journalist says that even if Tay's writing "may seem, at first glance, to be a mish-mash of green, New Age-ist, pro-Asian agendas, it cannot be dismissed on the ground of sounding intellectually trendy because such dismissal disregards the fact that Tay has been on about architecture, identity and climate for several decades now" (*The Business Times*, 22 Jan 1997).

[147] His vision of Singapore as a tropical city is based on the combined utilization of information, technology, and the qualities of the tropics (that is, the sun, rain, wind, and lush vegetation) to produce an efficient living environment in a positive and imaginative way, and one that is conducive to a good lifestyle.

'kampungs'[148] and barrios (settlement patterns that tend to emphasize) a high degree of interpenetration of shared spaces, which result in a high degree of social interaction among the users of the spaces."[149]

In Tay's vision, a tropical city should be like shophouses—"living upstairs and working downstairs"—but on a bigger scale, with sheltered walkways which connect all activities and other buildings. Tay says, "it is not the kind of compactness that is mono-cultural (just offices or just housing); we are talking of poli-cultural compactness, mixing all kind of living styles, working, recreation, education, and so on. But this intensive cultural exchange should be comfortable, conducive and enchanting."[150]

Tay takes the climate as an architectural anchor point and believes that architecture begins with the climate above all else.[151] He says that "politics of a place can mutate, but the climate does not."[152] It is in this respect that he argues that Singapore "is not a tropical city simply by virtue of its location in the equatorial belt, but (should be) a city at peace with its environment"[153] and he attests that one of the principal issues of designing in the tropics is the discovery of a design language of line, edge, mesh, and shade rather than an architecture of plane, volume, solid, and void. It is because of this climatic perspective that Tay succeeded in deconstructing a core, underlying and Western architectural concept—namely, the wall.

Tay has argued that all along, Western-trained local architects had learnt that the building is a box, with a flat plain as the principle of design. But to him, walls are not the absolute means of expressing architecture. Western architecture[154] is determined by its climatic conditions and is therefore a weathertight, enclosed system, exploiting the tensions between solids and voids, volumes and mass. It is a "total climate enclosure while creating the illusion and the actual possibility of plasticity in space with the visual and real interpenetration between the inside and the outside."[155] This has been ultimately realized in the technology of rolled metal and plate glass, culminating in the "curtain wall"—the glass wall—that provides at once "total closure" as well as the means of defining a luminous lightweight skin of a building.

However, in an equable climate in the tropics, the building enclosure does not need to be the absolute limiting barrier. The wall is therefore not the main feature nor does it need to be the delimiting factor in the design of building enclosures.

---

[148] A Malay term for a village type of settlement. It carries a connotation of home and roots and belonging.

[149] *The Straits Times*, 18 Jan 1998.

[150] *The Straits Times*, 8 May 1989.

[151] He also says that he takes climate seriously because: "The scientist, the artist, the historian and intellectual parts of me find the geographical facts of place a very interesting theme in which form-making, building, designing, and thinking come together" (*The Business Times*, 22 Jan 1997).

[152] *The Business Times*, 22 Nov 1997.

[153] *The Straits Times*, 8 Aug 1990.

[154] Tay prefers to call the Western architecture—"North" architecture because this is a geographic, climatic reference rather than a political one.

[155] 18/1998. Also in Powell (1997) op. cit., p. 40.

It is therefore not the most important architectural element in a building. Instead, he emphasizes "line, edge and shade, rather than flat, solid plains."[156] Against the desire for enclosure, he juxtaposes the necessity for openness to the environment, and against an architectural aesthetics of enclosure defined by solid walls in vertical planes, he juxtaposes an aesthetics of openness defined by "fuzzy" walls. These walls are "interpenetrating rather than enclosing, which are partial enclosures, movable at will and not arranged at any fixed plane."[157] A core concept of his alternative architecture is then that instead of sheer walls, buildings should be "soft-edged buildings." The "fuzzy walls" conceptualization offers, instead of enclosure, an "openness" by allowing interpenetration, insulation, and interlocking geometries.

Tay argues that in designing for the tropics, one should move away from steel and glass boxes like "those crisp, shiny air-conditioned towers that one sees in the city center" toward "fuzzy," permeable enclosures that emphasize shade, shelter, shadow, and profile.[158] These walls could be made of "meshes, fretwork patterns or trellis screens," creating degrees of transparencies that are about air, light, and comfort—responsive to conditions peculiar to this part of the world. It follows that walls as such do not need to be aligned vertically nor do they have to be on one plane. They can be quite freely positioned as required and to achieve whatever effects desired.

Such a conceptualization opens a whole new range of spatial possibilities in design. "In terms of the development of form, space and surface treatments, this leads to spatial differentiations by layering and the development of transitional zones with various degrees of transparencies. The elaboration of the 'fuzzy' wall brings tremendous possibilities in integrating use functions and variations into it"[159] and results in a whole new type of architecture.

Following the deconstruction of the Western wall, a climatic implication on architecture and a core aspect in Tay's ideas is that a main aspect of architecture in the tropics is not the wall—but the roof. It is therefore bound to emphasize shade and shadow rather than volumes and solids. Following this line, Tay constructed the "umbrella concept" that expresses the idea as well as the form of an alternative architecture.[160] Tay thinks that the idea of the "umbrella aesthetic" is not only architecturally sensible but also a fitting symbol for the tropical climate and the region's culture: "The umbrella does not just represent shelter, it also suggests the culture, the openness of Asian hospitality, the informality. It's a product of the climate, an echo of the balconies and shaded areas."[161]

---

[156] *The Straits Times*, 21 Jun 1997.

[157] *The Straits Times*, 18 Jan 1998.

[158] Ibid.

[159] Powell (1997) op. cit., p. 41.

[160] While Chua says that for those who are familiar with the architecture of Southeast Asia, as exemplified in the Malay house, Tay's architectural vocabulary "is highly reminiscent of what has been in practice in the vernacular architecture of this region," but Tay does not advocate "simplistic pastiche appropriations of the vernacular in new urban environments" because to him, such approach "will produce hoary hybrid buildings, and indigestible quotations of the vernacular that insult rather than celebrate the local" (*The Straits Times*, 18 Jan 1998).

[161] *The Straits Times*, 15 Apr 1984.

Tay says that when the umbrella aesthetic is applied to low buildings, it is easy to imagine what the forms may be like, but for tall buildings and complex structures, it is a challenge indeed. He proposes that we imagine a city where the architectural language is composed of distinctive roofs, with plenty of shade, ledges, and covered passageways linking one building to another, and argues that continuous sheltered linkages on the ground (owned by various entities), executed within a coherent design style, "need to be made possible."[162] In short, "big overhangs will be the order of the day."[163]

Yet for a modern tropical language to translate into built forms, prevalent concepts of the city forms themselves may have to change to enable groups of buildings to be linked at upper levels to create a new design language, and Tay argues that new building regulations and legal provisions would also be necessary for these connections between buildings owned by different owners. He gives us one such example when he relates to the current bus and taxi shelters in Singapore and what they could look like, if the idea of "umbrella architecture" were applied. It should be noted here that he implies that an implementation of the idea requires a change in the current basic assumptions and regulations without which such a change is impossible. He says:

> It is strange that living in the tropics where we have abundant rain and scorching sun, there are inadequate shelters when alighting from taxis, buses or cars at buildings or at kerbsides. This is because of property rights and regulations derived therefrom. (All canopies or shelters thus have to be within property boundary lines and nothing can extend into public spaces or road verges. This is a legacy inherent in the laws and building regulations handed down through the years).
>
> All that needs to be done is to modify the conceptual assumptions behind the laws to include the right not to be baked by the sun or drenched by rain.
>
> If such a change can come about, it is easy to imagine bus shelters overhanging the full width of the bus at a bus stop. Of course, they will have to be as tall as elevated pedestrian bridges to allow the passage of tall vehicles. Similarly, covered canopies can extend from entrances of buildings over public or even private land for the same effect. High canopies can span buildings too. A truly tropical city of continuous shelter can be achieved beyond the cosmetic and the rhetoric and be a real boon to pedestrians and motorists alike.[164]

Indeed, Tay feels that the main problem blocking the construction and implementation of such new design concepts is rooted in the basic assumptions of Singaporeans as well as the current architectural Western paradigm. He thinks that the main problem inhibiting an authentic architecture relates to deep social assumptions, referring to the frame of mind of both people and government as being inadvertently inclined to Western paradigms.

Tay argues that in Singapore's zeal to modernize, they may have unwittingly imported Western styles wholesale[165] and that "we are so inundated by these styles in our education, in the books and magazines that we read, in the design models that we emulate, that it is difficult to be different." Therefore, although the prospects for building a great tropical city are brightest in Southeast Asia, the odds against building

---

[162] *The Sunday Times*, 29 Apr 1984.

[163] *The Straits Times*, 8 May 1989.

[164] *The Straits Times*, 2 Mar 1996.

[165] The references in this paragraph come from *The Sunday Times*, 29 Apr 1984.

it are very great because such architecture contradicts deep Western social assumptions. He argues that Singaporeans always assume that West is best, even if they don't say so publicly, and that this is the main thing that is blocking the designers' authentic response to Singapore's climate and history.

He therefore argues that, as a first step, it is necessary to deconstruct the societal assumptions that the West is better. He says, "We need to first go beyond all our contemporary wisdom and to shed the inferiority that makes us slaves to ready made skills, ideas and vocabularies."[166]

Arguing that "applying Western standards has weakened our creative will,"[167] he makes a plea to Singaporean architects (as well as to the public) to pause and to reevaluate Western architectural styles.

Tay says, "if our people are to be able to realize that which is unique in themselves, they have to adopt a critical attitude (meaning penetrating and discerning)—towards the barrage of Western ideas as well as their own heritage. They must come to terms with the West, albeit on the basis of a critical understanding of who and what they are."[168] In other words, Tay argues that for such an alternative authentic architecture to develop, there should be more mechanisms for expressing alternative and critical views. However, he thinks that Singapore does not have appropriate mechanisms for expressing such views. He says:

> There is little critical thinking in design because criticism is usually mistaken in Singapore to mean disparagement and is, therefore, frowned upon. Only when there is good quality criticism can improvements come about. Talent is also sharpened and focused by criticism. (But) in the Singapore context, such a condition does not exist and therefore design is not pushed and the ideas are not stretched. The result is a mediocrity of ideas.[169]

Tay believes that such mechanisms and mentality are important in order to become conscious of Singapore's own design situation—that is, its natural or national identity in design.[170] He says, "Criticism must be there to sharpen thinking and to clarify ideas"[171] and adds, "for excellence to grow there has to be a critical climate of opinion with appropriate mechanisms for criticism."[172]

---

[166] Powell (1997) op. cit., p. 14.

[167] *The Sunday Times*, 15 Apr 1984.

[168] *The Straits Times*, 30 Jul 1994.

[169] See Tay (1990).

[170] Concomitantly, Tay laments that planning procedures are based on certain norms which have never been challenged or tested, nor any alternatives investigated. Such a situation is a circular process because "the norms produce the master plan, the master plan generates rules, the rules produce the buildings (and consequently, the buildings themselves) which confirm the norms. No progress will ever be made until there is an experimental building program, which is free from existing regulations, to find new things" (*The Straits Times*, 24 Jun 1992).

[171] *The Straits Times*, 4 Jul 1990.

[172] Tay thinks that such critical view should be asserted in all realms of life and not only architecture. He includes all social and cultural assumptions as well, saying for example: "Until and unless we begin our own critical review of our cultural heritage, and not fawn over the past, we will find it hard to overcome the negative aspects of inherited cultural presuppositions. Chinese Singaporeans should not allow their sense of cultural obligation to Chineseness prevent them from critically examining their heritage" (*The Straits Times*, 13 Feb 1991).

Tay argues that criticism or the expression of critical views is more than simply being disparaging, which seems to be a common, mistaken notion in Singapore. To him, one of the major characteristics of criticism and autonomy of reason is the ability to finely differentiate categories and meanings. He says: "Criticality is therefore the capacity to uncover the underlying assumptions behind an action or a design. It is the process of cutting through to the nub of an issue so that the thinking is stimulated and ideas examined knowledgeably."[173]

To sum up, Tay has been concerned with a good variety of issues, but above all, he has been trying to articulate and construct an alternative architectural language and morphology that, to his opinion, would be consistent and coherent (rather than transplanted and incoherent) with the climate, the times, and the people.

But the mere development of such concepts juxtaposes various dominant assumptions. It juxtaposes dominant assumptions of the government on the proper design of public housing for Singapore; it juxtaposes the professional paradigms in the field of architecture regarding walls and solids as the main architectural concepts; and it juxtaposes the socially dominant orientation toward the West and its ideas and designs as being superior and as sole sources for truism and emulation.

Emerging Patterns

The data presented in the above enfolds a few important points that we would like to note. First, it is clear that the classification of the charismatic ideas as unique is endemically relativistic and contextual. This is because the coining of a certain idea as "unique" can be done only in relation to its being "different" from its context. For example, to describe Tay's struggle for the construction of an alternative form of architecture is one thing, but to see it in the context of solid Western architectural paradigms and a strongly centralized government with fixed ideas as to how public housing should look, coupled with an extremely efficient bureaucracy that implements and executes such policies, is another perspective altogether. Likewise, to present Kuo's ideas on the need for an intangible dimension to social life is one thing (the radical nature or uniqueness of which Western readers might not even understand). But to see it in the context of a society "possessed" by a demand for quick, tangible, economic results is really an altogether different story.

This relative "difference" or "contrast" is crucial for the establishment of the revolutionary aspect of charisma, because this difference also means a direct juxtaposition to other given basic social assumptions. Therefore, the meaning of the leader's vision and the degree of their "revolutionary aspect" can only be grasped and understood vis-à-vis the context they act upon, and the nature of the basic assumptions that they set out to deconstruct, and reconstruct. It is in this respect that charismatic leaders are "products" of the situation, not in the sense of being "created"

---

[173] Ibid.

by the situation, but in the sense of being assessed, and being relevant, meaningful, and revolutionary—only in line of the specific social system that they are contrasted with and which they wish and attempt to transform.

One more interesting feature that rises from the cases relates to the intertwined relations between the leaders' alternative constructions and their engagement with the deconstruction of other given basic social assumptions. We think that although we have tried to separate the two (for the purpose of analytical clarity), it is still quite evident that, in reality, they interest and depend on each other. The leaders articulate and promote their own construction along the deconstructive process that they engage in. The further they deconstruct the basic assumptions, the more they are able to promote their alternative construction, and vice versa.

The deconstruction is activated not only by the mere repudiation and "attack" of the current basic assumptions. For the deconstruction to take place, equally important is the presentation of a meaningful construction that offers a coherent "internal logic of its own." The deconstruction is therefore possible only along the articulation of an alternative construction that is at least equally meaningful. This should be no surprise since people would not, as it were, deconstruct their own basic assumptions out of a self-destructive attitude. Instead, they might be willing to get rid of their taken-for-granted, solid social assumptions and constructions—only for an alternative reality construction that is, at least, equally meaningful.

Hence, it is basically an interconnected process, whereby deconstruction and reconstruction depend on each other and occur simultaneously. This is also the reason why the "internal logic" that the leaders' ideas and constructions offer is as important as their ability to question the validity of other current given underlying social assumptions. Charismatic leadership is therefore not an altogether anarchist agency, simply repudiating and destroying the status quo (as could have been understood from Weber's own emphasis on revolution). It is also a creative agency. It is, hence, essentially dialectical in being both a disruptive and a constructive social agency at one and the same time. In other words, to become a charismatic leader, it is not enough to be able to destroy. Equally important is the leader's ability to offer an alternative "order" that is at least equally coherent and meaningful. Furthermore, these two components are not parallel, but interrelated in nature.

The last point that we want to make here was less explicit in our empirical presentation, but nevertheless implied in our data. By this, we refer to the underlying thematic content of the leaders' visions. Tay's "modern tropical architecture," Kuo's "intangible dimension of social life," and Prema's "social welfare service" contain an underlying profound preoccupation with existential dilemmas. More particularly, they seem to focus on identity questions such as "Who are we?" both as selves and as a society and consequently, "What ought we to be?" It is our view that, in spite of the distinct content of each leader's construction, there are some underlying thematic concerns that encompass all three leaders' ideas, and that this "meta-content" may be a core aspect in their ability to engage with the symbolic societal core, as well as to construct social meaning.

In the next chapter, we will explore all these three issues further and correlate them to the charismatic leadership's agency in the social construction of reality and meaning, and in its transformation.

Chapter 8
Charismatic Leadership's Agency: Social Construction and Transformation of Meaning

This chapter will offer an analysis of the charismatic leadership's agency in the construction and transformation of reality and meaning. The level of analysis will be mainly confined to the micro and messo levels and will focus on the followers' perceptions and engagement in these processes.

This chapter can be also seen as an empirical demonstration as well as an exploration of the theoretical postulations that we suggested back in Chap. 4. There, we argued that charismatic leaders negotiate the symbolic structure by deconstructing and reconstructing the underlying basic social assumptions with regard to notions about the self, society, and the world. We will see how the uniqueness of the leaders' ideas is endemically contextual (in the sense of addressing particular underlying basic assumptions and paradigms in each leader's field of action) and how the nature of the constructivist and transformative processes entail distinct perceptual and philosophical aspects.

The following analysis is by no means a literary or artistic review of Kuo's plays and theater. Similarly, the analysis of Sister Prema's social service will not be analyzed from the point of view of social welfare, and Tay's ideas, designs, and texts will not be analyzed from an architectural point of view. Instead, it is a sociological analysis of their work, attempting to analyze leadership's agency in the transformation of the professional fields, as well as of the people whom they engage with.

We will first analyze each case separately and then attempt to draw theoretical postulations with regard to the charismatic constructivist and transformative patterns. The analysis of Kuo's case will be a bit longer because the artistic nature of his socially objectified artifacts (his artistic texts) requires some interpretation.

Kuo Pao Kun: Redefining Social Identity

An interviewee's statement reflects the crux of Kuo's social influence. He says:

> I think that theater was one of the art forms that Singaporeans, or people living in Singapore, had a connection with, since perhaps the earliest times the Western civilization has kept records of Singapore's development. But if you were to ask the question, 'how much of this

Dayan Hava and Chan Kwok-bun, *Charismatic Leadership in Singapore:*   155
Three Extraordinary People, DOI 10.1007/978-1-4614-1451-3_8,
© Springer Science+Business Media, LLC 2012

theater is really *Singaporean*, how much of it is really theater that *reflects our conscious-ness, that reflects our history, that reflects our anxieties?'*—then I think that that can only be answered by the fact that it was over the last twenty or thirty years that such a conscious-ness in theater evolved. And, then if you were to ask the question, 'who is the most impor-tant artist in developing this consciousness?'—The answer to that must be Kuo Pao Kun.[1]

The citation describes a social transformation in the development of Singaporean theater. It does not refer to the development of the stage in professional terms (like props, acting, choreography, staging, lighting, and others) but to its development as a meaningful social construct. In other words, it refers to the theater's development in reflecting and exploring a Singaporean consciousness and a particular social identity. It suggests that theater, as such, has transformed into something that reflects a unique psyche.

A journalist says: "His (Kuo's) works, which are critical perspectives on life, people and society, are said to come closest to reflecting a genuine Singapore life on stage."[2] Interviewees observe that "some of the plays that really embody the Singaporean consciousness are Kuo Pao Kun's plays,"[3] and that "Pao Kun's works are also 'political/sociological,' (because his plays are), actually not just comments on the political situation, but comments on the type of society that we live in, the kind of psyche almost, of the Singaporean."[4] Implicitly, they seem to suggest that theater, through Kuo's involvement, has become more meaningful to Singaporeans, and indeed, an interviewee says, "It was through Pao Kun that the culture of belong-ing"[5] developed and that whatever was going on the stage was meaningful or, in other words, "ours."

So how did this process come about? How did people engage in exploring and constructing a notion of their selves, the world, and the meaning of their existence? And extrapolating from that, can we learn from this process how social meaning is constructed?

Latent Existential Predisposition

It is of significance that Kuo's followers[6] anchor his point of departure (as a charis-matic figure) to an era that was for them characterized by uneasy feelings with regard to their identity. This implies that his leadership, at least in their eyes, was not

---

[1] Transcript A/4/1.

[2] *The Straits Times*, 14 Nov 1989.

[3] Transcript A/4/4.

[4] Transcript B/17/1.

[5] Transcript B/12/12.

[6] This is especially for the English-speaking theater practitioners. The term "English-speaking" here refers to Singaporeans of Chinese descent, whose education at school was in the English language.

the sole originator of the "social-reflective process," but rather was in congruence with existing vague feelings of having a fragmented or an incoherent identity. See, for example, how an interviewee connects Kuo's leadership to this predisposition:

> Pao Kun's influence was very much *felt* in the English language theater scene, (from mid-80s to early 90s) because the English language theater people were looking, searching for their *identity*: who are we, who are we as Singaporeans? What is a Singaporean play? What is Singaporean English? (...) And Pao Kun was one of the *routes*, one of the *roads*, one of the avenues, because he was very deeply Chinese to us, but yet he could talk to us in English. So that's why a lot of people went to him, and in a sense he became a modern guru in many ways.[7]

This may suggest that people were already willing to question or doubt their "taken-for-granted" formulations about themselves prior to or in tandem with Kuo's rise as a leader. It is therefore probable that such people were attentive to explorative processes that deal with the meaning of human existence and identity and were therefore receptive to Kuo's quest to explore, question, and maybe even reconstruct such social dimensions.

However, this is not to say that Kuo just happened to match people's anxieties and quest for meaning nor that his agency was restricted to a mere "supply" of people's specific needs. The term "amplifier," used by an interviewee to describe Kuo's role, offers some clues about the nature of Kuo's social role. "He was the loud-speaker or the amplifier of that whole issue, and through this person Singapore theater began to reassess its own identity."[8] It suggests that he enhanced, reinforced, and exposed given social tendencies that were previously in a latent or amorphous form. He was an agent to the crystallization, clarification, and articulation of covert, latent, and formless dilemmas, and to their transformation to overt, urgent problems to be dealt with. Kuo thus reinforced tendencies that were linked to self-exploration or in an interviewee's words: "In the '80s he disturbed us, and because we were disturbed, we went to find out more (about ourselves)."[9]

Once exposed to Kuo, people felt driven to fully immerse themselves in intro-spective explorations of "what and who should they be, in this place and time." It is by no means an easy task to drive people into the deconstruction and reconstruction of preconvictions about their selves and the world because such self-introspection is both cognitively and emotionally demanding, even disturbing. Words such as "inter-rogation," "investigation," and "excavation" (to use the words of one interviewee)[10] suggest the amount of effort, energy, commitment, and perseverance needed for such processes. Indirectly, it also implies how significant Kuo's agency was in driv-ing people into such processes.

We can therefore perhaps discuss Kuo's role as an "intermediate variable" between latent, formless, cognitive attitudes of people and their social activation. His agency filled the role of a "missing link" between people's latent cognition and

---

[7] Transcript B/7/1, 3.

[8] Transcript A/2/9.

[9] Transcript B/7/12.

[10] Transcript A/1/5.

their mobilization into social action. Hence, he did not create the change himself; rather, he helped people in the activation and realization of their own initiation into processes of self-introspection and transformation.

The Plays as a Platform for Existential Exploration and Expression

Kuo used theater to explore and expose the existential dilemmas because he believed that "the cultural mode of behavior (theater included) provides further access into the complexities (or simplicities) of our existence—our inner and our outer world."[11] It is therefore not surprising to hear interviewees say that Kuo's art "is always the art about asking questions."[12] Indeed, by and large, Kuo's plays are said to deal with the existential relations between the individual (self) and the collective (society and culture).

While these relations between the self and the society are usually semiconscious and "taken for granted,"[13] Kuo's plays bring the interaction between the self and the sociocultural dimension "up" to the realm of consciousness and can therefore be seen as a medium that reveals, unveils, and exposes these interactions. What was previously "passively" or reflexively taken for granted is uncovered and brought to the forefront of an active, reflective, conscious, existential social discourse.

It is in this respect that people refer to his plays as a strong intellectual plea for deep and complex investigation into the essence of things, saying, "It is always asking questions like who we are, where we are, why should things be like this? (and) the best art is that kind of art, which forces you to look at the world in another kind of way, and ask questions about it. And it is that asking of questions which his theater is always doing."[14] Indeed, in the ceremony where Kuo was made a member of the Order of the Chevalier des Arts et des Letters by the French government, the French ambassador said:

> You wrote: 'Not questioning can be very comforting.' French philosophy is based on questioning. As Descartes puts it: 'I think or if you like it better, I question, thus, I do exist.' You have spent great part of your life questioning your self and the Singaporean audience, in a very inspiring way, through your artistic creations. This is the main reason for today's award.[15]

Let us take, for example, the play, *The Coffin Is Too Big for the Hole*, which is probably the best known of his plays, and which, for many people, marks the beginning of a social discourse on the Singaporean identity (a discourse that Kuo is said to have triggered and led). In the play, a man's grandfather has prepared an unusually large coffin for himself while alive. Alas, upon his grandfather's death, the man discovers

---

[11] Kuo (1997a) op. cit., p. 1.

[12] Transcript A/4/5.

[13] See, for example, Herbert Mead's (1934) treatment of the formation of the self.

[14] Ibid.

[15] *The Straits Times*, 20 Jan 1997.

that the standardized hole in the public cemetery is too small for the coffin. In front of the crowd of family members, friends, and onlookers, the protagonist, being the eldest grandson, feels deeply responsible for fulfilling his grandfather's wish. But the large coffin, distinct in character, looks odd in the presence of row upon row of well-ordered standard graves in the cemetery.[16] The man is caught, as it were, in the middle of his grandfather's funeral, with an "unusually big" coffin that "wouldn't get into the hole."[17] But the problem worsens along the official plot's regulation policy that would not allow the allocation of another plot to fit the unusual coffin's size.[18]

The play seems to raise a question about the relations between man and society. It brings these relations to the realm of consciousness and provides a platform for the exploration of these existential relations. The coffin, representing individuality and uniqueness (which can be like the coffin—"charismatic" and special but also "damn heavy" or demanding), is juxtaposed with the notion of "society" as triggered by the government officials (representing standardization, regimentation, and homogenization) and the family members (representing tradition, family, kinship, heritage, and culture). As we engage with the plot, we feel the burden of such tensed relations and their irreconcilable constraints and demands. Through the play, we engage in the exploration of human beings, both being constrained by their own society's homogenization and regimentation and, at the same time, empowered by tradition, culture, and individuality—to negotiate the constraints within which they act.

Thus, it also exposes the fragility of society's rules and basic assumptions or symbolic structure as being constantly pushed, negotiated, and redefined by unique individuals (that are, just as the coffin, "unique," "damn heavy," "charismatic," and "unusually big"). To be sure, the relations between self and society are not reconciled,[19] in spite of the technical and exceptional solution that was forwarded by the

---

[16] Yu Yun in Kuo (2000).

[17] The man recalls thinking at that point: "Can you imagine that the coffin of your grandfather cannot get into the hole specially dug for him on the day of his funeral? And in front of two hundred people? We were speechless. We were literally stunned. We just stood there and looked at each other. Nobody said a word. It must have been the funniest thing that had ever happened in the entire funeral history of mankind."

[18] For which the government official says: "Look at all these graves in the cemetery. See? All same size. No two graves for one person. Everyone standard size!…(To allocate another plot) will be running against our national planning. You are well aware of the fact that we are a densely populated nation with very limited land resources. The consideration for humanity and sympathy cannot over-step the constraints of the state policy!"

[19] The Protagonist says at the end of the play: "As for me, the funeral somehow stuck in my mind and it would often come back to me. In a dream. Especially when I'm frustrated.
I'm sure you'll agree with me that grandfather's coffin had its special charisma and unique character. But the problem was it was too big for the hole. So, under the circumstances, to be pragmatic, it seems I have to get a standard-sized one. But then, whenever I get to go to the cemetery and see those graves—those rows after rows of standard-sized graves, I cannot resist thinking about the other problem, and this is what really bothers me a lot: 'Now, with them all in the same size and the same shape, would my sons and daughters, and my grandsons and granddaughters after them, be able to find me out there and recognize me?'
I don't know…I just don't know…"

government officials in their will to resolve this particular case. They are left as an unresolved dilemma.

By presenting this kind of exploration in the form of a "dilemma" (which is opposed to dogmatic, didactic answers) the play, as a discursive platform, "forces" (or at least invites) a complex, ambivalent mode of thinking that rejects simplistic resolutions. The form of the play as a "dilemma" forwards an in-principle argument about the multifaceted and complicated nature of reality. It hence invites an exploration of its ambivalent, irreconcilable sides, which bear no "right and wrong" kind of answers. The dilemma thus reinforces the explorative nature of the discourse that is triggered by the content of the play.

The dilemma form used in the play is not only a technique. It implies that fundamental existential dilemmas indeed do not really have "technical solutions" but are a matter of eternal debate, negotiation, and choice. Hence, the irreconcilable nature of these relations implies that each social working assumption pertaining to these relations is a matter of choice and is (or should be) therefore forever prone to be socially contested, debated, and negotiated.

The issues presented in Kuo's plays are not perceived by people as parochial, concrete, or "petty" problems. Instead, they are seen by interviewees as "exploring very profound elements, very very deep and profound levels of the Singaporean society (such as) our relationship with this place, Singapore, this land, the system, the people, and things that happen around us. It is about an individual or a human being within his land, in a bigger scope."[20] Through the plays, people engage with fundamental social issues, such as heritage, homogenization and regimentation, alienation, tradition, intergeneration relations, communication, socialization, and others.[21] In other words, Kuo's theater provokes, evokes, invokes, and explores issues that relate to questions of social meaning in a philosophical, deep reflective mode of thinking.[22] In an interviewee's words, "he is able to address and bring you or push you to a higher level of thinking rather then looking at something very petty."[23]

---

[20] Transcript C/1d/8–9.

[21] The theme of heritage comes up in *LaoJiu—The Ninth Born Son*, (1990); homogenization and regimentation are explored in *The Coffin is Too Big for the Hole*, (1985); *No Parking on Odd Days*, (1986) looks at alienation; the play *Kopitiam* (1986) explores tradition; communication is a theme in *Mama Is Looking for Her Cat* (1988); and socialization is an issue in *The Silly little Girl and the Funny Old Tree*, (1987).

[22] People say this about him, "he is a thinking man, constantly thinking, asking himself, dialoguing with himself and dialoguing with other people. And his plays actually show this thinking process." (Interview C/1d/8). Indeed, many people subscribe to the notion that Pao Kun is an extremely serious person. For example, one interviewee says: "If you ask me to go and socialize with Pao Kun, I can't, he's too intense for me. (…) I need *levity*, I need fun, and I need relaxation. (But) with Pao Kun it's hundred percent on! (…) Too intense (for me). Too serious, too serious. (…) There is a lot of humor in his plays but in real life he is not funny. He is very serious, he talks *to* you and you know that he *thinks* about what he talks to you, he is *very deliberate*. Every sentence is thought through. He doesn't give you a sentence off the cuff like what I'm doing now, that some of it is rubbish, right? He doesn't. Nothing comes out of him must be rubbish, so it's like he thinks it through and then he talks to you. So what do you do? Then I can't talk to him the way I talk to you now" (Transcript B/10/20).

[23] Transcript C/1d/9.

Through these plays, people engage with notions that are "larger than the self," so to speak, and engage in an explorative journey and self-expansion that transcends into a meta-world, a meta-thinking, a meta-self.

It seems that people see Kuo's plays as platforms that enable the exploration of existential issues and dilemmas. One such example can be seen in the 1986 play, *No Parking on Odd Days*, which, along with *The Coffin Is Too Big for the Hole*, marked for people the beginning of a conscious discourse on social identity. The underlying theme in the play deals with the notion of the "human fighting spirit." This notion is explored through the story of a man who is traumatized by his past confrontations with the bureaucracy. In one such particular encounter, the man recalls that he was unwilling to accept the parking offense ticket because two conflicting parking signs were displayed 50 meters apart. He then shares with the audience his trials and tribulations in trying to earnestly argue with the authorities, hoping that the authorities would amend their error. Alas, after months of tedious appeals and court proceedings, the authorities finally accept the driver's suggestions by displaying clearer parking signs but he is fined all the same for having contravened the formerly displayed signs, and he has to choose between going to jail and paying the fine. That event, as well as other similar encounters with bureaucracy, leaves him traumatized—and rather submissive.

Throughout the play, the protagonist is caught between his own rendering passive submission to arbitrary rules erected by officialdom, and his son's naïve, fighting spirit, saying: "My boy's seriousness, that bright spark in his eyes, the fighting spirit in his voice, hit me hard somewhere inside." This dilemma triggers a reflection on the notion of the human fighting spirit and its fragility or resilience. But what is excruciatingly painful for the protagonist are the unintended implications of his own past experiences—on the socialization of his own son. He realizes through the play that his own traumas affect the way that he had unintentionally socialized his son—to be submissive as well. So much so, that by the end of the play the son, who used to be "observant," "creative," and with a "fighting spirit," is eventually portrayed as someone quiet, who has been neutered, and has lost his vitality (or in the protagonist's macabre/laconic comment, "someone matured").[24]

With this man's story, and through his trials and tribulations, the audience reflects on the meaning of the human fighting spirit, its implications on social life and conformity, on self dignity, on the way we socialize our children, the kind of values that we pass to them, and the kind of future generations that we thus create. Though these issues are presented in a simple, light, and humorous way in the play, they nonetheless trigger serious existential dilemmas, or in an interviewee's words, "it's a very simple thing, it is very funny but in the end you cannot laugh anymore."[25]

---

[24] The protagonist says: "Now. 'That's a sign of him growing up,' I said to my wife. 'He's maturing,' I said. 'That's normal, they get more quiet as they grow, as they get wiser. You know wise men are always more thoughtful, quieter characters.' Well, he didn't ask me about that story again. He became more and more quiet and gradually the questions didn't come anymore." (Kuo, 1990, p. 68).

[25] Transcript A/4/5.

The issues exposed and explored in the plays are universal in that they deal with human nature and with dilemmas that are universal. At the same time, they are particular because they are concretely situated, socially, culturally, and geopolitically.

In the play, *The Coffin Is Too Big for the Hole*, for example, a meaningful cultural notion underlies the universal dilemma—not only because the protagonist speaks Singlish,[26] but more so because of that language form's social and cultural grounding.

For instance, the place where the story is situated (the cemetery) is of particular symbolic significance in eliciting and invoking the whole cultural notion of "paying respect to the ancestors," which is a core concept in Chinese societies. Also, the particular event in the play—the funeral—is of particular significance because it brings with it the "whole tradition of the filial son and the father, (in which) the most important duty that the son can do for the parents is 'the last rite,' (the burial), which is a very important symbolic ritual in the life of the Indians and the Chinese."[27]

K.K. Seet says that the play relies for its impact on an understanding of the infra-structure and traditions of the extended Chinese family, which is linked to the idea of the role in the network of filial piety with its concomitant duties and obligations. These duties and obligations are articulated by the concept "to be answerable to one's ancestors" that implies an ongoing process of honoring and paying homage to one's progenitors through appropriate gestures and deeds. Hence, in not giving his grandfather a proper burial, the narrator has a lot at stake since, according to the Chinese belief, the spirit of one's grandfather permanently watches over (and thus, there is a greater felt need to fulfill one's obligations and do what's appropriate and decorous).[28]

The dilemma and relations between self (or individualism) and society (or social homogenization) that is presented in this play is therefore meaningful to the audience—not only because it raises universal, human dilemmas, but more so because it touches upon unique cultural and social aspects. It thus deals with a particular case of a universal existential dilemma. This particular exploration turns the universal human dilemma from being "abstract, placeless and timeless" to being meaningfully grounded in the social, cultural, and political idiosyncrasies of Singapore. Hence, the plays enable a platform for exploration of both the universal as well as the particular levels of human existence. This "uniqueness" and particularism transforms the universal dilemma into something meaningful that belongs to the audience, or in an interviewee's words, it "talks about *us*"[29] and is like "telling a story with our own voices."[30]

---

[26] Singlish is briefly explained in Chap. 7.

[27] Transcript A/4/4.

[28] Seet (1992, pp. 244–245).

[29] Transcript A/2/5.

[30] Transcript A/4/4.

Negotiating Identity Formation

Although humorous, Kuo's plays are not a kind of light, entertaining art form.[31] People say that Kuo's "plays make *demands*"[32] and that "Pao Kun totally *de-glamorized* theater, made theater *painful*."[33] His theater form is demanding and painful, "very *mind provoking*, makes you *think*"[34] and "forces you to rethink who you are."[35] The "pain" expressed by the audience is not only due to the demanding intellectual effort that is required in an explorative process but more so because, through that exploration, people face themselves and realize that these were some things that were previously avoided or overlooked. That realization is painful because it points at gaps, fractures, or inconsistencies in their self and social collective identity.

Interviewees refer to the 1988 play, *Mama Is Looking for Her Cat*, as an example of such a painful realization. The play is considered a seminal work in theater because it represented for the first time a multilingual play that uses various languages and dialects in one production.[36] In this way, it presented the multilingual reality of Singapore as well as explored the implications of such multilingualism on the people and the communication problems that sometimes result. At the same time, this theatrical piece transcended the linguistic barriers in the society because it is a play that people could understand in spite of the language barriers. Krishen Jit says (about this play) that Kuo was the first to creatively integrate Chinese, English, Malay, Tamil, Hokkien, and other languages used in Singapore in one production, allowing Singapore audiences from different cultures and language streams "to sit in the same theater, watching a play which belongs to them all."[37]

The play is about a Hokkien-speaking mother who cannot any longer communicate with her children because they can only speak "official languages" (English and

---

[31] More so with the later plays which lost the previous humoristic, light style. An interviewee says later plays like *The Spirits* (1998) and *The Eunuch Admiral* (1995) that "He doesn't care, having a full (play) talking with spirits. It's just *HEAVY*, and you are asked to swallow heavy issues with a tough stomach. I think he goes to less pleasing plays and his latest works are more difficult to be entertained by. But they are serious and good works. Like (his version of the 'Eunuch' (play is like) the bad ginger—and gunshot—and you can see what he really wants (to say): A lot of oppression, suppression, a lot of being pushed and fighting back—by time, by issues, by concepts, by yourself, by many, many things." (Transcript A/2/4).

[32] Transcript B/13/5.

[33] Transcript B/10/11.

[34] Transcript B/2/8.

[35] Transcript A/4/4.

[36] One theater practitioner said about it: "*Mama Is Looking for Her Cat* introduced a multilingual element into playwriting. The idea was enormously influential in the sense that everybody thought that plays from now on ought to be written in this way (…) When he implemented this idea, multiculturalism as a philosophical idea became influential (…) I think many people saw as a landmark." (Transcript A/13/2,4,8).

[37] Kuo (1990) op. cit., Introduction.

Mandarin) and not their parents' dialects.[38] The play was not only a powerful theatrical piece, in terms of staging, but was also a mirror for self-reflection. An interviewee describes the audience's response to the play, saying:

> I went that night to see (the play). A lot of people in the audience could not understand the dialect or Tamil for instance. But the response was tremendous, I mean it hit them very hard because many of the people in the audience were kids who spoke English and they had a dialect relative (say grandmother or grandfather) whom they couldn't relate to. And it really hit home very deeply. It made them realize 'Hey, I got a problem' (…) It touched them.[39]

Through the play many in the audience came to the painful realization of the intergeneration miscommunication and alienation between themselves and their close relatives. An interviewee says:

> (The play) is about this old lady who was unable to communicate with her children any-more! And this is a terrible thing. (…) And that was the first time I realized how traumatic the change must have been for these people, who were completely unable to voice the trauma. They had no choice in Singapore, they had to fall-in-line, and they had to learn, and they had to suffer, and they did it quietly. This is how Singaporeans are. They say the Russian soul is a soul that can take a great deal of suffering. I think that in Singapore we also take a great deal of suffering, we just don't talk very much about it, and we don't have the art to describe that kind of suffering.[40]

The play was not a political commentary per se (on the government's language policies promoting the usage of English and Mandarin over other dialects). It was first and foremost a social commentary, a reflective debate on the social and human consequences of social policies. It was painful for people because by personifying, mirroring, and voicing the social traumas, the audience was forced to empathize with her situation and reflect on their own similar fragmentation.

The mother in the play is socially and physically lost, in addition to their inability to communicate with her when she was still around, her children do not know when and where she has gone to. But what was painful for people is that equally so, the children in the play have lost their own mother in various ways: physically, because they could not communicate and she left home; literally, in that they had lost their own "mother tongue"; and symbolically, since they had lost the roots of their social identity. For those people who watched that production, the play triggered profound questions about the meaning of their life. An interviewee says, for example:

> The kind of questions that he asked in that play related very much to the community, to very simple things like what kind of language should a person learn? And what happens if that language is suddenly removed overnight by the law, which says that you have to only learn and speak another language? What happens to you as a person? What happens to you as a

---

[38] There are four "official languages" in Singapore: English, Mandarin Chinese, Malay, and Tamil. In the past, Singapore's ethnic Chinese population would often speak the Chinese dialect of their forefathers and in the early 1970s, for example, it was possible to find advertisements in the "Classified" section of *The Straits Times* for language classes instructing in Hokkien—a dialect from Fuchien Province in China. In the mid 1970s, the decision was taken by the government that all Chinese instruction, and the national usage of Chinese, would be in Mandarin.

[39] Transcript B/10/7.

[40] Transcript A/4/5.

mother? What happens to you as a grandmother? What happens to you as a human being? (…) Could we have come so far economically, or materially, without making those sacri-fices? I don't know, maybe not. But then you have to ask yourself; *do we really want to come this far? Is this all we want to do in life? Do we want to give up so much to get so much?*[41]

In a similar way, the *Descendants of the Eunuch Admiral*[42] was a painful play because it made people realize that they may have a distorted, malformed self. The play is historically based on the story of the Chinese Great Admiral Zheng-He, an Emperor's eunuch who had reached high rank having helped to extend the empire territorially and who had a lot of power and wealth. But like other eunuchs, the play portrays him as someone whose "life will come to an end after he has lived his own: there would be no after life for his children. Even when he is a great man, a great sailor, a great diplomat, a great soldier, he would forever remain man in limbo, a stranger, a wanderer—and the very end of a long, distinguished lineage of life." The eunuch (having been taken from his family and castrated, was unable to reproduce and have his own family) is hence not only anatomically speaking but more so, socially, symbolically, and emotionally—a castrated, mutilated person.

One such symbolization of this "fragmented self" is described in the play, saying that when eunuchs died, they had to be "reunited" with their cutoff penises, because otherwise in their next life, they "can never come back to the world as a man any-more." The play says:

There are records saying that Zheng-He died in Calicut in India, or on the ship on the way back from his 7th and last expedition to the Western Ocean. Now if that was true, then how could he possibly get his 'treasure' put back in place? So, my discovery is: the great admi-ral, grand Eunuch Zheng-He, despite his very high status, was not buried with his full body! (…) How fragile all these big men and women are—and how temporary and transient is the power, status and authority of these people occupying high positions really are—when we found that a supremely powerful grand eunuch like Zheng-He could end up so pathetically.[43]

Symbolically and metaphorically, the play suggests, in various ways, the dispar-ity and contrast between the social and power status of the Eunuch Admiral and his own physical, social, and symbolic loss of humanity dignity.

The play raises, for reflection, the forms of social and cultural castration—a real-ization that was painful and devastating for people, to say the least. An interviewee has this to say: "it is a very *difficult* play. There is a *deep* message behind it that could be enlarged to the *whole generation of the Chinese* (as us having) no guts, no balls, no courage!"[44]

The play deconstructs taken-for-granted social assumptions with regard to the value of material achievements and suggests that although people may have gained

---

[41] Ibid.

[42] The play is based on the history of Great Admiral Zheng He, a eunuch of the Ming Emperor of China who, over a period of 3 decades, had extended the Emperor's gaze over territories from India to Arabia.

[43] Kuo (1995, pp. 4–5).

[44] Transcript B/8/5.

significant wealth and status, they may have lost a lot in terms of identity and dignity. This self-realization is painful, because it implies that they might have been "distorted" and "disfigured," as an interviewee says:

> (As) we grew wealthier, the wealth made us feel stronger to assert ourselves, and then there was a point when confidence went over into cockiness. We were damn cocky; we are the 'best,' 'we are the most efficient' and all that! And again through the plays we realized how *inadequate* we were, how *nothing* we were![45]

We can therefore say that other than structuring a platform for existential exploration, the plays offer an examination of a particular collective social identity. As such, the plays seem to negotiate the inclusion or exclusion of certain identity components. Through these explorations, some components are revalidated or reintroduced (such as heritage elements, local dialects, historical and cultural background, and others), while other social components are presented as being worthy of reevaluation, reassessment, or exclusion (like material goals, social control, regimentation, and homogenization). The exploration of the social identity definition is achieved both through the thematic issues in the plays as well as the particular form in which the plays are staged (including the usage of a structure which is based on a dilemma, the particular characters presented, the language used on stage, the particular social situation presented).

Kuo is said to have promoted a redefinition of identity by helping people in shifting the point of reference of their own identity formation. Prior to this shift (that according to interviewees occurred around the mid-1980s), there was a tendency to keep looking toward external sources for identity formation. English-speaking interviewees say that they were looking toward the "West"; Chinese-speaking interviewees were looking toward "China"; Peranakan[46] Singaporeans were looking toward both Malaysia and China, and so forth. The main point is that they were all looking to external sources and none were considering their selves (in terms of language, food, culture, mentality, and so forth) as a valid point of reference for their own identity formation. Look, for example, at the following account of a theater practitioner, who is of Chinese descent and was raised in an English-speaking environment:

> We would feel more connection at that time with let's say Madonna, and Michael Jackson, than watching a Chinese movie (...) (we were) just looking at pop music, and Western influence, we would watch an American sitcom, or talk American, and not feel that it's strange for (us). So many of us were not questioning why we were behaving this way, it was natural to us.[47]

However, around the 1980s, interviewees began to have feelings of identity inconsistency. Although they still continued to look toward external sources for

---

[45] Transcript B/10/12.

[46] "Peranakan" is the term applied to Straits-born Chinese people who have adopted some Malay customs. "Peranakan" is a Malay word meaning "descendant." It comes from the root word "anak" meaning "child."

[47] Transcript B/7/3.

self-affirmation, they already vaguely felt the inadequacy of that tendency. An interviewee commented:

> English language is in a sense our first language now and we all use it as a most natural
> language. But yet, a lot of the artistes were aware that this meant that they were discon-
> nected from their own ethnicity, because English is not something that is natural to the
> Chinese people (although) it seems natural to us.[48]

The following interviewee's account shows how his peers' external point of
reference correlated with a sense of fragmented identity:

> We were just growing up and the point of reference was the '*West.*' Life was elsewhere; life
> was not here, so everything here was not real. What was real? London, New York and every-
> thing that was happening there.
> (…) (The) social changes (where Pao Kun's impact was felt were) mainly an arrival at a
> sense of ourselves because just 20 years ago, we were not sure who we really were. As I
> said, life was elsewhere and especially more marked among the elite, life was really else-
> where; London, New York, Europe, and Paris. We had no sense of who we were. There was
> even a certain inferiority complex.[49]

Interviewees say that through Kuo, they began to appreciate "what they were"—
not as a pale imitation of someone else but as someone valuable, authentic, and
unique. This self-validation has consequently relocated the point of reference from
the previous external sources toward the local and their very own "here and now." In
other words, they say that Kuo had a role in the social transformation of the point of
reference for a Singaporean identity definition and formation.

This is not a mere "fine tuning" of identity but a systemic change. The shift from
an external toward an internal source of affirmation and formulation is a change of the
meta-structure for identity formation. Kuo did not advocate Malay, Japanese, French
or, for that matter, any other possible external source. The point of reference has
changed many times in the course of the history of Singapore and to advocate yet
another external source would have been a change *in* the content of identity but not *of*
the way that identity is formed (which, in other words, is a systemic type of change).
Kuo's impact is in helping to create a systemic transformation where the source ceases
to be external (and where there are many such possible sources) and becomes internal
and primordial (where there is only one such possible authentic source).

For the interviewees and the audience, never before was Singapore the locus of
its own identity formation (having for all of its modern history been occupied and
controlled by an external power). This type of change, therefore, deconstructs the
systemic working assumption that Singapore's identity should derive and form
along external forces or sources. At the same time, it reconstructs a new systemic
assumption regarding this place as valid for the formation of identity definition.
A theater practitioner describes a great sense of "self-affirmation" that accompanied
this shift of the reference point in identity formation:

> (For the past 20 years or so) Singapore theater is talking more on our own lives, our own
> culture, backgrounds and our own thinking. And I would say that how this happened would

---

[48] Ibid.

[49] Transcript B/10/7,12.

have to be linked with Mr. KPK.[50] I would say that he is the one who taught us to just like ourselves, rather than just idolize other people. (…) It is like for example if your child is always telling you 'I want to be Brad Pitt,' 'I want to be Keanu Reeves,' and this father comes to you and says; 'you are beautiful as yourself,' 'tell us your own story,' and 'live your own life,' and that kind of things. And it is difficult, it is not as easy as we can think because in Singapore, what we are? We are watching American movies, we are 'little Hollywood,' we eat continental food and we have this 'British' in us, everyone. And then our ancestors, my ancestors come from China and I don't know anything about China.[51]

Self-Affirmation and Validation

Indeed, there is something in Kuo's form of writing that elicits feelings of self-affirmation and self-validation. This may be related to the fact that Kuo's plays are said to focus on "ordinary people" who tell their "very own stories" in their "very own words." The plays do not portray "heroic figures" but tell the tales of ordinary people, like the man who would share with us the trials and tribulations of parking his car, a little girl who is emotionally attached to an old tree, a mother who tries to communicate with her children,[52] a young boy who loves to play with puppets, and other such "ordinary" figures.

What is common to all these figures is that they were able to "talk to us, about *us*." In an interviewee's words:

> It was the first time that ordinary Singaporeans were put on stage and their anxieties, their troubles, their weaknesses, their humanity became something which was interesting, which was worth watching. With Pao Kun, the hero was the ordinary Singaporean. He was the guy who will take a bus, or who might be a taxi-driver, who might be a hawker-seller, but his life became important, the ordinary Singaporean's life became something worthy of being put on stage. Ordinary Singaporean's life became worthy of drama, became worthy of witness in theater. And I think that's very, very significant. I think this is where the consciousness of the Singaporeans really developed to the fullest (…) Pao Kun writes about us, you and I, living in Singapore, and I think that's very, very significant.[53]

Such simple characters reinforce our introspection because we can see ourselves through them, and at the same time, they contribute to our self-validation because we can see that we exist in each one of them. Audiences could empathize and identify with these ordinary people in a way that was not possible with exceptional figures like heroes or the elite.

Interviewees say that Kuo promoted the self-affirmation of the "ordinary Singaporean" through his other projects, for example, the Memory Project in the

---

[50] "KPK" was the interviewee's own abbreviation for Kuo Pao Kun.

[51] Transcript A/2/9.

[52] These three themes can be found in *No Parking on Odd Days* (1986), *The Silly Little Girl and the Old Tree* (1987), and *Mama Is Looking for Her Cat* (1988).

[53] Transcript A/4/4.

Substation.[54] In that initiative, Kuo emphasized the notion that each person's particular existence and perception is meaningful and valid. As part of the Memory Project, the public was invited to contribute articles that were significant to them. These articles were then displayed with written texts that explained what they were and how they were significant and meaningful to their owners.

An interviewee says about this collective exercise, that "this is a very simple way but it makes a person relate (to himself), and every single person's memories counted, and not just always memories from the "godfather." And that space, that path that he has opened up with this project, was really important"[55] for the process of self-reflection and identity formation:

> When he talked about memories, he was not talking about using memories as an art form. He was talking about how memories are important to the *lay man*, to people in the *street*, what it *MEANS* to have memories. You see? It's not just about art, humanities, sociology, its about history; it's about the individual and the society and the country, and *who* and *what* he is! His *identity!* [56]

Through this exercise, he emphasized that it was not only the memories of "heroic figures" or the elite that were worthy of display but that each one's memories—down to the most ordinary of people—was worthy and is meaningful and significant enough to be included in the formation of the collective identity. By way of self-affirmation, this collective exercise promoted a collective social identity that was larger than the self, yet at the same time included and contained (rather than exclusively excluded) the particular individuality of many ordinary people, which together and apart felt, for the first time, socially significant.

The validation of the local was also promoted by Kuo's inclusion of "Singlish" and other local language forms on stage. This inclusive attitude seemed to audiences to be an authentic mirroring or reflection of a "real" slice of their life. The multilingual, multicultural nature of Singaporeans was literally expressed in their own voice and words and was in fact more than a mere authentic reflection of reality—it was a "celebration of the local." The following interviewee expresses how the inclusion of such languages was perceived as a social celebration of their particular social identity:

> I don't know whether anyone before Pao Kun had displayed this consciousness that there are regional variations of Mandarin. And of course the sub-underlying assumption is that they all have their own validity; that they are not to be all downgraded in favor of some hypothetical pure Beijing style Mandarin. People knew that there was such a thing as 'Singlish,' or 'bazaar' language or whatever but they did not treat it with respect, they did not accord it validity.
> He used local language and gave it this recognition, gave it validity, it is like you tell people that their experience is important and that their culture is significant and they are not just a bastardized version of the mother tongue or another central country. It is like saying that your local culture (which is let's say thirty years old, forty years old) has its own validity

---

[54] Between the years 1991 and 1993, Kuo launched a project (within the Substation's programs) that embarked on the recovery and reflection of people's memories, and cognitive and emotional reflections that were *meaningful* for people, focusing on things that are intangible, nonmaterial yet valuable and meaningful to the sense of self.

[55] Transcript B/18/15.

[56] Transcript A/5/4–5.

without having to refer back to Beijing all the time. I presume this is just as big a step for the Mandarin speakers as for the English speakers.[57]

For people, the representation of the "Singaporean" as speaking local dialects was far more coherent and meaningful than representations of Singaporeans using Queen's English or "BBC English," or Beijing Mandarin. The usage of Singlish and other language forms represented the local linguistic versions not only as a "lingua franca" but as a significant and relevant component of a valuable social identity and was, for people, a message that they were worthy, meaningful, and relevant. An interviewee says, "it touched something *very, very deep inside them* that Mandarin can never do, that English can never do"[58] or, in other words, it was a significant validation of the Singaporean culture and psyche.

Implied Deconstruction of the Systemic Assumptions

The inclusion of "ordinary" people in the process of identity formulation is not as simple as it may seem. It contains a quasi-social "drama" with regard to the eligibility to deal with and define the Singaporean social identity. The affirmation of this kind of "simplicity" and "ordinarity" means that it is significant enough to be included in the reconstruction of the "dominant" social identity. Yet the inclusion of many "ordinary" people in the process of such redefinition is squarely juxtaposed to Singapore's paternalistic, authoritarian, sociopolitical practice.

The practice to leave such matters in the hands of a few in power is both grounded on a cultural inclination toward authority and paternalism as well as on the government's policy of confining such issues to what is defined as the political arena.[59] In a social context characterized by paternalism and political centralism, the inclusion of many "ordinary" people is squarely juxtaposed to the dominant systemic working assumptions. The change is not only advocating a larger number of people to be included in the identity definition (which tends to be by the few vs. the many) but also that the criteria for the people who have a decisive voice do not require that they have political power or social status but only by the fact that they are mere "ordinary people" who live here, now.

Also, the staging of Singlish and other local language forms was not sociopolitically trivial. It enfolds an attempt to deconstruct the sociopolitical assumptions with regard to English or Mandarin being the "proper" languages for Singaporeans.[60] Their inclusion

---

[57] Transcript B/5/3.

[58] Transcript B/10/5.

[59] These contextual dimensions were elaborated in Chap. 6.

[60] It was a dramatic government decision to have Singaporeans speak English in order to be competitive in the international economic market. Later on, a similar decision was made in regard to Mandarin, both as a means to unify all Chinese dialects and to be economically viable to deal with China that was opening at that time to the global market. This decision indeed contributed to Singapore's appeal for multinational corporations that could then efficiently communicate with the Singapore labor force. Singaporeans admit that such language was economically "profitable," but lamented its consequences on other dimensions of life.

on the stage contested the social assumption that Singlish and other language forms are not "refined" enough for formal public mediums. Instead of considering them as something to "hide" or confine to the private realms, not worthy of public and official exposure, and something almost to be ashamed of, Kuo pulled them off the "backstage" of the everyday social life. What was previously acknowledged as residing in the "backstage" (in the home, in bazaars, and on the streets but never in official mediums such as TV and radio) was brought right into an "official" social forefront. This act seemed so revolutionary that people treated it as an example of Kuo's ability (as well as tendency) to "push boundaries" and break social "taboos." An interviewee says about it:

> At that time there was no outlet for it in the public arena and it was very private. (It was a) taboo, meaning that on television and on radio you are not allowed to speak dialects (until today, you're still not allowed to do that, and in Singapore, when these are the rules, you don't push it). So someone like Pao Kun always pushes. He always pushes and he has taught the younger artist to push (but the thing is how far you push so that you do not get into trouble). At that time, as we grew up, he pushed, he pushed. There was no (explicit rule against it), but we sort of inferred that if dialect wasn't allowed on TV, on radio, then it probably wouldn't be allowed on stage. But no one questioned that assumption. So there he was doing that, and he was very brave.[61]

The staging of Singlish, as well as the inclusion of "ordinary" people, "negotiated" as it were, the legitimacy of various possible components of social identity as "authentic." It seems to advocate that the "everyday life" (Singlish, Chinese dialects, other languages, and the "trivial" anxieties and problems of ordinary people) is equally significant for the representation and exploration of the Singaporean identity and thus meaningfully reconstructs the social reality.

Similarly, the inclusion of different languages and language forms implies that language itself is a matter of values, social meaning, and identity. This assumption is squarely juxtaposed with the perception of language as a matter of rational, instrumental, and pragmatic calculations and policies. It implicitly advocates that language has a deeper meaning that cannot be subjugated to arbitrary, current, or future pragmatic goals or needs because it is the very essence of social and self-identity. As such, it cannot be changed randomly or instrumentally without destroying vital parts of social identity and meaning.

Such underlying assumptions collided with the systemic implementation of the policies to speak languages (like English or Mandarin) for the purpose of promoting instrumental (economic) goals. While such policies regard language as instrumental (and thus carry the potential to keep changing the particular language at any time), Kuo's underlying messages tried to reconstruct the notion of language as that of being inseparable from a people's social identity.

In conclusion, it seems that Kuo's plays offer to his audiences a platform for existential exploration and, through that, promoted the possibility of reconstructing the self and the collective social identity. These plays enable a platform for self-reflection that includes positive self-validation and affirmation (by this implying the inclusion of certain identity elements), as well as painful realizations to be

---

[61] Transcript B/10/6, 7.

reconsidered (and by implying the exclusion of other elements). On the whole, the plays are a medium for social discourse, negotiation and redefinition of the social meaning, significance and relevance of various elements to the formation of the self and collective social identity.

Sister Prema: Concretizing and Socializing Spiritualism

A long-term volunteer in Prema's Heart to Heart service asked her to be a witness in his marriage registration. His reason was because he wanted her to be with him and his wife that special day. He says:

> Apart from the tremendous respect for her, we wanted her blessing for our marriage, and we wanted that her presence will serve as a reminder for us in every anniversary. Every year we will remember the things that she does, to whom she helps. And it would be a reminder of a moral example of a human kind…(and) every year, at least once a year, in our anniversary, she will be there as a 'judge' and we will ask ourselves what have we done over that year. You can visualize her standing there and asking: 'O.K., over the last year, what have you done, both in the worldly life and in the spiritual?'[62]

The use of words such as "judge," "reminder," and "moral example" imply that Prema is, for this interviewee, a "role model of morality," with which he can reflect, measure, and redirect his life.

A similar perception is described by a journalist from *Her World* magazine who interviewed Sister Prema in April 2000, on the occasion of Prema's special award as "The Woman of the Year." Sharing with her readers an account of how she felt while conducting the interview, we notice how Prema's presence elicits in the journalist a kind of moral self-awareness and self-reflection. When Sister Prema asked her, "What is it you want to ask me?" the journalist recalls her sense that "For a moment I feel I am at Virgil's Mouth of Truth, about to have a finger bitten off for not being true."[63]

Such a feeling is not only an expression of awe, but an expression of being morally self-aware. The more the journalist hears about Prema's frugal lifestyle and lifetime devotion to the needy, the more her uneasiness grows, implying by that an inner accountability of the way she lives her own life. She says:

> All this talk about religion disarms me. I attribute my uneasiness with this saint-like creature to my self-absorbed world of bills, back-stabbing friends and postnatal cellulite. Suddenly, the cashmere cardigan on my shoulders feels heavy, and the 'Yves St Laurent' gloss sticks uncomfortably to my lips.[64]

Prema's days are taken up not only by the daily running of the Heart to Heart service but also by many personal requests for appointments. People ask to come

---

[62] Transcript E/8/7–8.

[63] *Her World* magazine April 2000, p. 178.

[64] Ibid., p. 180.

and talk to her, and generally, these talks deal with the person's dilemmas in implementing spiritual notions in the realm of the everyday life.[65] A volunteer says:

> I turn to her for advice, because in this world you have to balance between the spiritual part
> and the worldly part. So, the best person to ask is a person who has some knowledge in
> spirituality—so that he can guide you when you are doing worldly work, if you are still
> maintaining your spiritual discipline. So that is very important. I can ask anyone (for advice)
> but they will give me comments on how to make more money, and all this—but this does
> not protect my spiritual discipline, and I should not neglect my spiritual discipline.[66]

Interviewees say that Sister Prema reinforces self-reflection, soul-searching, and a moral account on the meaning of their life. Furthermore, they relate to this "soul-searching" as an element that had played a role in the transformation of their own lives. An interviewee says, for example, "I used to think that 'we just live and make a living,' and I never asked if there is anything *beyond that*. But after having met her, I understood that there should be a *purpose in this life*, and that you are here not only to work and just go on with your life."[67]

People use words such as "purpose," "direction," "rethink" and "understand," implying Prema's agency in the process of self-search, particularly in the search for meaning. It is in this respect that people say, "whenever I meet her she brings us back to the ground, makes us rethink about our spending and makes us sit-back and think about ourselves and our direction in life. She makes us think about the other non-materialistic (spiritual) things in life."[68]

Another general pattern pertaining to the stories that come from Prema's volunteers is that they all have a similar ending, one that points at the fact that they eventually "found more meaning for their life." Their stories typically end by saying: "I came to find out more about the meaning of life," "it made my life more fulfilling and meaningful," and other similar expressions. In other words, they all describe a personal transformation of their life, a change that made them feel more contented, saying things such as, "we are now happy" or "generally I am more happy."[69]

But all this begs a question: Was Prema the sole cause in triggering the soul-searching process, self-reflection, and the finding of meaning and happiness?

A Predisposition to Existential Quests

It is of significance that many of the people who joined Prema's Heart to Heart social service mention that, prior to their joining, they were already in a cognitive

---

[65] For example, an interviewee said that he even came for Prema's advice in regard to the frequency of sex that people should have. (That is in spite of the fact that Prema herself avoids sexual activities). Her advice was: "if it is a spiritual husband then twice a month should be enough. Otherwise he wastes energy that should be spent on spirituality" (Transcript E/9/7).

[66] Transcript E/3/12.

[67] Transcript E/8/3.

[68] Transcript E/16/4.

[69] Examples of this can be found in transcripts E/3/4, E/20/4, E/7/1, and E/10/5.

and emotional state of "looking for the meaning of life." For some, the search for meaning was triggered by events (that could be negative or positive) that led to a general feeling of disorientation. For example, an interviewee links the search for meaning to her mother's passing away, saying; "In '93–'94 I had a feeling that there is *more to life*. It had to do with me coming to *think about life*, because when my mother was dying, I suddenly realized that *everyone dies in the end*, and it was a trigger to think about the *meaning of life* and how we really ought to live them."[70] Others do not link their trigger for existential reflections to a specific negative event. One volunteer, for example, says, "after having fulfilled social expectations like academic education, marriage, children and a good career, I was asking myself, what is the meaning of my life? I got all these things; I got good education, all these things, but what is the next step? What is the meaning of my life?"[71]

Not all the interviewees point at a concrete moment or event (whether negative or positive) as the trigger for such a search. Some point toward a general sense of dissatisfaction in spite of having accomplished various achievements. Such volunteers describe having had a general feeling of "disorientation," using words such as "emptiness" and "meaninglessness." Such words suggest a state of "existential anxiety,"[72] of not knowing exactly who and what they are, and what they really ought to be and do.

This anxiety was more or less a chronic state of dissatisfaction and disorientation as expressed, for example, by an interviewee saying: "I wanted to know, I was looking for answers for questions like 'Who am I? Why am I here? Where will I go when I die? Is there a God?' I wanted to do more and know more. Somehow I was not satisfied; I felt that there should be more! Life should be more!"[73] Similarly, another says that the search for meaning "was related generally to the way of life, that you do all sorts of things, but you still feel meaninglessness and emptiness. And it was more like I wanted to check more about life."[74]

People say that this soul-searching process ledness them to engage in substantial reading. The books that they read were not confined to a particular religion but were "spiritual" and metaphysical in that they dealt with notions about the nature of existence, particularly about the relations between the self and the world (in a transcendental sense). This vast combing of various religious corpuses was an expression of their eagerness to find meaning. An interviewee says, for example, "I started to read on God, on Yoga, on Buddha, on spiritualism, Christianity, Confucianism, every book that I could put my hand on. Because I wanted to know. I was looking for answers to questions like who am I?"[75]

---

[70] Transcript E/1/9, 11.

[71] Transcript E/15/1.

[72] According to Erikson's typology (1967), such a condition would be considered as a type of crisis that makes people "charisma hungry."

[73] Transcript E/14/4.

[74] Transcript E/19/2.

[75] Transcript E/14/3.

Hence, Prema's volunteers were probably in a "reflective" predisposition prior to their joining the Heart to Heart social service. Their search was consonant with this social service's spiritual notions because, as we have elaborated in the previous chapters' presentation of Prema's unique ideas, the social service's underlying ideology addressed questions such as "Who are we?," "Who is God?," "What is life?," "What is the world?," and "What is society?"

However, such existential notions were incorporated in all the other religious books that the volunteers read and chose to follow.[76] So what was in Prema's social service that people could not find in the written metaphysical, religious texts? What was missing in those spiritual texts that Prema's Heart to Heart social service offers?

Engaging the Particular, Subjective Self in Social Action

Prema's social service was not the sole source of the "meaning of life" that volunteers had gained. Rather, she and the social service are said to complement in some ways, the religious and spiritual systems that people have chosen to practice (following their "soul-search" and quest for meaning). Prema had a significant role in the concretization of the metaphysical spiritual notions that they encountered in their chosen religions. In other words, Prema contributed to the people's finding of the "meaning of life" by helping them to adjust, adapt, concretize, and customize the abstract metaphysical religious notions to their own particular cases. In that respect, she offered a bridge or link between the transcendental spiritual notions and their individual implementations.

One such volunteer, for example, says that Prema had a role in her own construction of meaning and mission in life:

> I was searching for the meaning of life, what is my mission, what am I doing in this life. And every time I met Prema, she gave me some clarification of thoughts and ideas. I needed her advice in my search of meaning of life. After my search I found what is my mission. She helped me to find it. She did not point exactly at it, but she helped me to find it through our conversations, and through what she is doing. After a few months of talks with her I found my (own) mission in life.[77]

It seems that Prema helped by linking abstract spiritual notions with possible particular, individualized implementations and adaptations. In other words, the clarification of the metaphysical notions was not achieved by the solitary reading of books but through an interactive social process that included conversations and advice. Such clarification required that the person referred to is considered as an

---

[76]Most of the volunteers link the "reactivation" of their own belief systems or disciplines (like Buddhism, Taosim, Hinduism, Christianity, Yoga) to a sense of existential meaning. Their "turning" to religions enabled a kind of existential framework, but they all sensed that, although it gave some answers and directions, it did not fully turn their life into something meaningful. In other words, there was still a need for a well-rounded sense of meaning.

[77]Transcript E/15/2.

epistemological authority in various religions, or considered (as Prema is) a "spiritual guru."

Such spiritual attributions legitimized, in people's eyes, Prema's role in the practical interpretation, concretization, and mundane adaptations of the metaphysical, religious, spiritual, and abstract notions. In one such case, Prema helped a volunteer to interpret and translate the metaphysical notion of "God" into the particular idea of "Mother Earth's" preservation (in the "Green movement"). This interpretation has also retained for the volunteer the spiritual notion of "loving God"—as an equation for "loving his creations" (of which "Mother Earth" happens to be one). Together with Prema, the volunteer was able to "personalize" and particularize the abstract metaphysical notion of "God" in a way that was meaningful for her and consistent with her own beliefs.

We can see another example of the importance of particularization in the following interviewee. He says that although he was previously inclined to do social service work because of his religion (in his case, Buddhism), it was only when this notion was internalized that charity work became meaningful. In other words, it was only when his own particular self was engaged that the spiritual notions were internalized and accorded meaning. This process may imply that the construction of meaning requires a particularization that is relevant to each individual's idiosyncratic self. The interviewee says:

> (The social service) *made my life more fulfilling and meaningful.* Before, if I had any spare time, I would ask myself how to spend the time and how to enjoy by going out and hanging around. But today, if I have time I prefer to go and help others, and this *gives a meaning to my life.* And sister Prema has *inspired* me to do that, although in the beginning, Buddhism pushed me to do the charity work. Today, I know in *my heart, inside,* that *I* want to do this, *myself.* Now it *comes from me, inside.*[78]

Here, words such as "comes from me," "inside," "my heart," and "myself" all imply that it is only when the metaphysical ideas had been internalized and the self has been engaged that they had the power to transform the self and construct a new, meaningful reality.

Other than Prema's role in adapting and "customizing" abstract spiritual notions to particular individuals, we can ask the question: What was the social service's role in the "internalization" of ideas and in the gaining of meaning in their lives?

People who join Prema's work indeed came already with an inclination toward social service. Some say that they were inclined by their own religious doctrines to appreciate such service. For example, some cite Christianity's notion of "love and compassion" as a basis for charity work, Buddhists cite the notion of "service to humanity" as implying social and charity work, Hindus refer to the notion of "karma and reincarnation" as suggesting charity work, and practitioners of Yoga mention the notion of "self-perfection" as pointing toward social welfare service.

Yet although most volunteers had a previous inclination to do charity work, it was only when they joined Prema's social service that they really "understood" the meaning of these metaphysical notions. People refer to a "deeper understanding"

---

[78] Transcript E/20/4.

gained from their actual participation in her social service. For example, the following volunteer had feelings of "meaninglessness and emptiness"—feelings that had driven him to "check more about life."[79] He read a lot of Buddhists texts and came to hear a tape recording of a talk that Sister Prema had given in the Buddhist library back in September 1991. What he had read related to "charity through the Buddhist notion of 'service to humanity'," but it was only through Prema's emphasis on action that he "really understood" the abstract written texts. He says:

> I am a Buddhist. I'm interested in the philosophy of Buddha's teachings. I was interested in Prema because she puts Buddha's teachings into action. Although she is not a Buddhist, for me—she is the *embodiment of compassion*. I read a lot and learned about Buddhism from books, *all* my studies were from books, all in black and white—but she put Buddha's teaching *into action*.

This may imply that meaning and understanding are not independent but embedded in social action and that alternative ideas or constructions become subjectively meaningful and understood only when the particular, subjective self is actively engaged in action. In other words, it is through the actual, active participation that a subjective, "deep understanding" of the ideas are experienced as coming from "inside."

Indeed, volunteers say, for example, that "this kind of things you cannot learn from books, you have to *do* it yourself."[80] In that sense, we should note which words the following volunteer uses to describe the degree to which he internalized the ideas:

> For 3–4 years we went once a month to visit these people, bringing with us food and money for bills like water, electricity, school fees, rental and so on. And when you are actually doing—it gives you a different feeling. It is different from seeing it in the streets and not really realizing it. When you see it in your own eyes—(you understand that) that is really all! This is it! One room, one kitchen, five children, one mother and all children go to school!—You feel very much that every human being, as a human being, you have a duty to watch your fellowmen. So when you can, when you are not busy with your family—we should look after these people. Before we met her we knew all these things, but we did not feel strongly about it. After being with her, it penetrates to the awareness, to the consciousness in such a way that you yourself want to contribute and give a hand to help.[81]

Instead of simply "knowing," he uses words such as "different feeling" and "feeling strongly" to express how deep the understanding has gone. Also, his usage of words such as "penetration," "awareness," and "consciousness" imply a process of subjective internalization and the penetration of the idea to the realm of awareness and consciousness, subsequently leading to a deeper experience of "understanding."[82] The use of phrases like "duty to watch," "should look after," and "contribute and give a hand" can also be seen as indications of the degree to which ideas were internalized because the deep internalization is then correlated with the volunteer's increase of personal commitment to *do* social charity and service work.

---

[79] Transcript E/19/1.

[80] Transcript E/17/3.

[81] Transcript E/8/3.

[82] This implies that joining Prema's social service is not only a symptom of the personalized interpretation of metaphysical ideas but also further internalizes the ideas by intensifying the measure of the understanding and the acceptance of the ideas.

Indeed, following the subjective internalization of the notion of "helping the needy," many volunteers further enlarged the scope and spectrum of their social welfare voluntary work. One volunteer says that in addition to having gained a more enjoyable, fulfilling life, he has also become more committed to social work. Notice how for him the "meaning of life" is intertwined with an active participation in and an increased commitment to social work. He says:

> In a way, I am grateful because she provided for me an opportunity to help, because some-times you feel you want to help but you do not know how. After we started to help, the *more* we did, the *more* we helped—the *more* we enjoyed. So much so that after some time *we started to look for other areas to help*. In this respect, this is how my life has changed, and I feel happier, definitely! And this is a contradiction to human nature, because you would think that when you are sacrificing for others—you would feel miserable, but in fact the more you help others—you feel *more happiness and joy!* And this had *changed my life*, and it makes my life more *fulfilling*.[83]

For this volunteer, the personal transformation from having a "meaningless and empty" life to a life that is "joyful," "happy," and "fulfilling" takes place simultane-ously with his growth of commitment. He moved from a point of vague, "formless," inclination to charity work to a point where he personally searched for additional areas of social service.

Many of the interviewees describe a similar pattern of increased commitment to social charity work. For example, among those who used to help to carry the monthly distributions to the needy, some started buying the required provisions for the monthly distributions (like rice, sugar, and oil), as well as donating money for that purpose. Another couple of volunteers began to collect vegetable leftovers from the weekly Friday market to distribute to various old folk's homes. On Sundays, this couple collects pastry leftovers from a hotel's Sunday high tea and distributes them among foreign construction workers from countries like Sri Lanka, Thailand, and Bangladesh, and from time to time, they also help to cook free public meals for old people. Similarly, other volunteers say that, in addition to their work with Prema, they started to support people in need, like sick people needing surgery, children from single-parent families, and so forth.

All these *additional* acts of personalized social service are not within Prema's social service, but people say that the increase in their personal commitment and the desire to "do more" originated from their experiences with Prema's social service. The increase in their commitment and social action can, in fact, be seen as indica-tions of the depth of the "subjective understanding" gained by those who joined Prema's social service.

Bridging the Spiritual and the Mundane

Prema's social service is literally a very "down-to-earth," "nitty-gritty" form of social action. There is nothing glamorous or spiritual about people gathering clothes,

---

[83] Transcript E/19/4.

food, and money and distributing them among the poor. Neither is it glamorous to spend their Sundays carrying heavy parcels for poor people, many of whom are old, frustrated, lonely, and at times "very demanding, and hard to satisfy."[84] It is a gray job, to say the least. Yet for Prema's social service volunteers, these actions are accorded meaning. They provide an existential expression of "who they are" and, consequently, of what the "mission" in their life is.

Notwithstanding the volunteer's particular religions and cutting across those different religious backgrounds, they all see in Prema's social service the ultimate implementation of their own particular religious notions. Volunteers say that she is "the embodiment" or "the personification" of their own basic religious notions. For example, Buddhists say that "her social service practice is totally based on Buddhism" and that "she is a personification of Buddhism"; Hindu volunteers say that her actions show that "she is a 'Bodhisattva,' a reincarnation" and that her service is a practice of "karmic and self-purification" notions; Christian volunteers say that her social service and she herself are a "personification of compassion" (as a core notion in Christianity); and practitioners of Yoga say that she is a practical realization of the Yogic notions of "selfless service" and of "service to humanity and service to God."[85] Cutting across religions and ways of life, different people feel that Prema's Heart to Heart social service offers a concrete implementation of abstract notions with regard to the self and the metaphysical world.

It is also possible that Prema is seen by the volunteers as a bridge between the unbridgeable—the spiritual and the mundane—and that their participation helps them build a link between metaphysical religious notions and their everyday, perhaps mundane, lives. Prema's own lifestyle seems to reinforce the connection between the spiritual and the mundane social world. That lifestyle, bearing as it does a striking affinity to a "monk's lifestyle,"[86] promotes the idea that spiritualism is (or should be) an integral part of the everyday, social, secular world. Just as the monks do, Prema renounces all possessions and expects lay generosity to provide the supplies necessary for her subsistence: clothing, food, shelter, and medicine. In her daily life, she rises very early and devotes herself to meditation, and, twice a month at least, fasts. Other similar practices relate to the avoidance of sexual activity and to dietary practices; she is a vegetarian, eats very small portions, and no nourishment is taken after midday except liquids.

Indeed, there is nothing new in following a monastic lifestyle, but its integration with everyday life constructs the possibility of a convergence between two seemingly juxtaposed realms. Her practice uproots the lifestyle of the monk from the sacredness

---

[84] People say that the rate of people burning out is high among those who do social service work. Volunteers say, for example: "those people are very difficult people to deal with because they are very bitter and angry and frustrated" (Transcript E/5/1) or "It is very difficult to do charity. You get burned out very fast. They are not easy people, they are frustrated and unhappy, so they are demanding and it is hard to keep on doing it (...) actually in her Prema's case it is very difficult to be compassionate because some of the old folks can be very demanding" (Transcript E/17/3).

[85] Examples of this can be found in transcripts E/1/1, 4; E/13/2; E/14/2; E/9/5; and E/14/2.

[86] See Bunnang (1984, pp. 159–170).

of the monastery's institutional system, and implicitly, by relocating it in the social world, it reconstructs a kind of spiritualism that is not ascetic and reclusive but actively immersed in "this" (literally, "down to earth") world. By following a monastic lifestyle within the everyday community, Prema seems to articulate the notion that spiritualism does not solely reside in religious institutions but is in our very simple social life. Hence, for people, Prema's social service (and her own lifestyle) constructs a substantial connection—a link between the metaphysical realm and the social world. Such a social interpretation of spiritual notions offers an experience that meaningfully engages the self by integrating it with both the spiritual and the social.

For volunteers, spiritual self-realization can therefore be achieved through active participation in the nitty-gritty of everyday life. This is in fact a reconstruction of the notion of spiritualism—not as secluded, untouchable, and divine—but as one that is intrinsically embedded in social action. Such a construction is directly juxtaposed to the ascetic, reclusive tendency of people who practice spiritual notions and offers a very practical, action-driven translation and implementation of spiritualism.[87]

This alternative reconstruction of spiritualism is reinforced by Prema's own behavior and beliefs. She believes in action. A volunteer says that Prema "thinks that there are no limits to what she can do and that she is full of this 'can do' spirit."[88] Indeed, Prema would usually say to others, as she did in February 1998, in her monthly meeting of the volunteers, "don't talk about it. Just do it." To those who try to understand her philosophy, she suggests a very simple way: "you watch, you do, you understand."[89] In Prema's view of things, "real" understanding of the underlying notions follows action and is not prior to that. It is in this respect that volunteers say that "she inspires by her example, by her action: You see her. You do. You learn." A volunteer says that before she joined Prema's social service she occasionally contributed money and thought about helping the needy, "but Prema made my thoughts meet my *physical body* and caused my body to work as well!"[90] Similarly, another volunteer says:

> Through all the years, I have been sending money to charity. But this was the first time that I did physical effort. I always donated money, I was very liberal with money and it was very easy for me to give away money. But I was very stingy with my time and physical effort. And it was she, who made me understand the importance of practically spending time and effort in doing charity.[91]

---

[87] This type of charisma is what Marcus (1969) would have called "transcendental charisma." He argued that there exists a particular type of transcendental charisma, one that is "in contrast to various movements of withdrawal, (but) is identified with participation, and that seeks its goal within time." According to Marcus, such charismatic leader "finds the 'break-through' in the individual's contribution to the purposes of history," and "focuses his quest for transcendence back into worldly and social activism" (1969, pp. 236–237).

[88] Transcript E/10/4.

[89] The simplicity of her approach and the obviousness of it to her was the probable reason why Prema was irritated by our research. She told other followers about the research interviews and said of the interviewer: "why does she need to ask so many questions, so many people? It is very simple: there are many people in need, and we have to help. Why can't she understand?"

[90] Transcript E/5/5.

[91] Transcript E/10/3.

Prema seldom engages in talks, discussions, or polemics. She quietly and subtly helps people with hardly anyone knowing about it. Volunteers say that she never "talks" about it. A long-term volunteer says: "her role is very subtle, she is playing a very subtle role, she doesn't talk, she is very subtle. She does not publicize herself, does not advertise herself."[92] When she does talk, however, she consistently emphasizes action. This is reflected also in the fact that her philosophical and spiritual comments generally end up with a "doing" emphasis (and more particularly, "doing charity work"). She therefore would conclude a comment on the meaning of reincarnation by saying, for example: "(...) *and now I know what I have to do*. And what I have to do is to put my head down, go forward and do it, and do it, and do and do."[93] Similarly she would rather conclude a comment on the human notion of "brotherhood," saying: "(...) so my thought became universal—everybody who needs—and I can help—it is my *duty to go and help*"[94] or would conclude a comment on the philosophical and social notions of "sharing," saying that "Only when I do that (sharing)—that I am part of the great good nature."[95]

Consequently, however secular and as mundane a social service can be, for Prema's volunteers, the experience of helping needy people is a practical expression of spiritual and existential notions. Volunteers say, for example, that eventually, "You feel very much that every *human being*, you have a duty to watch your fellow men (...) (and that) helps you understand more about *life, human beings*, and even about *yourself*."[96] Others say that helping needy people without expecting any recognition, gratitude, or return is an expression of the understanding of human beings as "brothers" because: "You treat everyone as brothers and sisters, and this is really a fundamental basis of the world."[97] For others, helping old, lonely, and frustrated people is an expression of "pure love and compassion to humanity."[98] And yet, for other volunteers, mere helping is an expression of "love" and "care," and therefore helping old, poor, frustrated people (as part of God's creation) is a concrete implementation or expression of "loving God."[99]

---

[92] Transcript E/3/14.

[93] 1995: 18/90–100.

[94] 1995: 5/203.

[95] 1995: 14/344.

[96] Transcript E/8/3.

[97] Transcript E/1/4.

[98] Transcript E/4/2.

[99] A volunteer says, for example: "service to God is service to humanity. To love God means to service humanity. It goes in parallel...if you have love for God—you have love for his created beings. It means that you can see God in each created being. It is one of the ways to show your love to God, to express your love to God" (E/6/2–3). In a similar way, for a Hindu volunteer, helping the needy is a practical implementation of the belief in self-purification and perfection that his belief system preaches about. He says that "As a Hindu, I believe that we are part of God, and we are here to learn and correct, so that we will be able to unite with him. And as long as we will not learn and correct ourselves, we will have to come back to this life again and again. So if I correct myself in this life (by helping the needy), I will not have to come back to this world, and I will be able to unite with God" (E/10/5).

There is evidence for a prior disposition for a search for identity and meaning among Prema's volunteers, which implies that Prema did not trigger the soul-searching processes but complemented it by enabling individual adaptation and a particular customization of abstract and spiritual notions.

It also seems that, for Prema's volunteers, the participation in the Heart to Heart social service resembles a purifying and uplifting experience or, in other words, it is perceived as spiritually meaningful. The combination that the service offers—of concrete human activity with an orientation to what is perceived as the "sources of being" and human existence—constructs social meaning and creates for the followers a *sense of being, doing and borrowing* at the active center of a symbolic order where self, society, and the cosmos coherently blend.

Prema's social welfare service also seems to offer a convergence of seemingly juxtaposing realms. It offers a meaningful link between the metaphysical, the abstract, and the spiritual—and the mundane, the practical, and the active, and this link seems to intrinsically engage each individual's self within the social as well as the metaphysical world.

Tay Kheng Soon: The Expansion and Contextualization of Architecture

Architects who were influenced by Tay's ideas (mostly the younger generation of architects) describe an expansion of their professional self-definition, followed by a symbolic expansion of the "self." This symbolic professional expansion offered a social meaning that, in particular, enabled an exploration and expression of the nature of relations between "society" and "place." The following analysis will attempt to show how both expansions—the professional and the symbolic—developed and how these two expansions correlate with one another.

Interviewees say that "Tay did a lot for the profession[100] by looking at the profession: what it is, what kind of work architects are doing, and the process that it involves."[101] Some say that:

> Tay is a very deep thinker in relation to architecture itself, in examining architectural trends, architectural forms, pedagogy of architecture and so on. He is very stimulating to talk to

---

[100] It is peculiar that architects use the words, the "voice" of the profession (e.g., D/8/1; D/13/6; D/16/14; D/18/3, 10) when referring to Tay. It may literally imply Tay's tendency to explore issues of concern to the profession (its content, process, training methods, and others). It may symbolically express his stature in the community (e.g., people say that he is "guarded quite as a sort of icon, one of the towering architectural figures," D/8/12). And it may figuratively express Tay's tendency for very vocal articulations of his views on various diverse issues. In a "parodic" self-reflection, Tay commented on his tendency to react to many issues, saying: "there is this concept of '*kaypoh*.' *Kaypoh* means 'busybody'—the image of a loud-mouthed housewife, who interferes in, who interjects, who makes her views and comments very loud and interferes with people's affairs. And that is regarded as very, very degrading or downgraded to take on that kind of role in society. It is reprehensible. So I am a *kaypoh*, I am a very big *kaypoh*!" (T/5/6–7).

[101] Transcript D/17/10.

when it comes to issues of that nature. He is able to categorize thoughts, and ideas, and to be able to examine those categories; and compare those categories with other categories and with life examples, so that the thought or idea are put into perspective, in a context.[102]

An interviewee says that there is "a core group that sees Tay as someone with great passion and great love for the profession, trying to push very hard for it to move and change, to take a quantum leap so to speak."[103] Indeed, "at the end of it all, architects do look at him as a person who has contributed tremendously to the profession in many ways."[104] Others would add that he has influenced the profession's status,[105] saying, "he has changed the status of the profession by defining what the profession means and some of the things that can be done by the profession."[106]

Stimulating Thinking

By and large, the interviewees source the roots of Tay's influence to the style and the content of his thinking. They say that he has a "deep thinking" and an ability to "see the big picture."[107] An architect who talked about his working experience with Tay described the impact of Tay's thinking in the following way:

When I worked with him, I have found it immensely frustrating at times but also very immensely rewarding because he will not dwell on core thing for far two long, he is constantly

---

[102] Transcript D/1/12.

[103] Transcript D/16/6.

[104] This quotation is taken from transcript D/6/6. Indeed, many interviewees refer to his reports when he was president of the Singapore Institute of Architects (1991–1992). For example, they say that his survey on the bidding process resulted, for example, in a fixed fee scale, so as not to create a downward spiral where the cheapest work (rather than the best work) wins. Another example cited by people is his report on the economic cycles of the private firms, experiencing very deep troughs at the top and the bottom of economic cycles, causing eventually to a loss of expertise and quality work (due to the need to constantly recruit and train new people). People cite this report as one that managed to convince the government (as the biggest developer) to hand a portion of the work usually given to the public sector—to private firms.

[105] A possible social implication of the profession's improvement of social status may be seen by the fact that people say that architecture as a profession has gained "a say" in social issues: "(Tay) has put the professional organization (the Singapore Institute of Architects)—on the map" (D/8/3). The professional organization gained social power not only in terms of its larger size and membership but more importantly, because it gained a consultative role in social issues. An interviewee says, for example: "With him and several others, it came across as an organization with ideas that should be consulted. He was one of the most articulate of the members of Singapore Institute of Architects…(and it is) today actually one of the largest professional organizations (…) and one of the most respectable organizations here as well. They are given a place in committees, which are set up to solicit representation from professional organizations. I don't think that kind of due recognition would be accorded to an organization automatically. They earned it" (D/8/3). Also, the fact that an interviewee who used to be the president of the Singapore Institute of Architects says that the number of applicants to study architecture, as well as their academic profile, has risen over the last few years, which may support this argument (D/16/14).

[106] Transcript D/17/10.

[107] These examples are in transcripts D/1/4 and D/1/7.

thinking of new ideas (…) It's a constant creative method, he was constantly thinking, thinking about something, concretizing it into built forms, tearing it apart again and another idea, concretizing that, tearing it apart again and moving on, in that sort of a process which is a little bit refreshing, it's an invigorating method.[108]

To use our interviewees' words, this kind of thinking is "refreshing," "invigorating," "provoking," and "mind blowing," and it "triggers thinking," "raises consciousness," "stimulates," causes "rethinking" and other similar terms.[109] By and large, this kind of thinking is felt as being "bigger"/"higher"/"broader"—terms that imply a sense of expansion. Particularly, it implies a process of cognitive expansion, in which people's minds expand and reach out to "unknown territories," so to speak.

However, the ability to see a "bigger picture" is not only admired but also used by people to mold and form their own definition of what architecture should be. For example, we can see how the following architect correlates Tay's "thinking style" to a professional role modeling:

It is that process (of thinking, rethinking and pushing the discussion) that is very enduring for people, because we actually keep on thinking about and proving things, finding ways to solve problems. (…) And this is something that is consistent with what architecture should be doing: Always finding out new ways to look at things and improve. And this needs someone who is really well versed with quite a lot of things; construction, technology, science, everything. And that is why Kheng Soon is a model of 'a good architect'—because he is what he is—and he looks at many things in life and takes note of everything. (So he is a model) for a lot of people.[110]

An architect who used to work with Tay recalls that the firm is "run very much like a think-tank,"[111] referring not only to the style of thinking but also to the content as one that encompasses a large canvas of diverse disciplines. Another architect in Tay's firm describes the firm's design's perception as working, "not in a very narrow sense but in a much more comprehensive manner, a manner that encompasses various diverse issues." For example, he says that their "design encompasses social aspects, cultural aspects and political aspects (…) lifestyles, space, climate, geometry and landscape."[112]

Venturing into Other Disciplines

Architecture, redefined as such, encompasses a broader spectrum that includes various and diverse additional dimensions and disciplines. To a large extent, the introduction of such dimensions as relevant to architecture is based on an inclusive

---

[108] Transcript D/13/3–4.

[109] These examples are from transcripts D/13/4; D/13/4; D/17/6; D/18/18; D/16/1; D/18/1, 3; D/15/2; and D/2/12.

[110] Transcript D/17/3.

[111] Transcript D/18/9.

[112] These two quotations are from Robert Powell (1997). op. cit., p. 25.

(rather than an exclusive) attitude that invites and opens (rather than closes) the boundaries of the profession.

Trying to characterize the nature of the professional expansion, we can generally divide the various dimensions that Tay has reintroduced to architecture into two broad areas. One area would include fields such as economy, sociology, politics, culture, and history, which we can refer to as social dimensions. The other realm would include fields such as ecology, geography, and climate, which we can refer to as environmental or physical dimensions.

Examples of such inclusions can be seen in the sociological aspects that Tay includes in the architectural treatment of the kind of "loud architecture" favored by the new middle class—the "nouveau-riche,"[113] the economic advances of including small and medium local enterprises and their particular social and cultural contribution to the "intrinsic identity in containing our essence,"[114] the inclusion of historical and heritage dimensions in the architectural discussion of urban conservation,[115] the inclusion of cultural and national identity dimensions in architectural discussions,[116] and so forth. One such concrete example of the way that cultural and social dimensions intersect with architecture can be seen in his treatment of the design plans of the Singapore Arts Center (SAC). To take a short passage by way of example, note how the architectural design is intrinsically embedded with symbolic and social identity issues:

> The few concessions to local features do not detract from the modernist stance of the design…But all this still begs the question: What should an Asian arts center in Singapore at this time be architecturally? As far as I can see, this is still an open question. The present design inspires no clarification of this central question. Moreover, what message it may have is distracted by the large globular structures, which dominate the appearance. The large lumps obscure in more ways than one…On the cultural symbolic plane of reckoning the acceptance of the dominance of the hall structures is symbolic of an implicit acceptance of the dominance of western arts in the consciousness. That the huge structures were allowed to overshadow actually and symbolically the diminutive Asian arts performances spaces and received no effective correction in the design is demonstrative of either a timidity and/or an insufficient consciousness of the importance of this as a cultural issue (…) And, in an unintended way, this disparity between East and West is, unfortunately, to be endorsed culturally through the mere building of the SAC in the manner designed.[117]

---

[113] See, for example, "Wah, so Obiang One," *The Straits Times*, 28 Mar 1990; or "Architectural crisis of Singapore's new middle-class?" *The Straits Times*, 16 Dec 1993; or a paper on "The Tropical City—Cultural Implications of High Density Development," at the PAM-AKP International Conference, Kuala Lumpur, 1985.

[114] See Tay (1994, p. 162).

[115] See, for example, Tay's (1990) paper on "Heritage Conservation—Political and Social Implications: The Case of Singapore" at the international conference on "Heritage and Conservation and Challenges to Asia/Pacific Basin," Darwin, Australia.

[116] See, for example, Tay (1990, 1991).

[117] *The Straits Times*, 30 Jul 1994.

It is evident that, for Tay, the SAC project should force architects to consider many societal, cultural, and artistic issues over and above the technical concerns of architecture and that for him "the project brings up deep issues of cultural aware- ness, cultural innovation and expression of the national psyche and identity."[118] Hence, the perception of the building is that "it is not just another building, it is stimulating a national creative consciousness, (and) a critical moment in the history of a nation."[119] When he uses phrases such as "national quest," "exploration into areas unknown and unfamiliar," "hidden areas of the national psyche," "conscious- ness," "identity," "dilemma," and so forth, he emphasizes the symbolic social mean- ing that could be both expressed as well as explored through the project.

For Tay, the building is intrinsically linked to the dilemma of constructing an "authentic identity," and hence, as a design work, it is seen as an opportunity to explore and express "the dilemma of being Asian and Modern at the same time."[120] To him, the building is seen as an important step in the quest for a new Asian iden- tity," and he says, "what it takes culturally to achieve a modern identity in the con- text of a closely networked globalized world is, the essence of the challenge today, and the building of the Singapore Arts Center is the symbol of this."[121]

Different in content but with a similar intersecting pattern would be the inclusion of physical dimensions such as environmental issues (like global warming and pol- lution) in the architecture of megacities in the equatorial belt,[122] as well as climatic issues (like heat, sun, rain, and humidity).[123] As an example, it is interesting to see how he introduces Sham Sani's findings on trapped heat in the cities[124] and explores its implications to tropical architecture.

Tay argues that air-conditioning in Singapore accounts for 50% of the total energy bill, which to him is an incredibly large amount that Singapore is spend- ing.[125] He then goes on to examine how climatic research can promote modern solu- tions for tropical architecture and cites climatic findings about the increase of 4° of temperature caused by "the heat island effect" in the city center (as opposed to the open field). He also cites the "canyon effect" in megacities in the tropics—an effect which is caused by the buildings trapping the air and trapping the heat, and the heat then reradiating within the space, which then builds up and causes further heat.

The fact that the tropical rainforest is typically 4–5° temperature lower than the ambient temperature in an open field situation is for him "a strong suggestion for

---

[118] Ibid.

[119] *The Straits Times*, 26 Oct 1992.

[120] *The Straits Times*, 30 Jul 1994. See also ST 26 Sep 1992.

[121] These two quotes are from *The Straits Times*, 30 Jul 1994.

[122] See, for example, "The Specific Conditions for 'Green Architecture' in Asian States Undergoing Rapid Modernization," Melbourne, RMIT Program.

[123] See, for example, Tay (1989)—"Towards a More Ecologically Responsible Urban Architecture," Quartenario Conference.

[124] Dr. Sham Sani's research (1986), University of Malaya, Geography Department.

[125] See Tay's (1989, p. 25).

shading and evaporative cooling to be part of a tropical Urban Design Agenda." He says that if we can conceptually merge these two environments (tropical forest and modern megacities), we should be able to settle for somewhere around 4–5° reduction in the city area. To him, this is "the critical area for climatic and design research,"[126] and the architectural agenda for the tropics should therefore try to "imitate" the tropical rainforest with its natural system for evaporation (with features like shading, evaporating systems, vertical plantation, special screening windows, and so forth). He says:

> We should be looking into evaporative cooling of buildings and open public places as well. The cooling of a group of buildings indicates for example the exploring of a mist of water on buildings so that plants can grow and thus also cool the building in the process. And if you want air-conditioning, then your air-conditioning bill could be 25% less.[127] (Therefore there must be) landscaping and evaporative cooling and high level shading and so forth. You must shade the buildings. You can even have fans that drive wind through public spaces during the 50% of the time in the tropics when there is no wind. We are talking about giant fans driving winds through city spaces, and these propellers can be driven by turbines from the rain water stored on the roof tops.[128]

Tay argues that "how we design single buildings and groups of buildings in the tropics which produce a cooling of the spaces in and around them is the real challenge"[129] of architecture and adds that this kind of research will be valid all over the tropical world because there are not enough studies on the intersection of architecture and tropical climate. In other words, the climatic synthesis with tropical modern architecture constructs a new professional agenda.

Contextualizing Architecture

These additional disciplines and dimensions are not studied separately. Rather, Tay focuses on how these various dimensions interact and interplay with architecture. An interviewee says that Tay talks "about people's lives in relation to economics, (talks) about people's lives in relation to large issues (like) social issues (and that) he has constantly been able to make the link (between) communities, histories and architecture."[130] Therefore, when he discusses climate, he "zooms in" on issues pertaining to architecture (such as heat traps and evaporative systems), and when he talks about culture, he focuses on its architectural representation (and not on culture in general).

In other words, the perceptual expansion of the profession correlates with the construction of links and connectors between architecture and other disciplines.

---

[126] Ibid., p. 70. Both this and the preceding quote are from the same document.

[127] Ibid., p. 62.

[128] Ibid., p. 74.

[129] Ibid., p. 64.

[130] Transcript D/1/4.

Hence, the cognitive professional expansion is achieved through the inclusion of various cross-discipline intersections and their linking as integral parts of the profession. The opinions of our interviewees that "these (various dimensions) are things that the profession must see" are indications for the internalization of these dimensions as integral parts of the profession. Touching on the interplay between different disciplines and dimensions in Tay's thinking, one interviewee says:

> (Tay) reads very widely, (and) discusses architecture in a very wide scope in terms of ecology (like the CO_2 factor in terms of pollution), how the world economy affects Singapore and its architecture (and others). And I think *that these are things that the profession must see* (because) that is how it actually and eventually drives architecture along a certain route. Architecture is (in fact) influenced by the social and political economic situation of the country and economic surrounding.[131]

Furthermore, a thematic inspection of the various added dimensions that intersect with architecture shows that they are not universal but particularly relevant to this part of the world, in this current time. His treatment of the SAC therefore deals with the Asian culture and the Singaporean national identity (and not with universal humanistic notions), his treatment of Confucian pragmatist notions deals with its implications on the teaching of architecture and aesthetics, and his treatment of the climatic dimensions does not treat snow or desert conditions but tropical conditions such as rain, humidity, and heat.

Hence, while it is generally true that Tay expanded the field by introducing other dimensions within other disciplines and by synthesizing and integrating them into the architectural field, at the same time, the various intersections that he introduced were particularly relevant to the local and current context. To use an interviewee's words:

> He has this talent for making it situationally, making it relevant. He is a person who is able to actually zoom in on an idea, take it out and actually apply it to what he feels that should be debated now, today…(turning it into) something very *current* at the time. (He) brings *it here* to Singapore…to the *situation*…and then *ties* it together. (…) He uses ideas and puts them into the current situation, (and it is) relevant because he places it into the local context.[132]

While the intersecting disciplines expand the field theoretically, the particular focus symbolically "brings the field back" to the local and current context and turns it into "our very own" architecture.

In other words, the synthesis of the field of architecture with a range of disciplines, and with various local and current perspectives, contextualizes that architecture. In this respect, the inclusion of economic, social, political, cultural, and historical dimensions intersecting with architecture, together with the particular focus on elements that are relevant to this place, people, and time, promote the social contextualization of architecture. Similarly, the inclusion of areas where architecture intersects with ecology, geography, and climate, and the particular focus on elements that are relevant and particular to this Southeast Asian region, promotes the physical contextualization of architecture.

---

[131] Transcript D/16/2.

[132] Transcript D/8/4.

Theoretically speaking, this contextualization culminated in the construction of modern tropical architecture as a separate body of ideas. The contextualization of the field created a coherent and unique body of ideas that stemmed from, and was consistent with, the particular setting. The field of tropical architecture was not entirely new as, in the 1950s, British architects such as Maxwell Fry and Jane Drew had initiated the field in their attempt to adjust their type of architecture to the British colonies in the equatorial belt. They indeed tried to cater to climatic and geographic considerations (like the elevation of the building from the ground), but their attempts were culturally and socially decontextualized. Moreover, these initiations, which catered to single buildings and were referred to as "bungalow" architecture, do not meet the needs of highly dense modern megacities. In the introduction to his 1989 work, *Mega-cities in the Tropics*, Tay writes that there were hardly any new ideas regarding the whole city or the tropical environment of urban areas. He says:

> Tropical architecture as a discipline virtually became defunct because the implied architecture style became dated and because the design of tropical buildings as individual buildings did not really solve the noise, dust, and heat problems which are created by the city itself, and which no single building can hope to solve except by air-conditioning.[133]

In this respect, Tay's "modern tropical architecture" tried to address this conceptual gap in the planning of dense tropical urban environments, which took into consideration cultural and social aspects as well as modern times (modern urban living style and its technological possibilities). The development of the field along such parameters resulted in the construction of a field that was qualitatively different, so much so that to an extent, it "separated" itself from mainstream architectural paradigms. In people's eyes, Tay "made a conscious effort to work in the tropical region, he consciously tried to practice it within his own work"[134] and became the "forerunner" of the idea of modern tropical architecture. As an interviewee explains:

> I would say (he is) the *forerunner*. He did not invent the idea but he was *the one who made it conscious* to people (before perhaps it was in the subconscious of people), but now *he made it conscious, so that could be attributed to him*. And he tries in his projects (whether small or big) to achieve that consciousness.[135]

From the paradigmatic point of view, the theoretical contextualization of architecture (that culminated in the ideas of "modern tropical architecture") was revolutionary, or in one interviewee's words, "It challenged the established authorities on architectural dialogue and theory."[136] Indeed, the kind of tropical city that Tay propounds is distinctly different from the cities we all know. Imagine the following:

> We are talking about large covered outdoor areas for outdoor activities with shelter from the rain and sun spanning between buildings. We are also talking about bridging structures between buildings so that you can move from one building to another without having to go down to the ground if you so choose. We are also talking about rooftops being connected

---

[133] Tay (1989). op. cit., p. 4.

[134] Transcript D/6/13.

[135] Transcript D/15/9.

[136] Transcript D/15/5.

throughout the city. So in effect we create two grounds; one on the earth and one on the podium rooftops. And we are also talking about landscaping the roof tops and introducing community and recreational facilities at the upper levels, features which at the moment are not at all considered in any of the cities in the tropics.[137]

An architecture that is based on overhanging roofs and shelters covering a whole range of built forms, interlocking and interpenetrating each other is in direct juxta-position or contrast to the architectural paradigm that sees the city as a conglomer-ate of built forms, enabling spatial enclosures and walls as the most distinctive and basic form of architecture.

The conflict in paradigms lies with the fact that one of the principal issues of designing in the tropics lies in the discovery that we have discussed earlier: The idea of a different design language and morphology (of line, edge, mesh, and shade) which collides with the paradigm that views architecture as the manipulation of plane, volume, solid, and void. It is precisely the discovery of such an alternative language (that is authentic to the context but foreign to the mainstream paradigm) that requires, in the interviewees' eyes and in Tay's own words, "an unlearning pro-cess, given the dominance of European architecture which forms the substance of the training of architects over the past 200 years."[138]

In other words, it requires the deconstruction of the dominant paradigm, which according to Tay, is the main thing that is blocking the designers' authentic response to this particular climate and history, and for which he argues that "we have yet to decolonize our minds."[139] The direct paradigmatic juxtaposition requires the decon-struction of the perception of the Western as superior, for which Tay argues:

> We need to pause to reevaluate whether these styles made practicable through extensive air-conditioning and insulation are the appropriate poetic images to express ourselves as Asians living in the tropics within a dynamic modern economy. We will need courage and patience if we want to invent new architecture to resist dominating international styles which consistently emphasize the enclosing walls and skin of buildings as the main aes-thetic language.[140]
> We have to take on the conceptual tasks ourselves.[141] (And) we owe it to ourselves to value our own creativity and our own self expression.[142]

This professional as well as social deconstruction of basic assumptions and para-digms met additional resistance from the particular context of public housing in Singapore. Chua Beng Huat relates that 85% of Singaporeans live in public housing estates, 90% of whom are owners of 99-year leases on their subsidized flats.[143] This implies the government's monopoly over the entire field of architecture on the island

---

[137] Tay (1989). op. cit., p. 29.

[138] Robert Powell (1997). op. cit., p. 13.

[139] Ibid., p. 14.

[140] *The Straits Times*, 29 Apr 1984.

[141] Powell (1997). op. cit., p. 14.

[142] Ibid., 2 Sep 1989.

[143] See Chua Beng Huat (1997, Cover page).

of Singapore. Chua has described the government's monopoly on public housing through the establishment of the Housing and Development Board (HDB) in 1960 and says that this board "is entrusted with extensive powers in land acquisition, resettlement, town planning, architectural design, engineering work and building material production—that is, all development work except actual construction of the buildings which is undertaken by private contractors."[144]

In other words, and especially in regard to planning and design, the scope and degree of the government's control is such that private contractors can only participate in its concrete, physical execution, but hardly in its planning and design. This condition, coupled with other sociopolitical factors that we have elaborated in Chap. 6, constrains[145] alternative voices as such and further reinforces the strength of the architectural paradigms to resist negotiation, questioning, debate, and alternative ideas.

The Expansion of Professional Self-Definition

Symbolically speaking, the theoretical contextualization of the architecture that Tay offers is socially meaningful. It is not the treatment of volume, void, solids, and mass, but a conscious and deliberate treatment of "us," living "here," in "this" "time." The contextualized architecture therefore deals not only with "what does it mean to be an architect" but, more importantly, with "what does it mean to be an architect *here*" in Singapore; it deals with "architectural ideas of what is possible for Singapore and architects here."[146] An interviewee says, for example, that through such construction:

> You get to explore ideas and possibilities, it is broad-minded, and innovative and always pushing the boundaries of what is possible. And boundaries are for example 'what does it mean to live in a place like Singapore and what kind of buildings can be built in Singapore?' Questions that are quite close to us, because we stay here. We are not just building one building after the other, (rather) the building becomes a way to ask questions, a way to find what is the best solution for Singapore, so that it relates to a lot of social issues, a lot of design issues and other important issues.[147]

The use of words like "explore ideas and possibilities," "pushing boundaries," "asking questions," and "a way to find" emphasize a cognitive expansion. But the cognitive expansion is at the same time related to existential notions, as implied by the use of words and phrases such as "what does it mean to live," "close to us," "social issues," and "important issues."

Along this theoretical and symbolic expansion, people could use architecture as a medium for reflection. In other words, it introduces architecture as a medium for

---

[144] Chua Beng Huat (1995, p. 129).

[145] For example, conditions such as centralized political control and an attitude of social and cultural compliance.

[146] Transcript D/17/11.

[147] Transcript D/17/2.

exploration and the expression of the relations between the "self" and the "place." People could use such exploration (or "internal struggle," to use one interviewee's words) to define their self and profession in this time and place. For example, an architect in Tay's firm says:

> There is a struggle which has an internal dimension, everyone of us comes to this. It is a private struggle within oneself, what I call the 'unfinished business': In this time of rapid economic expansion, how do we stand with the rest of the world? How then should we design? What is the authentic response? If you are a conscientious architect in the Third World, you want to be involved in this.[148]

It is in this respect that young architects (in particular) correlate the theoretical expansion and contextualization of architecture to their professional definition. They say that their perception of what architecture is about—and consequently, what they are and what they do as architects—expanded and developed.

This means that Tay's influence is not confined to the disciplines of "broadening" architecture but also to its "socializing" in terms of enabling architects to deal with social and identity issues. It is in this respect that interviewees say that "Tay is very interested in the social development of the people of Singapore and its relationship to architecture; he has always been like that. He likes to see very broad and very far vision of what the society or what architecture can be."[149] His ideas "are wonderful and always have a very strong social concern."[150]

This "socialization" of architecture correlates with Tay's own belief that "an architect's role is to give order and meaning to the settings in which life takes place."[151] Tay's feeling is that "Singapore is at a significant moment in its history when it is important to define itself by visions of what it can be as well as where its people come from and what they are"[152]; hence, architecture becomes a medium that can both express, explore, and help define Singapore's identity. Such perception sees architecture as a built dimension that invariably expresses and explores meaningful realms of life—realms that enfold notions about what and who we are and what we want to be. Or in Tay's words, "here architecture can project modernity, tropicality and promote a style of life that is true to the place so that we can be what we are and not a parody of something else."[153] The perception of architecture as having a social role is also echoed by a young architect, saying:

> Actually an *understanding of what society is about* is really the role of architects. Really, (to deal) with *what life in a city, or in a country, or in a built space—should be*. And that's his job. His job is to deal with *the interaction of human life and the built space*, at the very much larger level—at the level of the city.[154]

---

[148] Powell (1997). op. cit., p. 28.

[149] Transcript D/16/1.

[150] Transcript D/2/4.

[151] *The Sunday Times*, 12 Apr 1987.

[152] *The Sunday Times*, 29 Apr 1984.

[153] Tay (1990, p.15).

[154] Transcript D/1/4.

In this redefinition of architecture, the professional expansion therefore encompasses a much broader perspective of what architects deal with—not with mere "building forms" but with "life in built structures." It is in this respect that another interviewee says that "for Singapore and Singaporean architects Tay probably fulfills the role of an inspirational figure, (because) he gives the young people an *inspiration, a hope* that what they are doing *is more than simply manipulating objects* in space and so on, and that architecture is not simply an art form—but that it has a *social purpose* as well."[155] This sense of "social purpose" is described by interviewees as a feeling of "going beyond"; for example, an interviewee says:

> When I talk about the architect's role; (I think it means) to be able to imagine, imagineering, imagining engineering solutions. Not just aesthetic solutions. He is more than an engineer is because he can *imagine*. And I think that is what the role of an architect is. I think Kheng Soon fits that very well because his solutions *go beyond just the aesthetics*. When he talks about (issues such as) high rise/medium/low rise buildings, urban densities, conservation, countryside, and transportation—(he talks about) ideas in terms of *making a better society*.[156]

This "going beyond" does not relate to architecture's content as merely "going beyond" aesthetic issues (to issues such as climate, ecology, society, and so forth). It also refers to the profession's role definition as "going beyond" from merely dealing with buildings toward having a social role in relation to the "betterment of society."

Indeed, interviewees say, for example, that Tay asks, "what is the role of the architect in the society" and "what does it mean to live in a place like Singapore and what kind of buildings can we build for Singapore," and they say that "he always believes that architects should take a stronger role in molding the whole urban scene."[157] All these suggest that the profession's goal or the "end-result" is not a "good building" but a better society. In other words, Tay seems to imply that architects could, and perhaps also should, play a significant role in "imagining" and "engineering" a better society.

For Tay, the commitment to "betterment" means that "it is essential that unless you can create an environment that is really demonstratively better than the cities people are used to, the concept of modern tropical architecture is not on. Why should anyone live in a tropical city just because it is labeled as such? It has got to be significantly better."[158] This "social role" of architecture indeed correlates with Tay's own definition of the discipline (and hence his self-definition for himself as well as a possible "prototype" definition for those who follow him). He says:

> We must regain that special position in society wherein we serve the role of mediator between the mundane and the sublime. We must insist that our essential role is to project a vision of life's special potentialities ... Only when we see such a role for ourselves, can we regain our lost seat in that special position reserved for the '*undangi*' (the Balinese term for the divinator) of place and time.[159]

---

[155] Transcript D/14/8.

[156] Transcript D/1/7.

[157] For these references, see transcripts D/1/2, D/17/2, and D/18/4.

[158] Tay (1989). op. cit., p. 74.

[159] *The Straits Times*, 18 Jan 1998.

Tay's use of phrases such as "givers of orders," "mediator between the mundane and sublime," and his use of the term "*undangi*" communicate a notion of architecture as the "originator" and the "creator" of the symbolic center of the society.

Notwithstanding a possible interpretation of the use of these particular words as having a "megalomaniac" flavor, such a perception implies a preoccupation with existential notions and the symbolic order of the society as a core characteristic of the architectural profession and a profound perception of architects as meaningful participants in the shaping of the society and the place that they are part of. In other words, in the minds of the followers, architecture (and consequently their self-definition as architects) is symbolically tied to the meaningful center of the society, allowing them to draw such conclusions as the idea that "we still have a role *even* in Singapore."[160]

Establishing Social Discourses on Identity Formation

Our discussion seems to offer some indications with regard to the process and patterns whereby charismatic leadership constructs an alternative reality and transforms meaning. A social transformation is evident in all the three case studies, and that transformation seems to be linked to the concept of identity.[161] Volunteers in the Heart to Heart social service, for example, said that their lives became more meaningful by coherently blending spiritual notions in their self-definition and in their everyday life. Young architects said that their professional self-definition expanded to one that (other than strictly concentrating on building design) encompasses the dimensions of many more disciplines and that entails a social role in the shaping of their society. Young theater practitioners (mostly English-speaking) talked about the redefinition of their "Singaporean social identity" with and through the medium of the theater.

Overall, it seems that these social transformations generally relate to identity reformation, but each case concentrates on a particular type of identity. While Prema's case relates to the volunteer's individual self-identity, Tay's relates to the professional identity, and Kuo's relates to the Singaporean social identity.

It also seems that each case differs in the sources from which the identity components derive. While Kuo's concept of identity derives from "primordial" sources, such as tradition, heritage, language, culture, and history, Tay's conceptualization of identity emphasizes more "rational, scientific" and academic sources for such

---

[160] Transcript D/1/4.

[161] In November 1997, this research was discussed in a meeting with Eisenstadt, and he commented that he was currently working on a paper with regard to the comparative patterns of collective identity formation. He added that he thought that charisma could be one possible pattern, an observation that still requires further theoretical and empirical clarification.

formulations (as in his emphasis on "modernity" and the "autonomy of reason")[162] and Prema's conceptualization of identity sources from spiritual, transcendental, and "other worldly" notions.

These different sources for identity formation could have potentially triggered a debate within each other, since theoretically speaking, Tay's emphasis on rational constructions may contradict Kuo's emphasis on culture and tradition and may also contradict Prema's emphasis on religious,[163] transcendental notions. Equally so, we can see a contradiction in principle between Prema's and Tay's "universalistic" tendencies for identity construction and Kuo's emphasis on "particular" components. While Prema's conceptualizations cut across religions, nationalities, and races and Tay's conceptualization strives to transcend cultural particularism by climatic and geographical meta-structures and meta underlying themes,[164] Kuo tends to emphasize the very particularistic, primordial components that, in his opinion, would counter-balance the current "rootless drift." This means that the three leaders could have, at least potentially, debated with each other as there are enough grounds for controversy and polemics among their different identity contentions.

All three identity contentions seem to be set against the government's dominant assumptions (the government's contention of identity is distinct in that it relies mainly on instrumental, pragmatic, and economic parameters). Seen as such, conceptually speaking, there are at least four different contentions with regard to identity formation, and each builds on different grounds and sources.

However, it is interesting that while, in principle, the leaders could have addressed each other, at least two of the leaders (Kuo and Tay) seem to correspond their arguments mainly to the government's identity contention. Structurally speaking, this locus of reference could derive from the nature of the power structure. It is possible that the dominant nature of the government's contention (vis-à-vis the marginal

---

[162] Tay says: "Modernity is the assertion of the primacy of reason, morality and aesthetics as fields freed from the dictates of power and piety. Modernity or autonomy relies on an implicit scientific chain of cause and effect, which is capable of being independently verified. Thus, a thing is true or valid only if it satisfies reason and not because the powerful or the pious deem it so. To the extent that such autonomies in a given society are generally deficient, individuals and social institutions, such as contracts, law and human relations, become subject to the dictates of the mighty. A blurring of the truth becomes entrenched" (*The Straits Times*, 19 Aug 1998).

[163] An interviewee said once: "There was once he gave a lecture and he started by saying: 'if you are religious, you will never be a good architect,' because immediately being religious means that you follow a particular faith and you follow a particular faith means that you subscribe to a certain power of hierarchy (and not to the rational, autonomy of reason)" (Transcript D/18/14).

[164] Tay said in this regard: "Of course we were aware that we couldn't do a Malay architecture, nor should we do a Chinese architecture, or an Indian architecture, or a mix of all three. It just wasn't right. Aesthetically, it just wouldn't gel, to mix the different kinds of ethnic icons and symbols and design ideas into one. (...) We couldn't accept the idea of an architecture that was based on that kind of strategy of mixture. A kind of fusion, to use the word. The whole strategy of blending to me cannot work. You have to find a deeper level of unity in the study of expression. You cannot just add and subtract things. It's like grafting parts of different things together. You will never be successful."

power of the other three leaders' contentions) drives (in what seems to be a centripetal force) the polemics toward the power center. Hence, instead of having a variety of simultaneous, parallel, ongoing social discourses on identity, the structural properties may have shaped the plural nature of such social discourses into one main unilineal type of dialogue: periphery vs. center.

The Philosophical, Existential Nature of the Transformations Led by the Three Charismatic Leaders

The nature of the processes by which charismatic leadership (both leaders and followers) construct (or structurize) reality and meaning has a distinct intentional, reflective flavor. These processes do not rely on semireflexive, "taken-for-granted" social action nor "typificatory schemes" as we might find in the work of Berger and Luckman nor "structurizing patterns" that are described by Anthony Giddens.[165] The construction of such reality has an abrupt, rather than ongoing, nature and seems to be an intense social exercise that engages people in a conscious exploration and negotiation of the mere, underlying, taken-for-granted assumptions of the structure that they are part of. This is not to say that Berger and Luckman and Giddens do not accord to an individual's reflection, intention, and choice but that the difference lies in the fact that the leaders rely precisely and mainly on these aspects for social action and transformation.

In other words, it is not a process that relies on patterning or long-term social processes of socialization, or incremental, accumulative influences of recurrent typificatory schemes. To the contrary, it is a process that relies on focused reflection and acknowledges the "man-made" origins of the structural patterns (or at least the parts that are open for contention) and generates efforts in attempts to deconstruct and reconstruct or at least negotiate and redefine the man-made structural patterns.

A meta-thematic characteristic of these processes of reality construction and identity reformation is that the exploration, expression, and construction of identity are intertwined with philosophical reflections on existential dilemmas. These dilemmas relate to the nature of the self, the society, and the world, as well as the relations between them and the way by which these relations affect identity.

The cases therefore imply that in the charismatic reality construction, aspects such as reflection, intention, and choice are intrinsically related with philosophical dilemmas of "who we are" and what exactly the world that we live in is. Consequently, it is an intentional choice and decision about how people want to live their lives, the type of world they want to live in, and what they are prepared to do in order to construct such a life in such a world.

Within the wide range of dilemmas and reflections, each leader seems to concentrate on a particular spectrum. For example, Tay's case concentrates more on

---

[165] The "typificatory schemes" are found in Berger and Luckman (1966) and the "structurizing patterns" in Giddens (1984).

dilemmas about the relations between the "society" and its "physical place." Kuo seems to be more engaged with the relations between the "society" and the "self," and Prema deals more with the relations between the "self" and the "metaphysical transcendental world." The deliberate, conscious, and philosophical debate over these notions accords meaning to the term *Homo sapiens*." It further emphasizes the cognitive, perceptual, and reflective nature of the way that human beings contest, negotiate, redefine, and shape their own reality.

The Role of Socially Objectified Artifacts in the Transformation Process

The transformative processes were not solely created by the leaders, but with the help of messo level, socially objectified artifacts that the leaders constructed: Kuo's plays and his setting up of the Substation, Prema's ideas and her Heart to Heart social service, and Tay's ideas, designs and his company, Akitek Tenggara. In other words, the leaders were not the sole cause in the generation of reality construction and transformation. The socially objectified constructs that they created participated (once objectified) in the process of transformation and identity redefinition.

The objectified social artifacts participate in the transformation process by enabling institutionalized platforms for the active participation of others in a reflective and explorative social discourse on identity. These platforms were crucial for identity formation because they enabled profound reflections on various societal levels: micro, messo, and macro.

For example, Kuo's plays enabled a platform for exploration and discourse on the relations between the self (or micro) issues, societal (or macro) issues, such as homogenization, tradition, heritage, and others, and messo issues, such as family and community, and dealt with the various implications of these dimensions on the Singaporean social identity. Prema's social service enabled a platform for reflection as well as actual expression of the relations between the self (micro level), the transcendental spiritual world (macro level), and welfare groups (messo level) and explored the implications of these various dimensions on self-identity. Similarly, Tay's ideas explored the relations between (messo level) built forms, macro dimensions such as climate, environment, culture, and society, and professional (or micro) definitions and the implications of such dimensions on the way that local architecture should engage with and express social identity.

Crisis as Contextual Predisposition

There are indications that in the cases of Kuo and Prema, individual people may have been initiated to engage in transformational processes by a prior state of identity crisis. In Prema's case, most volunteers refer to a kind of personal identity crisis that either followed a specific event or just a general feeling of identity and meaning disorientation. In the case of Kuo, the younger generation of English-speaking practitioners was preoccupied with the theatrical expression of an authentic Singaporean identity. These identity crises could have established a social predisposition for the exploration of existential dilemmas, which may have then "prepared" the ground for Prema's and Kuo's social influence on self-transformation and on the social construction of meaning.

But even if this is the case, the crisis did not generate the leaders, and their agency is still evident in the way that both Prema and Kuo helped people to clarify covert, formless, or latent notions and mobilized concerted efforts and resources to squarely deal with these notions and dilemmas. Other than initiating people into conscious processes of self-reflection, both Kuo and Prema enabled social platforms for such explorations to take place, as well as assisted with the content and components of the particular identity reformations.

In Tay's case, there is no explicit evidence for a predisposition among the people whom he influenced.[166] This may have made his attempts to promote an architecture that deals with social identity more challenging[167] and his attempts to deconstruct professional and social paradigmatic assumptions harder.

Simultaneous Deconstruction and Reconstruction of Social Reality

In constructing the objectified artifacts (ideas, designs, texts, plays, organizations), all three leaders seem to have adopted an "inclusive attitude"[168] toward their social constructs. Prema's beliefs "opened up" religious boundaries to include various

---

[166] For the record, we should add that among the architectural community, at the time of the inception of Singapore as an independent nation (the mid and late 1960s), many architects who were interviewed described having had an urgent and profound quest to participate in the planning of Singapore. This quest found a channel through their voluntary participation in the Singapore Planning and Urban Research Group. However, the organization eventually ceased to operate in the early 1970s (some would say it was disbanded), on account of having overt and covert confrontations with the government's policies. (Some say these confrontations were over the direction being taken in Housing and Urban Planning, and others say that the group was perceived by the government as challenging their political authority.) Anyhow, most of the active members (with the exception of Tay Kheng Soon and William Lim) have never resorted to participating in independent kinds of organizations. In any case, since these people do not constitute the bulk of Tay's followers, their previous existential predisposition did not promote the emergence of Tay's influence.

[167] An interviewee says: "In the context of Singapore in the sixties, in those times, *nobody* was talking about tropical architecture. Everybody was trying to do modern buildings like the English and the Americans were doing (…) And then after that nobody talked about it and then now it is coming back again, but now it is an uphill battle because people are so used during the last twenty years to do this type of steel and glass building, people were not interested in identity in the last twenty years" (Transcript D/15/9).

[168] It is not clear to what extent this "inclusive" attitude could be seen as a counter reaction to the regulated, regimented structure, in particular, to the government's own formation of social identity. These reactions may be related in ways that are still in need for further study.

selected themes from different religious corpuses. Kuo "opened up" the normative definition of the "Singaporean identity" to include a variety of additional dimensions such as "ordinary people," local dialects, and other intangible, nonquantifiable, nonmaterial aspects of life. Tay "opened up" the boundaries of architecture's definition to include various intersecting disciplines such as climate, geography, culture, and others.

At the same time, this "opening up" and the inclusion of whole new realms and dimensions eventually enabled a process of alternative reconstructions, particularly by focusing on the various ways that the included dimensions intersect with local aspects. Consequently, this "opening up" culminated in proposed redefinitions or reconstructions of reality that seemed meaningful, coherent, and symbolically authentic.

For example, Prema's spiritual/social construct included various religions (thus deconstructing the formal religious definitions and blurring the boundaries within the different religions), but, at the same time, it reconstructed a notion that was spiritual/social/universal/humanitarian and that enabled the volunteers to have a meaningful reconstruction of their selves and their lives. Similarly, Kuo included various dimensions in the definition of the "Singaporean collective identity" (and by this, deconstructed the dominant sociopolitical definitions of collective identity). Simultaneously, this deconstruction enabled a reconstruction that included a whole realm of intangible dimensions that seemed to audiences and theater practitioners authentic and meaningful and resulted in the symbolic transformation of the theater—becoming "ours." Tay also included various disciplines into architectural framework (thus deconstructing the architectural confines as well as deconstructing the Western architectural paradigms as the sole base for professional truisms). But by doing this, he was promoting, at the same time, an architecture that was in touch with the place, the time, and the people and thus constructing an architecture that was synchronized with the context.

The inclusion of the additional dimensions into the identity definitions was not an easy task. In all three cases, the transformation of social identity was intertwined with the deconstruction of other underlying existing systemic assumptions. These social redefinitions "competed," so to speak, with other dominant social orientations. In that sense, Tay's modern tropical architecture was seen as an attempt to deconstruct prevailing professional paradigms as well as an attempt to deconstruct the narrow definition of architecture as a profession that is confined to building design. Kuo's inclusion of various additional primordial elements to the Singaporean social identity juxtaposed the dominant sociopolitical assumptions regarding the content of social identity, as well as the eligibility to participate in identity formative processes. Similarly, Prema's synthesis of various religious ideas into one spiritual/social belief system deconstructed the religious paradigm that regards such corpuses as "untouchable."

It is in this respect that terms referring to the leaders (such as "painful," "disturbing," "provoking," "pushing the boundaries," "breaking taboos," "extraordinary," "rocking the boat," "controversial," "provocative," "nuisance," and "constant threat") can be seen as symptoms of the underlying systemic resistance—to be negotiated, debated, deconstructed, and more significantly, transformed. It is a resistance that originates from the power of the underlying structure and basic social assumptions. Equally so, these "resisting symptoms" are indications of the leaders' agency and role: to negotiate the underlying structure of which they are a part, even if this "negotiation" means that they are bound to engage in endless attempts to "push" the constraining structure and being pushed back by it.

The Active Engagement of the "Self" in the Social World

A feeling of professional self-expansion followed Tay's redefinition of architecture. Feelings of self-validation and self-affirmation followed Kuo's redefinition of Singaporean identity. And feelings of self-expression followed Prema's redefinition of spiritualism (in its concrete social form). In other words, in all three cases the social transformation is linked to the "deep engagement" of the particular, idiosyncratic individual self.

The way in which the self was engaged differs in each case, but what is of significance is that all three cases point at a very peculiar kind of self-engagement. This type of self-engagement is intrinsically linked to the collective social arena. Perhaps it is in this respect that all three leaders are perceived as having "resocialized" their own professional fields, linking them with processes of identity formation. Tay's ideas "resocialized" architecture by promoting it as a possible medium for the exploration and formation of an authentic, local architecture. Kuo "resocialized" theater by promoting it as a discursive medium for the reflection, exploration, and redefinition of the "Singaporean collective psyche." And Prema "resocialized" spiritual transcendental themes by linking them into the daily, secular, mundane, social welfare realm.

It seems that, in a certain sense, the leaders' agency (and the process of charismatic reality construction) is related to a general notion of "links," "bridges," or "connectors" between different realms.[169] Indeed, Tay's architecture thrived on the elaboration of the linkages between architecture, other disciplines, and contextual elements; Prema's social service was precisely constituted on the links between the spiritual, daily, individual, and social realms; and Kuo's plays elaborated possible links between various intangible dimensions of life and the formation of a meaningful social identity.[170]

---

[169] These links were instrumental to the process of reality construction and deconstruction in that they clarified concepts that seemed unbridgeable. For example, Kuo's bilingualism deconstructed as it were, the social and theatrical boundaries that existed between the two entities (English-speaking and Chinese-speaking practitioners). Prema's monk lifestyle was a clear articulation of the deconstruction of the boundaries between sublime and mundane, religious and social, and Tay's multidisciplinary attitude and knowledge deconstructed the perceived boundaries between various disciplines.

[170] Perhaps it is also of significance that Kuo is perceived by many as a "bridge-maker" between various social communities: between the English-speaking theater and the Chinese-speaking theater, between the artistic community and the theater people, and between the artistic community and the intellectual, academic community.

But it is in the link between such notions of the self and the society that the crux of the construction of meaning lies. In Tay's case, social meaning was constructed when the architect's self-expansion was intrinsically linked to a social role (as in the "betterment of the built forms of the society"). In Kuo's case, social meaning was constructed when the feelings of self-affirmation and self-validation were linked to their social participation in the process of a Singaporean identity formation. In Prema's case, a meaningful life and self were constructed when the abstract metaphysical notions were actively translated and linked to the welfare of needy people.

This "linking" agency promoted the construction of meaning because along these links, life was intrinsically intertwined with philosophical, meaningful notions on existentialism, humanism, society, the self, and the world. Through this link, people (Prema's volunteers, young architects, and English-speaking theater practitioners) developed a sense of being at the active centers of the social system and of having a say in the shaping of their selves and their lives. In other words, it was precisely through this link that social meaning was constructed and, consequently, a subjective understanding developed, a sense of personal commitment increased, an existential meaning formed, and a transformation took place.

The next chapter will illustrate unique patterns of managing to transmit macro, public articulations of alternative views along a constraining (yet not totally delimiting) structure. The chapter will illustrate the relations between context and charisma, that is, it will show how the context influences the content and the form by which leaders engage in the negotiation of structure. Equally, it will show how charismatic leaders find indigenous ways to express themselves and negotiate structure while in it and being part of it.

Chapter 9
Structural Constraints and Alternative Sociopolitical Discourses

In spite of the constraining structural aspects that were mentioned in Chap. 6, we have seen in Chaps. 7 and 8 that within the micro and messo level realms (particularly within face-to-face interactions), transformations took place. However, as was suggested in Chap. 6, at the macro level of social action, there are probably more severe structural limitations on mass mobilization, mass organization, and public articulation of views. This chapter will focus on this realm of action and show how the interaction between charismatic leaders and structural aspects result in unique patterns and modes of expression, articulation, and argumentation of views in public.

Indeed, structure forms and shapes charisma by limiting the scope and degree of public discourse on sociopolitical issues. What would be very interesting to see, however, is how the charismatic leaders articulate their views, even in very constraining conditions. In this sense, they overcome the structure even if they are unable to completely transform it. Perhaps, it would be more accurate to relate to the patterns of social action as expressions of the leaders, both being pushed by the structure and pushing back the structure, by utilizing its endemic dialectical, dual character.

We will illustrate this notion by describing particularly how Kuo Pao Kun elaborated structural gaps into indigenous, unique ways for the public articulation of dissenting sociopolitical views. Instead of relying on official channels that were constructed by the establishment, Kuo (and also Tay Kheng Soon, but to a lesser extent) made use of alternative, quasi-centralized channels for sociopolitical discourse that, though less encouraged were, at least in principle, permissible.

Kuo created a "metaphoric" and "allegoric" alternative to engage in public sociopolitical discourse. No doubt this kind of discourse is extremely restricted, but at the same time, no one can negate the fact that Kuo created an indigenous medium for this discourse. This medium has its own particular language, content, and structure, and it enabled theater practitioners and audiences alike to participate (perhaps for the first time) in a public discourse that relied on channels that were not formally set by the establishment. Again, even if structurally speaking, the discourse was very restricted in form and content—subjectively and symbolically speaking, it was a great social departure for those involved.

Dayan Hava and Chan Kwok-bun, *Charismatic Leadership in Singapore:*   203
Three Extraordinary People, DOI 10.1007/978-1-4614-1451-3_9,
© Springer Science+Business Media, LLC 2012

In a similar way, Tay has also found a unique public way to articulate his views, capitalizing on a few permissible structural opportunities, namely, the letters column in the *Straits Times* newspaper,[1] the format of semiacademic abstract writing, and the reliance on the professional field to anchor a legitimate point of departure on his sociopolitical commentary. If we will follow through the exchange of letters, the content, the frequency, and the people involved (to the point of successfully "forcing" the establishment to engage in public accounts of policy matters),[2] we may be able to see that to a certain extent, this social action managed to constitute and establish a particular form of sociopolitical discourse, even if it is very restricted in nature and form.

---

[1] He makes use of a structural gap that derives from the dual nature of the newspaper (as having to adhere to balanced, informative, journalistic ethics and as being an organ for the transmission of the government's views). Tay takes advantage of the newspapers' aim for professional and ethical journalism (which requires a certain appearance of balance). An interviewee says about this: "to a certain extent, however suppressed it is, *The Straits Times* must still maintain some kind of appearance of balance. Just like the government, however authoritarian it is, it must still maintain some kind of appearance of democracy (…) Because I think that as Singapore becomes more and more globally important, there are external pressures on Singapore to be a democratic society (…) Singapore is not limited by its small size. Singapore has a very big presence in spite of its small size! So there is an international image question (…) So because Singapore is covered by international press, it needs public relations, it is very important to the state! (And the newspaper is a good platform for that), there is no other place to place it. If you look at the forum page, it props the government's claims to be a democratic society (Transcript D/20/10–11). It is perhaps this structural gap that "invites", as it were, its exploitation by certain people. An interviewee even says in this respect, "there are certain people in Singapore who have a certain privileged position with *The Straits Times*. In a certain sense it is ironic, (because) even though these people may be very critical of the government, they publish almost everything they write, especially if it's just letter to the forum. (There are indeed very) few people who do consistently give another point of view, and the (newspaper) takes that (because) in a certain sense it's useful to them" (Transcript D/20/3–4).

[2] Tay engages readers in polemics and debate over urban issues (e.g., over the "nouveau riche" type of architecture, over Confucian notions and their implications on aesthetics and creativity, on modernity and modernization, on the China-town conservation, on tropical architecture, and others). But in addition, Tay manages to trigger a kind of alternative dialogue (even if very restricted) between government officials and the readers. His persistent and various letters to the editors requesting information or offering feedback on policy matters seem to engage, as it were, the government officials in a public dialogue, over the newspaper. Just to bring a few examples: On 14 Sept 1974, 26 Sept 1974, 12 Oct 1974, the then Secretary of Road Transport Action Committee responded to Tay's comments on the inefficiency of the usage of buses as a central system for mass transportation. On 3 Jan 1998, two responses were published, with regard to his and Tommy Koh's comments on energy conservation (from 24 Dec 1997): one on behalf of the Director-General of Public Works, Ministry of National Development, and the other on behalf of the Permanent Secretary, Ministry of the Environment. On 17 Nov 1995, a response from the Corporate Communications Officer, Singapore Post Pte. Ltd., was published with regard to Tay's comments on the need to find more efficient ways to collect registered mail at post offices (published on 15 Nov 1997). On 2 Mar 1996, a response from the Corporate Communications Officer, Land Transport Authority, was published with regard to Tay's suggestions to extend shelters for alighting passengers (from ST 19 Feb 1996). On 18 Sept 1998, a response from the Head of Public relations for Chief Executive Officer and Chief Planner Urban Redevelopment Authority was published with regard to Tay's suggestions for nature conservation (from ST 15 Sept 1998), and so forth.

Since some interviewees also mention other people as having contributed to the construction of such channels (e.g., Tommy Koh—Singapore's former Ambassador to the UN, William Lim, and others), it cannot be singularly attributed to Tay (although he may be seen by some as the most persistent in its usage and expansion). Hence, for analytical clarity, we will focus on Kuo's case only and use the example of Tay to further ground our arguments with regard to the particular patterns of this sociopolitical discourse.

Structural Avenues for Public Sociopolitical Discourse

As a principal point of departure, we would like to clarify that in our view, social discourses are political in nature, even if people in Singapore seem to refrain from calling them so. The definition of politics is not confined to the legislative electoral politics, or the administrative and technical aspects of party politics, but encompasses public discussions, commentary, and the exchange of views on social issues as such. Though Kuo and Tay do not form constituencies and neither stands for election[3] (or, in the words of Chan Heng Chee, they have "no organization or action behind"[4]—they are "political" by virtue of the fact that they publicly articulate social and political commentary, and thus "participate in politics."

Douglas Sikorski argues that, to a large extent, in the context of political participation in Singapore, the framework for social debate and discourse is established in advance by the government.[5] Similarly, Chan has described[6] how the government "sets 'out-of-bound markers' for the media to ensure that discussion of racial, language, and religious issues does not get out of hand." She says:

> The articulation through newspaper columns can only be on limited issues. These issues concern the demand for a better or a more efficient administration rather than an argument on goals and values (…) there are obvious notions of what is permissible.

---

[3] Tay says, for example: "I don't 'mobilize' people—(therefore) I am not political. I don't have a constituency and I do not spend time cultivating a constituency. If I did, I would be *totally wiped out*. (So acting as an individual) is a *survival mechanism*. If (readers) did (admit publicly that they identify with me), if they *did*, I might be in *trouble*! You see how strange? Supposing hundreds of people express support, I would be in *deep trouble*! (…) I have used the term 'the politics of ideas' to describe this process many years ago. Yes, I would agree it is part of the politics of ideas, but politics of ideas is not politics of mobilization. I don't think so. Mobilization has to do with some kind of a coalescing of opinion and actions following therefrom. That is my understanding. (Though theoretically actions may follow from ideas) I am very skeptical about that in Asian societies. It may happen in Europe, I don't know. In Asian society, no. (…) I don't think there is a (real threat of people being actively mobilized by my writing). It's only a theoretical risk, because I know the culture well enough. That will never happen. People do not express themselves in public!" (T/5/7–9).

[4] See her 1975 essay, "Politics in an Administrative State: Where Has the Politics Gone?" p. 56.

[5] See "Resolving the Liberal-Socialist Dichotomy: The Political Economy of Prosperity in Singapore." 1991. p. 420.

[6] In her 1993 essay, "Democracy: Evolution and Implementation, an Asian Perspective." p. 16.

Administrative issues are permissible while obvious political issues are not and the extent
to which newspapers can pursue an issue too determinedly can be construed as anti-national,
as the editors of Nanyang Siang Pau and the Singapore Herald discovered.[7]

Sikorski argues that these "boundaries" are set to professional activities as well,[8]
as we can infer from a high-ranking official's comment, saying, "the professional
bodies were set up to look after the interest of their members. It was not their role to
get involved in public policies that did not affect their professional interests and
were not within their objectives."[9] Also theater performances are controlled in that
they have to be approved by a censorship mechanism, the Drama Review Committee,
prior to being allowed to be performed. "Script-less" plays (as those that allow for
the script to evolve through spontaneous interaction with the audience) are not
possible under this rule. Nor can the scripts include sensitive political and social
issues pertaining to government policies, race, religion, homosexuality, and international relations.

A few avenues for the public articulation of views and participation in a centralized system of government institutions can be located, for example, to name just
two, the Citizen's Consultative Committees (CCC) and the management committee
of the community centers, among others. The government indeed tries to maintain
an open dialogue with the electorate at various forums and platforms. But Chan
Heng Chee notes that "the participation is limited in number and in kind." Therefore,
"Grievances and dissatisfaction in the political system cannot find an alternative
leadership which can aggregate and articulate their views effectively. Over time, a
pattern of compliance sets in for want of a leadership to focus dissent."[10]

More institutionalized channels were set up by the government, especially after
the 1984 General Election, which showed signs of discontent and an increase in the
votes won by opposition parties. These channels included the representation of
dissenting views in Parliament, and for this, the government created the institution
of Non-constituency Member of Parliament (NCMP) to allow up to four members
of the opposition who had garnered the highest number of votes to be appointed to the

---

[7] Chan (1975) op. cit., pp. 56–57.

[8] As reflected in the government's decision to disband the Law Society and prosecute its then
Chairman, Francis Seow, for issuing a statement in May 1986 which was critical of the proposed
Newspaper and Printing Presses (Amendment) Bill. This Bill was passed to limit circulation of for-
eign publications, which published unwelcome criticism on domestic issues. (Sikorski, 1991:420).

[9] Reported in *The Straits* Times, 7 Jul 1986.

[10] This reference is from Chan (1975) op. cit., p. 55. Similarly, an interviewee says: "The sad part
about Singapore is that a lot of people, because of their sort of so-called memory and heresy about
political detentions and all, end up suppressing themselves, for no reason! Cause there are
Singaporeans who say, 'I can't talk freely because I'm afraid of being arrested.' Come on! You
think the bloody government has time to arrest everybody who says anything *stupid*? Or intelli-
gent? (When they say) 'I can't speak freely because I'm going to be watched,' that means you're
actually putting (censorship on yourself). Sometimes I think people who say that think too much
of themselves. I don't think they are all that important in a certain sense! The ISD (Internal Security
Department) doesn't have time to go about following every idiot who writes to *The Straits Times*.
There are only so many ISD agents!" (D/20/14).

House (if none or fewer than four opposition members were elected).[11] And in 1989, it created the category of Nominated Members of Parliament (NMP) to add articulate dissenters to the voices of the Parliament.

In spite of the government's attempt to officially contain and control public discourse, it is possible to detect at least five alternative channels that enable the articulation of ideas, without using the centralized establishment's system. In this respect, all these channels are "structural gaps" in a centralized system, or what Giddens would refer to as examples of the structure's enabling sides, consequently facilitating social action and agency if manipulated efficiently.

These channels include the analytical semiacademic mode of professional discussion, the articulation of views through the letter columns in the newspaper, the usage of interpretive art (most notably the theater)[12] and "coffee shop talk." Chan Heng Chee argues that, of the outlets for political commentary, the one that is the most "free" is the "coffee shop":

> Singaporeans love to talk. I think there is an unwritten law here that political discussion no matter how critical and even libelous, so long as it is not on the public platform nor in print is permissible. Those who depict Singapore as a police state are not quite correct. There is a qualitative difference. Singaporeans do not really have to look over their shoulders before they spout their political viewpoints. Whilst Singaporeans do not make politics, they gather in coffee shops, in bars and at cocktail parties and dinners to talk politics (…) I do not know whether there does exist a rumor-manufacturing machinery somewhere in Singapore as a new opposition strategy, but the fact that the Singapore public strives so heartily on rumors is perhaps indicative of their search for a safe avenue of political participation.[13]

Yet however "free" this coffee talk channel may be in terms of its content and scope; it is severely restricted in form. It can only be "casual," "informal," and a kind of "small talk" and, consequently, has a rather marginal effect on government policies, if at all.

All these channels would constitute "political action that is permissible for not having organization and action behind it; it is not viewed as disruptive. In fact, it lets off steam."[14] Kuo used the channel of the theater, and Tay (and others) used the professional channel (allied to that of the social commentator that uses semiacademic,

---

[11] Sikorski argues: "although political opposition is constitutionally permitted (…) Those who vociferously disagree with the established government policy are expected to not only be constructive and tactful, but be ready to defend their position against often-superior government resources in information and expertise. The few political opponents who managed to succeed at the polls have found it very tough going in Parliament, as the PAP concentrated every effort to discredit (or even jail) those who were regarded as troublesome. All action against dissenters was taken within the law and openly, but the legal system in Singapore gives the authorities strong prerogatives" (Sikorski, 1991:418).

[12] The role of interpretative arts has been reflected, for example, by Art Installation artists and painters, especially towards the second half of the 1980s, in the Artist's Village, and artists as Tang Da Woo, Amanda Heng and others.

[13] Chan (1975) op. cit., p. 58–59.

[14] Ibid., p. 56.

abstract, and sometimes obscure language).[15] These channels are actually structurally given—they are not, as it were, "created de novo" yet significantly and skill-fully expanded and transformed by persistent social participation into meaningful "social spaces."

The Construction of the Interpretive Sociopolitical Discourses

Phenomenologically speaking, interpretive discourses are only possible because they are supported by a widely shared culture or subculture, or basic, shared, common knowledge underlying the discourse. One needs cite only the famous example of a rapid closing and opening of a single eyelid, used by Gilbert Ryle and elaborated on by Geertz, to illustrate the extent to which the meaning is attached to the event. "Is it a twitch or a wink? Mere observation of the physical act gives no clue. If it is a wink, what kind of wink is it: one of conspiracy, of ridicule, of seduction? Only the knowledge of the culture, the shared understandings of the actor and his observers can tell us." [16]

This underlying, taken-for-granted, and shared meaning supports the discourse and enables the decoding of the indicated and encoded messages in the subtext, so that a discourse is established without necessarily engaging in concrete, overt, ver-bal articulation. It is this shared knowledge that is so crucial for the maintenance and functioning of interpretive discourses.

How do they all understand the same thing? How do all theater audiences come up with the same interpretation? How is it that different readers interpret Tay's comments in a similar manner? According to the interviewees, it is nothing more and nothing less than "because they know."[17] It is precisely this basic, prosaic

---

[15] In a self-reflective insight, Tay says, for example, about his own style of public comments: "I think any kind of long-term observer of Singapore's political scene cannot but realize that quite often it is not what you say but how you say it that matters (…) Certain words, certain phrases trigger certain reactions and it is unthinking. It is like automatic. So if you use the wrong words then you are immediately labeled, so your whole argument is defeated straightaway. They don't bother about it or you are branded. Quite apart from vocabulary, let's talk about sound; the sound of the voice. (…) a kind of *cool rational* presentation of an argument would be well received, even if it was disagreed with, because it was *cool*! That means the *tone* is not *inciteful*. (…) If the state-ment was made in an academic journal, then the latitude of permissibility is greater. If the state-ment is made in the public newspaper or on radio or TV, then the latitude is very small. So it is the tone, the place and then the words. The words have to be non-emotional (…) So that is the kind of distinction that one has to make. (So the housing policy should not be described as the 'social engineering of obedience'; it should be described as *'Housing a Nation'*!!) (And also) since one cannot speak in public without an organizing permit to speak, then by definition to organize is to mobilize and to speak is therefore political. Whereas writing, especially if you write in semi or academic, semi-academic or academic papers, who cares? Only academics read academic papers—so it is okay" (T/5/11–12, 16–17).

[16] Clifford Geertz (1973). *The Interpretation of Cultures*, New York: Basic. pp. 6–9.

[17] In relation to Tay, people comment on his writing, saying, for example: "It is so typically Kheng Soony" (a comment from an interviewee in the preliminary survey). Another interviewee says about Tay's writing in the newspaper: "people who know Kheng Soon very well, enjoy reading what he writes in the papers because it is like 'there he goes again'" (D/18/17).

understanding that illustrates the existence of a vast shared knowledge that enables a nonverbal, implicit interaction to replace an explicit, literal dialogue.

The reason why we refer to this kind of interaction as a "discourse" rather than calling it "dialogue" is that it is not confined to verbal exchange but typically involves other forms of social interaction—most predominantly, the business of "understanding without words." This culturally bounded phenomenon of "unspoken common knowledge" is actually the reason why everyday life can continue on the basis of its being "taken for granted," to use Shultz's phenomenological terms. It is this rootedness of the experience that enables one to embark on an interpretative discourse.

The texts therefore would rely on cultural knowledge that is not possible to translate literally, but encoded in the cultural understanding of the words. K.K. Seet, for example, refers to the "cultural untranslatability" of various aspects in Kuo's plays (both the English and the Chinese versions) as something that can be grasped intuitively, without requiring concretization. He argues that "the texts occasionally contain culture-specific concepts that resist smooth translation, gradations in the expressive meaning of words, modulations in the tenor of discourse, or units which are semantically complex. This cultural 'shared knowledge' decreases his need to spell out an idea explicitly or semantically."[18] This implies that the interpretive discourses are a shared process; the leaders bring something but so do the audiences.

The grasp of the literal text requires the departure of both audience and readers into the sphere of symbolic meaning and reflection, which is more than a mere passive reception of a literal or a nonliteral text. It is because of the requirement of a predominantly active engagement in the usage of allegories that we can speak of the audience actually establishing and engaging in a social discourse, even though it is not overtly or directly manifested and even when it is severely confined to the realm of a virtual, or "psychic discourse."

Kuo's Metaphorical, Allegorical Interpretive Sociopolitical Discourse

Theater, literature, and the arts in general enrich their texts by exploiting symbolic connotations and associations attached to objects and events. It is here that imagination, fantasy, and meaning engage the reader or observer in an active way. Aristotle related to the fact that metaphorical expressions are always obscure, but appreciated their capacity to "name that which has not been named."[19] And it is precisely the imaginative, ambiguous feature of the metaphors that allow an alternative discourse to take place—one that engages the participants in a vivid mode of

[18] See Seet, K.K (1992). "Cultural Untranslatability as Dramatic Strategy: A Speculative Look at the Different Language Versions of Kuo Pao Kun's Plays." Thiru, Kandiah (Ed.). *Beyond the Footlights, New Play Scripts in Singapore Theatre*. Singapore: UniPress. NUS. pp. 244–245.

[19] See Ong, Siow Heng, and Nirmala, Govindasamy-Ong. (1996). *Metaphor and Public Communication*. pp. 2–5.

interpretation—and may even contribute to the extension of the understanding and comprehension of ideas on social issues.[20]

Metaphors are grounded in common experience within a culture and include images and ideas. It is therefore possible for a metaphor to be properly recognized and its pertinence accounted for within its total context. Ong Siow Heng, for example, suggests that metaphorical utterances can be identified only if we take into account some knowledge possessed by speakers outside of the sentence and outside of their linguistic symbols. He argues that the audience identifies something as a metaphor from their perception and understanding of the context, from their own worldview, and from their own assumptions about the speaker.

It follows that a metaphorical discourse is intellectually and imaginatively demanding because the mind has to go through "an imaginative leap that is not governed or determined by rules or convention and so is not reducible to literal paraphrase." In this regard, imagination, feeling, and culture do not substitute, but instead complete the cognitive content of metaphor—and it is up to the active engagement of the audience to blend these two components coherently. Ong says that a metaphor cannot be understood by someone with insufficient knowledge because it is enigmatic or useless to a person without the knowledge of what the expressions represent, and who only has a lexical grasp of the meaning of the words.[21] Indeed, this notion is echoed by interviewees, one of whom says:

> I think that in all political plays in Singapore, the audience must bring something with them (…) It must be an audience which is *receptive*, and *knows in a way*, what Pao Kun wants to say. Well, all political plays in authoritarian societies need to do that because there is censorship.[22]

One reason a metaphor works is because the audience willingly suspends the literal lexical system at appropriate moments, and engages the imagination to think out what the metaphor is about, to try to find the unstated or the encoded subtext. This can only be done if the audience is familiar with the attributes that are considered as common knowledge about the metaphors. Ong says, in this respect, that "the speaker and the audience are thus personae in a dramatic, interactive exchange, which emphasizes the idea that human communication is a dynamic enterprise rather than the mere passing on, of static information in rigid, literal terms."[23]

Alongside the political constraints on sociopolitical commentary, allegorical discourse can be safely transmitted through nonliteral "structural gaps" in censorship systems, since censorship relies mostly on explicit, official, literal objective

---

[20] This is contrary to the positivists' and empiricists' devaluation of the metaphor as predominantly a distortion of communication because of its "senseless and ambiguous use of words in other sense than that they are ordained for." This means that the metaphors should thereby be discarded as deceiving rather than clarifying, and certainly not essential for communicating truth or logic, phrased literally (Ong & Nirmala, 1996: 6–7).

[21] For the quotes in this paragraph: Ibid., p. 22.

[22] Transcript B/17/3.

[23] Ong and Nirmala (1996) op. cit., p. 22.

understanding of words rather than on implicit, ambiguous, subjective, interpretations of the symbolic connotations of a text. In other words, explicit, literal texts render themselves more easily to censorship, but subjective connotations and associations prove to be resistant to censorship. Thus, it is here that a virtual, interpretive discourse can be set free. The discourse operates through an encoded verbal text that is up to the audience to decipher: It is the subtext within the text that conveys the underlying, decoded messages.

Kuo has never admitted that the metaphors or allegoric subtexts were intentionally constructed. Instead, he has always spoken of the "interpretive" nature of art and theater, as initially enabling various readings that are subjected to each observer's individual interpretation. Ultimately and objectively, it is thus never not what Kuo himself says, but what the audiences make of it. Kuo has always stressed that the interpretations are individual, and therefore not something situated, as it were, "in" the text, but in the minds of the interpreters. He says: "The Coffin, a one-man show, is subject to different interpretations. It is just a story. What you make out of it depends very much on your experience."[24] He also says, "on the part of the audience, (I) have heard of some very different interpretations—things that I had never dreamed of. People watch it and form their own opinion, most of which is very subjective."[25]

Various interpretations of the allegories are indeed possible, yet interviewees suggest that such comments may also be a "defense mechanism" or a tactic to overcome censorship. An interviewee says:

> Different people of course have different interpretations. They can interpret in their way. Pao Kun always says: "Yea, this is so called art: it is *up to you to interpret*." You know? 'It is up to you to *interpret* it, you can discuss it, you can debate, you can agree, you can disagree' (…) (but we all understand what is the message behind) even though he didn't 'say' all these…[26]

It is the "minimalist," cost-effective nature of the allegories and metaphors that enable them "to say a lot with very little," and thus relieving the need to engage in prolonged interactions that may easily cross the "out of bound" markers of what is permissible and slip into "subversive sociopolitical discourse." The usage of such language connotations requires a mastery of language, a skill that Kuo possesses not only in English, but in Chinese as well. The minimalist profile, short-term, and fragmented nature of this discourse, together with its predetermined structure, as occurring during predetermined, structured form (theater plays) is less constrained, at least sociopolitically.[27]

---

[24] *The Straits Times*, 3 Jul 1985.

[25] *The Straits Times*, 19 Jul 1985.

[26] Transcript B/8/5–6.

[27] Serge Moscovici (1992) notes that generally, the permission of carnivals and holidays in the religious, social and intellectual realms are linked to the fact that societies in general are willing to tolerate deviant behaviors (even if undesirable)—if they are restricted in such patterns as occurring at predetermined times.

Such encounters are predispositionally controlled, since they were already screened and approved by the censorship process, and are limited in terms of time, audience, and content. For example, the audience's scope is limited because the discourse is established with the participation of people who have the ability to decode plays and semiacademic texts. Those who cannot decode it, cannot engage in the discourse and thus are not sensitive to the leaders' argumentation. This radically restricts and confines the scope and nature of the audience. One interviewee argues that such interpretive plays are obviously permissible only because of the restriction in number and in the kind of audience[28]:

> From the government's point of view, I think they have changed also and become far more sophisticated. They have come to realize that the art group is really by and large, (I wouldn't say this of every artiste in Singapore, I wouldn't say this of every group), but by and large the arts community in Singapore is harmless politically, because they have very little influence politically (…) My guess is that the government has begun to realize that at the most, we are talking about a thousand people going to see the same stupid plays over and over again, and they spread out right around the country. So how many votes do they make, really? And how much of a threat to the system? Are they? Hardly, really. And how many of them want to be a threat to the system? Not really. …So they are safe, there is nothing for the government to worry about (…) The theater scene alone, is one of those areas where it is clearly more liberal, so why? So if you ask me that, my conclusion would be that the people are less of a political threat. And the intelligence service has become more intelligent, so to speak, and realizes this.[29]

An Example of Metaphorical Subtext

We will now focus on the analysis of one particular metaphor that is conveyed in Kuo's play, "The Descendants of the Eunuch Admiral." Kuo relates a historical (past time) story of a Eunuch Admiral—yet at the same time, he uses metaphorical clues that point to modern-day Singaporeans. This synthesis creates a new concept: that of the "modern-day eunuchs." The theme of castration, a vivid and figurative metaphor, not only describes the realities of the past Eunuchs, but conveys a critical message about the present "deals" that modern-day eunuchs make, in order to enjoy materialistic and other related sociopolitical pleasures.

Eunuchs have been instruments of rule in most of the classical empires of the Far East and the Near East. In China and Byzantium, as well as in the Arab, Mesopotamian, and Persian empires, eunuchs held a variety of positions at the court, in government and in the army. In Ming China, whole departments of eunuchs came into existence at court, and these were soon made use of for the confidential businesses of the emperor, outside the palace.[30] Max Weber has commented on how they headed

---

[28] Tay says that a high-ranking official commented on the "unthreatening" nature of the "virtual" "intellectual audience" saying: "You are a dispensable constituency (…) (politically) immaterial" (T/5/10).

[29] Transcript B/11/7, 9.

[30] Wolfram, E (1960). *A History of China*. Berkeley and Los Angeles: University of California Press. 253.

armies and at times controlled the bureaucracy, so that counselors could communicate with the emperor only through the intermediary of eunuchs.[31] In the earlier Han Dynasty, "they were established in the center of the governmental machine (and) soon obtained control of the civil service."[32]

Eunuchs originated when masters of large harems needed dependable harem guards who could not be led into temptation and betray their masters. Emperors required men who would owe them total allegiance and bear no competing loyalties. These men were typically from poor social backgrounds. They might be peasants, slaves, or young boys acquired in military operations, and who had lost contact with their families, uprooted from their kinship and region of origin. Having been castrated, they could not found their own families of procreation, and in the words of Lewis Coser, they became therefore "literally or figuratively, aliens."[33]

From the description given by Coser, "eunuchs were utterly alone. Socially rootless, they owed everything they were to their ruler; since eunuchs had no other groups of reference, the ruler—and his court—became for them the unique object of reference, the unique protector and the major point of repair, and their doglike devotion to him therefore resulted (...) consistently from their position."[34] This total devotion enabled them to implement the ruler's policies with an utmost single-mindedness that could not have been distracted by any peculiar tendencies to any other reference group.[35]

According to Weber, there was a constant struggle between the literati and the system of eunuchs in China, without which "Chinese history is most difficult to understand."[36] Although bureaucracy had claimed to be devoted to the rulers, it also developed tendencies toward being an autonomous body with its traditions and its ethical professionalism which, at times, imposed pressures on rulers. Bureaucratic officials were therefore exceedingly distrustful of the eunuch system because it negated the emphasis on rationality and on disciplined and methodical behavior. In contrast to the rationalism of the bureaucrats, the eunuch system practiced favoritism and particularism while the Chinese scholars advocated universalistic, rational standards. Eunuchs gave the emperor a governing class to be trustworthy since they could never covet hereditary power. Therefore, eunuchs were appropriate tools for

---

[31] Hans Gerth (1951) op. cit., p. 285.

[32] Fitzgerald, C.P (1954). *China: A Cultural History*. New York: Frederick Praeger. 252.

[33] Lewis Coser, *Greedy Institutions: Patterns of Undivided Commitment*. (1974). p. 23.

[34] Ibid., p. 24 (quoting Wittfogel, 1963).

[35] Eunuchs were loyal only to the rulers. Coser concludes that the social rootlessness from all group involvement makes for the eunuch's "objectivity" vis-a-vis all subjects, and conversely for his nearness to the ruler. He is hence "an ideal instrument of the ruler's subjectivity." (Coser, 1974: 25).

[36] Weber's words are in Gerth, op. cit., pp. 138–139. According to Coser (1974), "the eunuchs exploited (their) position near the person of the ruler and his family. Their basis of operation was attendance on persons, while the bureaucratic official based his power upon his position in an impersonal system. They thrived on nearness, where bureaucrats cultivated distance." He says "eunuchs controlled appointments to government posts, long-established practices of bureaucratic administration were eliminated and the court, i.e., the emperor and his tools, the eunuchs, could create a rule by way of arbitrary decisions, a despotic rule" (in Coser, 1974: 28).

the rulers who wished to escape the control of both the aristocratic class and the bureaucracy.[37]

Kuo's play takes no shortcuts on descriptions of the castration process and describes various modes of castration. Yet the plastic and figurative descriptions of castration methods are not included out of a sadistic pleasure. Each method described is "less cruel" and "more enlightened" in the sense that the castration itself is less painful. There are even methods that are so subtle that the castration is achieved without the full awareness of the castrated, albeit that the results are the same: castration is achieved. One thing that is common to all those methods—the "primitive" and "cruel," as well as the more "enlightened"—is that the castrated person cooperates with his own castration.

We will only cite the last method of castration, which is described at the end of the play, after having established the eunuch's paradoxical existence betwixt and between mighty powers yet suffering solitude, loneliness, rootlessness, and tormented fragmentation. This last method describes an "enlightened" castrative method, where people even willingly collaborate and cooperate with the process of castration, a process delivered by a "trusted caretaker."

The people's cooperation in their own castration is related partly to the "trust" they have in their "caretaker" and partly in the mere "indulgence" in the "pleasures" that the process offers. This method relies on a very long-term, prolonged process of castration and on the incremental pain that can be constantly added. Every time there is an increase in pain—enough time is given until the next increase—so that, in the process, people adjust to the level of the pain as "natural." Eventually, there are no "visible" signs of castration, and those same people being castrated can even recall some pleasures derived along the way. But, all the same, they are eventually castrated. The play says:

> Indeed, life had not been too kind to Zheng-He. The greatest of all ancient Eunuchs he was subjected to the most savage form of mutilation. Had he lived much later, he would have suffered only the minimal trauma by applying a more modern, and by far the most sophisticated, method of cutting and cleansing, which is the least painful and the least traumatic. Some say it was even comforting and pleasurable.
>
> You need highly trained specialists to do this. And again you have to do it when they are very young. The operation is usually handled by specially trained nannies, applied to the boys when they are still very young children. When the nanny has won the confidence of the little boy, she would begin to massage his testicles—perhaps after a bath, during playtime or before bedtime. Massaging softly, very softly at the beginning, so that there is not only no pain but is actually comforting and pleasurable.
>
> As the boy gets used to it, the nanny would gradually increase the pressure of the massage—again, always making sure it is done below the pain tolerance level of the child. As time goes by, the nanny would have increased the pressure of her massage to such a degree that although the boy still finds it pleasurable, she would have actually started to crush the testicles so hard that the impact begins to damage the inside of the organ. Of course, the child, by which time his pain tolerance level would also have risen so high, would continue to perceive the massage as not only benign, but also pleasurable. Very soon, the functions of the testicles are completely destroyed and the job is done.

---

[37] See Coser (1974) op. cit., p. 28. This resulted in an interaction that enabled the rulers to pursue with their policies without the threats and pressures of any other alternative autonomous powers such as the aristocratic class or the administrative machinery.

Apart from the absence of any perceived pain, and the advantage of retaining all the organs intact—nothing is cut off, all the parts are retained—the greatest merit of this method is that it is received by the subject as comforting, enjoyable, and even highly desirable. Externally, everything looks exactly same. Nothing would be missing. Everything looks normal and untouched. The only difference is that life will come to an end after he has lived his own: there would be no after life for his children (…) even when he's a great man, a great sailor, a great diplomat, a great soldier. He would forever remain man in limbo, a stranger, a wanderer (…) and the very end of a long, distinguished lineage of life.[38]

The metaphor of castration is very powerful and relies on the usage of imagination. But it is the process of the castration that gives the clues to the understanding of the metaphor: an accumulative, incremental, and prolonged process that is delivered by a "trusted caretaker," where people cooperate with their own self-castration (believing it to be for their own good, attributing good intentions to the caretaker, and even sometimes feeling that it is actually pleasurable). The process is not only "noncoercive" but, in fact, even supported conceptually and technically by all group members, including the family—and the ones to be castrated as well.

It is the "noncoercive" nature of castration as a social self-sacrifice that offers clues with regard to the encoded message: people cooperate with their own castration, thinking that it is good for them, without being aware of its invisible destructive nature. The castration process is not a clear-cut event (both literally and nonliterally); rather, it is a slow, "nonpainful" decay of the penis that results, eventually, in its being totally neutered. It does not require any surgical cuts because the organ is already destroyed physiologically.

Modern-day eunuchs are therefore people who cooperate with their own castration, blinded by the trust they have in their caretakers, and the hedonistic pleasures that they think they would gain. Also the fact that the increase of pain is done over such a long time span (and with lengthy intervals in between each increase of pain) contributes to their rendering themselves submissive to the castration, as they may already have become used to that level of pain as "part of their lives."

The understanding of the message is partly supported by the fact that the audience knows Kuo and knows what he wants to say. His recurring public statements in regard to the destructive side effects of the rapid and massive economic development that was not balanced with an equal process on social issues such as tradition, culture, social identity, and creativity are well known to the audience[39] and a recurrent

---

[38] *The Descendants of the Eunuch Admiral*, 1995. p. 22.

[39] In the "Notes on Memory" (a draft for a collective paper presented in the Substation's Conference, 16–18/9/94), he said, for example: "we are descendents of people who went through very hard times; they toiled for life to ensure that we would live in comfort and abundance. They made sure that we were protected from the harshness of life. They even avoided exposing us to the stories of their hardship. With all good intentions, they molded us into a people with short and shallow memories. We were taught, under loving protection, to focus our energy in things that ensure our material wellbeing. We were spared all the embarrassments of family stories, all the distractions of history, all the frustrations of art and literature and all confusions of philosophy. In the process, we gained a material home and lost a spiritual homeland. We lead the life of a fresh pack of international newly rich, as we lead the life of a new generation of cultural orphans. In effect, we were isolated from the source of knowledge where ideals spring from, where moralities derive from. But as we approach adulthood as individuals and as a nation, the thinness and shortness of our consciousness are facing more and tougher challenges as we awaken to the other dimensions of life as modern humans."

topic in his plays. Also his views with regard to the over-centralized control of the government and its demand for social compliance, as well as its emphasis on economic and material aspects of life, are not new to the audience.

The image of castration in the Eunuch play is strong: the message is clear and yet is not "there." It is not explicit in the text. It is implicitly situated somewhere in between the text's subtext and its being deciphered by an active, knowledgeable, participating audience. It is within the interactive understanding that the message is understood without being explicitly put forward.

The metaphorical structure works by creating a new concept that synthesizes two different concepts—eunuchs and modern-day Singaporeans. The substitution is made by portraying that A (the Eunuch Admiral) is powerful, though castrated. Yet by way of similarities, it substitutes A with B (modern-day Singaporeans) and leaves the substitute of the emperor to the audience. The substitution is achieved not by explicit naming, but by stating similarity affiliations between A and B (like saying that "A is similar to B in being 1, 2, 3").

The metaphorical similarity between the eunuch and modern-day Singaporeans is introduced with the presentation of three different clues transplanted in the play.

First, the eunuch in the play is a Chinese eunuch. Although Kuo could have spoken about eunuchism by citing examples from other empires, he mentions only the Chinese eunuchs. This immediately situates and contextualizes the play as part of the audience's remote collective history or collective archetype (at least because quantitatively speaking, 76% of the population is of Chinese descent). Second, Kuo states right at the beginning of the play that he himself feels as if he is a descendent of the great Eunuch Admiral Zheng-He (and he sees himself as an example of a "modern-day Singaporean"). Third, by stating a similarity between the way the eunuch's relative status was displayed (the penises being stored in a special room, displayed in boxes hanging in accord with the relative status of their "owners") and formulating an affinity with the similar design of contemporary modern organizational charts. For example, the play says:

> Now, I'd like to share a funny thought with you. Now, you look at us: together like this, don't you think we look like the organizational chart of my company. You know-lah, my chairman and the directors on the top, then the MD, the section heads, then us and the *kaki-tangan*[40] below us, we are all on the floor level. What I mean is, don't we look like a network of pricks? [41]

The metaphor is only partially stated. While Kuo offers clues for the similarity between the eunuchs and modern-day Singaporeans, he does not offer any similar clues for the metaphor of the emperor. He does not indicate that the emperor can be substituted metaphorically by having certain affinities and similarities with any other possible social entities. Yet is it not obviously implied by the mere grounding of the first half of the metaphor which points at the similarity between modern-day

---

[40] "*Kakitangan*" is a Malay word meaning "staff." (Literally, the feet "kaki" and hands "tangan" of an organization).

[41] *The Descendants of the Eunuch Admiral.* p. 3.

Singaporeans and eunuchs? Since the other half of the metaphor is self-explanatory, it could have been left entirely intact to be decoded and grasped in the audience's minds.[42]

Articulating Sociopolitical Dissent Through Aggression Sublimation

Other than metaphors, the interpretive characteristics of the discourse suggest that Kuo makes use of various social, cultural, and psychological dimensions that result in "overt aggression sublimation." Yet those who share the same phenomenological background are able to decode the conflictual and dissenting flavor of these "mild statements." Most of the particular techniques that Kuo uses take the form of passive-aggressive modes of interaction. The passive-aggressive mode of conflict management is not only more prevalent in Asian cultures in general and in the Chinese one in particular[43] but also enables political commentary in the face of contextual sociopolitical constraints.

As suggested by literature on Chinese culture,[44] the indirect, passive-aggressive nature of the discourse is supported by a cultural inclination for indirect verbal interactions, especially in regard to modes of conflict management. A sublimation of the aggression into a passive-aggressive mode is, according to Michael Bond, a characteristic of Chinese culture:

> Of course there are less obvious ways of being hostile towards others. Anger and opposition may be expressed in playing helpless, going slow, backbiting, not understanding, forgetting important promises, and other forms of passive-aggressive behavior. In authoritarian contexts this is a sensible strategy to adopt, as open rebellion will unleash repressive measures. Passive resistance is rarely labeled as 'aggressive' and hence is not punished, although it may be equally effective in undermining the pressure of superiors (…) Cross-cultural studies involving the Chinese would do well to include measures of these 'quieter' forms of aggression. I would expect them to be more frequent in any more hierarchical social system, like the Chinese.[45]

This tendency can be seen also in other cultures in the region. In his research on Malay peasantry resistance, James Scott notes similar passive-aggressive patterns. He says:

> The everyday forms of peasant resistance—the prosaic but constant struggle between the peasantry and those who seek to extract labor (…) most of the forms stop well short of collective outright defiance. Here I have in mind the weapons of the relatively powerless groups: foot dragging, dissimulation, false compliance, pilfering, feigned ignorance, slander,

---

[42] Again, this is only one of the possible interpretations, and not an explicit argument made by Kuo.

[43] See Michael Bond (1991). *Beyond the Chinese Face: Insights from Psychology.* pp. 14–16.

[44] Ibid., Also see Peter Smith and Michael Bond, (1993), *Social Psychology Across Cultures: Analysis and Perspectives.*

[45] Bond (1991) op. cit., p. 16.

arson, sabotage, and so forth. These Brechtian forms of class struggle have certain features in common. They require little or no coordination or planning; they often represent a form of individual self help, and they typically avoid any direct symbolic confrontation with authority or with elite norms.[46]

Passive-aggressive forms of discourse are suitable for expressing conflictual ideas because they convey the message yet do not seem too aggressive as to block any possible reconciliation or negotiation.

In the interpretive discourses, the passive-aggressive effect is achieved by incorporating simultaneous clues of both aggression and compliance in the text.[47] The passive aspects modify the aggressive message to the extent that its aggressive scope and degree is not explicit in a literal reading of the text. Yet the inconclusive manner of presenting the conflict can be decoded by applying the culturally shared knowledge on conflict management. An interviewee says this about Kuo's plays:

His plays were largely, well, almost allegorical. So he doesn't so much, sort of attack the system directly, as attack situation, look at situations and explore possibilities, the inner conflicts and allow that to speak for itself. So he never, I think, attacked the system. I mean even the 'No parking on Odd Days' play, is not an attack on the system, but yet I think, because it's so subtle, the more you think about it, that's where it's power comes from…and I think Pao Kun also achieved that "directness in subtlety," because if you're

---

[46] James Scott, *Weapons of the Weak: Everyday Forms of Peasant Resistance.* (1985). p. 29.

[47] For example, it is of significance that Tay tends to conclude his public comments with a "positive" or "constructive" tone. Just to show a few examples, he ends his comments on the lack of nature conservation saying: "to the authorities, I offer a plea to please consider the points made in the spirit of open dialogue." (ST 15 Sep 1998). He ends his comments on the need to be more efficient in energy using "flattering" terms: "Singapore can be the showcase for enlightened energy-efficient practices as it is small and well-governed. It has brains in both the private and public sectors" (ST 24 Dec 1997). He ends his comments on the lack of infrastructure for creativity pointing at a possible positive, bright future, saying: "our essential space limitations can be pushed back further by creative administration. Innovation can grow from this new partnership. Small space needs big hearts" (ST 28 Mar 1998). He ends his comment on the plans for the Singapore Arts Center reminding of other past, shared, collective experiences, saying: "such a major architectural and cultural undertaking must at least draw the kind of enthusiastic response from Singaporeans as did the new Changi International Airport and the Benjamin Sheares Viaduct when they were completed." (ST 30 Jul 1994)

These end remarks sublimate the text and "legitimize" it by adding features of "constructive criticism." There is a difference in kind in the legitimization given to "destructive versus constructive" commentaries because constructive criticism seems to imply an in-principle acceptance of the government's policies, and a willingness to cooperate with the system by suggesting ways of improving its function. In contrast, destructive criticism is perceived as a delegitimization of the authority of the powers that be, both in principle and in content, and thus a threat to social harmony and stability. It seems that a "final note" that includes a few possible ways for "improvement" or some positive remarks, colors the whole text with a legitimate shade, even if these comments are vague, too general or impractical. Their applicability is of less relevance. What is relevant is the fact that those suggestions are attached to the body of the text and apparently express and imply an acceptance of the powers that be. Therefore, the final notes work as textual clues for political framing of the semantic text—since it suggests ways for improvement, it is not an in-principle rejection. It is neither a threat to social cohesion, nor politically subversive. They do not totally legitimize the text but at least ensures that the discourse stops well short of being liable for formal persecution.

too conjectural—then you don't get to the core of it, but if you're too direct—then you get into trouble, so he managed to be both conjectural and get to the nub of the issue. (…) The way in which (he says things), the style is so subtle that you can't put a finger on it…So it is finding that balancing, because if you don't go near enough to the point, then people say what's the big deal he is talking about, right? But I think he's managed to find a way.[48]

Each of the "passive-aggressive" techniques that Kuo employs shows us how they are a reaction to the constraining structure, yet at the same time, they are an example of how structural gaps can be used for the purpose of commenting on that same mere structure. This is true also of the other such techniques that Tay employs, like using closing remarks that color his statement into a kind of constructive, positive remark, using semiacademic, abstract language.

In the following section, we will describe some of the aggression-sublimation techniques used by Kuo. These will include such techniques as the "fable" kind of story, the use of messengers, questions instead of exclamation marks, the usage of dreams and of wit, and the usage of generalizable, universal interpretations.

Fables

Kuo's messages are conveyed in the format of very "simple," almost "childlike" stories. The plots are not complicated. A theater practitioner relates to Kuo's "fable like theater," saying that there is a very positive sense of a naïve, childlike spirit in his plays, "Yet it can be very deep and highly spiritual. I think that in introducing these productions he started (a trend) again: we saw that theater does not need to have complex sort of story line in order to bring over a complex attitude or psychological (issue)."[49] The format of a fable carries with it a simple story that conveys a moral lesson to be learned. The simplicity of the plot is crucial for the easy grasping of that lesson that a more complex story lines may obscure. They are then a structure that makes the task of deciphering easier, if not obvious.

The Usage of Messengers

Another technique of aggression sublimation refers to the delivering of the message through an "unthreatening" third party. The aggression is thus modified by the fact that the message is never protested bluntly nor actually transmitted by the protagonist of the play, but by another character. Michael Bond argues[50] that in Chinese conflict management situations, the message is always conveyed by a third, unthreatening party so that the strategies include indirect confrontation through mediators or arbitrators. It is imperative for the sublimation that the transmitting character would

---

[48] Transcript B/17/3.

[49] Transcript A/2/3.

[50] Bond (1991) op. cit., p. 66.

have an "unthreatening" nature. This transference of aggression makes use of a "third party" and is consonant with Chinese and other Asian cultures.

One example of this is in Kuo's play, *The Silly Little Girl and The Funny Old Tree*. Here, he transmits critical messages through children, who seem naïve and innocent. The protest against the demolition of tradition in the face of economic modernist developments is voiced by a little girl who is remarkably "unthreatening": it is a girl (and not a boy); a little one (not an adult); and "silly" (as if all the rest were not enough to "disarm" her). The strong critical message is not channeled through a smart, potent adult vociferously protesting, but through an unheard voice of a hopeless, helpless, silly, little girl. Still, the underlying message seems to be transmitted very clearly, as a newspaper critic suggests, in writing: "the girl's not silly, and the tree, more than funny."[51]

In *No Parking on Odd Days*, it is the young son who is the one who urges the father to "fight back" against a punitive system that enforces too many regulations, restrictions, and fines. Still, the underlying message that criticizes the scope, degree, and content of regulations in Singapore is clearly read by audiences and journalists alike. A newspaper review of the play says:

> Minutes into *No Parking On Odd Days*, however, it was clear one did not have to be a motorist to appreciate this one-man, one act original which gave the bureaucracy an extra-sharp elbow in the ribs and kept the audience in stitches (…) the cost of compliance as the play reveals, is not just a matter of fines that he pays at the Maxwell Road police station… Each time, the man's son urges him to challenge the parking ticket ("fight daddy, fight!") only for their outspoken and honest attempts to be beaten down by the bureaucratese.[52]

Similarly, in *Lao Jiu—the Ninth Born*, it is the youngest son who "rebels" against family pressure to comply with the meritocratic, scholastically oriented, educational system that puts at its forefront science and neglects cultural and traditional dimensions. And in the play *Kopitiam*, it is an aging, lonely grandfather who resists his "educated, businessman" grandson who plans to sell the coffee shop (just because it is not economically viable). It is the voice of a lonely old man who conveys the message with regard to the very limited, narrow, economic perspective that modern Singaporeans have toward life.

Questions Instead of Exclamation Marks

This technique uses not only straightforward questions but also posits incomplete answers, which would also include Kuo's frequent usage of the dilemma form that we discussed in Chap. 8. A more literal indicator of the fact that he "frames" the play within a "question" is the repeated usage of phrases like "I don't know."

---

[51] *The Straits Times*, 15 Aug 1989.

[52] *The Straits Times*, 4 Jun 1986.

For example, the play, *The Coffin is Too Big for the Hole* begins with an implied question ("I don't know why") and ends with the implication of that question hanging, unanswered: "I don't know." The play offers no resolution of the question; instead, it just posits the question and the dilemma in a figurative manner and with no answers.

In the view of one theater practitioner, this tactic was "safer" in terms of posing critical messages and was more prevalent in Kuo's plays after he was released from detention. He says:

> Kuo would always end his plays with a *question* meaning that he would *expect* the audience to *ask questions*. It was what I think he hoped, that the audience would be *aware* of some of the problems, of some of the dilemmas that were occurring in the socio-political conditions of Singapore at that time. (The question mark) replaced the heroic stuff. (While all his plays, in the '60s, '70s were heroic times of revolution)—after his detention—the clenched fists were no longer there.[53]

Dreams

Dreams are a subconscious, or a nonconscious, state of mind. They are a field free of "superego" restrictions, where the "mind" is set free even when it sets to express aggressiveness. Yet at the same time, precisely because of the unintentional nature of dreams, their messages cannot be held against the dreamer (since he is not "really" in a conscious state of mind while dreaming). It sublimates aggressive messages, as "unintended" and "unconscious" and, as such, whatever aggression it conveys, is unintentional, and the person hence should not be liable, but in fact excused.

Kuo often starts or finishes his plays with dreams, and it is often in these dreams that the message is most clearly conveyed. *The Coffin Is Too Big for the Hole* starts with the words: "I don't know why, but it keeps coming back to me. This dream. Every time I get frustrated, it comes back to me." The narrator already points at the aggressive encoded message by mentioning that the dream always occurs whenever he is frustrated, which serves as a clue, an implication, or an introduction for the implied aggressive message. The play also finishes with a dream, saying, "As for me, the funeral somehow stuck in my mind and it would often come back to me. In a dream. Especially when I'm frustrated."

In a similar way, the *Descendents of the Eunuch Admiral* starts with the metaphor of the modern-day eunuchs by the protagonist's statement of his own resemblance to the historical and mythical eunuch. This gives us the first clue for the message to be conveyed. Yet the message is squarely positioned in the realm of a subconscious dream. We include a short extract from the play to show how the dream is a crucial component in the way Kuo conveys his messages—for example, how he comes to

---

[53] Transcript B/12/7.

say that he (and probably other Singaporeans) have close affinities with eunuchs. The play says:

> I have come to realize of late that dreaming has become the center of my life. Yes, dreaming. Dreaming all by myself. Alone, painfully alone, and floating away. But this loneliness is a potent one: it is an inviting loneliness. There's a vast space all around me. Endless. Haunting. Unknown. But promising. And seemingly reachable. I have a fear of this unknown. And yet this fear is also part of the yearning to depart, to leave the place I'm so used to—even when I know what I am going away from is a terrible insanity. Yes. Everyday. Everyday. I long to return to my nightly unknown.
>
> Was he also like this? Was he also like this when he was sailing across the vast ocean in the dark of the night, looking into the eerie distance, alone at sea, forgetting the pain created in him by the removal of his manhood?
>
> In these dreams, the days were no more just fun, no more just being cheerful and full of hope. In these dreams, being alone, I was able to look at myself, look inside myself and look through myself. And as I dived deeper and deeper into the stark loneliness of myself, I felt I had become closer and closer to him, closer to this 600-year old legend of a molested and incarcerated man.
>
> Yes, each night, through my own fear and uncertainty, I discover more agony in him, more respect for him, and more suspicion of him. And the more I do it—longing for him in the day and taunting him in the night—the more I do it, the more I am convinced that we were related, closely related—so closely related that I had to be a descendent of the eunuch admiral.[54]

Wit

Kuo's plays are largely seen as employing wit, as indicated from the audience's responses to them as being sarcastic, metaphorical, humorous, parodies, and satires. This humor is, however, also serious. A newspaper review of the *The Coffin Is Too Big for the Hole* said that "it is painfully funny and achingly serious (...) Kuo scores in his play, a sardonic commentary on the rigidity of a system that will not budge."[55] In the same vein, another review says:

> It's only about 35 minutes long, is full of apparent lightness and innate humor, and takes veiled digs at society and establishment alike…the upshot of the whole lightly macabre affair—grandpa got his special grave, his funeral was voted as the Story of the Year, and the official was awarded a medal for being sympathetic towards the grave plight…very funny and very tragic…perhaps the laughter is not so much at the absurdity, but because its "unintentional" irreverence and mockery comes too close to the bone?[56]

Lewis Coser has quoted Freud saying that "Wit permits us to make our enemy ridiculous through that which we could not utter loudly or consciously on account of existing hindrances, (and that) wit is used with special preference as a weapon of attack or criticism of superiors who claim to be in authority. Wit then serves as a

---

[54] *The Descendents of the Eunuch Admiral*, 1995. p. 1.
[55] *The Straits Times*, 29 May 1990.
[56] *The Straits Times*, 20 Nov 1985.

resistance against such authority and as an escape from its pressures."[57] Citing examples of wit as social practices that provide a "socially recognized channel for the expression of the culturally disallowed,"[58] Coser argues that wit is a socially approved, controlled, and limited act of conflict that "clears the air." But we should not overlook the fact that, at the same time, wit is also a way to safely convey an aggressive message.

The Presentation of Generalizable Meta-interpretations

Encoded messages can reach an abstract level by conveying a message that is generalizable, and the messages in Kuo's plays convey multilayered interpretations that can be concrete and parochial but, ultimately, generalized. In other words, the play can be interpreted as an abstract, universal, philosophical discussion which "has nothing to do," as it were, with the particular context. Yet at the same time, the messages permit a very concrete, local subtext. By way of example, newspaper reviews of *The Coffin Is Too Big for the Hole*, describe the various possible interpretations that the production entails:

> The onus of interpretation is on the individual onlooker, so you can easily—and validly—view *Coffin* as just a light, humorous piece. Or you can probe it for depths of meaning, from what happens to individualism in a rigidly bureaucratic society to whether tradition is a boon to our sense of 'roots,' or a deadweight burden…is it Chinese because it deals with an aspect of that tradition? Is it Singaporean in highlighting the obsession with standardization and regulation? Or is it universal in its questioning? *Coffin* is all those.[59]

Though grounded in the particular history of the Chinese Eunuch Admiral, the *Descendents of the Eunuch Admiral* entails more universal interpretations of conformity to social pressures. The director of the English version of the play, Ong Keng Sen, says that he discovered that universal angle when the play was well accepted in Europe. He then realized that the play conveys a universal message on the sacrifices that we all make in order to become part of society, or become materially successful: an interpretation that made the play relevant to other audiences, cutting across time, place, and culture. He says:

> (The play enabled the audience) to look at the castration of Singapore, either politically, or in the economic sense, because I think a lot of us subvert ourselves to making money, to the point where we don't even realize that we've lost ourselves. So you can look at it (also in this way). And recently we played it in Berlin and Hamburg, and they looked at it more in terms of the loss of self because of capitalism and commercial enterprise and all that. While, I think that in Singapore it of course has a much deeper meaning because of the politics, and you lose yourself, I think, as soon as you belong to a system.[60]

---

[57] Freud, Sigmund (1938). "Wit and its Relations to the Unconscious." In *Basic Writings of Sigmund Freud*. New York: The Modern Library. p. 697.

[58] Coser, Lewis (1956). *The Functions of Social Conflict*. p. 42.

[59] *The Straits Times*, 20 Nov 1985.

[60] Transcript B/7/8.

Another interviewee said, for example, that, to him, *Kopitiam* was the best example of "couching the text in humanitarian terms"[61]:

> I saw and loved (this 'universal/humanitarian notion) on performance of *Kopitiam* (...) Can you see what the direction is? The direction is that the computer expert, the son that comes from Canada—is Singapore in terms of development. And the father represents humanity— caring for friends. (The old man) could not close the coffee shop because where would his friends go? Because they come there to have a cup of coffee and read newspapers! Yeah, and that play was full of debate. Pao Kun led me to appreciate what he was doing in the 80s, that he realized that he has to crouch it in humanitarian terms rather than in socio-political terms. The humanitarian personalities that he represented, could be said to be subtle representatives of his specific political position; (by showing) human pain and how complex the situation is (...) It also was sort of a 'safe play,' right? He wasn't advocating revolution or anything like that. It is a humanitarian play, right? This is part of what I said, of him being, becoming more and more humanistic in his orientation. And I don't think, by choice. But I also think that he got deeper and deeper into formulating the characters of the play, and things like sub-text, became more and more important for him.

The Social Functions of the Alternative Sociopolitical Discourses

As we have already attested at the beginning of this chapter, interpretive and encoded messages can be deciphered because the audience knows what Kuo is going to say. But if indeed the audience already knows what he has to say, why is the metaphorical, allegorical, (or in Tay's case, the abstract, semiacademic) discourse still needed? It may be because the imaginative "stretch" and the reflective cognition that the metaphorical discourse enables expand the subjective understanding of social issues and ideas. The concept of "further understanding" is expressed in the following remarks from an interviewee:

> (It) is both *affirmation*, as well as to make life (apprehensible) it doesn't mean that it has to be something *new* (...) what it does is to *intensify* the experience, through new facets of it, and I think what Pao Kun does, his plays, just like Pavel's plays: the *experience* of going to seeing it. You *know* it! But do you *feel* it? Do you *realize* it to that extent? That's the art of it.[62]

In this respect, it is possible that the alternative sociopolitical discourses function as a mechanism of "social affirmation," serving as a reassurance for the audience's own convictions, beliefs, and ideas. Such interpretation may be reinforced by the fact that the audience of Kuo's plays (and the readers of the letters column in *The Straits Times*) tend to comprise a more or less regular group of people. To use Robert

---

[61] This is from transcript B/12/7 and B/12/7, 9. Basically, the play is about an old coffee shop owned by an old man, who worked very hard to finance his grandson's studies in Canada. Though economically the coffee shop was not doing well, it was important for him to maintain the coffee shop because of his camaraderie with his friends (who frequent in the coffee shop). His grandson becomes a computer expert in Canada and returns to Singapore, and wants to sell the coffee shop in order to invest in a business that "makes money."

[62] Transcript B/17/6–7.

Merton's conceptualization of social function,[63] while the manifested function of the plays refers to watching an art performance (and the reading of the newspaper is regarded as "informative"), the latent function refers to the social affirmation of people's ideas and values.

Perhaps the people's affirmation is needed all the more because they are constantly undermined by contrary dominant sociopolitical assumptions of both the majority and the power center. This interpretation would also support the argument of Serge Moscovici, that the corrosion of ideas is all the more susceptible in a social system that tends to conformity and that values harmony, preservation, and compliance.

Alternatively, or in addition to being self-affirmation rituals, using Lewis Coser's conceptualization of social mechanisms of social conflict, it is possible to see the role of these practices as bearing the potential within them of being "alternative safety-valve institutions." In his classic work on conflict,[64] George Simmel argues that social structures differ as to the degree of conflict which they tolerate, and that where the structure inhibits the expression and acting out of hostile feelings, substitute mechanisms for the venting of such feelings can be expected to exist.

Following Simmel, Coser assumes that the need for safety-valve institutions increases with the rigidity of the social structure, that is, with the degree to which the social system disallows expression of antagonistic claims. He adds that in cases in which conflict behavior against the original object is blocked, hostile feelings may be deflected upon substitute objects, or substitute satisfaction may be attained through mere tension release.[65]

Coser observes that there are certain social settings that repress overt expression of certain themes, and argues that in such conditions, the means of the dialogue or expression would be replaced or substituted. Our Interviewees express a similar notion—one uses the words "hot air" to refer to the public articulation of views as mere "ventilation." He says:

> Whatever the government wants to communicate will be communicated. There will be no miscommunication and they will make sure that there is no miscommunication. What they want to communicate is control, but there is room for other things. There is room. In fact, they welcome it, I mean, if they were to give no room, I don't think that the society could carry on. (They may in fact welcome it) because they know that there are people who want to know that there is space for such people. If you take the educated class, they want to know that there is space for such people. Once in a while, they may hear reports of them 'shouting on the mountain,' but they may not care what is being shouted but it makes them feel better that 'some shouting on the mountain' is allowed. And the government knows

---

[63] According to Merton (1968), the introduction of the concept of "latent functions" affords the sociological interpretation of many social practices, which persist even though their manifest purpose is clearly not achieved. In cases where a "group does not—and, indeed, often—cannot attain its ostensible purpose there is an inclination to attribute its occurrence to lack of intelligence, sheer ignorance, survivals or so-called inertia…yet given the concept of latent function, however, we are reminded that this behavior may perform a function for the group, although this function may be quite remote from the avowed purpose of the behavior" (1968: 118).

[64] Simmel, *Conflict*. (1955). pp. 16–20.

[65] Coser (1956). op. cit., pp.40, 45.

that, so it is not that (restricted). Well, if you want to be cynical, ultimately it is hot air and it won't change society. The authorities are still in full control of anything, everything that happens on the island. But you are welcome to say what you want to say.[66]

Emerging Patterns

Indeed, while discourse entails an ongoing, incremental argumentation that builds on mutual ongoing responses, this kind of discourse seems sporadic, circumscribed, somewhat silent, erratic, and finally, virtual. Instead of amounting to mature crystallized arguments that build on each other, it retains a more initial, somewhat crude, preliminary, anecdotal nature, and, as a "public" channel, it is severely limited to those who attend theater performances (or, in Tay's case, those who read the letters column).

Indeed, the audience's response is never direct, overt, nor public. Instead, there may be some private "in-group" discussions (mostly between close acquaintances, or a kind of "coffee shop talk"), which are only rarely echoed or transmitted back to Kuo (or to Tay and the other people who engage in public commentary through the newspaper). If there is any at all, they would take the form of sporadic and indirect feedback.[67] These findings resemble Scott's observations that we have already mentioned, with regard to the public resistance responses of Malay peasantry, as

---

[66] Transcript D/21/10.

[67] Though interviewees say that "there is a mute audience" (D/21/3), it is still possible to sense the discourse that is constituted along indirect, erratic feedback. An interviewee says: "Very often the dialogue isn't even necessarily in terms of other people writing on the same issue. It's an interesting thing. If a person is actually known in the media, you will get very often, people who come, total strangers who say: 'Oh, by the way aren't you so and so who write on the government'? There is actually an audience out there, and you'll know because they'll come out and they'll meet you for the first time and they'll tell you that they have read your columns and that they remember what they have *read*. So there is an effect even if people don't, even if the writing does not accumulate by other people also contributing directly (to the same issue) (…) (so) *You know!* You know (that there is an audience) because people like Kheng Soon (are always in public meetings), and every time he will go to a public meeting there will be some new people there, and very often they'll say: 'Oh I'm glad to meet you, I've read your things all the time, and I like what you say, and I particularly remember what is that you wrote.' So you will get very face-to-face feedback of things you've written a while ago. So the audience is not abstract" (D/20/1–2). Even with regard to the government as a (reluctant) participant in the alternative sociopolitical discourse, though it is much more difficult to get a direct response, an interviewee says: "In fact, I think every time you get a response of a certain kind, you're surprised by it. Usually they just ignore it. Or they would pretend that they're ignoring it. The government very seldom responds directly. It is much more difficult (to get some direct feedback from the government). Because so often it depends on how closely in touch you are with people who have connections with the government. But still you will know indirectly. (You will know that) not only they have read you, but that they have made comments about it. But it's not comments directly to you. It's comments to a third party who they have contact with and whose opinions they value" (D/20/11, 5).

always taking the form of nonorganized, noncollective, and nonpublic practices. Scott commented on the patterns of such social action, saying:

> They are, however, forms of resistance that reflect the conditions and constraints under which they are generated. If they are open, they are rarely collective, and, if they are collective, they are rarely open. The encounters seldom amount to more than 'incidents,' the results are usually inconclusive, and the perpetrators move under the cover of darkness or anonymity, melting back into the 'civilian' population for protective cover.[68]

This kind of ambiguous interaction could be easily dismissed by Western categorizations of public discourse on the ground of having an ambiguous, inconclusive, erratic, incidental, and intangible nature. But that would be failing to see the other half of the picture. Indeed, these discourses are a fitting example of how structural constraints form the way that charismatic leaders work and deliver messages in public. But, however ambiguous and elusive the articulations of the leaders are and however mute, virtual, or "psychic" the response of the captivated audience is,[69] the introduction and patterning (or institutionalization, if you wish) of these discourses to the public arena in Singapore overcame the very many structural constraints— and still delivered the message.

For artists, Kuo's allegoric language manages to convey the message that it is the artist's prerogative to explore and express sociopolitical issues. One interviewee says:

> To us theater people, he is an important artiste who actually changed certain dimensions by saying that we should be socially committed; we should be able to make a statement! As an artist in this country. That was a big jump, for an artist to make a statement, because only politicians are allowed statements in this country. So you see the difference? If you are not in politics and you make statements—you are in trouble, you can be sued by this government, even the opposition party. But (he was saying) that if you are an artist you can make a statement through art. So Pao Kun, I would say, started the ball rolling.[70]

People feel that such channels are their own way to participate in the shaping and the making of their own society.[71] Commenting on the way that politics is perceived in Singapore and as to who has a role in it, an interviewee says:

> The government as well as the public tend to think of politics as something that political parties do. Whereas *we* have a different view of politics; that it is not just for parties, it is for all concerned Singaporeans (…) *for* individuals like us, who are interested in politics and public issues, who want to contribute ideas, but don't want to form a party, don't want to

---

[68] Scott (1985). op. cit., p. 242.

[69] There are distinct characteristics of this audience, i.e., having tertiary education (mostly in western countries such as Britain, Australia, and America), or being referred to as the "intelligentsia." This suggests that at least there is a subgroup in the society, who do not wish to align itself with an "opposition" position nor rely on centralized mechanisms for their participation in the social and political affairs of their country.

[70] Transcript B/9/17.

[71] Tay says, for example: "(I use the newspaper media) because I have this belief that there is a possibility of a more enlightened society. And I want to live in such a society. And because I do not have such a society, I must try my best, try to do something to create such a society, isn't it? (…) I hope to live to that day. To live in such a society, of my own, is much better. I mean, there are such societies in England, in America, and so on (…) they do exist, but they are not my society."

join a party. And it is not something that we are shy about, we don't feel that makes us 'cowards or inferior,' or 'unwilling to get our hands dirty' or something. We feel that there is a legitimate role of citizens to want to be involved in political debate, without having to join a party.[72]

For interviewees, it was through these alternative channels that they could express, articulate, and exchange views on such issues (even if the articulation was indirect, and the communication was indirect, mute, and psychic). These were public channels that were not formed by the government and that, in a very symbolic way, became their very own. Though structurally the discourses are tiny little cracks, symbolically, they are perceived as much bigger: they are social spaces whereby people actively and meaningfully engage in the shaping of their lives.

It is the unique, authentic, and indigenous nature of these discourses that gives them a special social meaning. An interviewee says this about Kuo's plays:

I always see his plays as very metaphoric and very powerful because of the metaphors that they evoke and I think that, that kind of lyricism that he has given to Singapore theater (...) is a powerful thing to give to the theater scene. For me, this is his greatest gift, the fact that he has given us that metaphoric theater.[73]

---

[72] Transcript D/22/11.
[73] Transcript B/11/5, 6.

Conclusion

The structuralist camp in sociology (structuralism, Marxism, and structural functionalism) and the action camp in sociology (symbolic interactionism, phenomenology, some versions of the Weberian perspective, and post-structuralism) have not done much to study the theoretical as well as the empirical interactions between structure and agency. This research situated itself right in the middle of these two main camps, and relied on dialectical sociological approaches (such as Peter Berger's version of phenomenology, and Anthony Giddens's structuration) as a point of departure for the analysis of charismatic leadership. Such an approach promoted a sociological understanding of the dialectical relations between structure and agency by illustrating these interrelations with regard to the phenomenon of charismatic leadership. It thus demonstrated and promoted an understanding of how charismatic leaders shape, and are simultaneously shaped by, structure and the social reality of which they are a part. In so doing, it also contributed to the empirical demonstration of how a dialectical approach can be a fruitful way of analyzing social reality, structure and agency.

Following such a dialectical treatment of charismatic leadership, we have used a case study approach to attend to the nature of both agency and structure and their interrelation with regard to charismatic leadership. In doing so, the case study method illustrated how it is possible to deduce indigenous insights into the phenomena's particularized aspects, as well as to generalize theoretical observations that transcend contextual particularities. This method hence promoted the study of both the particular and generalizable aspects of charismatic leadership's agency and its relations with contextual factors.

The extent to which the charismatic leaders were shaped by the structure is evident in a number of ways: in the way that it shaped the particular content of their ideas; in the frequency of occurrence of such leadership; in the intensity of the attributions, manifestations and relations of the followers; in the scope and latitude of social action and transformation; and in the particular forms whereby the various actors interact. This, however, is not to say that the context "makes" the leaders. If this were the case, we should have people like Kuo, Tay and Prema occurring in abundance.

Dayan Hava and Chan Kwok-bun, *Charismatic Leadership in Singapore:*
Three Extraordinary People, DOI 10.1007/978-1-4614-1451-3,
© Springer Science+Business Media, LLC 2012

The fact that we could only locate few such people suggests that there is something about these individuals that transcends structure and particularisms of context. These people's agency is "universal" in the sense that no matter what the particular circumstances are, they would always, by nature, engage with the reflection on and the negotiation of the underlying structure of their own society. This means that wherever we find charismatic leaders, even in much more "opened" contexts, they will still be engaged in their reflection on the basic underlying assumptions of their own society, and will negotiate its meta, man-made structure (and whatever its underlying social structure would be). However, since underlying basic assumptions vary among societies, the content of the leaders' ideas, as well as the particular ways whereby they engage with the particular meta-structure and its transformation, will differ.

Charismatic leaders engage with and negotiate the meta-structure of their societies and in that process construct an alternative social reality. The way they construct reality is unique and differs from the emphasis that constructivist theories accord to typificatory schemes, ongoing socialization, and reproductive patterning of structuration. Contrary to these mechanisms, charismatic leaders construct reality by negotiating with the mere meta-social structure and by redefining the basic social assumptions. Such reality construction is qualitatively different because it relies on the acknowledgment of the "man-made" origins of the underlying structure (that governs and generates structurational patterns and typificatory schemes); it perceives the meta-social structure as mutable, contestable, debatable, negotiable, and workable; and thus, it reconstructs the very roots, origins and foundations of social reality.

Therefore, an interesting feature of the charismatic agency is that the articulation of an alternative social reality and meaning is always simultaneously intertwined with a juxtaposition and deconstruction of given basic social assumptions. It is hence essentially a constant, ongoing, simultaneous, dialectical process, both disrupting basic social assumptions and reconstructing alternative social meaning. In that sense, Tay's modern tropical architecture deconstructed professional Western architectural paradigms and, simultaneously, promoted an architecture that was coherent with the Southeast Asian context and meaningful to the young generation of architects. Similarly, Kuo juxtaposed his quest for the inclusion of the intangible dimensions onto social life with the dominant socio-political assumptions that tend to emphasize the pragmatic and economic dimensions to social collective identity. At the same time, he attempted a creative redefinition of social identity that would be meaningful to a young generation of theater practitioners and audiences alike. In like fashion, Prema deconstructed the paradigm of "untouchability" with regard to religious corpuses, and simultaneously synthesized various religious ideas into one spiritual/social belief system, thus promoting a philosophy and a way of life that was more meaningful for her volunteers.

We have also seen that the charismatic leadership agency constructs social reality by engaging people in a meta-thematic, philosophical discourse. As the three case studies suggest, in spite of the distinctness of the content of each leader's reality construction, there is a "meta-existential-content" that underlies all three cases. While all three cases are similar in that they encompass notions about the self, society and the world (as well as the links between these dimensions and social meaning and identity), each case represents a different reality contestation by focusing on a particular spectrum from the wide range of existential dilemmas. Therefore, though they all contain meta-existential dimensions, their different contentions produce alternative versions of what social reality is, or should be. This meta-thematic emphasis relies on reflection, exploration, intention and choice. The deliberate, conscious, perceptual, and philosophical aspects emphasize the cognitive and reflective nature of the way that charismatic agency contests, negotiates, redefines and shapes its own social reality, and accords meaning to the term "homo-sapiens." In keeping with Shmuel Eisenstadt's theoretical postulations, we saw that the charismatic leadership agency indeed relied on institutionalized dimensions such as organizations, texts, designs and plays. However, these institutionalized dimensions promoted the charismatic leadership's agency by enabling social platforms that particularly facilitated collective reflection, exploration and redefinition of human dilemmas, of basic social assumptions, and of social identity.

Following Shils's symbolic conceptualization of charisma, as well as with recent arguments of scholars in organizational behavior studies, who emphasize the link between charismatic leadership and self-concept,[1] our three cases also suggest that charismatic leadership is linked to the formation of identity and self-concept. However, other than suggesting the link with identity and self-concept, our cases suggest that the agency of charismatic leadership intrinsically and symbiotically grounds the self-concept within the social arena. That grounding may be a key factor in the understanding of the ability of such agency to mobilize people into social action, and engage people with their own society. In fact, it ties the particular, micro-level self with an entity that is bigger than their own selves: with their own macro society. By grounding the self concept within the social arena, people (leaders as well as followers) develop a sense of identity, of being at the active centers of the social system, and of having a sense of significant social participation in the shaping of their selves and their lives.

Singapore proved a tempting subject for empirical study for a number of reasons. First, research on charismatic leadership in the Southeast Asian context is scant – with the exception of monumental leaders like Mao, Gandhi and Sukarno, most of the studies on charisma rely on Western cases, most notably of business leaders. Second, studies that treat contextual factors relate to leadership in general but not to charisma. Third, research on charismatic leadership (in its pure Weberian sense as opposing and repudiating the power center) is scarce in one-party-dominant political contexts. Indeed, the very particular characteristics of the cases (or in Abbott's words, the "idiosyncrasies of the cases") were tremendously valuable to the conceptual generalizations of the relations between macro contextual factors, and charismatic leadership. In fact, they were so salient that they enabled an almost "laboratory"

---

[1] The most notable examples come from Shamir, House and Arthur (1993). But whereas these scholars also link charisma with self-efficacy and followers' empowerment, the link to self-concept formation is more general in the sense that it enables the analysis of charismatic leaders who promote followers' identity formation, though they may not contribute to their self-efficacy like Jim Jones who, for instance, created a deepening sense of dependency (Lindholm, 1990: 152) and Hitler who undermined the power of subordinates by promoting factionalism in the Nazi Party (Nyomarkay 1967; Lindholm 1990: 110–112).

type of inquiry, and facilitated the analytical clarity of the generalizable relations between context and charismatic leadership.

To start with, the unique socio-political context compelled us, in a way, to further clarify charisma's revolutionary aspect to suit cases with no obvious mass revolutionary movements or macro large-scale changes. In doing so, our research contributed a possible interpretation of the revolutionary aspect of charisma, as situated in the realm of ideas. Indeed, the emphasis in our research on ideas being a core aspect of the charismatic phenomenon is in accord with Weber's initial formulation of ideas as a core historical force, and with the recent emphasis on vision in the current leadership theories. However, the case studies show that the content of the charismatic ideas relates to underlying paradigms, basic social assumptions and the meta-structure of the particular social reality. It is in this respect that whereas various recent scholars have referred to the charismatic ideas as "uplifting," "raising" and pointing to "higher ideals," our research emphasizes the way in which charismatic ideas "go down," "go deeper," and "dive," so to speak, into the depths of human existence and to the underpinnings of social reality. In constraining contexts (but not only here in Singapore), it is in this nature of ideas as "cutting through the nub" of the meta-social reality, that the charismatic revolutionary aspect may be situated.

This also means that, ultimately, the revolutionary aspect is by definition relative and contextual because it can only be grasped vis-à-vis the underlying assumptions that it juxtaposes and deconstructs, and with the particular content of the discourse that is generated. As we suggested in Chap. 7, it is in this respect that charismatic leaders are "products" of the situation – not in the sense of being "created" by the situation, but in the sense of being assessed, and being perceived relevant, meaningful and revolutionary in line with the specific social system that they are contrasted to, and which they wish and attempt to transform.

The charismatic leaders not only confronted their particular power center and its assumptions, but also the basic social assumptions of the members of their own society and, therefore, their agency corresponded to the particular nature of the power center, and the nature of the society of which the leaders are a part. Tay Kheng Soon, for example, was perceived as "radical" not only because his ideas were articulated in a tightly-controlled political field, but also because he juxtaposed those ideas against the solid social and cultural inclinations towards Western paradigms. Kuo was perceived as "pushing the boundaries" not only because his quest to include intangible dimensions in the social identity question the power center's definition as to who is eligible to participate in the redefinition of collective identity, but also because this quest confronts the dominant orientation of the society towards economics and pragmatism as the most valid components of social identity. Similarly, Prema's mixture of religious themes into a synthetic philosophy was seen as one of "rebelliousness,"[2] not only because this eclectic philosophy is

---

[2] Prema says that with regard to her "stubbornness" in questioning the teachings of the Christian teachers in Sunday school: "Other children asked: 'Everybody accepts it, why can't you accept? Why is it so difficult? Why do you get yourself into trouble? (…) So I was always a rebellious child. A difficult child. They called me: 'asking questions' " (1995: 2/240, 7/93).

critical about the dogmatic, exclusive nature of religious corpuses, but also because this mixture confronts people's perceptions about mundane life and spiritualism as unbridgeable.

There are also indications with regard to the ways that the context shapes the latitude, scope and nature of charisma: for example, its interactions, behavioral manifestations, social transformations and the articulation of views. We saw that social action seemed to enjoy greater latitude at the micro and messo levels of society, and we also saw a clearer social influence in these two levels of analysis. However, the latitude for social action at the macro level of society is much more confined, and therefore the leaders' social influence at that level was harder to be identified.

There are also indications to suggest that contextual factors effect the frequency of idiosyncratic charisma. The impediments placed on alternative authority in general, including charismatic leadership, result in there being a smaller number of idiosyncratic charismatic leaders. At the same time, some contextual factors reinforce charisma attributions towards outstanding people, precisely because of their scarcity. This means that the reinforced attributions are a corollary of the constraining context and can only occur in constellations where only few people stand out. Therefore though contrast-effect processes of impression formation may reinforce charismatic attributions, they cannot generate charisma (once again, the context therefore cannot "make" leaders, but to a large extent can shape the particular intensity of the social attributions towards the leaders).

It is also the case that the intensity of idiosyncratic charisma seems to be effected, for example, in the smaller number of followers (due to contextual restrictions on collective organized action); in less overt manifestations of followership (because of both socio-cultural and political factors); in the inclusion of negative attributions towards the leaders (because of collective, compliant tendencies to brand extraordinary, revolutionary people as "controversial" or as "trouble makers"); and in the loss of personal charisma (because, in an efficient and successful system of co-optation, idiosyncratic charisma may automatically transform into "office charisma").

Also the scope, degree and nature of the processes of social transformations seem different from what the current literature on leadership suggests. Rather than abrupt, total, dramatic processes of large-scale structural reformation, the social transformations are confined more to a type of action that relies on a constant, ongoing "exploitation," "manipulation" and the "taking advantage" of tiny structural gaps, cracks or niches within the tight structure. These charismatic leaders must make painstaking efforts to work out delicate, feasible measures to cope with system-conservative political pressure while conducting their activities in the negotiation or breaking of system boundaries. The more they intend to deviate from existing boundaries, the more risky their business becomes, and the more delicate they have to be in their social action.

This type of social action requires absolute mastery and knowledge of "the rules of the game," of "knowing thy enemy," and of acting as "smooth and shrewd operators." The usage of terms such as "exploitation," "taking advantage," "opportunism," and "manipulation," may sound "negative." Indeed, such a "Machiavelistic" conceptualization of charismatic leadership does not agree with the "idealistic" treatment of extraordinary leaders in the current organizational behavior literature. A more "value-free" interpretation of this type of action would therefore refer to the leaders' ability to work within utmost constraining contexts, and it would thus be more accurate to see their agency in terms of an ongoing "negotiation" with the underlying social structure a negotiation where the power center itself participates, even if not willingly so. In other words, these leaders exploit little cracks; expanding, amplifying, and broadening them into social spaces that offer the participants a meaningful way to engage with their own structure, and with their own social reality.

Contrary to the "universal" assumptions with regard to extraordinary leadership in the recent leadership theories (see Brynman, Stephens, & Campo, 1996.) it seems that specific contextual factors may result in unique patterns of charismatic interaction, social action and transformation. These contextual propositions are not in agreement with the current "universal" leadership paradigm, and suggest that a reflective perspective is first and foremost required to be willing to resurrect our conventional convictions[3] on charismatic social action. In this study charisma did not result in clearly defined and obvious manifested ways, but rather unique patterns of indirect and ambiguous interaction, ambivalent and passive-aggressive modes of discourse, and restricted social action and change.

Our research observations in this field suggest that the study of charismatic leadership in centralized, constraining contexts, requires an approach that takes antinomies, paradoxes, latency, liminality and ambivalence, as part and parcel of such social action,[4] and can locate, identify, diagnose, interpret and account for such patterns. Such an understanding of social action and change posits a real challenge for positivistic and quantitative research because it differs from the "tendency in behavioral science to read mass behavior directly from statistical abstracts on income, caloric intake, newspaper circulation, or radio ownership" (Scott, 1985: 38). Even within qualitative approaches there is still a need to further conceptualize, operationalize and methodologically clarify ways of analyzing such patterns, and in fact, our research points at the need to further develop such language and tools.

---

[3] In particular relation to cultural variances, Bond (1991: 1–2) says that whenever empirical findings stem from the given paradigms, people may "claim that the investigator did not adequately understand the culture examined, that the measures distorted the real cultural phenomena, or that the interpretations of the results are biased. The typical response is thus to dismiss the researcher's findings."

[4] Moscovici says, for example, that "one can visualize a purely public compliance without any private acceptance, as illustrated, tragically, by concentration camps, and a private acceptance without public manifestation as witnessed by secret societies and, during certain epochs, Christian heresies" (Moscovici 1980: 211).

Bibliography

Abbott, A. (1992). What Do Cases Do? Some Notes on Activity in Sociological Analysis. In H. S. Becker & C. R. Charles (Eds.), *What Is a Case? Exploring the Foundations of Social Inquiry* (pp. 53–82). Cambridge: Cambridge University Press.

Archer, M. S. (1985). Structuration Versus Morphogenesis. In S. N. Eisenstadt, H. J. Helle, S. N. Eisenstadt, & H. J. Helle (Eds.), *Macro-sociological Theory, Perspectives on Sociological Theory* (Vol. 1, pp. 58–87).

Argyris, C. (1976). *Increasing Leadership Effectiveness*. New York: Wiley.

Avolio, B. J. (1995). Transformational Leadership. *Leadership Review Quarterly, 1*(2), 4.

Avolio Bruce, J., & Gibbons, T. C. (1988). Developing Transformational Leaders: A Life Span Approach. In J. A. Conger & R. N. Kanungo (Eds.), *Charismatic Leadership: The Elusive Factor in Organizational Effectiveness*. San Francisco: Jossey-Bass.

Avolio, B. J., & Bass, B. M. (1988). Transformational Leadership: Charisma and Beyond. In J. G. Hunt (Ed.), *Emerging Leadership Vistas* (pp. 29–49). Lexington: D.C. Health.

Bass, B. M. (1981). *Stodgill's Handbook of Leadership*. New York: Free Press.

Bass, B. M. (1985). *Leadership and Performance Beyond Expectations*. New York: Free Press.

Bass, B. M. (1988). Evolving Perspectives on Charismatic Leadership. In J. A. Conger & R. N. Kanungo (Eds.), *Charismatic Leadership: The Elusive Factor in Organizational Effectiveness* (pp. 40–78). San Francisco: Jossey-Bass.

Becker, H. S. (1992). Cases, Causes, Conjunctures, Stories, and Imagery. In H. S. Becker & C. R. Charles (Eds.), *What Is a Case? Exploring the Foundations of Social Inquiry*. Cambridge: Cambridge University Press.

Bell, R. S. (1986). Charisma and Illegitimate Authority. In R. M. Glassman (Ed.), *Charisma, History and Social Structure*. New York: Greenwood.

Bendix, R. (1962). *Max Weber: An Intellectual Portrait*. Garden City: Doubleday.

Bendix, R. (Ed.). (1968). Reflections on Charismatic Leadership. In *State and Society*. Boston: Little, Brown.

Bennis, W., & Nannus, B. (1985). *Leaders: The Strategies for Taking Charge*. New York: Harper and Row.

Bensman, J., & Givant, M. (1975). Charisma and Modernity: The Use and Abuse of a Concept. *Social Research, 42*(4), 570–614.

Berger, P. L. (1963). Charisma and Religious Innovation: The Social Location of the Israelite Prophecy. *American Sociological Review, 28*, 940–950.

Berger, P. (1967). *Invitation to Sociology: A Humanistic Perspective*. Garden City: Doubleday.

Berger, P. L., & Kellner, H. (1981). *Sociology Reinterpreted*. New York: Anchor Books.

Berger, P. L., & Luckman, T. (1966). *The Social Construction of Reality*. Garden City: Doubleday.

Dayan Hava and Chan Kwok-bun, *Charismatic Leadership in Singapore:*   235
Three Extraordinary People, DOI 10.1007/978-1-4614-1451-3,
© Springer Science+Business Media, LLC 2012

Berlew, D. E. (1974). Leadership and Organizational Excitement. *California Management Review, 17*, 21–30.

Blau, P., & Scott, W. R. (1962). *Formal Organizations*. San Francisco: Chandler.

Boal, K. B., & Bryson, J. M. (1988). Charismatic Leadership: A Phenomenological and Historical Approach. In J. G. Hunt, B. R. Baliga, & H. P. Dachler (Eds.), *Emerging Leadership Vistas* (pp. 12–26). Toronto: Lexington.

Bond, M. H. (1991). *Beyond the Chinese Face: Insights from Psychology*. Hong Kong: Oxford University Press.

Bosserman, P. (1968). *Dialectical Sociology: An Analysis of the Sociology of Georges Gurvitch* (p. 227). Boston: Porter Sargent.

Bradley, R. T. (1987). *Charisma and Social Structure: A Study of Love and Power, Wholeness and Transformation* (pp. 29–72). New York: Paragon House.

Brynman, A. (1992). *Charisma and Leadership in Organization*. London: Sage.

Brynman, A., Stephens, M., & Campo, C. (1996). The Importance of Context: Qualitative Research and the Study of Leadership. *Leadership Quarterly, 7*(3), Fall. 353–370.

Bunnang, J. (1984). The Way of the Monk and the Way of the World: Buddhism in Thailand, Laos and Cambodia. In H. Bechert, R. Gombrich, H. Bechert, R. Gombrich, H. Bechert, & R. Gombrich (Eds.), *The World of Buddhism* (pp. 159–170). London: Thames & Hudson.

Burke, K. (1962). *A Grammar of Motives and a Rhetoric of Motives*. Cleveland: World Publishing.

Burns, J. M. (1978). *Leadership*. New York: Harper and Row.

Calder, B. J. (1977). An Attribution Theory of Leadership. In M. B. Staw & R. G. Salancik (Eds.), *New Directions in Organizational Behavior*. Chicago: St Clair.

Chan, H. C. (1971). *Singapore: The Politics of Survival*. Singapore: Oxford University Press.

Chan, H. C. (1975). Politics in an Administrative State: Where Has the Politics Gone? In S. C. Meow (Ed.), *Trends in Singapore*. Singapore: Singapore University Press.

Chan, H. C. (1993). Democracy: Evolution and Implementation, an Asian Perspective. In R. Bartley et al. (Eds.), *Democracy and Capitalism: Asian and American Perspectives*. Singapore: Institute of Southeast Asian studies.

Chua, B. H. (1995). *Communitarian Ideology and Democracy in Singapore*. London: Routledge.

Chua, B. H. (1997). *Political Legitimacy and Housing*. London: Routledge.

Cicourel, A. (1964). *Method and Measurement in Sociology*. New York: Free Press.

Cicourel, A. (1981). On the Integration of Micro and Macro Levels of Analysis. In K. Knorr-Cetina & V. A. Cicourel (Eds.), *Advances in Social Theory and Methodology: Towards an Integration of Micro and Macro Sociologies*. Boston: Routledge & Kegan Paul.

Conger, J. A. (1988). Theoretical Foundations of Charismatic Leaders. In J. A. Conger & R. N. Kanungo (Eds.), *Charismatic Leadership: The Elusive Factor in Organizational Effectiveness* (pp. 12–40). San Francisco: Jossey-Bass.

Conger, J. A. (1989). *The Charismatic Leader: Behind the Mystique of Exceptional Leadership* (pp. 21–93). San Francisco: Jossey-Bass.

Conger, J. A., & Kanungo, R. N. (1988). Behavioral Dimensions of Charismatic Leadership. In J. A. Conger & R. N. Kanungo (Eds.), *Charismatic Leadership: The Elusive Factor in Organizational Effectiveness* (pp. 78–98). San Francisco: Jossey-Bass.

Coser, L. (1956). *The Functions of Social Conflict*. London: Routledge & Kegan Paul.

Coser, L. (1964). The Political Functions of Eunuchism. *American Sociological Review, 29*, 880.

Coser, L. (1967). *Continuities in the Study of Social Conflict*. Glencoe: Free Press.

Coser, L. (1974). *Greedy Institutions: Patterns of Undivided Commitment*. New York: Free Press.

Daniel, F., & Hugh, A. (1983). *Managing Individual and Group Behavior in Organizations*. London: McGraw-Hill.

Douglas, M. (1966). *Purity and Danger: An Analysis of Concepts of Pollution and Taboo*. New York: Praeger.

Dow, T. E., Jr. (1969). The Theory of Charisma. *The Sociological Quarterly, 10*, 306–318.

Eisenstadt, S. N. (1968). *Max Weber: On Charisma and Institution Building*. Chicago: University of Chicago Press.

Eisenstadt, S. N. (1995). *Power, Trust and Meaning*. Chicago: University of Chicago Press.

Emmerson, K. D. (1995). Singapore and the 'Asian Values' Debate. *Journal of Democracy, 6–4*, 95–105.

Erez, M., & Early, C. P. (1993). *Culture, Self-identity and Work*. New York: Oxford University Press.

Etzioni, A. (1961). *A Comparative Analysis of Complex Organizations*. New York: Free Press.

Etzioni, A. (1975). *A Comparative Analysis of Complex Organizations: On Power, Involvement, and their Correlates*. New York: Free Press.

Eu Meng, K. (1995). *Singapore's Extraordinary People*. Singapore: Television Corporation of Singapore and Landmark Books.

Fabian, J. (1968). Charisma and Cultural Change. *Comparative Studies in Society and History, 11*, 155–173.

Fiedler, F. E. (1978). The Contingency Model and the Dynamics of Leadership. In L. Berkowitz (Ed.), *Advances in Experimental Social Psychology*. New York: Academy.

Fitzgerald, C. P. (1954). *China: A Cultural History*. New York: Frederick Praeger.

Foucault, M. (1989). From the Order of Discourse. In P. Rice & P. Waugh (Eds.), *Modern Literary Theory: A Reader* (pp. 221–233). London: Edward Arnold.

Freud, S. (1938). Wit and its Relations to the Unconscious. In A. A. Brill (Ed.), *Basic Writings of Sigmund Freud*. New York: The Modern Library.

Friedland, W. H. (1964). For a sociological concept of charisma. *Social Forces, 43*, 18–26.

Geertz, C. (1973). *The Interpretation of Cultures*. New York: Basic.

Geertz, C. (1977). Centers, Kings and Charisma: Reflections on the Symbolics of Power. In J. Ben-David & T. N. Clarck (Eds.), *Culture and its Creators* (pp. 150–171). Chicago: University of Chicago Press.

Gerth, H. H., & Mills C. W. (Eds. and Trans.). (1947). *From Max Weber: Essays in Sociology*. London: Routledge & Kegan Paul.

Giddens, A. (1972). *Emile Durkheim: Selected Writings* (pp. 1–69). London: Cambridge University Press.

Giddens, A. (1976). *New Rules of Sociological Method: A Positive Critique of Interpretive Sociologies*. London: Hutchinson.

Giddens, A. (1984). *The Constitution of Society: Outline of the Theory of Structuration*. Cambridge: Polity.

Gouldner, A. W. (1965). *Studies in Leadership*. New York: Russell and Russell.

Hemphill, J. K. (1954). A Proposed Theory of Leadership in Small Groups (Chap. 1). In J. K. Hemphill et al. (Eds.), *Leadership Acts*. Columbus: Ohio State University.

Hofstede, G. (1980). *Culture's Consequences: International Differences in Work Related Values*. Beverly Hills: Sage.

Hofstede, G., & Bond, M. H. (1989). The Confucius Connection: From Cultural Roots to Economic Growth. *Organizational Dynamics, 16*, 5–21.

Hollander, E. P. (1958). Conformity, Status and Idiosyncracy Credit. *Psychological Review, 65*, 117–127.

Hollander, E. P. (1964). *Leaders, Groups and Influence*. New York: Oxford University Press.

Homans, G. C. (1950). *The Human Group*. New York: Harcourt, Brace.

House, J. R. (1977). A 1976 Theory of Charismatic Leadership. In J. G. Hunt, L. L. Larson, J. G. Hunt, & L. L. Larson (Eds.), *Leadership: The Cutting Edge*. Carbondale: Southern Illinois University Press.

House, J. R., & Shamir, B. (1993). Toward the Integration of Transformational, Charismatic and Visionary Leaders. In M. Chemers & R. Ayman (Eds.), *Leadership Theory and Research* (pp. 81–107). San Diego: Academic.

House, J. R., Woycke, J., & Fodor, M. E. (1988). Charismatic and Non-charismatic Leaders: Differences in Behavior and Effectiveness. In J. A. Conger & R. N. Kanungo (Eds.), *Charismatic Leadership: The Elusive Factor in Organizational Effectiveness* (pp. 98–122). San Francisco: Jossey-Bass.

Howell, J. M. (1988). Two Faces of Charisma: Socialised and Personalised Leadership in Organizations. In J. A. Conger & R. N. Kanungo (Eds.), *Charismatic Leadership: The Elusive Factor in Organizational Effectiveness* (pp. 213–237). San Francisco: Jossey-Bass.

Hunt, J. G., & Osborn, R. N. (1982). Toward a Macro-oriented Model of Leadership: An Odyssey. In J. G. Hunt, U. Sekaran, & C. Schrieshein (Eds.), *Leadership: Beyond Establishment Views* (pp. 196–221). Carbondale: Southern Illinois University Press.

Kanter, R. M. (1984). *The Change Masters*. New York: Simon & Schuster.

Kelman, H. C. (1958). Compliance, Identification and Internalization: Three Processes of Attitude Change. *Journal of Conflict Resolution, 2*, 51–60.

Kluckhohn, F. R., & Strodtbeck, F. L. (1961). *Variations in Value Orientations*. New York: Harper and Row.

Kuo, P. K. (1990). *The Coffin is Too Big for the Hole and Other Plays*. Singapore: Times Books International.

Kuo, P. K. (1993). Commentary by Kuo Pao Kun. In *Arts Versus Arts, Conflict and Convergence*. Singapore: The Substation Conference.

Kuo, P. K. (1994). Opening notes for *Our Place in Time – A Conference on Heritage*. Singapore: The Substation Conference.

Kuo, P. K. (1995). Complexities and Contradictions. In *Space, Spaces and Spacing*. Singapore: The Substation Conference.

Kuo, P. K. (1997a). A Need for a Cultural Layer. A paper delivered at a conference held by the Institute of Policy Studies, Singapore

Kuo, P. K. (1997b). A conversation with Kuo Pao Kun. In *Lives: Ten Years of Singapore Theatre, Essays Commissioned by the Necessary Stage* (pp. 126–142). Singapore: First Printers.

Kuo, P. K. (2000). *Images at the Margins: A Collection of Kuo Pao Kun's Plays*. Singapore: Times.

Lindholm, C. (1990). *Charisma*. Cambridge, MA: Basil Blackwell.

Maranell, G. M. (1970). The Evaluation of Presidents: An Extension of Schlesinger Polls. *The Journal of American History, 57*, 104–113.

Marcus, J. T. (1969). Transcendence and Charisma. *Western Political Quarterly, 14*, 236–241.

McCann, S. J. H. (1997). Threatening Times and the Election of Charismatic U.S. Presidents: With and Without FDR. *The Journal of Psychology, 131*(4), 393–400.

McClelland, D. C. (1975). *Power: The Inner Experience*. New York: Irvington.

McClelland, D. C. (1985). *Human Motivation*. Glenview: Scott, Foresman.

McHugh, P. (1968). *Defining the Situation: The Organization of Meaning in Social Interaction*. Indianapolis: Bobbs-Merrill.

Mead, H. G. (1934). *Mind, Self and Society from the Standpoint of a Social Behaviorist*. Chicago: The University of Chicago Press.

Meindl, J. R. (1990). On Leadership: An Alternative to Conventional Wisdom. In B. M. Staw & L. L. Cummings (Eds.), *Research in Organizational Behavior* (Vol. 12, pp. 154–203). Greenwich: Jai.

Meindl, J. R., Ehrlich, S. D., & Dukerich, J. M. (1985). The Romance of Leadership. *Administrative Science Quarterly, 30*, 78–102.

Merton, R. K. (1968). *Social Theory and Social Structure*. New York: Free Press.

Misumi, J., & Perterson, M. F. (1985). The Performance-maintenance (PM) Theory of Leadership: Review of a Japanese Research Program. *Administrative Science Quarterly, 30*, 198–223.

Morgan, J. L. (1986). *From Simple Input to Complex Grammar*. Cambridge: MIT.

Moscovici, S. (1980). Towards a Theory of Conversion Behavior. *Advances in Experimental Social Psychology, 13*, 209–239.

Moscovici, S. (1992). *Minority Influence*. Chicago: Nelson-Hall.

Moscovici, S. (1993). *The Invention of Society* (W. D. Halls, Trans). Cambridge: Polity Press.

Nadler, D. A., & Tushman, M. L. (1990). Beyond the Charismatic Leader: Leadership and Organizational Change. In R. M. Steers, P. W. Lyman, B. A. Gregory, R. M. Steers, P. W. Lyman, & B. A. Gregory (Eds.), *Motivation and Leadership at Work* (pp. 689–707). New York: McGraw Hill.

Nannus, B. (1992). *Visionary Leadership*. San Francisco: Jossey-Bass.

Ng, S. K. (1980). *The Social Psychology of Power*. New York: Academic.

Nyomarkay, J. (1967). *Charisma and Factionalism in the Nazi Party*. Minneapolis: University of Minnesota Press.

Oberg, W. (1972). Charisma, Commitment, and Contemporary Organization Theory. *Business Topics, 20*, 18–32.

Olsen, E. M., & Marger, M. N. (Eds.). (1993). *Power in Modern Societies*. Boulder: Westview.

Ong S. H., & Nirmala G-O. (1996). *Metaphor and Public Communication*. Singapore: Graham Brash (Pte) Ltd. 1–37.

Oomen, T. K. (1968). Charisma, Social Structure and Social Change. *Comparative Studies in Society and History, 10*, 85–99.

Osborn, R. N., & Hunt, J. G. (1974). Environment and Organizational Effectiveness. *Administrative Science Quarterly, 19*, 231–246.

Osborn, R. N., & Hunt, J. G. (1975). An Adaptive-reactive Theory of Leadership: The Role of Macro Variables in Leadership Research. In J. G. Hunt & L. L. Larson (Eds.), *Leadership Frontiers* (pp. 27–450). Kent: Kent State University.

Ow, C. H. (1984). Singapore: Past, Present and Future. In P. S. You, C. Y. Lim, P. S. You, & C. Y. Lim (Eds.), *Singapore: Twenty-five Years of Development*. Singapore: Nan Yang Xing Zhou Lianhe Zabao.

Parsons, T. (1960). *Structure and Process in Modern Societies*. Glencoe: Free Press.

Parsons, T., & Henderson, A. M. (Trans. and Ed.) (1964). *Max Weber: The Theory of Social and Economic Organization* (pp. 358–373). London: The Free Press of Glencoe.

Perinbanayagan, R. S., & Wilson, R. A. (1971). The Dialectics of Charisma. *The Sociological Quarterly, 12*, 387–402.

Peters, T. J., & Waterman, R. H. (1982). *In Search for Excellence*. New York: Harper & Row.

Popper, K. R., & Eules, J. C. (1977). *The Self and its Brain*. London: Routledge & Kegan Paul.

Popper, K. R., & Notturno, M. A. (Eds.) (1994). *Knowledge and the Body-mind Problem: In Defence of Interaction*. London and New York.

Powell, R. (1997). *Lines, Edges and Shades*. Singapore: Page One.

Radcliffe-Brown, A. R. (1957). *Natural Science of Society* (p. 87). New York: Free Press.

Redding, G. (1990). *The Spirit of the Chinese Capitalism*. Berlin: W. De Gruyter.

Roberts, N. C., & Bradley, R. T. (1988). Limits of Charisma. In J. A. Conger & R. N. Kanungo (Eds.), *Charismatic Leadership: The Elusive Factor in Organizational Effectiveness* (pp. 253–276). San Francisco: Jossey-Bass.

Rosen, D. (1984). Leadership Systems in World Cultures. In Kellerman, B. (Ed.) *Leadership: Multidisciplinary Perspectives* (pp. 39–61).

Ross, L. (1977). The Intuitive Psychologist and his Shortcomings: Distortions in the Attribution Process. In L. Berkowitz (Ed.), *Advances in Experimental Social Psychology*. New York: Academic.

Runciman, W. G. (1963). Charismatic Legitimacy and One Party Rule in Ghana. *Archives Europeenes de Sociologie, 4*, 145–165.

Runciman, W. G. (Ed.) & Matthews, E. (Trans.) (1978). *Max Weber: Selections in Translation*. Cambridge: Cambridge University Press.

Sartre, J.-P. (1992). Existentialism. In E. B. Forest (Ed.), *Human Thought and Action*. Lanham: University Press of America.

Sartre, J.-P., & Mairet, P. (Trans.) (1952). *Existentialism and Humanism*. London: Methuen.

Sashkin, M. (1988). The Visionary Leaders. In J. A. Conger & R. N. Kanungo (Eds.), *Charismatic Leadership: The Elusive Factor in Organizational Effectiveness* (pp. 122–160). San Francisco: Jossey-Bass.

Schein, E. H. (1985). *Organization Culture and Leadership: A Dynamic View*. San Francisco: Jossey-Bass.

Schernerhorn, J., Hunt, R., Jr., & Osborn, R. N. (1991). *Managing Organizational Behavior*. New York: Wiley.

Schrag, O. C. (1961). *Existence and Freedom*. Evanston, IL: Northwestern University Press.

Schutz, A. (1967). *The Phenomenology of the Social World*. Evanston, IL: Northwestern University Press (Original work published 1932).

Scott, J. C. (1985). *Weapons of the Weak: Everyday Forms of Peasant Resistance*. New Haven: Yale University.

Seet, K. K. (1992). Cultural Untranslatability as Dramatic Strategy: A Speculative Look at the Different Language Versions of Kuo Pao Kun's Plays. In Kandiah Thiru (ed.), *Beyond the Footlights, New Play Scripts in Singapore Theatre*. Singapore: UniPress, National University of Singapore.

Shamir, B. (1992). The Charismatic Relationship: Alternative Explanations and Predictions. *The Leadership Quarterly, 2*(2), 81–104.

Shamir, B. (1995). Social Distance and Charisma: Theoretical Notes and an Exploratory Study. *The Leadership Quarterly, 6*(1), 19–47.

Shamir, B., House, R. J., & Arthur, M. B. (1993). The Motivational Effects of Charismatic Leadership: A self-concept-based Theory. *Organizational Science, 4*(4), 577–594.

Shils, E. A. (1965). Charisma, Order and Status. *American Sociological Review, 30*, 199–213.

Shils, E. (1968). Charisma. In *International Encyclopedia of the Social Sciences* (Vol. 2, pp. 386–390). New York: Macmillan.

Shils, E. A., & Finch, H. A. (Trans. and Ed.) (1949). *Max Weber on the Methodology of the Social Sciences*. Glencoe, IL: Free Press.

Sikorski, D. (1991). Resolving the Liberal-Socialist Dichotomy: The Political Economy of Prosperity in Singapore. *International Journal of Politics, Culture and Society., 4*(4), 403–433.

Simmel, G. (1955). *Conflict*. (Translated by Kurt, H. Wolff). Glencoe, IL: Free Press.

Sister Prema (Hsu, Teresa). (1991). Service to Humanity. A recorded talk delivered at the Buddhist Library. Singapore.

Sister Prema (Hsu, Teresa). (1995). An Oral History Interview with Hsu, Teresa. Singapore: Oral History Department, National Archives. *Wheels* 1–11.

Smith, P. B., & Bond, M. H. (1993). *Social Psychology across Cultures: Analysis and Perspectives*. London: Prentice-Hall.

Smith, P. B., & Peterson, M. F. (1987). *Leadership, Organizations and Culture*. London: Sage.

Spencer, M. E. (1970). What is Charisma? *The British Journal of Sociology, 24*, 341–354.

Stodgill, R. M. (1959). *Individual Behavior and Group Achievement*. New York: Oxford University Press.

Stodgill, R. M. (1974). *Handbook of Leadership: A Survey of the Literature*. New York: Free Press.

Tambiah, S. J. (1984). *The Buddhist Saints of the Forest and the Cult of Amulets*. Cambridge: Cambridge University Press.

Tay, K. S. (1975). *Transport Dilemma in Singapore*. Singapore: National University of Singapore.

Tay, K. S. (1988, November). *The Committee on Heritage Report*. Singapore: Committee on Heritage.

Tay, K. S. (1989). *Mega Cities in the Tropics: Towards an Architectural Agenda for the Future*. Singapore: Institute of Southeast Asian Studies.

Tay, K. S. (1990). Architecture and National Identity. *Journal of the Singapore Institute of Architects, 161*, 13–15.

Tay, K. S. (1994). Domestic Enterprises: Levelling the Playing Field. In *Debating Singapore: Reflective Essays*. Singapore: Institute of Southeast Asian Studies.

Tay, K. S. (1991). Singaporean Taste beyond Food. *Journal of the Singapore Institute of Architects, 166*, 32–34.

Tong, C. K., & Yong, P. K. (1998). Guanxi bases, Xinyong and Chinese Business Network. *The British Journal of Sociology, 49*(1), 75–96.

Trice, H. M., & Beyer, J. M. (1986). Charisma and its Routinization in Two Social Movements Organizations. In L. Cummings & B. Staw (Eds.), *Research in Organizational Behavior* (Vol. 8). Greenwich: Jai.

Tucker, R. C. (1969). The Theory of Charismatic Leadership. In D. A. Rustow (Ed.), *Philosophers and Kings: Studies in Leadership*. New York: Braziller.

Turner, V. (1967). Betwixt and Between: The Liminal Period in Rites de Passage. In *The Forest of Symbols* (pp. 93–111). Ithaca: Cornell University Press.

Watzlawick, P., Weakland, J. H., & Fish, R. (1974). *Change: Principles of Problem Formation and Problem Resolution*. New York: Norton.

Weber Max and Hans H. Gerth (Ed and Trans) (1951). *The Religion of China : Confucianism and Taoism*. New York: The Free Press..

Weber, M. (1924) 1947. *The Theory of Social and Economic Organization*. In Henderson, A. M. & Parsons, T. (trans.), Parsons, T. (Ed.) New York: Free Press.

Weber, M. (1974). On Subjective Interpretation in the Social Sciences. In M. Trozzi (Ed.), *Verstehen: Subjective Understanding in the Social Sciences* (pp. 18–37). Reading: Addison-Wesley Educational.

Wittfogel K. (1963 [1957]). Oriental Despotism: A Comparative Study of Total Power. New Haven, CT and London: Yale University Press.

Willner, A. R. (1984). *The Spellbinders: Charismatic Political Leadership*. New Haven: Yale University Press.

Wolfenstein, E. V. (1967). *The Revolutionary Personality*. Princeton: Princeton University Press.

Wolfram, E. (1960). *A History of China*. Berkeley: University of California Press.

Wuthnow, R., Hunter, J. D., Bergesen, A., & Kurzweil, E. (1984). *Cultural Analysis*. Boston: Routledge & Kegan Paul.

Yukl, G. (1989). Managerial Leadership: A Review of Theory and Research. *Journal of Management, 15*, 251–289.

Zaleznik, A. (1977). Managers and Leaders: Are They Different? *Harvard Business Review*, 15(3), 67–78.

Zaleznik, A., & Kets de Vries, M. F. R. (1975). *Power and the Corporate Mind*. Boston: Houghton Mifflin.

Index

Lightning Source UK Ltd.
Milton Keynes UK
UKOW06n1238080316

269803UK00011B/330/P